GHOSTS O
ATLANTI

C000051925

"Kenyon has covered all the bases on Atlantis in this exciting new book!"

DAVID HATCHER CHILDRESS, AUTHOR AND CO-STAR ON
THE HISTORY CHANNEL'S *ANCIENT ALIENS*

"*Ghosts of Atlantis* introduces a thought-provoking sampling of Atlantean themes and their ramifications. With his inviting style, Kenyon explores Atlantis in popular culture and our subconscious, archaeological and scientific evidence for forgotten civilizations, religious implications, conspiracy theories, extraterrestrials, time travel, cosmic catastrophes, and much more. *Ghosts of Atlantis* provides numerous insights and a fascinating path to navigate through the Atlantis phenomena."

ROBERT M. SCHOCH, PH.D., AUTHOR OF *FORGOTTEN CIVILIZATION*

"Kenyon has a superior perspective on the history and progress of alternative viewpoints. *Ghosts of Atlantis* is a valuable and timely contribution to the field—it brilliantly elucidates how similar the fundamental ideological forces in the world play out, regardless of the period of time or culture we live in. Beautifully written."

CHRIS DUNN, AUTHOR OF *LOST TECHNOLOGIES OF ANCIENT EGYPT*

"*Ghosts of Atlantis* takes the reader on a magical mystery tour through many of the great puzzles and enigmas of our world, expertly weaving them together into a cohesive and alternative picture of our most ancient past. A deeply thought-provoking compendium that updates and reenergizes this long-running debate and will surely keep alive the age-old question of humanity's lost past and its true origins. A tour de force that delivers a timely wake-up call to scientism in all its forms; a work that will surely be discussed and debated for many years to come."

SCOTT CREIGHTON, AUTHOR OF *THE GREAT PYRAMID VOID ENIGMA*

"Kenyon has written the widest-ranging, most comprehensive, and most convincing argument that a prehistoric civilization actually existed and was all but erased from human memory by a natural catastrophe. A must-read."

GREGORY L. LITTLE, ED.D., COAUTHOR OF *DENISOVAN ORIGINS*

"No one handles the mysteries of protohistory more deftly than Doug Kenyon. He has done more than any single individual in recent time to uncover the secrets of planet Earth, once and for all dispelling the orthodox myth of a barbaric 'Stone Age.' His new book is a magnificent synopsis of our knowledge of the advanced arts and sciences of lost civilizations."

SUSAN MARTINEZ, PH.D., AUTHOR OF
THE MYSTERIOUS ORIGINS OF HYBRID MAN

"Skillful writing guides us smoothly through complex subjects toward an exciting place where mysticism and materialism might intersect to provide a greater understanding of the universe. An exciting book, wrapping deep subjects in a fascinating style that invites you to delve into the writer's intriguing multiverse vision."

RAND FLEM-ATH, COAUTHOR OF *ATLANTIS BENEATH THE ICE*

"Kenyon offers us a thorough, up-to-date survey of the current state of the world of alternative science. He's an accomplished researcher and author, as is convincingly demonstrated by this book. May the ghosts of Atlantis continue to haunt a world gone astray!"

MICHAEL A. CREMO, AUTHOR OF *FORBIDDEN ARCHEOLOGY*

"*Ghost of Atlantis* is a fascinating read, integrating many threads of research. This book allows for hope—we've collectively forgotten much wisdom, yet it's not too late to recognize our spiritual nature and choose to build a higher civilization."

JEANE MANNING, AUTHOR OF *THE COMING ENERGY REVOLUTION*

"A riveting read. Kenyon presents nonstop and impossible-to-ignore evidence for humanity's amnesia and offers compelling arguments for what lost memory means to humanity—we ignore the truth of the past at our peril."

JULIE LOAR, AUTHOR OF *GODDESSES FOR EVERY DAY*

"Kenyon has an ability no one else has—to pull in the fullness of place, timeframe, story, and fact so a larger view emerges. *Ghost of Atlantis* is his capstone. This one book ties together how the many worlds of the past reveal the singular path we humans have taken since the beginnings of all beginnings. I give Doug a huge thank-you for what he has done in this incredible book."

P. M. H. ATWATER, L.H.D., AUTHOR OF *THE FOREVER ANGELS*

GHOSTS OF
ATLANTIS

How the Echoes of Lost Civilizations
Influence Our Modern World

J. DOUGLAS KENYON

Bear & Company
Rochester, Vermont

Bear & Company
One Park Street
Rochester, Vermont 05767
www.BearandCompanyBooks.com

Text stock is SFI certified

Bear & Company is a division of Inner Traditions International

Cataloging-in-Publication Data for this title is available from the Library of Congress

ISBN 978-1-59143-391-0 (print)
ISBN 978-1-59143-392-7 (ebook)

Printed and bound in the United States by Lake Book Manufacturing, Inc. The text stock is SFI certified. The Sustainable Forestry Initiative® program promotes sustainable forest management.

10 9 8 7 6 5 4 3 2 1

Text design and layout by Virginia Scott Bowman
This book was typeset in Garamond Premier Pro and Museo with Leftheria Pro used as the display typeface

To send correspondence to the author of this book, mail a first-class letter to the author c/o Inner Traditions • Bear & Company, One Park Street, Rochester, VT 05767, and we will forward the communication, or contact the author directly at **https://AtlantisRising.com**.

✦

To my great-grandchildren, nieces, and nephews

Contents

The Great Forgetting
The consequence of collective trauma

Artifacts of Knowledge
Evidence of the superior technology of the past

Untaught History

What might really have happened

Domains of the Lost

Forgotten civilizations from around the globe

Inner Connections

How advanced civilizations have left their mark on our bodies

Other Worlds

Lost civilizations from outer space

Signs of a Crime

Cover-ups and conspiracies to bury the truth

Ancient Doom
The end of civilizations past and present

Stellar Dimensions
*How we might rediscover our history—
and avoid destruction*

Acknowledgments

As may or may not be clear by now, this book is the culmination and outgrowth of many years of work that went into the creation, development, and production of *Atlantis Rising Magazine,* which was sold on newsstands worldwide from the 1990s onward. Anyone reading our magazine or the various books, translations, and documentaries that flowed from it owes a debt to the many artists, writers, and advertisers who helped create it; and, in turn, all of those who worked on it are indebted to those who chose to support financially this very unique endeavor. It was a good deal while it lasted, but—confronted by the inevitable challenges of advancing age—I was forced in 2019 to close the doors of our cherished periodical. It is hoped, though, that with the publication of the present book, it will be clear that the mission continues, albeit in a somewhat different form.

In a project like this, where so many have lent their support, it is not easy to decide who to single out for the kind of special thanks we can offer here—but for all who have helped along the way, you know who you are and so do I. Thank you so much. We will always be in your debt.

Among those to whom I can honestly say that if it were not for you, this book would not have happened, there is first my wife, Patricia, whose years of loyalty and loving support have kept me going through some very challenging times. Also in the family category I include my granddaughter Jessica, without whose very practical assistance at a crucial moment this project would not have been possible.

Someone who, in the 1990s, played an indispensable role in getting *Atlantis Rising* up and running, and in introducing it to the public, was the late John Anthony West. I would like to acknowledge here just how critically important his help was at a time of great vulnerability for the publication. I hope that, wherever he now hangs his hat, John will be pleased to see the present book in print, and that he will welcome the unique attention being paid here to the latter-day recovery of lost ancient wisdom—the cause he served for most of his life.

I would also like to extend my very special appreciation to Robert Schoch. In the 1990s, he, along with John West, broke the ice on mass public awareness for the reality of advanced prediluvian civilization and its significance today. For the quarter century of *Atlantis Rising Magazine*'s existence, Schoch's many thoughtful contributions were essential to the high level of credibility that our work enjoyed everywhere. I could make similar statements about many of our writers, but, lacking the space here to say more, I will simply point out that you will find many of their insightful comments included in this book, and I am very grateful to them for that.

Also entitled to my gratitude is my friend and teacher, the late Elizabeth Clare Prophet. Without her patient encouragement and support for various projects of mine since the 1970s, there would have been no *Atlantis Rising Magazine,* nor this present book.

Ghosts of Atlantis is now in your hands, though, and I think you will agree that everything worked out well. For that and more, I am, and will always be, grateful.

Introduction

In the July/August 2016 issue of *Atlantis Rising Magazine,* researcher Steven Sora made a case for the possible identity of Queen Guinevere of Camelot fame. She was, he argued in "Guinevere Unveiled," a Pictish princess from a pre-Scottish tribe. While many believe that the stories of King Arthur and the knights of the round table are entirely fiction, Sora pointed out that the origins of the legend are probably factual, albeit of a much earlier era than we usually consider.

Popular British writer Graham Phillips is one of the leading authorities on the historical origins of the Camelot stories. He believes they derive from events that took place in the fifth century—the Iron Age, not the Middle Ages, as the Grail romances would have us imagine. In his book *The Lost Tomb of King Arthur,* Phillips argues that the bones of King Arthur himself can be found in Shropshire, and he is campaigning to have a specific site there dug up by archaeologists.

Whether or not the story is grounded in historical fact, however, is probably *not* the most important point. The enduring popularity of the Grail romances seems more related to the role they continue to play in our imagination. Like disputes over the literal truth of the Bible and other holy books, the most important thing for most of us probably has more to do with what the stories have come to mean symbolically. However, as our connection to the ideals—like chivalry, enshrined in the myths—is apparently fading away, the need to uncover the true facts of the story becomes even greater.

For those who have eyes to see and ears to hear—to use the biblical phrase—it is still possible to connect with the original spirit that animated important seminal events in Earth's long history, even as the quest for the concrete facts behind them often falls short. The inner truths are what matter, and the rest is superstition.

Like the knights in quest of the Holy Grail, we are pursuing an elusive goal. Whether we find it, we suspect, depends more upon what we are made of than on what we can actually touch. This should not discourage us from searching for the physical facts that gave birth to our mythologies, but it can remind us that the quest itself is the thing that matters most, and if the gods choose to smile on our endeavors, it is more likely to be for the ardor of our hearts than for the superiority of our intellects.

All of the above could just as easily be said about the story of Atlantis. In a 2017 survey on so-called paranormal beliefs, Chapman University in California found that 55 percent of the public "agree" or "strongly agree" with this statement: "Ancient, advanced civilizations such as Atlantis once existed." Of all the paranormal beliefs examined in the survey, the idea of a lost ancient civilization found the most support, but others were, surprisingly, also widely accepted. Fifty-two percent of Americans, for instance, believe that "places can be haunted by spirits." Also enjoying wide acceptance: "Aliens have visited Earth in our ancient past," at 35 percent.*

While the Chapman poll may be taken by some as a rare instance of honest reporting, it still fails to grasp the extent to which many of the ideas it considers to be outside the norm (that is, paranormal) are supported by a great deal of evidence (at least anecdotally), while views that our society might consider more "normal" often are not. If you are reading this book to learn the hard research facts about Atlantis, you may well miss our point. The Atlantis we are talking about comprises much more than you will learn from archaeology, though we certainly believe that recent discoveries now support once discarded notions of advanced prediluvian civilization. Atlantis, we believe, was not only an archetype, or dream, or cautionary tale, but a real place—and an advanced one at that; but here we are talking about what we might call the "greater" Atlantis, not just a city or even a continent but in fact a lost identity

---

*The full survey, officially called the Chapman University Survey of American Fears 2017, was published on October 11, 2017, on the blog *Voice of Wilkinson* on the Chapman University website. You can find it at https://blogs.chapman.edu/wilkinson/2017/10/11/paranormal-america-2017/.

for the human race, whose murdered corpse, like the ghost of Hamlet's father, still cries out to us as we confront the disturbing possibilities of our future.

According to the Greek philosopher Plato—whose dialogues *Timaeus* and *Critias* are usually cited by academia as the sole source of the Atlantis story—an Egyptian "priest of Sais" told Solon, Plato's ancestor, about Atlantis. After pointing out that Earth's history is far more ancient than any childish Greek could possibly appreciate, the priest said, "There have been, and will be again, many destructions of mankind arising out of many causes; the greatest have been brought about by the agencies of fire and water, and other lesser ones by innumerable other causes." The recurrent rise and fall of civilization, as reflected in the Atlantis story, has been noted often and provoked many warnings of what may lie in store.

In his haunting 1959 science fiction novel *A Canticle for Liebowitz*, author Walter M. Miller Jr. envisioned a post-apocalyptic future—one very much like our own ancestors must have experienced between ice ages or after the fall of a civilization like, perhaps, Atlantis—in which few fragments of the present civilization survive, and they are, at best, only dimly understood. In the book, set centuries after a nuclear holocaust, humanity has again—as suggested by the priest of Sais—fallen into the barbarism of a dark age. Struggling to preserve the fragile relics remaining from a more advanced, albeit forgotten, era, a handful of cloistered and dedicated monks seek to stave off the looming threat of total amnesia for humanity and to beatify the "blessed Leibowitz," founder of their order in the aftermath of the ancient war.

The brothers themselves, unfortunately, have lost most of the keys to understanding the mysterious culture that had preceded them, which was wiped out by a legendary deluge of "fire"—one that the reader will recognize as nuclear cataclysm. Their mistakes in interpreting the few treasured artifacts they possess are many. Some, to our sophisticated eyes, are funny. An electronic schematic diagram, for example, though incomprehensible, is yet seen as a thing of mystical beauty. One consecrated monk spends a lifetime lovingly "illuminating" it with gold scrollwork. Another fragment that inspires the brothers to the most sublime metaphysical speculations is a precious, though mysterious, fragment requesting "a pound of pastrami and six bagels." And within the cloistered walls of the monastery, tales of "fallouts"—the dreadful monsters that once devoured the ancients—are whispered about with much fear and trembling.

Ages pass in Miller's tale and an understanding of nature's processes once again begins to dawn. Electricity is rediscovered. Mechanical transportation develops, and so does powered flight. Technology is born again. And even as, in a flawed and distorted way, the knowledge of the ancients is slowly reconstructed, peculiar patterns from the previous age begin, ironically, to reappear. A fanatical religious dogma blocks recognition of the true nature of ancient advancements, and an arrogant new order seeks to stamp out any awakening to their world's true history by claiming its own achievements to be unprecedented. To buttress its own authority, the new establishment initiates an inquisition in which theologically and politically incorrect views are repressed and punished.

Somehow though, as Miller tells it, despite ignorance and tyranny civilization painfully climbs once again to the heights and eventually finds itself at a crossroads where, like its forebears, it must confront terrible dilemmas . . . or die.

If society were to survive, Miller believed, it must somehow come to understand and overcome the challenges that destroyed its ancient ancestors.

Yet today, to hear some tell it, the story of human evolution is one of almost unbroken ascent. From the darkness of the Stone Age, we have traveled inexorably to the so-called enlightenment of our present age. Certainly there have been setbacks, wars, plagues, and the like, but we have continued on, doggedly moving up the ladder. And just a few thousand years after cowering in the caves, here we are— masters of nature, technology, and all that we survey, at the pinnacle of achievement.

Or so we have been led to believe.

According to the narrative of mainstream history, primitive civilization emerged from the Stone Age just a little over five thousand years ago. With the first great labor-saving invention of the ancient world—the wheel—society crossed the great divide and headed irreversibly toward the modern world we know today. It was the wheel, we are told, that revolutionized primitive society and set the stage for the great achievements that followed.

Such is the conventional scenario for the dawn of civilization on Earth. The assumption has been that the rise of highly organized society was unprecedented. After all, if there had been an earlier advanced civilization, it is argued, we would have discovered unmistakable evidence of it. We would see the remains of its highways and bridges and electrical wiring. We would find its plastic bottles, its city dumps, its DVDs. . . . Those, after all, are the things that we ourselves will leave behind to puzzle future archaeologists.

But could an ancient civilization have risen to heights similar to our own and, perhaps, have traveled a different road? What would we understand of a world that might have employed fundamentally different—though perhaps no less effective—techniques to harness the forces of nature? Would we understand a world that could, for example, create and transmit energy by means other than an electric power grid, travel great distances without internal combustion engines, or make highly complex calculations involving earth science and astronomy without electronic computers? What would we make of a world without social media?

Are we capable of recognizing and respecting achievement along lines different than our own, or would we retreat to convenient stereotypes of superstitious and primitive ancients? Why, we wonder, is the subject of prediluvian civilization—like that suggested by Atlantis—so disturbing to conventional thinking? Why is the suggestion that our civilization is not the first to rise to such heights greeted with derision? Why, despite significant evidence, will no influential academics touch the issue of lost high civilization in our forgotten past? And moreover, why should anyone living in the third millennium CE care about something that history has forgotten? Why should we fight to learn the meaning of a civilization that may or may not have existed so long ago? What could the story of Atlantis, or whatever world may have once existed, possibly tell us about ourselves?

It seems the time has come when the general public is more prepared than ever to hear the facts. And quite disturbingly for mainstream academia, that does not necessarily mean the standard orthodox version usually served up in college classrooms and presented in the media. All of that may have to change, though.

Could such change require a great dramatic episode? Maybe so.

Poseidon beneath the waves, featured on the
cover of *Atlantis Rising Magazine*, September/October, 2015

The laws of change are the laws of drama. It's the way plants reach
the flowering stage and caterpillars become butterflies—the way of
metamorphosis, of redemption—and it was the heart of the ancient
temple practice that has come down to us as theater. From Sophocles

to Shakespeare, from Goethe to Arthur Miller, great playwrights have demonstrated the laws that can liberate souls from darkness. Some have understood and been transformed.

Profound insight into the nature of change illuminated psychoanalysts like Carl Jung, who wrote of a universal process through which the "base metal" of the lesser self could be changed into the "gold" of a higher self through application of "alchemical" principles. Some, such as historian Arnold Toynbee, saw cycles of change unfolding through history like the processes of nature, including birth, life, and death or transcendence for entire civilizations.

Knowledge of such things, though nearly forgotten by the modern alienated Western mind, nevertheless continues to inspire initiates of the original order. The perennial wisdom and sacred science in ancient teachings, from Egyptian to Hopi, from Gnostic to Confucian, guide a quest for illumination in our own time. And while some may listen to their inner voices and others will try to drown out their intuitions with the noise of the times, few can escape the sense that we stand at the portal of dramatic change—a spiritual initiation the likes of which has not been seen for eons.

Most of the pages to follow appear here in this form for the first time. Long-term readers of *Atlantis Rising Magazine,* however, will doubtless recognize previous writings of mine—columns from "Alternative News" and "Letters from the Publisher," articles by Martin Ruggles (my pen name), various sidebars, notes, and so on. (To establish points of facts, credited quotes from numerous *Atlantis Rising* contributors are also included, but without resort to the original article author's main content.) Old friends will certainly spot many themes that were regularly visited in our pages and were a major part of our branded identity and will hopefully be happy to learn that we remain in the fight.

THE GREAT FORGETTING

*The consequence
of collective trauma*

The Atlantis of Our Dreams

Searching for clues in the unconscious mind

In the early 1980s, when blockbuster movies like *Star Wars* and *Raiders of the Lost Ark* were making box office history, my friend, filmmaker Tom Miller, and I decided to take our own shot at celluloid fame and fortune with an action/adventure screenplay called *The Atlantis Dimension.* In our story, a group of contemporary explorers discovers the ruins of Atlantis beneath the waters of the so-called Bermuda Triangle. Unconsciously driven by forces set in motion during previous lives on Atlantis, our characters face some very ancient blowback, including heroic action, ancient technology, underwater archaeology, treachery in high places, and nature turned very bad. Our screenplay, we firmly believed, was fully in synch with the public's obvious appetite for exotic and thrilling entertainment—accompanying, of course, a good story. But alas, for reasons not entirely clear to us, it was never to be filmed, and the script itself was read by no more than a few dozen people.

Still, on other levels, our scenario was to prove strangely prophetic and suggested that there could well be larger forces at work here than those of mere pop culture. The site of our fictional account, for instance, was an island in the Bahamas where construction of a giant Atlantis-themed resort was under way. That development project was the work of the story's villain, whose luxurious Miami villa was situated in an exclusive community called Paradise Island. I ultimately learned that an actual Atlantis Paradise Island in the Bahamas had been around since 1968, though when I wrote our script, I had never heard of it. And

10

Artist Tom Miller's conception of the end of Atlantis (also see color insert plate 1)

when Atlantis the resort debuted in 1998 with a massive national advertising campaign, I was astonished to see how much, in my view, reality was imitating my art. (A further curious side note: the Atlantis resort was once owned by a Merv Griffin company, whose principal stockholder at one point was Donald Trump.)

I might also add that in 1985, in the midst of our search for funds to produce *The Atlantis Dimension,* the space shuttle *Atlantis* was launched for the first time, providing, it seemed, a clear omen that things could be ready to take off.

Never shy about exploiting popular mythology of any kind, Hollywood has long recognized the box office potential of Atlantis. Even before the 1980s, there had been many notable attempts to capitalize on the subject. Disney's *20,000 Leagues Under the Sea* (1954) and *Journey to the Center of the Earth* (1959), both based on novels by nineteenth-century French visionary Jules Verne, depicted discovery of the ruins of Atlantis. In 1961, MGM presented director/producer George Pal's *Atlantis, the Lost Continent,* which attempted to portray events leading up to the continent's final destruction. Derided as an example of the cheap and cheesy science fiction fare popular in drive-in theaters of the day, critics hated it, pointing out that many of its scenes were taken directly from *Quo Vadis,* MGM's 1951 film story of Roman anti-Christian tyranny.

The underwater ruins of Atlantis, illustrated by Rob Rath for the graphic novel version of *The Atlantis Dimension* by Doug Kenyon

In the Atlantis myth itself, we are left with a persistent tale that, while widely shared, is seldom taken seriously. Yet, no matter how much it is dismissed by academic authorities as nothing more than a kind of cartoon, its deep effect on our culture is undeniable. And while legitimate debate over the facts may rage, some of us believe that deep in the ocean of humanity's unconscious are the virtual remains of a lost history that still makes its demands on our thoughts and sensibilities.

The notion of a great lost civilization and our society's demonstrable amnesia on the subject eventually inspired me to launch a bimonthly magazine, which I dubbed *Atlantis Rising*, focusing on ancient mysteries, unexplained anomalies, and future science. After twenty-five years of continuous publication and several spin-off books and videos, in the spring of 2019 we closed our doors. Nevertheless, more than thirty years

Movie poster for *Atlantis, the Lost Continent,* directed by George Pal
(also see color insert plate 2)

after writing the *Atlantis Dimension* screenplay, I continue to believe that the echoes of long-forgotten worlds still reverberate and that if we could only translate their siren songs, we might exorcise some of the strange ghosts that trouble us yet.

PLANETARY AMNESIA

Probably no one over the past seventy years could be more directly linked with the notion that Earth's forgotten history has been punctuated by memory-destroying catastrophic events than Immanuel Velikovsky. The late Russian-American psychoanalyst's *Worlds in Collision* caused a sensation when it was published in 1950. His subsequent titles, *Earth in Upheaval* and *Ages in Chaos,* further elaborated his ideas and expanded the controversy. Here was a true scholar of considerable authority suggesting, among other things, that Earth and Venus might once have collided, leaving a vast chaotic aftermath that could do much to explain our

Immanuel Velikovsky

peculiar history. For such arguments, Velikovsky was, ever afterward, roundly ridiculed. Surprisingly, though, many of his predictions have now been verified, and some of his critics, including the late Carl Sagan, have since been forced to concede that he might, after all, in some ways, have been on to something.*

A psychoanalyst and associate of Sigmund Freud and Carl Jung, Velikovsky offered great insight into the psycho-sociological impacts of cataclysmic events. The psychological condition and case history of planet Earth is, he said, one of amnesia. The planet, he believed, is in a near-psychotic state, left so by traumatic events of an almost unimaginable magnitude. Collectively, we must now wonder: Have we compulsively closed our eyes to certain painful realities? Have we, moreover, cloaked that intentional blindness with an aura of authority, thus effectively turning things upside down—making right wrong and wrong right, if you will?

The church fathers of the Middle Ages, for instance, refused—because of Galileo's politically incorrect conclusions—to look through his telescope for themselves. His notion that the sun, not the Earth, is the center of the solar system was deemed heresy, no matter what the evidence might show. In other words, the minds of the authorities were made up, and they had no intention of being confused by troublesome facts.

---

*For more information on Velikovsky, his books, and his theories, seek out the Velikovsky Encyclopedia online.

Some believe that such blindness continues today and the ruling elite may be of a similarly intolerant religion. Around the world, the authorities of government, industry, and the academic world (along with their debunker hit squads) seem to remain determined to prevent any reawakening from the long amnesiac coma.

Sometimes, when it is difficult to find a rational explanation for the choices our leaders make, it is tempting to think in terms of dark conspiracies and treacherous hidden agendas. For Velikovsky, though, the explanation for behavior that some might describe as evil and others would view as at the very least self-destructive and unenlightened—or mad—lies in the mechanisms of a wounded mind seeking to regain equilibrium in the aftermath of a nearly mortal blow. The victim of a near fatal trauma is driven apparently by fear, both conscious and unconscious, in order to exorcise the record of such experiences, lest he be overwhelmed. How else can we get on with our lives, put the past behind us, and think about the future? As it turns out, though, fully forgetting such an experience is not such an easy thing. There are heavy consequences. Much more than the record of the trauma can be lost. In fact, the very identity—what some would call the soul—can be a casualty.

Galileo Galilei at his trial by the Inquisition in Rome in 1633.
Galileo pushes away the Bible.

What is true on an individual level, Velikovsky believed, was also true on a collective level. The process might move more slowly and allow for personal exceptions, but the institutions of society would, in time, come to reflect and enforce a deep collective subconscious wish that, for the good of all, certain doors stay closed and certain inconvenient and terrifying facts stay forgotten.

As in many a Hollywood mystery or in mythic tales from a host of ancient traditions, we, the victims of amnesia, are left with few clues to guide us through a maze of incomprehensible signs and images. Reduced to a primitive state, we find ourselves back in the Stone Age, so to speak, where we cower in our personal caves, thinking only of survival and forgetting entirely any past grandeur. The path to collective recovery from such a fate can be long indeed—many millennia, perhaps. Nevertheless, like a victim returning to the scene of the crime or disembodied phantoms haunting the house where death came suddenly and violently, we are drawn inexorably, no matter the cost, to retrace our footsteps. Again and again, we struggle to uncover the source of our pain and find a way back to the pinnacle from which we have tumbled.

Along the way, the incoherent fragments of a lost identity—the artifacts of forgotten worlds—haunt our dreams. Whispering sadly of a lost state of grace, we spin tragic tales of a "Garden of Eden" from which we have been ejected by some cruel and heartless god. Like Sisyphus or Prometheus, we rail against the harshness of our fate, and life seems indeed, as Shakespeare's Macbeth put it, "a tale told by an idiot, full of sound and fury, signifying nothing."

In such twilight realms, the princes of the darkness and their sycophants, whose seeming light and authority are but an illusion of the shadows, become the tyrants whom we permit to enslave us. Whether in government, orthodox religion, society, academia, or the "Twitterverse," such figures find the light of recovering consciousness a threat—one best stamped out, nipped in the bud, strangled in the cradle, silenced. Should we be surprised to learn that those dark princes will fight fiercely to preserve the perks and prerogatives of their dim domain?

Nevertheless, driven by ancient longings we have carried on, often blindly, in the attempt to penetrate at last the darkness and to learn the secret of our birth—our origin. And now, perhaps millennia later, after many harrowing trials, dare we hope that we have come full circle? Is our struggle finally nearing an end? Could this be the time when we transcend our fate and break free of the cycle? Or are we destined to plunge, once again, into the abyss?

Where can we look for answers to such questions? How can we uncover our history's forgotten prologue and learn the truth?

THE MYTHIC RECORDS

Until we uncover something more concrete, some wonder if the guidance we need could be found in our myths, legends, and dreams—also termed the universal unconscious. Could our planet's tragic history be unraveled from such subjective records?

Read between the lines, Plato's Atlantis story, along with other stories of cataclysmic destruction, is corroborated by the Bible, by the Indian legends of Central America, and by a thousand other ancient myths from every part of the world. Giorgio de Santillana, an authority on the history of science at the Massachusetts Institute of Technology, hypothesized in his great work *Hamlet's Mill* that an advanced scientific knowledge had been encoded into ancient myth and star lore. If it is true that those who cannot learn from history are doomed to repeat it, could these enigmatic messages from our past be something we ignore only at our peril?

If we accept that mythology may have originated with highly advanced people, then we have to think about what the myths are saying: that a great cataclysm struck the world, destroyed an advanced civilization and a golden age of mankind, and, moreover, may be a recurrent feature in the life of Earth. Some people believe that these messages from many ancient sources, including the Bible, point to the possibility of a recurrence of such a cataclysm in our lifetime.

Exploring such knowledge is like an undersea diving expedition—of another kind, but not without perils and monsters of the deep. Could the monster we must face be our own undiscovered selves locked away with the lost secret of our origins? And is what we can discover and prove objectively limited by the amount of light we can bear to cast upon our wounded subjective selves?

When the violent death of an entire civilization has proved too painful to deal with consciously, society has often suppressed the memory by

Plato and his story of Atlantis; art by Tom Miller

force of inquisition or academic sanction, depending on your historic period. Nevertheless, we are driven by irresistible subconscious forces to reenact the ancient tragedy again and again until the spell is broken and at last we awaken from our coma.

The popularity of the 1997 movie *Titanic* had Hollywood scrambling to clone the formula. The secret of unlimited wealth seemed to be at stake. Most theories about the movie's success had to do with star power and special effects combined with a good love story, but could something else have been involved? Call it an archetype, if you will, but the idea of an enormous technically advanced and arrogant world—supposedly impervious to danger—suddenly destroyed by nature itself and banished to the bottom of the sea may strike an even deeper chord than most Hollywood moguls would dare to consider.

If it is true that our civilization is, as Plato reported, but the latest round in an eternal series of heroic ascensions followed by spectacular falls, it makes sense that we share a deep need to comprehend better the nature of our predicament.

The bow of the *Titanic* at the bottom of the Atlantic

Velikovsky offered a compelling explanation for many of the world's pathologies. The cataclysmic destruction of a society and its subsequent descent into barbarism, he said, would result in a loss of collective memory, and whatever new order rose from the ashes of the old, a sense of self-preservation would tend to block any recollection of the former world. The forgetfulness of the amnesiac, however, is not a peaceful thing, as fragments of the lost self haunt the dreams and darken the prospects. Healing demands recovery of the shattered memory and the self that went with it. Unconsciously driven to retrace our footsteps, we, the victims, eventually come full circle and again confront the challenges that defeated us before, and now we must—once and for all—pass our test or die again.

At deeper levels, we all understand somehow that, before the dawn of recorded history—our collective memory—we once rose to the heights, but we then plunged into an abyss from which we have not yet fully recovered. Like the watery ghosts of the *Titanic,* we long to be awakened, but we dread it, too, and there's the rub.

Memory under Assault

To whom do we owe our condition?

In May 2015, the terrorist army calling itself the Islamic State in Iraq and the Levant (also known as ISIS) captured the historic Syrian desert city of Palmyra and soon began to trash its prized ancient ruins. The mostly Roman-era artifacts at Palmyra had been classified as a United Nations World Heritage Site that must be protected by the civilized world. *Civilized,* alas, was not a term that could be applied to Palmyra's new bosses.

For the invaders, the sites and statues were nothing more than heathen temples and idols, deserving destruction. For the rest of the world, such ruins serve as a window into the past, constituting society's very memory. Lose them and we might never learn who we really are.

The demolition of ancient ruins had become a hallmark of the truly terrifying ISIS campaign to establish a new caliphate in the Middle East like that of centuries past. In videos distributed on the internet, a horrified world witnessed—in addition to the savage murder of many innocents whose only crime was to be in the path of the marauders—the systematic destruction of numerous major archaeological locations. Men with bulldozers, sledgehammers, and drills attacked sites such as Aleppo, Khorsabad, Jonah's Tomb, Hatra, Nimrud, and Mosul in a region widely considered the cradle of civilization.

Some of the more valuable pieces, it was hoped, would yet survive, as ISIS—seeking to generate cash flow for its operations—worked to sell them on the international antiquities black market. Some believed,

Photo published by ISIS showing the destruction by bulldozer of the tomb and shrine of Ahmed ar-Rifa'i, founder of the Rifa'i order of Sufi mysticism, in Muhallabiyah, Iraq

in fact, that the entire campaign might be nothing more than a cover for sophisticated looting on a grand scale.

Looting aside, the tactic of completely destroying evidence of the very existence of one's enemies is certainly nothing new. According to some historians, after destroying Carthage in the Third Punic War (149–146 BCE), in an attempt to make sure that nothing survived of their hated adversary, the Romans sowed the ground with salt. Some question the truth of the salt story, but no one doubts the ruthlessness of the Romans in their campaign to utterly destroy Carthage. The so-called scorched earth tactic, used in some military campaigns to destroy anything that might be useful to a foe, has often led to the virtual erasure of entire cultures. Some have equated the use of such extreme force with attempts to completely destroy an entire ethnic group—what is now called genocide—and the practice itself is by no means extinct. Elsewhere in Iraq, the Yezidi, a Kurdish sect, has been virtually wiped out by the ongoing massacres perpetrated by the majority Muslims who surround them, including ISIS. In China, a similar threat is faced by Uighurs Muslims, Tibetan Buddhists, Falun Gong sect members, and others. In Pakistan, Ahmadiyya Muslims have been slaughtered by local Muslim majorities over issues such as "blasphemy." Genocide of the Darfur people of Sudan has been deplored throughout the world.

The greatest crimes, though, seem to be in actions for which no

An elderly Tibetan women holding a prayer wheel on Barkhor Street, Lhasa, Tibet

rationale—military, economic, social, or otherwise—can be offered as a defense. The Nazi holocaust against the Jews comes to mind. Could such practices point to an even deeper, unconscious agenda?

PSYCHOLOGICAL SCARS

Popular rage aimed at wiping out the "idolatry" of the "infidels" and knowledge of the very existence of earlier times induces and reinforces a collective planetary amnesia, but down through the history of civilization, it has often been a useful tool in the hands of powerful elites who benefit from the widespread ignorance.

Half a millennium ago, during the Spanish conquest of Mexico, Bishop Diego de Landa burned most of the pre-Columbian folding books now known as the Mayan codices, written by scribes in hieroglyphic script on bark paper. And that was but a small part of the conquistadores' ruthless campaign to remove all history of the native cultures and religions, which were in many ways clearly superior to those of the invaders. Everywhere Hernando Cortés and his soldiers went, he ordered the destruction of ancient temples and replaced them with Christian churches. The loss of the Mayan codices and the systematic destruction of other cultural resources have made it nearly impossible for scholars to reconstruct accurately the pre-Columbian history of ancient America.

In Europe, the inquisitions of the Middle Ages often saw forbidden

A modern mural by Fernando Pacheco in Mérida, Mexico, depicts Spanish bishop Diego de Landa burning figures of Mayan deities.

books and their authors consigned to the flames, but the worst tragedy for Western culture as a whole was the loss of the greatest repository of knowledge from the ancient world, Egypt's Library of Alexandria. Even now, many centuries later, that loss is mourned by historians and scholars who must struggle to piece together what the ancients truly knew. Containing more than a million ancient scrolls, the library was said to employ, in its prime, hosts of dedicated scholars. One curious irony in the loss of the great library is that historians cannot definitively decide who to blame—not for a shortage of suspects but from an abundance. Indeed, many historical figures have been indicted, academically speaking, for the crime. (Another curious irony is that when the Roman emperor Aurelian burned the library in the third century CE, it was part of an effort to crush a revolt by Queen Zenobia of Palmyra, the same city in Syria besieged by ISIS fighters in 2015.)

The list of cities, libraries, statues, documents, and other resources destroyed in every way imaginable during Earth's long and turbulent history is long indeed. Today, the campaign to destroy statues honoring

The Library at Alexandria, as depicted by nineteenth-century artist Otto von Corven

figures from American history who are now deemed politically incorrect may be the most recent example.

The relative geological stability that Earth has enjoyed for the past few thousand years is believed, in mainstream academia, to be typical of human history. Great planetary catastrophes of any kind are associated only with natural history from millions of years before the rise of humanity. The idea that the way things *are* is the way they *have always been* has been called uniformitarianism. Today's scientists challenge this doctrine only at their academic peril, yet a small but growing number of researchers persist in confronting that threat. These "catastrophists," as they're called, believe that the world we find today exists in the aftermath of a series of forgotten ancient catastrophes. Like the priest of Sais quoted by Plato, modern catastrophists tell us that the story of mankind is in actuality one of a never-ending cycle of ascents, followed by cataclysmic falls and ensuing great forgettings that must be labeled as collective amnesia.

More recently, psychiatrists have applied the term post-traumatic stress disorder to a group of mental disorders that can affect people after they have witnessed life-threatening events (such as military combat, natural disasters, terrorist incidents, serious accidents, or violent personal assaults). Symptoms include depression, anxiety, nightmares, and amnesia. Could such a diagnosis be applied to the culture of an entire planet? And could a collective unwillingness to explore and define our mysterious past—unconsciously dreading that doing so would open ancient wounds—eventually harden into a systematic repression of the truth and the enthronement of wishful thinking? Could the practice lead to actual physical tyranny?

Certainly our reluctance to honestly explore the past has led to many evils. Consider the actions of the Spanish conquistadores in the New World. Over time, such reluctance to embrace the truth of our origins has often become codified and institutionalized, culminating in nightmares like the inquisitions of the Middle Ages and the book burnings of Nazi Germany. How often have we watched as a marauding army or a brutal elite, acting in the name of God or the people, enforced a collective subconscious wish to keep such threatening—and thus forbidden—knowledge safely out of sight? All too frequently, believed Immanuel Velikovsky.

Supported by Carl Jung's notion of an innate collective unconscious undergirding all of human awareness, Velikovsky saw this vast and mysterious well of shared experience as a source of great collective psychological pain. Jung believed that many of our greatest aspirations, as well as our deepest fears, emerge from this domain, and its presence is exposed in our dreams and in our myths. In the subtext of such narratives, Velikovsky read the tale of monumental, albeit forgotten, ancient tragedies.

A few years before his 1979 death and the 1982 publication of his book *Mankind in Amnesia,* Velikovsky received an honorary doctorate degree from the University of Lethbridge in Alberta, Canada. At the accompanying symposium, a two-day event titled "Recollections of a Fallen Sky: Velikovsky and Cultural Amnesia," several other experts offered papers of their own on the topic. Despite ill health, Velikovsky himself made a presentation, arguing in his remarks that mankind forgets catastrophic events *consciously* while remembering them *unconsciously.**

Dr. E. R. Milton, chairman of the university's department of physics,

---

*In 1978, all the papers presented at the conference were gathered and published as a book, *Recollections of a Fallen Sky: Velikovsky and Cultural Amnesia; Papers Presented at the University of Lethbridge, May 9 and 10, 1974.* You can view the book online on the website of the Grazian-Archive at www.grazian-archive.com.

who led the symposium, explained in his published notes, "If the cultural amnesia theory is correct, then it is possible to suggest that every generation lives in a state of trauma induced by the conflict between subconscious memories of past catastrophic events and the refusal of the conscious mind to recognize that these events actually occurred in prehistoric and historic times." Could such trauma, as Velikovsky believed, be the cause for mankind's aggression and hostility? For anyone who worries about the possibility of nuclear war, the answer should be crucial. And what about the dangerous social instability that has become, almost a half century later, even more commonplace?

"The trauma," Milton said, "is also responsible for the inability and at times the outright refusal of science to recognize overwhelming evidence pointing to the catastrophic past of the Earth and the entire solar System." In fact, he added, "the trauma is also responsible, in part at least, for the actions of some scientists who denounced Velikovsky without even reading his work. Perhaps the men who did this really are saying that the truth is too awful."

One of the first clues Velikovsky cited at the Lethbridge symposium was from a century-old book by C. E. Brasseur de Bourbourg, a French missionary who wrote about ancient Mexican beliefs and history, as well as possible connections between Egyptian and Mexican beliefs. Brasseur's books, oddly, did not connect the ancient history of Mexico with similar accounts from biblical scripture. And Velikovsky "found it strange that [Brasseur], being a clergyman, did not observe, or did not dare to report that in the Scriptures many pages deal with the very same events he was describing." Brasseur wrote that cataclysmic events had been described in Mexican lore, events also recounted by several sixteenth-century Spanish historians. "These were," said Velikovsky, "events of great violence. Mountains rose and moved; many volcanoes erupted from the North-Pacific Coast of North America all the way to Tierra del Fuego at the southern tip of South America. The ocean rose like a wall and moved, accompanied by terrific winds. Fiery bodies were seen fighting in the sky. Stones descended from above, followed by rains of naphtha. Men were maddened by the din and the paramount danger. Houses collapsed and were carried away, hurricanes tore out great trees of whole forests with their roots. If such a great catastrophe occurred today, what impression would it leave in the survivors?"

For Velikovsky, biblical accounts and related traditions are replete with references to great cataclysmic events. "The catastrophe of the second millennium [BCE]," he said, "has been remembered on very many pages of the Biblical Prophets and the Psalms. Our whole life is pervaded by influences originating in these and other catastrophic events that took place in earlier ages. The catastrophes survive in the liturgy still used today, only we choose not to examine them as such. Whatever area of life we select to explore we find some vestige of the terrifying events of the past. The calendar is a good example, either the Jewish calendar or the Christian calendar or that of any other creed. Throughout the year the holidays are reflections of catastrophic events."

A great deluge like that described in the Bible's story of Noah was certainly not the first cataclysm to destroy life on Earth. Indeed, Plato's description of the end of Atlantis is a similar example, but many memories from very ancient times survive only in mythology. Very old Egyptian myths, Velikovsky pointed out, describe "battles and changes in the sky and of vast destruction on Earth, changes that we neglect to investigate and know in our desire to believe that we live on a planet that is stable and safe."

Could the fear that our world is not safe lead to a collective amnesia? We know that, at least on the individual level, it can certainly do that. Modern psychoanalysis has been built around the idea that forgotten traumas from childhood shape and scar the lives of adults. The phenomenon of racial amnesia, said Velikovsky, occupied Sigmund Freud's mind in the last decades of his life and, in fact, became his obsession.

"Initially," said Velikovsky, "Freud claimed that the impressions made upon a child's mind dictate the child's future and cause also neuroses in juvenile and adult life. Later Freud reversed his thesis and claimed that man's destiny is triggered by images which exist within the racial memory, deep within the unconscious mind."

But if Freud backed away from the idea of psychological damage from forgotten trauma, Velikovsky did not. "From psychoanalytic studies," he said, "we know that a traumatic experience, either of a physical or psychological nature, leaves a strong vestige deep within the human soul. Such vestiges are in the heritage that comes to us from antiquity. They are found in most of the written documents that survive from the civilizations of the past: from Mexico, China, Iceland, Iran, India, Sumeria, Rome, Greece, Egypt, and Judea. They also survive from traditions carried from generation to generation, by word of mouth, in races that do

Noah's Ark; engraving by
Gustave Doré

not know how to write. These latter traditions eventually are written down by anthropologists, who collect together stories of catastrophes from north and south, from west and east, from Lapland and the South Sea islands. We ask why we do not recognize this evidence the vestiges of which exist within the souls of men. The answer is that because these vestiges are buried so deeply we are unable to see the evidence before us."

Blindness of this type persists not only in the mad excesses of barbaric terrorists but in the citadels of Western civilization, where the "politically correct" ruling elite practice an intolerant "religion" not entirely unlike that of their forebears—more subtle, perhaps less violent and/or physical. John Anthony West sardonically labeled it the "Church of Progress." Others call it scientism.

In Velikovsky's theory of cultural amnesia, unconscious memory is transmitted genetically from one generation to the next, a concept already proposed by Freud and Jung but in contradiction of more recent biological research. Nevertheless, Velikovsky had his reasons for thinking that memory is indeed so transmitted, if not racially, then in some other way. As we will see, there are other ways that such memories could be passed from one generation to another, and not for just a few centuries but, in fact, for many millennia.

3

The Search for Lost Records

Could Atlantis have left us a library?

When director Stanley Kubrick presented *2001: A Space Odyssey* in the late 1960s, many saw the film as a remarkably prophetic vision daring to deal with themes untouched by the popular culture. Here, it seemed, was a larger vision of humanity's origins and destiny than the big screen (even super wide Cinerama) had ever attempted. Certainly the notion that ancient progenitors from the stars had left behind mysterious clues intended to guide a fledgling human race toward the ultimate recognition of its true identity was a stimulating one.

Oddly, the critics saw all that, but they ignored or dismissed the possibility that something very much like the film's enigmatic obelisk might actually exist.

Is it possible that our forebears left us such a marker, but that it points toward a more transcendent and spiritual destiny than the secular establishment is prepared to consider, challenging many of the assumptions underlying the existing order? What ancient artifact still confounds our understanding of its very shape and proportions, whose origins and method of construction remain a mystery, but whose pervasive influence as a symbol draws us onward to some more profound and transcendent awareness?

What better answer than the Great Pyramid of Giza? This was the view of esoteric brotherhoods throughout history, from the builders of the Gothic cathedrals to the founders of America (see, for example, the Great Seal).

A forming solar eclipse is marked by the "obelisk" in Stanley Kubrick's *2001*

In the 1990s, sensational discoveries on the Giza plateau in Egypt led millions to wonder whether ancient forebears—maybe even Atlanteans—had left behind a virtual hall of records, which might soon be discovered. Recently, a new academic paper by *Atlantis Rising* contributors Dr. Robert Schoch and Robert Bauval, joined by independent researcher Dr. Manu Seyfzadeh, revisited the ancient quest for a lost cache, or hall of records, in Egypt. More on their new discovery shortly, but first some background.

In the 1993 prime-time NBC television special *The Mystery of the Sphinx,* narrated by Charlton Heston, much of the public learned for the first time that the Great Sphinx might be thousands of years older than believed by mainstream Egyptology. Leading the debate was Schoch, a Boston University geology professor with a powerful argument that water weathering of the Sphinx conclusively proved a much greater age than widely thought. At about the same time, Bauval, a Belgian engineer, along with Adrian Gilbert hypothesized in their best-selling book *The Orion Mystery* that a correlation existed between the monuments of Giza and the constellation Orion. Early in 2017, Schoch and Bauval joined forces to write *Origins of the Sphinx,* and later that year, with Seyfzadeh, they published the peer-reviewed paper mentioned above, titled "A New Interpretation of a Rare Old Kingdom Dual Title: The

Charlton Heston narrating
The Mystery of the Sphinx
in 1993

King's Chief Librarian and Guardian of the Royal Archives of *Mehit*."
That paper presented new evidence that the Sphinx not only is much
older than previously thought but also may guard a hidden chamber
containing the archives of a lost ancient civilization.*

THE CLUES OF HISTORY

While the idea of a lost fountainhead of civilization remains controversial, the suggestion that civilization's origins are much older than previously supposed remains intriguing, and many wonder whether we may
yet find some previously undiscovered record of an earlier high culture.
Is it possible that a very ancient yet advanced civilization foresaw a coming dark age of many thousands of years and took measures to leave
a kind of time capsule that could survive the dark millennia between
their age and another of parallel advancement? After all, as we have
learned from the fate of the Library of Alexandria, the knowledge from
one age is not always easy to convey to another.

Could the original builders of the monuments of Giza have left
behind such records but have hidden them so well that they could elude
detection for millennia? Some researchers, like Schoch and Bauval,
think the answer is yes, and that a hall of records is yet destined to
be discovered. Such a discovery would, hopefully, help us understand

---

*See Manu Seyfzadeh, Robert M. Schoch, and Robert Bauval, "A New Interpretation
of a Rare Old Kingdom Dual Title: The King's Chief Librarian and Guardian of the
Royal Archives of *Mehit*," *Archaeological Discovery* 5, no. 3 (July 2017), https://doi
.org/10.4236/ad.2017.53010.

The Sphinx, as found in the early 1800s, buried in sand up to its shoulders

who we are, in a much deeper way than ever before, and, perhaps, lead us to the stars. For evidence, they point to many ancient and modern sources, including the ancient Egyptians, who left many texts referring to a remote golden age preceding their own era that they called Zep Tepi, or the First Time. Zep Tepi apparently ushered in the age of Leo around 10,500 BCE.

At the spring equinox in the age of Leo, the Lion constellation would have risen just before the sun. It would have been seen due east and in alignment with the Great Sphinx of Egypt. So it could be argued that the Sphinx was built to behold its own image, which appeared in 10,500 BCE on the horizon.

If Plato is to be believed, there was a civilization much older than

Egypt, indeed many thousands of years older. Could references in ancient texts to secret rooms and passageways under and in close proximity to the Sphinx and the Giza plateau be clues to the legacy of an even earlier age? Here are a few of the intriguing references from antiquity:

- On the walls of the Temple of Edfu are allusions to the "Sacred Book of Temples," which tell of objects kept in a secret hall, and then hidden still further to protect their secrets.
- The Westcar Papyrus, dating to the Fourth Dynasty, tells of a sage named Djeda who knew of "the secret chambers of the books of Thoth." The papyrus instructed the pharaoh Khufu, later credited by some with building the Great Pyramid, with keys that would someday open the "hidden place," a library room where scrolls were kept. Djeda also made prophecies indicating when the hall would one day be discovered.
- Engravings on the Dream Stele of Thutmose IV, located between the paws of the Sphinx, actually appear to reveal an understructure of some kind below the body of the Sphinx. Some researchers think their meaning could have been literal.
- The Greek historian Herodotus, writing in 443 BCE, said that hidden under the Giza plateau was a vast labyrinth of tunnels extending in all directions far beyond the pyramid, "whereon great figures are graven," and the way into it is to be found "underground."
- The Corpus Hermeticum (written early in the Christian era, if not sooner) tells how Hermes (the Greek equivalent of Thoth) hid the "secrets of Osiris" and put a spell on them to preserve them from being seen by the unworthy.
- The Roman Marcellinus wrote in the fourth century that there are winding subterranean galleries and passages beneath the pyramids in which, he said, the ancient priests (knowing the flood was coming, and fearing that memory of their sacred ceremonies would be obliterated) constructed vaults in various places. Such a vault, said Marcellinus, would be found between the paws of a feline monument.
- Several of the quatrains of Nostradamus are interpreted by some as referring to a "hall of records."

Artist Tom Miller's conception of a Giza hall of records (also see color insert plate 3)

- Edgar Cayce said that such a chamber housing a storehouse of records existed beneath the Sphinx and prophesied that it would be discovered around the end of the twentieth century.

A MESSAGE FROM THE AGE OF LEO

In a 2017 article for *Atlantis Rising* titled "The Sphinx Breaks Its Silence," Robert Schoch explained the origins of the paper he wrote with Manu Seyfzadeh and Robert Bauval, "A New Interpretation of a Rare Old Kingdom Dual Title: The King's Chief Librarian and Guardian of the Royal Archives of *Mehit*." In May 2017, Dr. Schoch and Bauval had participated in successive conferences in California and Arizona. One of the attendees was their colleague and friend Dr. Seyfzadeh (a dermatologist with a passion for ancient Egypt), who privately revealed a personal discovery he had made: hieroglyphic evidence dating back to earliest dynastic times that refers not just to the Sphinx but also to an archive under the Sphinx, corresponding to an underground chamber in the vicinity of the Sphinx's left paw. At Seyfzadeh's invitation,

The Dream Stele of Thutmose IV shows the Sphinx resting upon
some type of structure—which could be an underground structure;
photo courtesy of Robert Schoch and his wife, Catherine Ulissey

Schoch and Bauval joined as coauthors on the paper describing the discovery. Schoch believes the paper will have historic implications.

Dr. Seyfzadeh had pointed out that on the base of a statue of Hemiunu—vizier of the pharaoh Khufu, who is conventionally credited as the builder of the Great Pyramid—there is a dual/tandem title that has eluded full translation by Egyptologists. The title, the authors believe, goes back in time to well before Khufu, as it is also found on wooden panels of Hesy-Re, an official in the court of the pharaoh Djoser who would have lived before 2500 BCE, the date usually ascribed to the Sphinx. It consists of seven distinct symbols: (1) axe; (2) reed and inkwell, forming a single symbol; (3) sedge (a plant found in Egypt); (4) bread loaf; (5) axe; (6) bent rod (a mysterious, previously undeciphered sign); and (7) recumbent lioness.

The axe symbol usually denotes an overseer, master, architect, or some sort of high official in charge of something important. Two axes indicate a dual title. The reed and inkwell, sedge, and bread loaf generally mean that the official was overseer of the royal scribes and/or architects—an extremely important position.

But what could the second title represent? The axe of the second title is identical to and, presumably, has the same meaning as the first.

But what is the apparent "bent rod," and what does the lioness represent? The lioness of the second title appears to be the same lioness represented elsewhere on the Wepemnefret stele. (Wepemnefret was the son of Khufu. Archaeologists led by George A. Reisner found the stele on the wall of his tomb in 1905.)

Egyptologist William Stevenson Smith (1907–1969) translated the hieroglyphic title as "Craftsman of Mehit." But the meaning of the bent rod protruding from, or entering into, the back of the lioness has eluded Egyptologists, in part due to its extreme rarity.

Dr. Seyfzadeh's suggestion was that the bent rod represents a physical key used to open a physical lock. By the time of the Middle Kingdom (circa early second millennium BCE), the Egyptians had developed simple lock-and-key devices, and now there is evidence that such devices actually go back to a much earlier period. Most likely, however, at such a very early date locks and keys were familiar only to the elite, and thus references to such devices appeared rarely.

Sticking a key in the back of a lioness would make no sense, say the paper's authors, unless the lioness represents something else, such as a building or statue, protecting a locked chamber or vault. Was the physical structure securing or protecting a locked vault in the shape of a lioness? Immediately the Great Sphinx comes to mind. The Sphinx today has a lion's body with a human head, but the head was recarved in dynastic times. Schoch has long argued that the Sphinx was a recumbent lion. And during seismic work carried out around the Great Sphinx in the early 1990s, as described in *Origins of the Sphinx* (see pages 70–86 of that book), Schoch and geophysicist Thomas Dobecki identified a chamber of some kind under the Sphinx in the vicinity of the left paw.

We can interpret the second part of the dual title as a reference to an overseer, master, guardian, or possessor of a key that opened a vault that was, based on the first part of the dual title (referring to scribes and records), an archive, a hall of records guarded by a lioness. In the real, physical world, that archive could have been located in the chamber under the Great Sphinx, and prior to the recarving of its head the Sphinx would have represented the lioness Mehit. The dual title could thus be translated concretely as "Overseer of the Scribes of the King and Master of the Key to the Lioness" or, more fluently, as "The King's Chief Librarian and Guardian of the Royal Archives of Mehit."

Rendition of the dual/tandem title found on the base of the statue of Hemiunu (in front of the left foot), on the stele of Wepemnefret, and on the wooden panels of Hesy-Re; illustration by Catherine Ulissey

With all this in mind, Schoch believes, there is a strong case to be made that as early as the First Dynasty (when some of the first written records in Egypt were kept) the Sphinx—which at that time was a lioness named Mehit—existed on the Giza plateau and guarded a locked chamber where archives were stored.

THE SEARCH FOR THE HALL OF RECORDS

Efforts to find a chamber beneath the Sphinx were actively pursued as late as 2009 but produced little in the way of visible results. Dr. Joseph Schor, under the auspices of Florida State University, obtained permission in 1996 from then Egyptian director of antiquities Zahi Hawass to investigate the area. Schor and his partner Joe Jahoda, a representative of the Association for Research and Enlightenment (A.R.E.), the Edgar Cayce organization, planned to map the entire Giza plateau—with the aid of ground-penetrating radar—and to excavate any resulting discoveries. Unfortunately, all of that came to an abrupt end when the Egyptian antiquities authorities inexplicably called a halt to Schor's efforts.

Schor was reluctant to discuss his findings, but at a conference held by A.R.E. in 1998 he did comment. His group, he said, had pinpointed an anomalous area about 35 feet beneath the Sphinx, which he described as a chamber in the bedrock about 25 wide and 40 feet long, with parallel walls and a height of up to 45 feet. The Cayce readings refer to such a chamber as an antechamber to the hall of records, and it was said to be off the right front paw of the Sphinx.

In 2009, Zahi Hawass stated that he planned to drill under the Great Sphinx. The report of his intention was published in the February/March edition of *Ancient Mysteries,* the A.R.E. newsletter. Joe Jahoda, a longtime A.R.E. member, had convinced Hawass to drill for a chamber under the Sphinx, and Hawass told A.R.E. representatives that soon after the drill arrived, he would get his team together and begin the drilling.

The newsletter reported that Jahoda had asked whether A.R.E. would purchase the special drill necessary to drill at an angle into the limestone bedrock. Kevin Todeschi, CEO of A.R.E., approved, and A.R.E. patron Don Dickinson agreed to help with the purchase. Thus, the drill was obtained, crated, and shipped to Egypt.

Very little further information has been forthcoming, but also in 2009, Philip Coppens reported in *Atlantis Rising* that Egyptian authorities had been pursuing ground-penetrating radar surveys of the Giza plateau on their own. Nothing definitive on the subject has emerged, though many attribute this fact to chaotic conditions in Egyptian politics, as well as to visceral objections to the introduction of any evidence of advanced prediluvian origins for the monument of the Giza plateau.

Could a hall of records be the link between our world and another—perhaps similar—one that might have existed before the deluge, accompanying the end of the last ice age? Some investigators believe that a highly evolved civilization would want to tell its story to posterity, just as we like to do by planting "time capsules." If they are right, we may yet learn, directly from the participants, the truth of what happened to Atlantis. Proof that civilization has risen and fallen on Earth, not once but many times, not only would corroborate Plato but could well change much more.

ARTIFACTS
OF KNOWLEDGE

Evidence of the
superior technology of the past

The Crystal Planet

What might the ancients have known that we don't?

A 2019 study published in the journal *Nature* found evidence that stars, like our sun, are turning into immense crystals. Indeed, say astronomers at the University of Warwick in the U.K., our sky is filled with white dwarf stars like our sun, all in the process of solidifying into crystals. The research, led by Dr. Pier-Emmanuel Tremblay, is largely based on observations taken with the European Space Agency's Gaia satellite.*

In 2017, we learned that Earth's magnetic field is at least partially powered by "quartz" crystals at its core. That was the conclusion of researchers at the Earth–Life Science Institute at the Tokyo Institute of Technology investigating laser-heated diamonds under extreme pressures, like those believed to exist at Earth's core. The Japanese scientists, who, like the Warwick researchers, published their results in the journal *Nature,* appear to be challenging the established view regarding the chemical composition of Earth's core and to be corroborating a view, long held by many in the alternative science community, that our planet is at its heart a "great crystal."†

---

*See the press release from the University of Warwick: "Thousands of Stars Turning into Crystals," ScienceDaily (online), January 9, 2019, https://www.sciencedaily.com/releases/2019/01/190109142631.htm.

†See the press release from Tokyo Tech: "'Quartz' Crystals at the Earth's Core Power Its Magnetic Field," Tokyo Tech News (online), February 23, 2017, https://www.titech.ac.jp/english/news/2017/037545.html.

A white dwarf star solidifying;
art from the University of Warwick/Mark Garlick

Crystals have long excited the human imagination. Atlantis is said by some to have employed a high science of crystals to run an advanced technology. More recently, the Vikings are reported to have used them in navigation. Today, New Agers associate them with light and magic and carry them everywhere, but the late science fiction writer Kurt Vonnegut Jr. had a different take. In his 1963 novel *Cat's Cradle,* Vonnegut facetiously imagined a type of water crystal ("ice-nine") that froze at room temperature. When a few drops accidentally fall into the ocean, water everywhere soon freezes, thus ending the world as we know it. Few, though, dream of crystals anything like those discovered in Mexico's Cueva de los Cristales in 2015. This 1,000-foot-deep cave below Naica Mountain in the Chihuahuan Desert contains the largest natural crystals ever discovered. Some are over 30 feet long. Grown in gypsum deposits, the crystals are a phenomenon unique in the world. "It's the Sistine Chapel of crystals," Spanish geologist Juan Garcia-Ruiz gushed to the now defunct news service Cosmos Online.*

---

*The Naica cavern is so amazing that it is featured in the online version of Atlas Obscura, the well-known guide to all the weird and wondrous places on our planet; see "Giant Crystals of Naica," Atlas Obscura (online), n.d., https://www.atlasobscura.com/places/giant-crystals-naica.

Inside Naica Mountain's Crystal Cave (also see color insert plate 4)

The ability of crystals to tune electronic circuits was the basis of early crystal radios. One wonders what unusual electromagnetic and optical properties may be possible with crystals of such great size as those at Naica, or in the stars.

ANCIENT POWER GRID

Some believe that a single planetary energy system, long forgotten to modern humanity, flows across the world. And that, here and there along the energy pathways, a prehistoric global civilization once tapped into its power by building vast transmission and receiving stations, using various forms of monumental architecture. Such possibilities were the basis of "Our Crystal Planet," a 1996 article for *Atlantis Rising* by the late researcher Dr. Joseph Jochmans.

"Have today's historians been so out of touch with the obvious interconnections of all of these remains," he wondered, "that they have tried to explain the silent sentinel ruins as nothing more than 'primitive' construction projects having little meaning or purpose beyond localized superstitious needs?"

Ancient and modern indigenous peoples the world over, Jochmans explained, have very similar traditions of Earth energy patterns and how they were once utilized. In England, alignments among standing stones and stone circles are called leys, along which flowed the life force that fertilized the landscape. In Ireland they are remembered as fairy paths, and in Germany as holy lines. The Greeks knew them as the sacred roads of Hermes, while the ancient Egyptians called them the pathways of Mim.

The Chinese today, said Jochmans, still measure the Lung Mei, or "dragon currents," that affect the balance of the land, as practiced through the ancient art of feng shui. Much in the same fashion as the application of acupuncture needles in Chinese medicine facilitates the flow of chi or life force in the human body, so the placement of pagodas, stones, trees, temples, and houses in the environment was regarded as a way to heal the earth.

Native Australians still go on walkabouts or pilgrimages down their dream paths, crisscrossing the desert in an effort to seasonally reenergize the life centers of the region. They work with boards, called *churinga,* that map out the dream lines, and by meditating on them, they are able to predict the approach of storms and the location of game animals as they interact with the line systems.

The old Polynesians spoke of using the *te lapa,* or "lines of light," flowing in the ocean as a method of navigation. The stone heads of Easter Island and the sacred *ahu* platforms of Hawaii were so positioned as to receive their *mana,* or life power, along *aka* threads from over the watery horizons.

When the Spanish conquistadores entered Peru in the sixteenth century, they found the entire Inca empire organized around *huacas,* or sacred centers, situated along *ceque* lines, which all converged at the Coricancha, the temple of the sun in ancient Cuzco. Similarly, the Maya of the Yucatán interconnected their pyramid sanctuaries by means of *sacbes,* raised white roadways that were built in dead-straight segments through the jungle swamps.

In western North America, medicine wheels and kiva circles are often found in linear arrangements, and in the Midwest and East coastal regions, the Mound Builders left many of their great earthen works in geometric alignments covering large areas. In New England, mysterious stone chamber sites also fit into linear patterns, and many

An Italian tracing of the "sacred line of Saint Michael," a ley line running from Jerusalem to Ireland that intersects seven ancient monasteries devoted to Saint Michael

Native American shamans today speak of energies called *orenda, manitou,* and other names that flow through the earth to promote healing.

Not only did indigenous cultures around the world tap into their local terrestrial powers, but many ancient and modern traditions recognize that these local patterns are part of a much larger energy configuration: Earth's crystal grid.

The elders of the Native American Hopi nation say that Earth's surface is like the back of a spotted fawn. As the fawn grows, the spots move and change in number. Similarly, every time the Earth Mother "sings a new song" or shifts to a new vibrational pattern, her power centers also shift to a new configuration, interconnected by a complex sacred geometry.

In the 1970s, several students of inventor Buckminster Fuller performed a series of experiments that involved submerging a balloon in a liquid medium filled with blue dye and subjecting the balloon and liquid to a certain frequency of vibration. The students found that the dye collected at specific points on the surface of the balloon, and thin lines of dye also formed, joining the points in geometric arrangements. When the frequency of the vibration increased, the original dye points quickly dissolved and then a greater number of dye points began to slowly form, again joined by lines but now in a more complex configuration.

Based on this experiment, which has been repeated and expanded upon by other researchers, as well as other studies, many now believe that Earth has its own energy centers, much like the human body has chakras and acupuncture points. Like the growing fawn or the balloon subjected to a higher frequency, when Earth periodically moves into a higher energy state, so the overall planetary energy patterns shift into new crystal-like forms. This global phenomenon appears to have been going on for a very long period of time.

A study of map projections and worldwide geological patterns conducted in 1976 by Athelstan Spilhaus, geophysicist and consultant for the National Oceanographic and Atmospheric Administration (NOAA), revealed that when the supercontinent Pangaea first broke apart approximately 220 million years ago, forming the rudiments of our modern-day continental masses, the breakup occurred along equidistant lines forming the edges and points of a tetrahedron. This geometric shape, composed of four equilateral triangles, is the first and simplest of the sacred solids of Plato.*

The Platonic solids are a series of regular polyhedrons—that is, three-dimensional shapes in which every face is an equilateral, equiangular polygon of the same shape and size. There are five Platonic solids ranging from the tetrahedron to the cube to the dodecahedron, a twelve-sided figure with each face forming a regular pentagon.

Based on the research of Han-Shou Liu of the Goddard Space Flight Center, who analyzed stress lines in the Earth caused by polar

---

*For a closer look at Spilhaus's work, see Bojan Šavrič, David Burrows, and Melita Kennedy, "The Spilhaus World Ocean Map in a Square," ArcGIS StoryMaps (online), February 7, 2020, https://storymaps.arcgis.com/stories/756bcae18d304a1eac140f19f4d5cb3d.

and land movements over the last 200 million years, Spilhaus found that the planetary structure next organized itself around a combination of two Platonic solids: the cube and the octahedron. A cube is composed of six squares, and the octahedron has eight triangles arranged like two Egyptian pyramids end to end, or in the configuration of a fluorite crystal. Earth's crystalline evolution did not end there, however, but has since moved into two even more complex Platonic forms.

THE PLANETARY DODECA

In the 1970s, three Russian researchers—historian Nikolai Goncharov, construction engineer Vyacheslav Morozov, and electronics engineer Valery Makarov—announced in *Chemistry and Life,* a journal from the Soviet Academy of Science, their discovery of a geometric grid pattern that appears to interlink a wide number of natural phenomena into a single planetary system. Their work was based on the findings of American researcher Ivan T. Sanderson, who identified what he called twelve "vile vortices" or electromagnetic energy disturbances located equidistant over the surface of the globe—with two of them being the so-called Bermuda Triangle near the Caribbean and the Devil's Sea off Japan. The three Russians found an underlying framework linking these centers into a dual crystal structure, a combination between an icosahedron and a dodecahedron. Not surprisingly, these happen to be the fourth and fifth solids in the Platonic series, which were projected outward by the Earth for over the last million years or so. The icosahedron is composed of twenty triangles forming a ball, and the dodecahedron is made up of twelve pentagons as its sides.

Drawing from their combined experience of history, engineering, and electronics, the Russian researchers decided that there was nothing in theory to have prevented a latticework pattern—a "matrix of cosmic energy," as they put it—from being built into the structure of the Earth at the time it was formed, whose shape could still be dimly perceived today. (*Pravda,* once the official Russian journal for the younger generation, followed up the idea with a suggestion that Earth had begun life as a crystal, and that only slowly did it mold itself into the spheroid it is today.) According to the hypothesis, the crystal can still be seen in twelve pentagonal slabs covering the surface of the globe—a dodeca-

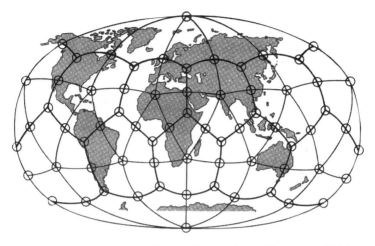

The dodecahedron of Earth, as theorized by Goncharov, Morozov, and Makarov

hedron. Overlaid onto this are twenty equilateral triangles. The entire geometric structure, they claim, can be seen in its influence on the siting of ancient civilizations, earth faults, magnetic anomalies, and many other otherwise unrelated geophysical phenomena, which are placed either at the intersections of the grid or along its lines.

That the ancients were very familiar with the Earth's crystal grid can be seen in their literature and in their archaeological remains. Plato, in describing how the planet would appear from space, stated that it looked like a ball sewn together with twelve pieces of cloth. These would be the twelve pentagons of the dodecahedron, which also forms the framework for the icosahedron grid. Gold objects found in the Khmer ruins in Southeast Asia and among Druidic remains in France, in addition to stone balls unearthed from the Neolithic period in Scotland, were all shaped to show the geometric progression of the crystal grid from tetrahedron to dodecahedron, and they're thought to have been used as teaching tools to help initiates to understand the evolution of the planetary energy systems.

THE SATURN HEXAGON

NASA's Cassini probe has been orbiting Saturn, the ringed gas giant, for years and has sent back to us some very detailed images of the planet's

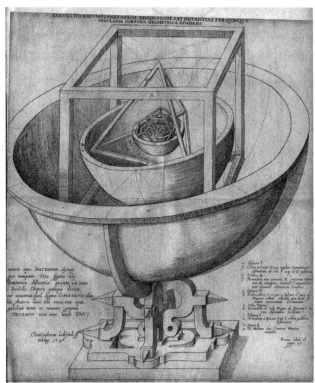

Sixteenth-century engraving of Johannes Kepler's model of the solar system based on the Platonic solids

stormy atmosphere. It seems that there is a gigantic (15,000 miles in diameter) perfect hexagonal cloud hovering over Saturn's north pole. What's more, it appears to be a permanent feature. First spotted by the Voyager spacecraft, the cloud was rephotographed years later by the Cassini space probe, still there and unchanged. So far NASA scientists have failed to come up with a satisfactory explanation for it, but that has not deterred a tide of internet speculation.*

Some think it is a manifestation of evil. Researcher Richard Hoagland sees it as evidence of hyperdimensional energy flow. Certainly it does appear to indicate the presence of some kind of geometric force field or standing wave, which would imply that the planet's underlying form is crystalline. Hoagland has suggested that Earth and Mars

---

*NASA has a video of the hexagonal cloud in motion available for viewing on its website: "Saturn's Hexagon in Motion," NASA Science (online), September 4, 2018, https://solarsystem.nasa.gov/missions/cassini/science/saturn/hexagon-in-motion/.

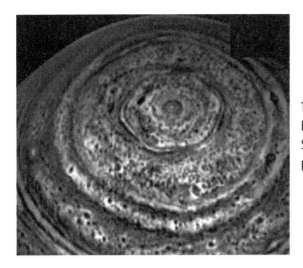

The 15,000-mile-diameter hexagonal cloud over Saturn's north pole; photo from NASA

are both basically tetrahedrons (four equilateral triangles) and that the ancient civilizations of both planets knew it. Most who see a geometric basis for the shape of Earth also acknowledge a connection with ancient grids and ley lines. To some mystics that suggests the possibility of a planetary consciousness expressed in forcefields or regions of influence. The Gaia hypothesis (Earth as goddess) is one example of such thinking.

For many in the alternative science community, the Saturn hexagon and accompanying aurora imply underlying geometric patterns that are thought to be at the core of all large natural structures, such as planets. Here on Earth, researchers have noted overarching geometric forms in events like earthquakes, storms, and volcanic activity, to say nothing of bird and animal migrations and many other natural phenomena. Changes in the planet's geomagnetic field have been associated with changes in its resonance and have been interpreted as indicative of some kind of process of ongoing, essentially organic change.

Whatever the cause of Saturn's mysterious hexagon, though, it is clear that some kind of symmetry is present where none was expected, at least by the science establishment.

For the researchers at the Earth–Life Science Institute (ELSI) at the Tokyo Institute of Technology, whom we mentioned earlier, the main issue appears to be which alloys can be found at the center of the Earth. According to a 2017 news release for Tokyo Tech News, "In 2013, Kei Hirose, now director of ELSI, reported that the Earth's core may have cooled by as much as 1,000°C since its formation 4.5 billion years ago. This large amount of cooling would have been necessary to sustain the geomagnetic field—unless there was another as yet undiscovered source of energy. These results were a major surprise to the so-called deep Earth community and created what Peter Olson of Johns Hopkins University referred to as 'the new core paradox.'"* The established understanding about Earth's core was not matching up with the new facts that ELSI and others were providing.

While the conventional view has been that Earth's molten core is mostly iron, the researchers at ELSI experimented with other alloys that might also be present, including some containing silicon and oxygen. They found that at the temperatures and pressures likely found at the core, these elements could combine to form quartz-like silicon dioxide crystals—and that crystallization could provide immense energy for the planet, thereby solving Olson's paradox. In other words, the notion of a crystal planet, and the sacred geometry implied, may not be so far-fetched after all.

---

*See Peter Olson, "The New Core Paradox," *Science* 342, no. 6157 (October 2013): 431–32, https://doi.org/10.1126/science.1243477.

5

Wisdom of the Ancients

Following the clues to a lost science

The vast Hebrew Torah—the first five books of the Bible, according to conventional scholarship—was passed down orally from generation to generation, long before being written down in the sixth century BCE. Similar claims can be made for many ancient scriptures.

Speech or song, folktales, ballads, chants, prose, and verses have been handed down in this manner for many thousands of years with astonishing accuracy. The phenomenon has caused many to wonder just how anyone could remember so much. Certainly, it is a gift seldom

A temple scroll of the Hebrew Torah

Stonehenge just before dawn

found in today's Google-driven and short-attention-span culture. It's certainly not an aspect of the "Twitterverse."

Australian science writer Dr. Lynne Kelly is convinced that sacred places, like Stonehenge, Nazca, Easter Island, and sites all over the ancient world have played a little understood but crucial role in the preservation of ancient memory. In her 2017 book *The Memory Code,* Kelly claims that Neolithic people were able to preserve knowledge by using the landscape as a mnemonic tool, much like with the memorization technique known as the method of loci. Operating as a kind of memory enhancement technique, the method employs visualizations and spatial memory—familiar information about one's environment—to facilitate the quick and efficient recall of information. The ancient Britons, says Kelly, could have built Stonehenge in an attempt to replicate locally a more distant landscape, helping them to memorize and store knowledge that would otherwise be forgotten. Circles and stones or timber posts could have represented the landscape, and each stone would have been associated with a segment of their knowledge system.

The henges across northern Europe, the elaborate stone houses of New Mexico, huge animal shapes in Peru, and the statues of Easter Island were all built, believes Kelly, to serve as "the most effective memory system ever invented by humans." However, the ability to manipulate abstract numbers and shapes may represent another kind of ancient memory with implications as great, or greater, for civilization.

THE NUMBERS OF DIVINITY

For one thing: learning arithmetic should not be such a big deal. That seems to be the implication of a recent study at the University of Nottingham and Harvard. According to the study, children who haven't yet learned the basic rules of arithmetic, like place value and the addition table, nevertheless can easily solve illustrated problems involving approximate addition and subtraction of symbolic numbers between five and ninety-eight. The children in the study performed well above chance and, in the process, astonished teachers accustomed to seeing their students struggle greatly in this arena. Dr. Camilla Gilmore, who led the work, said we may now be able learn new strategies for teaching primary mathematics and "making it fun." The research has lent weight to concepts, such as those modeled by the Montessori method, that children bring an innate knowledge to the learning process.

For those who believe that human intelligence begins and ends with the physical brain, such an idea is difficult to accept. On the other hand, for those who perceive the brain to be, at best, a link or tuning device that merely taps into knowledge that emerges from some kind of resonant nonphysical source, the findings in the new study make perfect sense.

Here's another clue to consider: the next time you find yourself attracted to someone's face, chalk it up to the golden ratio. As defined by *Webster's Dictionary*, the golden ratio is "a ratio of two numbers in which the ratio of the sum to the larger number is the same as the ratio of the larger number to the smaller." Put simply, that ratio is approximately equal to 1.618:1, and it's commonly represented by the Greek letter phi.

Long thought to be the universal key to growth, the ratio, which appears over and over in nature's structures, has been shown to play a key role in our perception of beauty. Whether or not the Golden Ratio is the key, the role that proportion plays in beauty seems evident. Dr. Kang Lee of the University of Toronto and his colleagues at the University of California at San Diego tested for the ideal facial feature arrangements on female faces by changing the distances between eyes, nose, and mouth.* According to the press release: "They discovered two 'golden ratios,' one for length and one for width. Female faces were judged more attractive when the vertical distance between the eyes and the mouth was approximately

---

*See the press release from the University of Toronto: "Researchers Discover New 'Golden Ratios' for Female Facial Beauty," EurekaAlert! (online), December 16, 2009, https://www.eurekalert.org/pub_releases/2009-12/uot-rdn121609.php#:~:text=They%20 discovered%20two%20%22golden%20ratios,percent%20of%20the%20face's%20width.

36 percent of the face's length, and the horizontal distance between the eyes was approximately 46 percent of the face's width. Interestingly, these proportions correspond with those of the average face."

Indeed, the mathematical face of divinity has appeared in many other surprising places.

In 2011, Aidan Dwyer, a thirteen-year-old seventh grader from Northport, New York, wowed the energy research community with a discovery relating solar energy to the Fibonacci sequence. He showed that when solar panels are arranged in the fashion of actual tree leaves, which follow a pattern named after eighteenth-century Italian mathematician Leonardo of Pisa (later known as Fibonacci), they produce from 20 to 50 percent more energy than when the panels are set up in the standard manner. Intrigued by the orderly way in which branches spiral upward around a tree trunk, Aidan realized that the natural pattern was one that optimized the collection of sunlight by tree leaves, yielding the greatest return over time. In contrast, standard solar arrays must be either moved mechanically to follow the sun—a costly, energy-consuming process—or placed in fixed positions that are most productive only during brief intervals when the sun is shining directly upon them.

The Fibonacci sequence is a variation on the golden ratio. It comprises a series of numbers, beginning at 1, in which each number is equal to the sum of the two preceding numbers. The following sequence results: 1, 1, 2, 3, 5, 8, 13, 21, 34 . . . Perhaps not coincidentally, the ratio between any two successive numbers in the Fibonacci sequence equals the golden ratio.

Many have argued that the pattern created by the golden ratio, which is pervasive in nature, is the virtual fingerprint of God, clearly revealing the presence of order in the universe. Widespread application of the golden ratio and other high geometric harmonies in classic ancient art and temple architecture, it is argued, is strong evidence for great advancement in ancient civilization, whereas the chaotic nature of modern civilization—obedient to no discernible order—could be taken as evidence of advanced and widespread decay.

THE GEOMETRY OF SPIRIT

Followers of the Sufi path in Islam have long believed that the spinning dancers known as dervishes are uniquely in touch with the spirit

Whirling dervishes in Turkey

of God. In a 2013 study published in the *New Journal of Physics,* an international team of researchers suggested that the long white skirts of the dancers generate mysterious patterns that mirror natural Coriolis forces—the apparent forces that, as a result of Earth's rotation, deflect moving objects (such as air currents) to the right in the northern hemisphere and to the left in the southern hemisphere. "Their skirts show these very striking, long-lived patterns with sharp cusp-like features which seem rather counterintuitive," said one of the paper's authors, James Hanna, from Virginia Tech. By employing the principles behind the Coriolis effect, the researchers were able to describe the strange skirt patterns mathematically.*

Whirling dervishes, though of ancient origin, remain a popular tourist attraction in Turkey. The celebrated Russian spiritual teacher G. I. Gurdjieff, himself a Sufi initiate, believed that the dervishes and other practitioners of ancient dance rituals were able to convey, through their complex movements, advanced ancient wisdom predating written communication such as that found in sacred geometry and art.

Another study, this one investigating the enigmatic Pict people of

---

*See a news release about the study from IOP Publishing: "A Whirling Dervish Puts Physicists in a Spin," IOP Publishing (online), November 27, 2013, https://iopscience .iop.org/article/10.1088/1367-2630/15/11/113055.

Hilton of Cadboll Stone, a Pictish stone from northern Scotland

Scotland, shows that as early as about 500 CE, Pictish artisans and architects were using the golden ratio in building Christian chapels. The Picts have long been considered a primitive, albeit very artistic, people. Archaeological investigations of a Pictish monastery at Portmahomack on the Tarbat peninsula in Scotland, however, reveal an unexpected mastery of advanced design principles.*

A similar revelation has been claimed by alternative scholars for builders of the Great Pyramid in Egypt, who are credited with incorporating the golden ratio into its design. In "Divine Proportion," a 2013 article for *Atlantis Rising*, writer Patrick Marsolek noted that the slope of the sides of the Great Pyramid is virtually identical to the slope of a theoretical "Golden Pyramid," incorporating the phi ratio as an integral part of its geometry. According to orthodoxy, there is no "historical"

---

*For more details about the Picts and their surprising advancements, see Ian Johnston, "The Truth about the Picts," *The Independent* (online), August 6, 2008, http://www.independent.co.uk/news/science/the-truth-about-the-picts-886098.html.

(i.e., textual) evidence that the Egyptians knew about phi, or could have been capable of making such a sophisticated calculation, but, Marsolek wondered, could its obvious presence be simply a coincidence?*

The great French scholar R. A. Schwaller de Lubicz, author of *The Temple in Man* (1981), an exhaustive study of the vast ancient temple at Luxor, Egypt, produced extensive evidence that the Egyptians knew about phi and encoded it throughout the temple. The Luxor Temple, indeed, displays a kind of proportional growth similar to the geometrical progression expressed in the Fibonacci series, in which the addition of a new copy or representation of a given figure to the existing pattern results in a larger version of the original structure, but with the same shape. This pattern is considered a physical signature of the golden ratio, and it can be seen in many animal bodies in the way that hard tissues like bones, teeth, shells, and horns develop; consider, for example, the shell of the chambered nautilus.

De Lubicz demonstrated that sections of the Temple of Luxor display such a progression (as do many Hindu temples), with additional sections of the temple building on the previous as guided by phi proportions. Furthermore, de Lubicz demonstrated, the entire temple corresponds to a complete human body, with different sections representing different anatomical parts.

However, de Lubicz emphasized, phi has a more abstract meaning beyond its physical measure in the temple structure. By analogy, he suggested, imagine a revolving sphere, which implies the presence of an axis. While we can *imagine* such an axis, it does not objectively exist. Still, such an imaginary axis can be used to calculate the properties, movement, and mass of the sphere. The stones of the Temple of Luxor, de Lubicz claimed, are a record of the numerical expression of phi. Phi in its universal aspect is unmanifest, yet it very much pervades the temple, just as the axis informs the sphere's physical manifestation.

De Lubicz was not the only one to see phi in this way. The seventeenth-century German mathematician and astronomer

---

*For an analysis of the use of the golden ratio in the Great Pyramid complex and other ancient Egyptian structures, see Gary Meisner, "Golden Ratios in Great Pyramid of Giza Site Topography," GoldenNumber.net (online), May 14, 2016, https://www.goldennumber.net/great-pyramid-giza-complex-golden-ratio/.

Shell of a
chambered
nautilus

Ruins of the Temple of Luxor in Egypt

Johannes Kepler believed that the golden ratio served as a fundamental tool used by God to create the universe. More recently, the twentieth-century Swiss architect Le Corbusier, focusing on systems of harmony and proportion, described the properties of the golden ratio as "rhythms apparent to the eye and clear in their relations with one another. And

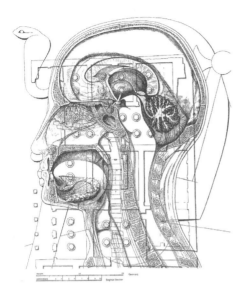

A section of the Temple of Luxor corresponding to the human head

these rhythms are at the very root of human activities. They resound in man by an organic inevitability, the same fine inevitability which causes the tracing out of the Golden Section [i.e., the golden ratio] by children, old men, savages and the learned."*

THE MUSIC OF THE SPHERES

In the January 2015 issue of *Atlantis Rising,* Julie Loar wrote about *musica universalis,* the "music of the spheres," an ancient Greek philosophical concept that sees the proportions of the movements of celestial bodies—the sun, moon, and planets—as a form of *musica,* the medieval Latin word for music. Music in this form is not audible but is understood as a mathematical concept. The Greek philosopher Pythagoras is usually credited with this idea, which stemmed from his mystical and mathematical philosophy and its associated system of numerology. The discovery of the geometric relationship between mathematics and music is also attributed to him. Pythagoreans believed that this relationship gave music powers of healing, as it could "harmonize" the out-of-balance body.

There is a legend, said Loar, that Pythagoras could hear the music

---

*See Le Corbusier, *Towards a New Architecture* (1927; repr., Eastford, CT: Martino Fine Books, 2014).

Greek philosopher Pythagoras in Raphael's sixteenth-century fresco *The School of Athens*

of the spheres, enabling him to discover that consonant musical intervals can be expressed in simple ratios of small integers. In an effort to win their confidence, Pythagoras told Egyptian priests that the god Thoth gave him the ability to hear this "music." He believed that only Egyptians of the right bloodline, passing successful initiations, could enter the temples and learn the mysteries set in place by divine beings at the beginning of time. Plato and others transferred Pythagoras's concepts into structural models of the universe, assigning the Platonic solids to the planets and alchemical elements: earth—tetrahedron, water—cube, air—octahedron, fire—dodecahedron, and quintessence—icosahedron. The spheres were thought to relate to whole-number ratios of pure musical intervals, creating harmonies.

According to Manley P. Hall, eighteenth-century British scholar Thomas Stanley was a leading authority on Pythagorean musical wisdom. In his 1731 book *The History of Philosophy,* Stanley offered the following explanation on why Pythagoras is now generally credited with discovery of the diatonic scale:

Having first learned the divine theory of music from the priests of the various Mysteries into which he had been accepted, Pythagoras pondered for several years upon the laws governing consonance and dissonance. How he actually solved the problem is unknown, but the following explanation has been invented.

One day while meditating upon the problem of harmony, Pythagoras chanced to pass a brazier's shop where workmen were pounding out a piece of metal upon an anvil. By noting the variances in pitch between the sounds made by large hammers and those made by smaller implements, and carefully estimating the harmonies and discords resulting from combinations of these sounds, he gained his first clue to the musical intervals of the diatonic scale.

After carefully scrutinizing the brazier's tools, Pythagoras noted the weights and returned home to build a wooden arm, extending from the wall of his room, with four cords attached at regular intervals and corresponding to the weight of the brazier's hammers: twelve pounds for the first cord, nine pounds for the second, eight pounds for the third, and six pounds for the fourth.

Pythagoras thereupon discovered that the first and fourth strings when sounded together produced the harmonic interval of the octave, for doubling the weight had the same effect as halving the string. The tension of the first string being twice that of the fourth string, their ratio was said to be 2:1, or duple. By similar experimentation he ascertained that the first and third string produced the harmony of the diapente, or the interval of the fifth. The tension of the first string being half again as much as that of the third string, their ratio was said to be 3:2, or sesquialter. Likewise the second and fourth strings, having the same ratio as the first and third strings, yielded a diapente harmony. Continuing his investigation, Pythagoras discovered that the first and second strings produced the harmony of the diatessaron, or the interval of the third; and the tension of the first string being a third greater than that of the second string, their ratio was said to be 4:3, or sesquitercian. The third and fourth strings, having the same ratio as the first and second strings, produced another harmony of the diatessaron. According to Iamblichus, the second and third strings had the ratio of 8:9, or epogdoan.

Stanley added, "The key to harmonic ratios is hidden in the famous Pythagorean tetractys, or pyramid of dots. The tetractys is made up of the first four numbers—1, 2, 3, and 4—which in their proportions reveal the intervals of the octave, the diapente, and the diatessaron. While the law of harmonic intervals as set forth above is true, it has been subsequently proved that hammers striking metal in the manner [work as stated]."*

In a chaotic world where discord seems to dominate, a shift to harmony may seem unlikely, but John Michell, the late author and scholar of Atlantean lore (*The View Over Atlantis,* 1969), remained optimistic. Dissonant music, he said, "will overcome itself." In a 1995 interview with *Atlantis Rising,* he explained, "It has always been recognized that music is the most powerful of the arts. As Plato said, forms of government eventually follow the forms of music. That's why the ancients were very careful in controlling music—no cacophony was allowed. The same music was heard at festivals every year and people were held under a kind of enchantment where the mind was held under one influence. Music is by far the most powerful means for therapy. Certainly the music—and the other art forms too—we see now is threatening society with chaos. It's a vessel that not only reflects what happens but actually determines what *will* happen. As to what will come about, I have no idea. I think more and more it's in the hands of God and that there is now working out an alchemical process and that changes come about through nature—through the natural process of cause and effect. Things are chaotic and we have a reaction and a yearning for a source of order—there's quest for that and an invocation of that, and then there follows a revelation."

---

*See Manley P. Hall, *The Secret Teaching of All Ages,* First Thus ed. (South Orange, NJ: A & D Books, 2013).

6

Secrets of the Portolans

*Where could the sailors of the
Middle Ages have learned their tricks?*

Ancient seafarers had no GPS, no radar, and no sonar to guide them. Getting where they wanted to go depended on the skill and experience—to say nothing of the daring—of their ship's pilot. The late thirteenth century saw the development of highly prized navigational charts known as portolans (*portolanos* in Italian), which mapped out the coastlines and provided directions and distances to various ports in the Mediterranean and Black Sea. With the dawning of the so-called Age of Discovery in the early fifteenth century, Spain and Portugal, both seafaring powers of the era, treated portolans as top state secrets. Later, the Dutch and the English would use them to guide raiding and trading missions.

Scholars have long thought the portolans to be a product of the accumulated experience of Mediterranean seamen, providing essential compass headings and distance estimates learned over generations of trial and error. Proof, however, of the actual origins of the portolan charts has been elusive, and to this day their true source remains an unsolved mystery.

According to intensive research published in 2016 by geodetic scientist Roel Nicolai of Holland's Utrecht University, these realistic sea charts, which first appeared in the late thirteenth-century Carta Pisana (an ancient map hand-drawn on sheepskin and depicting the entire Mediterranean Sea), could not possibly have originated in medieval

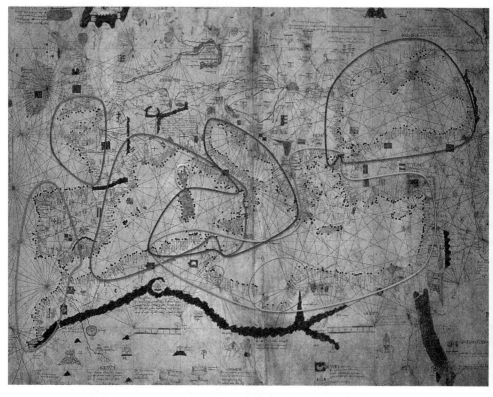

By averaging the data from numerous single sailing records, Dr. Nicolai attempted to replicate the presumed method by which portolan charts were produced.

Roel Nicolai

Europe. According to Nicolai's research, there are no signs of earlier, simpler precursors from which they could have evolved, and navigational equipment at the time was not sophisticated enough to have provided the data needed for the astounding accuracy of the portolans.

A press release about Nicolai's research notes:

> So far, it has been assumed that sailors carefully recorded data about their courses and distances they travelled on busy shipping routes. It was believed that their measurements were compiled in so-called portolans, books with sailing instruction, and eventually processed by cartographers [that is, made into maps]. Nicolai, however, has shown that it is unlikely that the nautical compass was available in time and that navigational methods used at that time were sophisticated enough to determine distances at such a degree of accuracy.*

In an attempt to replicate the presumed method by which portolan charts were produced, Nicolai averaged the data from numerous single sailing records detailing the location of harbors, the direction of travel, and so on. The accuracy of his results was worse, by a factor of ten, than that of the actual portolan charts. That was true even when he used methods to calculate averages that were not available before the end of the seventeenth century. Only in the nineteenth century did cartographers finally manage to re-achieve the accuracy of the portolans.

According to Nicolai, a recent analysis of the oldest surviving portolan—by Portuguese cartographer Jorge de Aguiar in 1492—revealed that its source data must have been derived, or copied, from some earlier unknown maps and not from any data jotted down by navigators of that time period. Indeed, the map copiers, who certainly used medieval parchment, probably had no idea of the incredible accuracy of the details they were transferring. "We immediately recognize [in the portolan] the shape of the Mediterranean," said Nicolai, "but even in the late Middle Ages, that shape was far from established on maps. Nobody really knew how all of the Mediterranean's shorelines ran."

Nicolai's research also made the case that the portolans were copied from various sources: "There are obvious differences of scale and orientation between different areas on portolan maps. Not only does that demonstrate clearly that they were collated from different maps,

---

*For more information, see the full press release from Utrecht University: "Origin of 'Medieval' Sea Charts Disproven," Utrecht University News (online), March 3, 2014, https://www.uu.nl/en/news/origin-of-medieval-sea-charts-disproven.

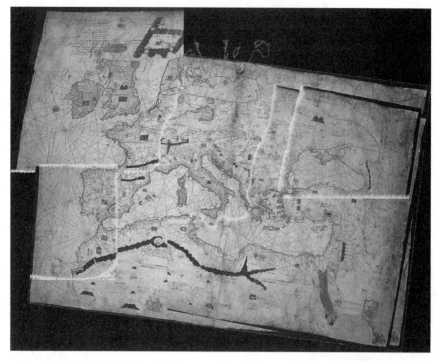

This full map is made from a mosaic of many portolans apparently copied from older sources. Portolan shorelines are in blue. Actual shorelines are in red. In the resulting composite, the Mediterranean is displayed with much more accuracy than the common sailing knowledge of the time would have permitted, suggesting that the source maps contained more advanced geographic knowledge than the map copiers possessed. (Also see color insert plate 6.)

it also shows that those medieval cartographers were not familiar with the techniques used to produce those different sources."

Nicolai also showed, amazingly, that three centuries before Mercator, the originators of the portolans had the mathematical sophistication to project the curvature of the Earth onto a flat surface. This is no easy trick.

The main reason most ancient maps look crude or primitive to modern eyes is their failure to reflect the Earth's roundness in the way we have come to expect. In 1569, the Flemish cartographer Gerardus Mercator unveiled a method of projecting the planet's surface onto a virtual cylinder, which made it possible to show lines of constant course,

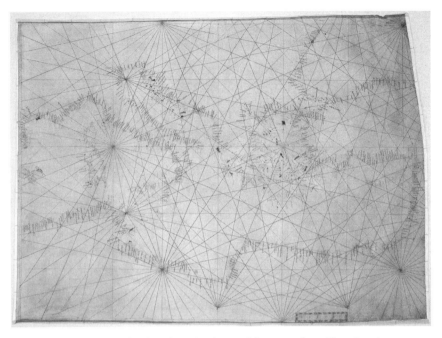

Reference chart, held at the U.S. Library of Congress, for sailing direction
and distance to various medieval ports

called rhumb lines or loxodromes. The technique preserved the angles
with the meridians. The linear scale was equal in all directions around
any point, thus simplifying the challenge of navigation. In other words,
straight lines on a map translate to straight lines at sea. The Mercator
projection, which required the use of an advanced mathematical conversion formula, had the effect of enlarging the apparent scale of areas
near the poles and shrinking those near the equator, but it represented
a great improvement over earlier methods.

No evidence has been found that the knowledge required for the
projection of curvature was available when the portolans were made.
The demonstration that the portolans were based on such projection
methods could be a true game changer.

In trying to identify the original source of the mysterious charts,
Nicolai did consider ancient Constantinople, but then he ruled it out.
The Byzantines, he believed, added little to the scientific knowledge
they inherited from the classical age, providing only a repository for
ancient Greek and Arabic knowledge. And he saw no reason why the

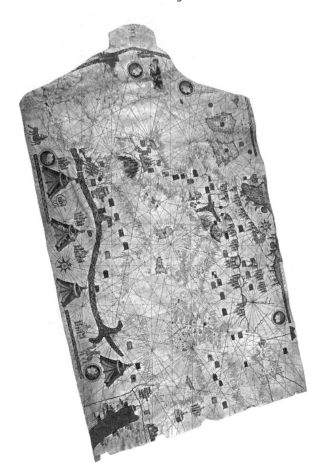

The Roselli map, a typical thirteenth-century portolan navigational chart (also see color insert plate 5)

Byzantines would even attempt to chart English and French coastlines that were well beyond their sphere of interest.

Could portolans have had an Arabic background? After all, the Arabs were keen astronomers and navigators. But, Nicolai contended, the accuracy of the portolans transcended the Arab navigational ability of the time and, for that matter, what we know of Roman and Greek scientific knowledge as well. Although he conceded that the Arabs were scientifically ahead of Europe and had considerable knowledge of chart projections, he did not believe it had been convincingly shown that they had the knowledge required to reduce observations of the Earth's curvature to a flat map surface.

The inescapable implication was, Nicolai believed, that part of history needs to be rewritten. "This needs to happen even if I am wrong," he said, "because [the portolan creators] were much further advanced in terms of knowledge in the Middle Ages than we think." For him, the idea that such medieval European developments could have existed (and that we have been totally unaware of them) is implausible. After all, he explained, charts of other parts of Europe were demonstrably less accurate than the portolans of the Mediterranean and Black Sea.

What does seem plausible, he argued, is that portolan charts originated from a tradition that is now lost. As for speculating about lost civilizations, he did not want to go there. For the moment, though, he was convinced that we must think our way back step by step.

If such sophisticated cartographic technology did not come from the Greeks, the Romans, the Byzantines, the Arabs, or even the Phoenicians, the burning question remaining is: Where, exactly, could it have come from?

Strangely enough, some believe, the answer may have been proposed a half century earlier by a pioneering small-college professor in New England.

THE MAP OF COLUMBUS

The portolans of the Mediterranean and Black Sea, as it turns out, were not the only highly accurate, albeit anomalous, maps that have survived from antiquity. In 1966, Charles Hapgood, a cartographer and Harvard-trained professor of anthropology and history at Keene State College in New Hampshire, published *Maps of the Ancient Sea Kings*. The book featured many maps that clearly revealed advanced knowledge from some unknown source. These maps, Hapgood believed, provided "hard evidence that advanced people preceded all the people now known to history."

Hapgood was no ordinary small-college professor. He had been an official in the administration of President Franklin Roosevelt, and in the 1950s he personally advised President Eisenhower concerning ancient map evidence. Albert Einstein himself wrote a foreword to one of Hapgood's books.

Regarding the portolan mystery, Hapgood acknowledged that most such charts were of the Mediterranean and the Black Sea, but he knew that well-authenticated maps of other areas also survived—maps that

Charles Hapgood

demonstrated similar accuracy but on a much larger scale. In the preface to *Maps of the Ancient Sea Kings,* he stated flatly, "The ancient voyagers traveled from pole to pole." As impossible as it may sound, he wrote, "the evidence nevertheless indicates that some ancient people explored the coast of Antarctica when it was free of ice. It is clear, too, that they had an instrument of navigation for accurately finding the longitudes of places that was far superior to anything possessed by the peoples of ancient, medieval, or modern times until the second half of the eighteenth century."

Discovered in 1929 in Topkapi Palace (or Seraglio), the former imperial residence in Constantinople, the most remarkable of Hapgood's maps was created by Piri Reis, a sixteenth-century Turkish admiral. Inscriptions on its margin claim that the western part, showing the American coasts, was copied from a map that had been in the possession of Christopher Columbus but had fallen into the hands of the admiral along with the booty seized from eight Spanish ships captured in a battle off the coast of Valencia in 1501 or 1508.

That very map, Hapgood believed, had been part of a larger one that in 1492 had guided Columbus on his epic journey of discovery. In correspondence with President Eisenhower, Hapgood promoted a renewed effort to find the chart, which he believed still to be in Spanish hands.

"The most remarkable detail of the Piri Reis map, indicating its

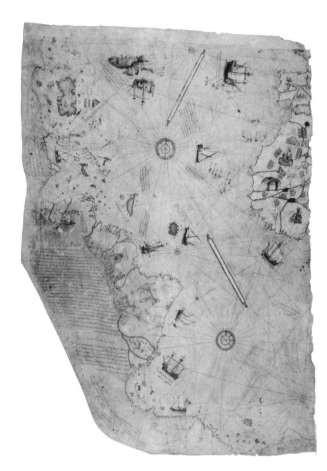

The Piri Reis map

enormous age," Hapgood wrote to Eisenhower, "was pointed out by Captain Arlington H. Mallery some years ago. [Mallery] stated that the lower part of this map showed the sub-glacial topography of Queen Maud Land, Antarctica, and the Palmer Peninsula. After four years of study of the map, we came to recognize that Captain Mallery's statement was correct, but desiring the most authoritative checking of our conclusions, we submitted the data to the cartographic staff of the Strategic Air Command." Hapgood appended the Air Force study to his letter. He continued, "Needless to say, this is a matter of enormous importance for cartography and for history. The Antarctic ice cap is at present one mile thick over the areas shown on the Piri Reis Map. Consultations with geological specialists have indicated beyond question the truth that the data on the map is many thousands of years old.

It seems that the Antarctic ice cap [has] covered the Queen Maud Land coast [for at least the last] 6,000 years. . . . The map information must have been obtained earlier, either by the Phoenicians or by some earlier (and unknown) people."

The ancient sea charts, including the Piri Reis map and others, Hapgood believed, reflected the possession of highly accurate information that had been passed down for thousands of years from people to people. It was possible, he thought, that the Minoans (the sea kings of ancient Crete) and the Phoenicians could have been involved in the transmission, if not necessarily the origination, of the information. In his book, Hapgood provided evidence that ancient maps were collected and studied in the great Library of Alexandria and compilations of them were made by the geographers who worked there. That library, as we noted earlier, had been totally destroyed by the end of the fourth century, with its contents completely lost.

Well, maybe not *completely* . . .

Hapgood also knew that copies of these maps had been transferred to Constantinople. Rand Flem-Ath, who, with his wife Rose, wrote *Atlantis beneath the Ice* (2012), was a frequent correspondent of Hapgood's. In his book, Flem-Ath says Hapgood thought these maps inspired the European "Age of Discovery and especially the expeditions under the direction of King Henry, the Navigator of Portugal."

In *Atlantis Rising* #78 (November/December 2009), in his article "The Lost World Map of Christopher Columbus," Flem-Ath explained how Hapgood feared that the Spanish would not pursue the search out of concern that it might reveal that someone other than Columbus deserved the credit for discovering America. Still, Eisenhower followed through on the professor's proposal, instructing John David Lodge, his ambassador to Spain, to attempt to locate the map.

To this day, though, its whereabouts remain a mystery.

THE ATLANTIS CONNECTION

In his professional academic publications, Hapgood preferred to attribute maps like the one that inspired Piri Reis to the ancient Egyptians and shied away from mentioning Atlantis. The very word was—and to a large extent still is—taboo. But with his students, he was quite open on the subject and even encouraged them to research it. And, according to Flem-Ath, who examined Hapgood's personal archives at Yale, the idea of Atlantis was at the root of his fascination with the maps of the ancient sea kings. The islands of Saint Peter and Saint Paul in the mid-Atlantic, Hapgood believed, in fact, matched Plato's description of the plain upon which the city of Atlantis once stood.

The Saint Peter and Saint Paul Rocks, as they are formally known, are situated 100 kilometers (62 miles) north of the equator and are the only Brazilian oceanic islets in the northern hemisphere. Their total land mass above water is about 4.2 acres, and their highest elevation, on Nordeste Island, is just 59 feet above sea level. According to Wikipedia, the archipelago is composed of several rocks, five small rocky islets, and four larger islets. In 1832, the rocks were visited by Charles Darwin on the first leg of his famous voyage around the world on HMS *Beagle*. Darwin listed all the fauna he could find and noted that he could not find a single plant or even a lichen on the island.

"When [Hapgood] spotted those mid-Atlantic islands," Flem-Ath told *Atlantis Rising*, "he immediately thought—Atlantis! He even tried to interest President Kennedy in the quest." His timing was terrible, though. After starting the ball rolling in October 1963, he hoped to see JFK before Christmas, but—as we all now know—events in Dallas intervened.

Many questions persist regarding what kind of lost ancient society could have possessed the knowledge needed to create the Piri Reis map and the portolans. For those who treat the matter seriously, though, there has been no shortage of clues that there was once a civilization on this planet possessing many great secrets, which have been lost. One need only consider the advanced technologies that must have been employed in the building of mysterious ancient monuments, like the Great Pyramid, Angkor Wat, or Easter Island, to see that we have forgotten a great deal.

Ciphers of the Initiated

How much can the rest of us expect to learn?

The quest for lost secret knowledge can take many forms. The survivors of Atlantis, some believe, might have taken steps to guard their advanced knowledge against the dark ages they saw were coming, preserving it for rediscovery by some future, similarly advanced society. Their knowledge, it has been speculated, could have been preserved in well-hidden archives. Edgar Cayce, the renowned sleeping prophet of Virginia Beach, Virginia, predicted that we would find more than one "hall of records," and to this day many continue to search for one. Whether or not such an archive is to be found, there may be another place to look for lost knowledge from the past. Some of the greatest thinkers and writers in history, it turns out, have embedded important secrets in their work, where only the initiated, who knew what to look for, could find them, and where, like the contents of a buried archive, they may still await discovery.

THE COPIALE CIPHER

According to a University of Southern California press release, "A strange eighteenth-century German manuscript seems straight out of fiction— a handwritten message in abstract symbols and Roman letters meticulously covering 105 yellowing pages, hidden in the depths of an academic archive. Now, more than three centuries after it was devised, the seventy-five-thousand-character Copiale Cipher finally has been broken. The mysterious cryptogram, bound in gold and green brocade paper, reveals the rituals and political leanings of an eighteenth-century secret society in Germany. The rituals detailed in the document indicate that the society apparently had a fascination with eye surgery and ophthalmology, though it seems members of the society were not eye doctors."*

Of course, biblical parables directed to those who had "eyes to see" might also have been considered by the uninitiated to be optometrically related, but that would have missed the point.

The Copiale translation "opens up a window for people who study the history of ideas and the history of secret societies," said computer scientist Kevin Knight, who was part of the team that finally cracked the code. "Historians believe that secret societies have had a role in revolutions, but all that is yet to be worked out, and a big part of the reason is because so many documents are enciphered."

To break the cipher, Knight and colleagues Beáta Megyesi and Christiane Schaefer of Uppsala University in Sweden tracked down the original manuscript, which had been discovered in the East Berlin Academy after the Cold War and is now in a private collection. The team transcribed a machine-readable version of the text, using a computer program created by Knight to help quantify the co-occurrences of certain symbols and other patterns.

"When you get a new code and look at it, the possibilities are nearly infinite," Knight said. "Once you come up with a hypothesis based on your intuition as a human, you can turn over a lot of grunt work to the computer."

With the Copiale Cipher, the codebreaking team began without even knowing the language of the encrypted document. But because they had a hunch about the Roman and Greek characters distributed throughout the manuscript, they isolated these from the abstract symbols and attacked it as the true code.

"It took quite a long time and resulted in complete failure," Knight said.

After trying eighty languages, the cryptography team ultimately realized the Roman characters were "nulls" intended to mislead the reader. It was the abstract symbols that held the message.

---

*See the press release from the University of Southern California: "USC Scientist Cracks Mysterious 'Copiale Cipher," University of Southern California (online), October 25, 2011, https://pressroom.usc.edu/usc-scientist-cracks-mysterious-copiale-cipher.

The Copiale Cipher

The team later tested the hypothesis that abstract symbols with similar shapes represented the same letter or groups of letters. Eventually, the first meaningful words of German emerged: "ceremonies of initiation," followed by "secret section."

As the USC press release explained, "Knight's plan was then to target other coded messages, including ciphers sent by the Zodiac Killer, a serial murderer who passed taunting messages to the press but has never been caught. Knight also aimed to apply his computer-assisted code-breaking software to other famous unsolved codes such as the last section of *Kryptos,* a sculpture bearing an encrypted message carved into four large copper plates on the grounds of CIA headquarters,* and the Voynich Manuscript, a mysterious medieval document that has baffled professional cryptographers for decades." Some of the most curious and complex ciphers, though, have been passed down to us by the greatest geniuses in history.

---

*For more details about the mysterious *Kryptos,* see Julian Borger, "Interest Grows in Solving Cryptic CIA Puzzle after Link to Da Vinci Code," *The Guardian* (online), June 11, 2005, http://books.guardian.co.uk/news/articles/0,6109,1504317,00.html.

Kryptos sculpture at CIA headquarters, Langley, Virginia

THE FRANCIS BACON ENIGMA

As millions of fans of Dan Brown's book *The Da Vinci Code* know, Leonardo is said by some to have buried deep secrets of Christian origins in his paintings and drawings. And he may not be the only Renaissance artist to have resorted to such tactics. Recently, two art-loving Brazilian doctors claimed to have uncovered secret lessons about human anatomy left by Michelangelo in his paintings on the ceiling of the Sistine Chapel in the Vatican.*

The unraveling of secret codes left by the giants of Western culture has become a passion for some researchers. Sleuths—both professional and amateur—still rummage through dusty archives and libraries in search of hidden knowledge. Of all the candidates for the title of "greatest literary mystery," some scholars argue, there are none more intriguing than those in the Shakespearean plays. Many wise men, including Mark Twain and Friedrich Nietzsche, have believed that the secret author of

---

*See Sam Savage, "Brazilian Doctors Uncover 'Michelangelo Code,'" RedOrbit.com, June 16, 2005, https://www.redorbit.com/news/science/156539/brazilian_doctors_uncover _michelangelo_code/.

the plays—or, at least, the leader of the group of Gray's Inn "wits" who produced and loaded them with secret messages—was Francis Bacon.

In 1880, Ignatius L. Donnelly, a U.S. congressman and author of *Atlantis: The Antediluvian World,* wrote in *The Great Cryptogram* that Bacon had revealed his authorship of the Shakespearean works by concealing secret ciphers in the text. A few years later, Orville Ward Owen took the idea a little further. A physician, Owen used a "cipher wheel" of his own devising to unlock many cryptograms found in Shakespeare's works. With the aid of his machine, Owen could quickly collate printed pages from the works of Shakespeare, Bacon, and other authors, combining passages that appeared to have some connection with key words or phrases. In his 1893 book, *Sir Francis Bacon's Cipher Story,* Owen claimed to have discovered nothing less than a secret history of the Elizabethan era hidden in the Bacon/Shakespeare works. Bacon is also said to be the man who, behind the scenes, guided the creation of the King James Bible. Owen and others have deduced that Bacon was the secret love child of Queen Elizabeth I and Robert Dudley, the Earl of Leicester, and was forced by the highly sensitive nature of his personal saga to rely on ciphers to disseminate his knowledge.

Ciphers are a system for writing codes, so that those with special knowledge—some might call them initiates—can find hidden messages left in places where the uninitiated would find nothing of interest. Bacon is widely credited with creating the bilateral cipher based on steganography (the hiding of a message's existence). Otherwise innocuous text could be made to carry a hidden message that could be extracted using a prearranged key to identify the letters forming the secret message. Only the intended recipient would know even to look for a message. Bacon wrote that he created his bilateral cipher when he was a young man in Paris. He and the Rosicrucian fraternity, which he founded, used several kinds of cipher. Placed in various published works issued outwardly under different names or pseudonyms, the ciphers were intended to convey messages to those in the know. Many of Bacon's coding techniques were later picked up by the clandestine services of various world powers, and, ultimately, by modern computer programmers to create binary and machine codes.

Researcher William Henry is among those who believe that Bacon used a cryptic double A (one light and one dark: A**A**) as a key to many

Orville Ward Owen's
cipher wheel

of his ciphers. Facsimiles of the *Sonnets, Hamlet,* and *Richard III* published during Shakespeare's time all bear the light A and dark **A** on their title pages. It also appears in the King James Bible of 1611.

Whether or not Bacon is actually Shakespeare, he is still universally respected as one of the greatest thinkers who ever lived, one gifted with extraordinary prophetic vision. "He seemed to be able to see through time," wrote Henry ("Bacon and the Double A," *Atlantis Rising* #45, May/June 2004), "describing inventions of great imagination such as a pillar of light at the center of the *New Atlantis.*" A true initiate, Bacon hid his secrets in cryptograms buried in writing products turned out by his workshop, many bearing the A**A** headpiece, including books written by other authors but under his direction.

Five rival publishers independently produced the works of Shakespeare bearing the A**A** headpiece, lending credence to the idea that this is the signature of a hidden author, Bacon.*

Bacon had his own wood blocks of devices or emblems, some of which were his own design, and every book produced under his direction, whether written by him or not, was marked by the use of one or more of these logos. His authors included Edmund Spenser, Christopher Marlowe, Shakespeare, Walter Raleigh, and others.

---

*For a look at some of the ciphers and codes in question, see Richard Tingstad, "Summary of Most Convincing Bacon Ciphers in Shakespeare," Rictin.com, 2010, http://www.rictin.com/a/bacon-cipher/.

Two examples of Francis Bacon's double-A insignia

Bacon's mastery of ciphers and symbols, say scholars, enabled him to use these works to send messages or teachings. According to Henry, Bacon's greatest code may be English itself. "The English language," wrote Henry, "as is widely acknowledged, is founded upon the English translation of the King James Bible (which, some believe, God enabled and Bacon guided) and upon the plays of Shakespeare. There are about 22,000 different English words in the plays, of which *7,000 are new words,* introduced—as Murray's Oxford Dictionary tells us—into the language for the first time."

THE TORAH PROPHECIES

If English itself is a code hiding many ancient secrets, Hebrew may well be another. Some, like best-selling author Michael Drosnin, have argued that God himself foretold the events of all times, including our own, in a code buried in the letters of the Hebrew Torah. *The Bible Code,* Drosnin's 1997 book, was based on the findings of Israeli mathematician Eliyahu Rips.

Widely respected for his research in geometric group theory, Rips became known to the general public following his coauthorship of a paper on what he argued was coded messaging in the Torah. In the late 1970s, Rips began using a computer to look for such codes. In 1994, with Doron Witztum and Yoav Rosenberg, he published an article in the journal

An example of the Bible code from Drosnin's book

○ YITZHAK RABIN   □ ASSASSIN THAT WILL ASSASSINATE

Statistical Science, "Equidistant Letter Sequences in the Book of Genesis," which claimed the discovery of encoded messages in the Hebrew text of Genesis. This became the inspiration for Drosnin's book.

In 1994, Rips wrote a letter about his research to Israeli prime minister Yitzhak Rabin, saying, "The reason I'm telling you about this is that the only time your full name—Yitzhak Rabin—is encoded in the Bible, the words 'assassin that will assassinate' cross your name. That should not be ignored, because the assassinations of both John and Robert Kennedy and Anwar Sadat (the Egyptian leader) are also encoded in the Bible—in the case of Sadat with the first and last names of his killer, the date of the murder, the place, and how it was done. I think you are in real danger, but that the danger can be averted."

On November 4, 1995, about a year after Rips's letter was delivered to Rabin by his close friend, the poet Chaim Guri, Rabin was shot in the back and murdered by a man who believed he was on a mission from God. The murder, said Rips, had been encoded in the Bible three thousand years before.*

---

*For an analysis of the Bible code and Drosnin's book about it, see Paul Ratner, "Scientists Claim the Bible Is Written in Code That Predicts Future Events," Big Think (online), November 19, 2018, https://bigthink.com/surprising-science/scientists-claim-the-bible-is-written-in-code-that-predicts-future-events.

In the years since Drosnin's book, the theory that the Bible contains such a hidden code has been dismissed by most experts, who say similar patterns can be found in just about any sufficiently large group of letters. The possibility of such divine coding, however, has fascinated many, not the least of whom was Sir Isaac Newton. In the book *Temple at the Center of Time: Newton's Bible Codex Deciphered and the Year 2012,* researcher David Flynn claimed to have unraveled Newton's "unified field theory of biblical prophecy" and suggested that the Temple of Solomon is more than a mere place of worship—indeed, that it intersects time and dimension, making it a prophetic and supernatural structure, virtually "God's Time Bomb."

Flynn catalogued a number of anomalies surrounding the temple, including the *prisca sapentia* (pristine knowledge) framework of Newton, which suggests that the distance between the temple in Jerusalem and the capital city of any nation historically affecting the chronicles of Jerusalem would be supernaturally connected. "The description of Jerusalem as a terrestrial center point is found in Philo's *Legatio and Gaium,*" Flynn notes. "The world is like a human eyeball. The white of the eye is the ocean surrounding the world, the iris is this continent, the pupil is Jerusalem, and the image in the pupil is the Holy Temple."

THE PLATO CODE

Many other potential ancient sources of secret meaning continue to come to light. Even the writings of the Greek philosopher Plato are now regarded by some scholars as veiling esoteric intentions. In fact, J. B. Kennedy, a science historian at the University of Manchester in the United Kingdom, claims to have cracked what he calls "the Plato code"—the long-disputed secret messages hidden in the great philosopher's writings.

Widely regarded as the greatest mind of Greece's Golden Age, the philosopher Plato laid the very foundation of Western culture and science. In a 2010 paper published in the journal *Apeiron,* Kennedy revealed that Plato used a regular pattern of symbols, inherited from the teachings of Pythagoras a century earlier, to give his books a musical structure. Pythagoras had declared that the planets and stars made an inaudible harmony, a "music of the spheres." Plato imitated this hidden music in his books.

Bust of Plato

The hidden codes, said Kennedy, show that "Plato anticipated the Scientific Revolution 2,000 years before Isaac Newton, discovering its most important idea—the book of nature is written in the language of mathematics. The decoded messages also open up a surprising way to unite science and religion. The awe and beauty we feel in nature, Plato says, shows that it is divine; discovering the scientific order of nature is getting closer to God. This could transform today's culture wars between science and religion."*

Kennedy spent five years studying Plato's writing and found that in his best-known work, *The Republic,* he placed clusters of words related to music after each twelfth of the text—at one-twelfth, two-twelfths, and so on. This regular pattern represented the twelve notes of a Greek musical scale. Some notes were harmonic, while others were dissonant. At the locations of the harmonic notes, he described sounds associated with love or laughter, while the locations of dissonant notes were marked with screeching sounds or war or death. This musical code was key to cracking Plato's entire symbolic system.

Kennedy said: "As we read his [Plato's] books, our emotions follow the ups and downs of a musical scale. Plato plays his readers like musical instruments."

---

*See the press release from the University of Manchester about Kennedy's project: "Science Historian Cracks the 'Plato Code,'" ScienceDaily (online), June 29, 2010, https://www.sciencedaily.com/releases/2010/06/100628111846.htm.

Plato's *Republic* on ancient papyrus

Plato did not, however, design his secret patterns strictly for his own amusement—like Bacon, he did it for his own survival. Indeed, his ideas were a major threat to the official Greek religion of the time. Mathematical laws and not the gods controlled the universe, he said. Socrates, Plato's own teacher, had been executed for heresy. Secrecy was common in ancient civilizations, especially for esoteric and religious knowledge, but for Plato it was a matter of life and death. Encoding his ideas in secret patterns was the only way to be safe, Kennedy believes.

Interest in secret codes of many kinds continues to grow. There is reason to hope that recent research may direct new light into some long hidden corners. Technology developed by NASA, for instance, for use with satellite imagery now holds promise as another tool for examining ancient manuscripts. The hope is that the faded ink of such texts may ultimately yield the secrets of lost worlds. Now, many scholars are eagerly waiting to see what the technique can tell them about such documents as the Dead Sea Scrolls, the Nag Hammadi texts, the Voynich Manuscript, or maybe some yet-to-be-discovered message from a lost civilization.

UNTAUGHT HISTORY
- - - - - - - - - - -
*What might
really have happened*

8

Time Line Tangles

*How ancient is human history
in the Americas, really?*

The idea that humans like us—with the ability to create tools and art—first appeared only about 40,000 years ago is being challenged as never before. According to experts across the world, a growing body of evidence—advanced harpoon tips from the Congo, sophisticated cave paintings from Indonesia, rock paintings from Australia, and more—is causing the entire time line of human development to be seriously questioned.* It has suddenly become respectable to argue that humans like us may have been around for at least 100,000 years—maybe much longer.

In fact, the skillfully created harpoon tips from Africa are more than 90,000 years old. Hand stencils on the walls of Indonesian caves are 40,000 to 50,000 years old—every bit as old as their amazing counterparts in European caves at Lascaux and Chauvet, indicating that the original development of such skill goes much further back in human history than researchers once believed possible.

Cave art, indeed, found throughout the world shows sophisticated drawings and paintings of many animal species dating to at least 10,000 years *before* we thought they did. The astonishing art clearly reveals the handiwork of brilliant artists whose mastery of line and anatomical

---

*To learn more about these and other discoveries, see Robin McKie, "Cave Art and Harpoon Tips Show African Roots of Our Creative Genius," *The Guardian* (online), October 11, 2014, https://www.theguardian.com/science/2014/oct/11/cave-paintings -indonesia-african-roots.

Stencil of human hand in Indonesian cave;
photo by Kinza Riza, courtesy of *Nature*

detail has impressed even many of today's most discriminating experts.

In the Chauvet-Pont-d'Arc Cave of France, the dating of charcoal and other residues found in paintings on the cave walls had previously assigned them to 22,000 to 18,000 BCE. In 2015, however, art in a cave on the Indonesian island of Sulawesi was found to date to 35,000 to 40,000 years ago. Soon a new paper appeared—the dating of the Chauvet Cave art was being revisited, and it could now be shown definitively to go back 33,500 to 37,000 years. Indeed, France immediately and proudly reclaimed for the Chauvet Cave (and its tourist industry) the title of possessing the oldest animal art on Earth.*

In Plato's story of Atlantis, the Greek lawgiver Solon was told by the Egyptian priests at Sais that civilization has risen and fallen many times. Now the theoretical time line of human development has finally become sufficiently extended that it is possible to allow for such long-term developments as civilization, not just once, but possibly multiple times.

The phrase "It's much older than anyone thought possible" is used so often in archaeology news that it seems like all modern time lines for

---

*See A. Quiles, H. Valladas, H. Bocherens, et al., "A High-Precision Chronological Model for the Decorated Upper Paleolithic Cave of Chauvet-Pont d'Arc, Ardèche, France," *Proceeding of the National Academy of Sciences* 113, no. 17 (2016): 4670–75. https://www.smithsonianmag.com/smart-news/new-timeline-zeroes-creation-chauvet -cave-paintings-180958754/.

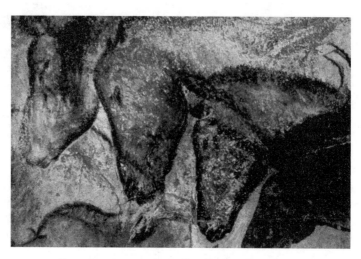

Horse drawings on the wall at Chauvet Cave, France

human history on Earth should be thrown out, and we should just start over with a new set of assumptions.

THE TIMEKEEPER'S REWARD

In *Timaeus* and *Critias,* in which Plato gives his account of Atlantis (written in 360 BCE), the island nation was said to have sunk in approximately 9600 BCE, after millennia of prior history.

In the seventeenth century, the bishop of Ireland, James Ussher, published a biblical chronology declaring that Creation occurred on Sunday, October 23, 4004 BCE (Julian calendar).

Today, mainstream natural historians insist that Earth is between four and five billion years old, and that the first humans like us arrived about a hundred thousand years ago, which still, they argue, doesn't allow enough time for us to have risen to our present "lofty height" more than once.

They can't all be right, and so the argument over who has the most credible time line still rages and will do so, apparently, for as long as people are around. There is more to be gained here, however, than scholarly bragging rights. At stake is the authority that comes with being proclaimed society's official custodian of truth, and reaping the perks that go with that. Indeed, most debates over time lines are really as much about who is in charge as who is right.

Take the claim that Atlantis was actually a Mediterranean volcanic island, Santorini (Thíra), that blew up during the Bronze Age. The theory reconciles itself with Plato by claiming a place error was made in the numbers he provided. Even though he said nine thousand years, what Plato really meant was nine hundred. Or so they say. The latter number, of course, is much more convenient for academia, conforming closely to the standard paradigm for the development of civilization. The conventional view is that in the time actually referenced by Plato, humans were but primitive hunter-gatherers incapable of civilization. Of course, the curious fact remains that the 9600 BCE date just happens to coincide with the well-documented end of the last great ice age—an event of which Plato was supposedly ignorant. Moreover, new discoveries at Göbekli Tepe in Turkey, Tell Qaramel in Syria, the Gulf of Cambay off India, and elsewhere make it clear that humanity could do civilization at least as long ago as Plato claimed.

The powers that be, whether in church, state, or academia, understand well the importance of controlling which time lines are accepted by society, and they fully comprehend the perils of losing control of that argument, so woe to anyone who might challenge conventional wisdom.

The idea that modern humans, or even Neanderthals or Denisovans, could have been present in the Americas over twelve thousand years ago has long been controversial, and discoveries supporting that argument have been denied, discredited, or disregarded by conventional science. In 1966, for example, respected archaeologist Virginia Steen-McIntyre used well-accepted dating methods, including uranium series and fission track, to demonstrate that an ancient site near El Horno in Mexico showed human activity nearly a quarter million years ago. Thereafter, she was scorned by academia and soon found herself unable to pursue her professional career. Her evidence, no matter how compelling, was dismissed out of hand. After all, it challenged accepted scientific doctrine, considered all but proven at the time, that the first human migration to the Americas was across the land bridge from Siberia to Alaska and took place a mere twelve thousand years ago. Dr. McIntyre's findings may still be considered too radical, but conventional wisdom is moving in her direction.[*]

---

[*]Read more about Dr. McIntyre's findings in "Hueyatlaco Site—'Extreme Dating Controversy'" (undated), on s8int.com, http://s8int.com/hueyatlaco.html.

At many paleological conferences today, you would be hard-pressed to find anyone still defending the so-called Clovis origins theory (named for Clovis, New Mexico, where the first humans supposedly settled). New evidence has swept that old paradigm aside and postulated dates going back three times as far, and farther.

Recent findings at what is now known as the Cerutti Mastodon site, near San Diego, California, are suggesting that more than 130,000 years ago, someone used stone tools to break the bones of mastodons.* The purpose, it is speculated, would have been to extract the nutritious bone marrow. According to archaeologist Steven Holen, the evidence is "fairly conclusive."

The magnitude of the discovery is difficult to exaggerate. "We often hear statements in the media that a new study 'changes everything' we knew," Chris Stringer of London's Natural History Museum told *New Scientist*. "If this result stands up to scrutiny, it does indeed change everything we thought we knew about the earliest human occupation of the Americas." Not surprisingly, the protectors of the status quo have responded angrily, asserting that "natural" processes might have produced the evidence. Others say it could be the work of Neanderthals or Denisovans rather than modern humans, but still, it shatters all conventional time lines. It is worth remembering, moreover, that—not even counting the findings of Steen-McIntyre at El Horno—this is not the first evidence of extreme antiquity in the Americas.†

As early as the 1990s, linguist Johanna Nichols wrote a paper demonstrating that the 150 languages of Native American people, which she had studied, could not possibly have evolved in less than thirty thousand to forty thousand years.‡ Now DNA evidence from Native American tribes is producing similar conclusions.

---

*The San Diego Natural History Museum has an exhibit, *The Cerutti Mastodon Discovery,* about the mastodon find. See "The Cerutti Mastodon Discovery" on the website of the museum for information, photos, and interviews with the archaeologists.

†See Colin Barras, "First Americans May Have Been Neanderthals 130,000 Years Ago," *New Scientist* (online), April 26, 2017, https://www.newscientist.com/article/2129042-first-americans-may-have-been-neanderthals-130000-years-ago/.

‡See the press release from the University of California at Berkeley: "Incredible Journeys of Our Native Tongues," by Patricia McBroom, in the *Berkeleyan* (a university newspaper), March 11, 1998, https://www.berkeley.edu/news/berkeleyan/1998/0311/linguistics.html.

Archaeologist at the Cerutti Mastodon site, near San Diego

Other DNA research published in 2016 has virtually ruled out the Siberian route for Americans before 12,600 years ago. The study, published in the journal *Nature,* reveals that prior to that time, the corridor would have been "biologically unviable"—in other words, impossible. The researchers concluded that while people may well have traveled the route after that point, it would have been impassable earlier, as it lacked crucial resources, such as wood for fuel and tools and game animals for food. The research was led by Eske Willerslev, a Danish evolutionary geneticist at Cambridge University in the U.K. "The bottom line is that even though the physical corridor was open by 13,000 years ago, it was several hundred years before it was possible to use it," Willerslev said. "That means that the first people entering what is now the US, Central and South America must have taken a different route. Whether you believe these people were Clovis, or someone else, they simply could not have come through the corridor, as long claimed."*

Smithsonian Magazine has chronicled a number of discoveries similarly testing the foundations of orthodoxy in places like Monte Verde

---

*Read about the study in *Smithsonian Magazine:* Jason Daley, "First Humans Entered the Americas Along the Coast, Not Through the Ice," *Smithsonian Magazine* (online), August 11, 2016, https://www.smithsonianmag.com/smart-news/humans-colonized-americas-along-coast-not-through-ice-180960103/.

in Chile and Aucilla River in Florida.* Evidence for alternative time lines also comes from the Chesapeake Bay. In an area that has not been above water for fourteen thousand years, a twenty-two-thousand-year-old mastodon skull, along with associated flint knives of considerable sophistication, has been dredged up. The artifacts, analyzed by geologist Darrin Lowery of the University of Delaware, suggest that rather than being colonized from the northwest, America may have been settled from the east (i.e., Europe) by very ancient seafarers. The so-called Solutrean theory has been gaining adherents for a while now, but many mainstream archaeologists remain unwilling to give up the cherished Clovis narrative.†

In recent years, there have been many discoveries of human-created artifacts in both North and South America dating to long before

Solutrean tools found in France

<hr />

*See Guy Gugliotta, "When Did Humans Come to the Americas?" *Smithsonian Magazine* (online), February 2013, https://www.smithsonianmag.com/science-nature/when-did-humans-come-to-the-americas-4209273/.

†Read about the Solutrean theory and Lowery's finds in the Chesapeake Bay, as well as other evidence of early human migrations to the Americas, in "Migration of Early Humans to America," factsanddetails.com (online), March 2020, http://factsanddetails.com/world/cat56/sub361/entry-5987.html.

Rock art at Pedra Furada in Brazil

13,000 years ago. Archaeologist Niede Guidon, for example, has discovered rock art at Pedra Furada in Brazil dating back 48,700 years.* If, as the new research establishes, the rock painters could not have arrived by way of the Siberia–Alaska corridor, where did they come from? The plot thickens, and once again the schoolbooks appear in need of a rewrite.

Whether in war or debate, history, it has been said, is written by the victors, which might go far to explain the gap between what passes for history today and actual truth.

ALTERNATIVE HISTORY

For thousands of years, the indigenous Heiltsuk Nation of British Columbia has relayed an oral tradition from generation to generation telling that its ancestors escaped the harsh conditions of the last Ice Age on a temperate island off the coast of Canada. In 2016, Alishu Gauvreau, an archaeologist from the University of Victoria, led a dig on Triquet Island on the Canadian coast. Notwithstanding the Willerslev study previously mentioned, artifacts from Triquet Island, including a spear tip and mastodon rib bone, have included charcoal flakes dating to about

---

*Read more about Guidon and Pedra Furada in "The Rock Art of Pedra Furada: Research by Niede Guidon," in the South America Rock Art Archive of the Bradshaw Foundation (online), http://www.bradshawfoundation.com/south_america/serra_da _capivara/pedra_furada/index.php.

14,000 years ago, making them among the oldest ever found in Canada.*

Where academia once accepted without question that the first Americans arrived from Asia over an ice-free land bridge from Siberia to Alaska, new evidence is leading many to believe it is more likely that early Americans arrived by boat. Even with those concessions, though, discoveries from South Carolina to Brazil to Chile are eroding confidence in the conventional wisdom as never before.

In southern Chile, at Monte Verde, freshly uncovered evidence now suggests that controversial conclusions drawn in the 1970s may, if anything, have undershot the mark, and that human antiquity in the Americas could be far greater than even many cutting-edge experts have supposed. When renowned Vanderbilt University archaeologist Tom Dillehay made his first paradigm-shattering discoveries in Monte Verde, he claimed an age for human habitation of 14,500 years ago—enough to earn the derision and criticism of his skeptical peers. The experience left him discouraged and uninterested in pursuing the research. But after some serious persuasion from the Chilean government and others, he reluctantly agreed to return in 2013 for a new survey of the site. The result has been that many *new* artifacts have been uncovered, and Dillehay's dating of human habitation has now been adjusted to as much as 19,000 years ago—more than 4,000 years earlier than his prior estimate, and several millennia before the end of the last major ice age.†

Once again, conventionally minded skeptics have been outraged, but Dillehay has now accepted that destiny may well tie him to the Monte Verde story and the rapidly evolving case for early humans in the Americas.

On another front, human waste found in Oregon's Paisley Caves has now been firmly dated by scientists at the University of Oregon to 14,300 years ago, more than a thousand years before Clovis settlements in New Mexico. It has also been shown that the diet of the Paisley community included aromatic herbs that would have required some time to

---

*See Brigit Katz, "Found: One of the Oldest North American Settlements," *Smithsonian Magazine* (online), April 5, 2017, https://www.smithsonianmag.com/smart-news/one -oldest-north-american-settlements-found-180962750/.
†See T. Dillehay, C. Ocampo, J. Saavedra, et al., "New Archaeological Evidence for an Early Human Presence at Monte Verde, Chile," *PLoS ONE* 10, no. 11 (2015): e0141923, https://journals.plos.org/plosone/article?id=10.1371/journal.pone.0141923.

Vanderbilt University
archaeologist Tom Dillehay

develop, an indication that this community had been around for a long time.*

From British Columbia's Triquet Island to Oregon's Paisley Caves, Chile's Monte Verde, and Virginia's Chesapeake Bay, many archaeological sites have produced a mountain of evidence challenging the once-unquestioned conventional time line. It is clear now that humans have been roving the Americas for millennia longer than the academic establishment would have us believe. Maybe much longer.

Although the megalithic sites at Sacsayhuamán and many other locations in Peru and Bolivia are officially associated with Andean imperialism going back only six centuries, temple complexes at Puma Punku and nearby Tiahuanaco provide extensive evidence of even more sophisticated stonework predating the Incas by thousands of years. According to the late Arthur Posnansky, the early-twentieth-century director of Bolivia's National Museum, the application of an archaeo-astronomical analysis to Tiahuanaco reveals that it was built seventeen thousand years ago by a people unrelated to local tribes of Aymara Indians. Posnansky further pointed out architectural similarities between Puma Punku and Easter Island, 2,180 miles west of continental Chile, suggesting that both locations had been independently influenced by an earlier high culture. The question arises: Do we know anywhere near as much about the very ancient past as we thought?

---

*See the press release from the University of Oregon: "Pre-Clovis Human DNA Found in 14,300-Year-Old Feces in Oregon Cave Is Oldest in New World," ScienceDaily (online), April 3, 2008, https://www.sciencedaily.com/releases/2008/04/080403141109.htm.

Human coprolite from Paisley Caves in Oregon

Consider this: Industrial civilization on Earth is usually thought of as a "human thing." The assumption is that *no* humans means *no* civilization—but do we know that for sure? A couple of NASA astrophysicists now say the answer is no. In a 2019 paper titled "The Silurian Hypothesis: Would It Be Possible to Detect an Industrial Civilization in the Geological Record?," Gavin A. Schmidt and Adam Frank took a look at the fossil records from the fifty-million-year-old Paleocene epoch and asked whether the massive amounts of buried carbon that we find today could suggest that an industrial civilization existed here long before humans. In the extremely ancient past, did some species other than humans evolve to the level that they could have caused global warming of their own? Based on the fact that all the records of our own time, except perhaps for nitrogen fertilizers and plastic containers, may be lost in a few million years, Schmidt and Frank conclude: We can't rule it out.*

---

*See Gavin A. Schmidt and Adam Frank, "The Silurian Hypothesis: Would It Be Possible to Detect an Industrial Civilization in the Geological Record?," *International Journal of Astrobiology* 18, no. 2 (2019): 142–50, https://www.cambridge.org /core/journals/international-journal-of-astrobiology/article/silurian-hypothesis -would-it-be-possible-to-detect-an-industrial-civilization-in-the-geological-record /77818514AA6907750B8F4339F7C70EC6.

9

The Neanderthal Connection

Has civilization's missing link been found?

A 2012 study published by a team of researchers from Eotvos University in Budapest, Hungary, declared that prehistoric artists were more scientifically accurate in depicting the movements of animals than are their modern colleagues. By comparing drawings of four-legged animals found on cave walls with roughly parallel drawings from the 1880s, the researchers were able to show that modern depictions of the walking or trotting motions of animals had the positioning of the legs wrong more often than did the ancients. Where the prehistoric artists had an error rate of 46.2 percent, the modern artists were wrong 83.5 percent of the time.[*]

Here, once again, we find the mainstream history of human life on Earth to be insufficient. The long-standing consensus has been that the processes that would ultimately lead to civilization didn't really get going until about six thousand years ago, when humans invented the wheel. Before that, in the four millennia following the great warm-up at the close of the last ice age, humans were, at best, just primitive farmers. Before that, we had been, for around forty thousand years, essentially

---

[*]See Gabor Horvath, Etelka Farkas, Ildiko Boncz, Miklos Blaho, and Gyorgy Kriska, "Cavemen Were Better at Depicting Quadruped Walking Than Modern Artists: Erroneous Walking Illustrations in the Fine Arts from Prehistory to Today," *PLoS ONE* 7, no. 12 (2012): e49786, https://www.researchgate.net/publication/233889775_Cavemen _Were_Better_at_Depicting_Quadruped_Walking_than_Modern_Artists_Erroneous _Walking_Illustrations_in_the_Fine_Arts_from_Prehistory_to_Today.

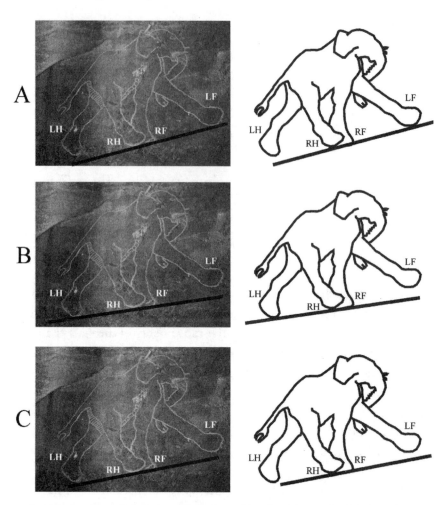

Prehistoric cave-wall depictions of elephants (line drawings on the right have been added for clarity). Researchers have shown that comparable animal illustrations from the 1880s (not shown) got the leg positioning wrong more often than did the ancients.

hunter-gatherers, savages or "cave men" incapable of much more than making good spear points. That is the story everyone learns in school. To suggest otherwise is to invite scorn from the knowledge establishment. Nevertheless, as readers of *Atlantis Rising Magazine* were well aware, there is plenty of powerful evidence to the contrary, and more is uncovered every day. Indeed, if nothing else, the amazing artistic sophistication of the cave painters seems enough, by itself, to turn conventional wisdom on its head.

A full thirty-five thousand years ago, painters in the Coliboaia Cave in Romania were producing sophisticated portraits of many animals, including a horse, bear heads, and a rhinoceros. The artists used black paint. The artwork is even older than the famous masterpieces previously found in other European caves like Lascaux and Chauvet (dated to almost twenty thousand years ago). Still older cave art has now been discovered, but more on that later.

Such findings certainly provoke many questions: Where did the ancient artists learn the techniques that would not be rediscovered for many thousands of years? Were they simply born geniuses, or did they learn their amazing skills at the feet of culture bearers from an earlier forgotten era? Indeed, could their awe-inspiring masterpieces be the last remains of a much more ancient and forgotten culture—one not at its dawn, but in its twilight?

From a strictly human perspective, the puzzles presented are complex enough, but what about when the story is expanded to include our so-called "country cousins," the Neanderthals? Now the story of the origins of civilization becomes very mysterious indeed. Many of the milestones that we think of as representing exclusively human achievement were, it turns out, also passed by this once derided group, albeit much earlier.

The GEICO caveman of recent television fame had a point. To say that something is "so simple a caveman could do it" does not give him the respect he deserves. Assuming that these "cavemen" were largely Neanderthal, they were certainly capable of much more than that for which they have been given credit.

Neanderthals, in fact, some believe, may well be the source of that great lost culture many of us have searched for. Researcher Dr. Robert Schoch is among those who argue that Neanderthals may deserve much more credit for very early developments that heretofore have been chalked up to so-called modern humans. Even mainstream science has now accepted that, at the very least, Neanderthals used body paint, wore jewelry, and worked with tools, and now we know that they produced exceptional cave art thousands of years before humans did.

Neanderthals probably came to Europe, science concedes, over a quarter million years ago, which means they had much more time to advance their culture than humans have had to evolve theirs. Modern humans, it is believed, did not arrive in Europe until about forty-two thousand years ago. And, yet, it now appears that Neanderthals were blowing paint over their hands to make stencils as long as thirty-seven thousand years ago. That is the age of art recently found in Spain's El Castillo Cave.*

Science now recognizes that all signs point to much greater antiquity for both humans and Neanderthals than was once believed. It is no longer controversial to talk in terms of at least a half million years. The question arises: Could the great, lost ancient civilization for which so many have searched have been, in fact, Neanderthal?

As Robert Schoch and Oana R. Ghiocel explained in "The Enigma of the Carpathian Sphinx" (*Atlantis Rising* #89, September/October 2011), some very ancient artifacts may exist that we simply have not recognized, regarding them simply as natural formations. According to Schoch and Ghiocel, one formation in particular, located in the southern Carpathian Mountains of Romania, the so-called Carpathian sphinx, could be evidence of a very old and very advanced lost civilization. Some scholars, including Romanian Dan Braneanu and Peruvian Daniel Ruzo, have made points in favor of such a theory, arguing that a

The Carpathian sphinx

---

*See Ker Than, "World's Oldest Cave Art Found—Made by Neanderthals?," *National Geographic* (online), June 14, 2012, https://www.nationalgeographic.com/news /2012/6/120614-neanderthal-cave-paintings-spain-science-pike/.

primordial civilization was destroyed long before the earliest civilization acknowledged by conventional historians.

ANCIENT SAGA

Named for the German Neander Valley, where they were first discovered in 1856, Neanderthals, a subspecies of the genus *Homo,* have been extinct for about thirty-two thousand years. Fossil remains of Neanderthals found in many parts of Europe have been dated to as long as six hundred thousand years ago. In Croatia, remains found in Vindija Cave have been dated to between thirty-three thousand and thirty-two thousand years ago. Much of the most recent and astonishing research has been conducted on the Iberian peninsula, where fossils have been dated to forty-five thousand years ago. Mainstream archaeology usually assigns several cultural classifications to Neanderthals, the earliest being the Mousterian stone-tool culture, which goes back about three hundred thousand years.

The Neanderthal brain is thought to have been at least as large as the human one. One study using 3D computer-assisted reconstructions of Neanderthal infants whose remains were found in Russia and Syria showed that while human and Neanderthal brains were the same size at birth, the adult Neanderthal brain was larger than a human's. Neanderthals were also physically much bigger and stronger than humans.*

Genetic studies now suggest that modern humans owe part of their DNA to Neanderthals, and there is much speculation that considerable interbreeding may have taken place between humans and Neanderthals from eighty thousand to fifty thousand years ago.†

---

*See Marcia S. Ponce de León, Lubov Golovanova, Vladimir Doronichev, et al., "Neanderthal Brain Size at Birth Provides Insights into the Evolution of Human Life History," *Proceedings of the National Academy of Sciences* 105, no. 37 (2008): 13764–68, https://www.researchgate.net/publication/23245353_Neanderthal_brain_size_at_birth_provides_insights_into_human_life_history_evolution.

†The Smithsonian National Museum of Natural History offers a simple explanation of the study of human-Neanderthal interbreeding; see "Interbreeding," on the museum's website at http://humanorigins.si.edu/evidence/genetics/ancient-dna-and-neanderthals/interbreeding.

Mitochondrial DNA from an 1856 specimen, for example, was extracted in 1997. Since the only source of change in mitochondrial DNA is random mutation, which occurs, it is said, at a fairly constant rate of 2 percent every million years, scientists consider this type of DNA suitable for study.

Studies of such DNA have shown that there are approximately twenty-five differences between the mDNA of modern humans and Neanderthals, suggesting that the two species separated in the human family tree about six hundred thousand years ago. This is consistent with the idea that Neanderthals first appeared about a half million years ago, as, it is believed, though unproven, there should have been some "intermediate" stages before they developed into their last known form.

Neanderthals lived during a time period usually labeled the Middle Paleolithic, also known as the Middle Stone Age. The Middle Paleolithic, we are told, is characterized by varied environments, from the richer and tundra-like conditions in Europe to the savannas and semiarid deserts of Africa. Food varied with the environment. In Europe, evidence has suggested that Neanderthals hunted many animals, but as we shall see, they were not strictly meat eaters.

Certainly new research has begun to radically change the stereotypical image of Neanderthals with which most of us are familiar—shambling hairy dunces, like the GEICO caveman. We now know they were much more sophisticated than previously believed. Startling new revelations from El Sidrón Cave in northern Spain are among many discoveries that make the point.

In the Asturias region of northern Spain, El Sidrón provides the best collection of Neanderthal remains in the Iberian Peninsula, and it is considered one of the most important research sites in the world. Discovered in 1994, it contains around two thousand skeletal parts of at least thirteen individuals dating back about fifty thousand years.

Recently researchers from Spain, the U.K., and Australia, says the study, "combined pyrolysis gas-chromatography-mass spectrometry with morphological analysis of plant microfossils to identify material trapped in dental calculus (calcified dental plaque) from five Neanderthals at the site."

Results, published in the journal *Naturwissenschaften* (Science of

Nature), offer molecular evidence that Neanderthals used medicinal plants. The finding is based on the fact that residue on teeth shows they were eating some bitter foods—plants. It had already been established that Neanderthals possessed the bitter taste detection gene. So, if they ate bitter plants despite the taste, it seems likely to some observers they understood it was good for their health. In other words, they knew how to self-medicate, something we humans did not learn for many millennia.

"El Sidrón has allowed us to banish many of our preconceptions of Neanderthals," says Antonio Rosas of the Museum of Natural History in Madrid. "Thanks to previous studies, we know that they looked after the sick, buried their dead, and decorated their bodies. Now another dimension has been added relating to their diet and self-medication."*

A burial site at Sima de las Palomas, also in Spain, underscores

Researcher in Spain's El Sidrón Cave;
photo courtesy of CSIC Comunicación (also see color insert plate 9)

---

*See the press release about the study from the University of York: "Neanderthals in northern Spain had knowledge of plants' healing qualities, study reveals," ScienceDaily (online), July 18, 2012, https://www.york.ac.uk/news-and-events/features/el-sidron/; see also Enrico de Lazaro, "Study Reveals Neanderthals Used Medicinal Plants," Sci-News.com (online), July 19, 2012, http://www.sci-news.com/othersciences/anthropology/article00476.html.

Antonio Rosas at work in Spain's El Sidrón Cave;
photo courtesy of CSIC Comunicación

Rosas's point. Here, three Neanderthal skeletons buried about fifty thousand years ago were found together with their hands raised in the same way. Archaeologist Michael Walker considers this a sign of some kind of ritual burial, suggesting concerns about the afterlife and, by implication, complex thought about the future.

As for cave painting, in caves at Altamira in Cantabria, Spain, images once attributed to humans have now been shown to predate the human arrival from Africa and, thus, are now attributed to Neanderthals. Some of these paintings are at least 40,800 years old, but, nonetheless, they reveal an advanced mastery of the medium.

Bison cave drawing, Altamira, Spain, thought to be about 36,000 years old

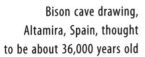

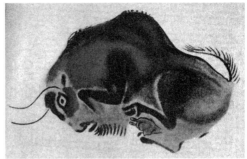

Art for the cover of *Atlantis Rising* (September/October 2013) based on facial reconstruction from a Neanderthal skull found in an Altamira cave and currently housed at the Smithsonian Institute in Washington, D.C. The lower symbol on the ceiling has been dated to at least 35,600 years ago, making it 20,000 years older than the bison at the top.

AN UNDERAPPRECIATED LEGACY

The late British psychologist Stan Gooch was among those who felt we owed the Neanderthals a complete rethink. In books such as *The Dream Culture of the Neanderthals* and *Cities of Dreams,* he argued for a radical reinterpretation of their legacy. While their brains were as large, or even larger, than ours, they were structured quite differently. In the human brain we find both a cerebrum and cerebellum, but, Gooch pointed out, the Neanderthal cerebellum is much larger. The cerebellum, he believed, is responsible for intuition, dreaming, insight, paranormal abilities, and magic, which he argued, once gave rise to a "high civilization of dreams." Neanderthals, he wrote, developed a deep understanding of the natural world, but they did not necessarily do so in the rational, logical, "scientific" manner that modern humans have come to expect and accept. Gooch stated, "I think that they [the ancient Neanderthals] obtained their knowledge not logically and scientifically but intuitively." Neanderthals were, he said, the original creators, the innovators of high culture, of symbolic values and religious sensibilities, which early modern humans (Cro-Magnons) copied and adopted without genuine understanding. Neanderthal culture was not a civilization of high technologies but one of the mind and spirit that survives today in our beliefs, myths, folklore, and religious practices (Schoch and Ghiocel).

In 2006, the late prolific alternative-science writer Colin Wilson published his book *Atlantis and the Kingdom of the Neanderthal: 100,000 Years of Lost History.* Writing later for *Atlantis Rising* #60 ("Atlantis and the Neanderthals," November/December 2006), Wilson explained how his own view of the Neanderthal contribution to civilization had evolved.

Citing research by writers Charles Hapgood (*Earth's Shifting Crust*) and Rand Flem-Ath (*Atlantis beneath the Ice*), Wilson explained that he had come to believe that civilization on Earth is very, very old. Two factors in particular had impressed him: (1) that Neanderthal man was far more intelligent than we assume, and (2) that ancient measures prove that man knew the exact size of the Earth millennia before the Greek Eratosthenes worked it out in 240 BCE.

"A little research of my own quickly verified both statements," said

Wilson. "Far from being a shambling ape, Neanderthal man had a larger brain than we have, was well acquainted with astronomy, played musical instruments, and even invented the blast furnace. As to the size of the earth, the ancient Greeks had a measure called the stade—the length of a stadium. The polar circumference of the earth proves to be *exactly* 216,000 stade. Yet the Greeks did not know the size of the earth. They must have inherited the stade from someone who *did* know." In the course of his research, Wilson found many other tidbits that made it plain to him that the highest knowledge from the very dawn of Western civilization must have been inherited from a much earlier civilization that knew much more than the supposed founders of our world.

Wilson's book detailed many remarkable discoveries, including the unearthing of a half-million-year-old plank that had been carefully planed on one side. He considered Neanderthal man possessed of a very high level of intelligence and cited the red ocher mines in South Africa, dating back one hundred thousand years, and the Berekhat Ram sculpture, dating to a quarter million years ago.

Civilization, believed Wilson, must be at least a hundred thousand years old, which means the Neanderthals must have been the civilizers, since humans, apparently, were not sufficiently advanced at that point. But he, like Gooch, believed that such advanced civilization would not necessarily fit our present-day model. Instead, it would have been more shamanic in nature and would have taken for granted group consciousness, "the kind of telepathic awareness that enables flocks of birds and schools of fishes to change direction simultaneously. Ancient man almost certainly possessed this same telepathic ability."

"Societies like ancient Egypt were almost certainly collectives," he argues, "which could explain their ability to lift massive weights." Such a society would have had a special understanding of proportion and would have been very adept mathematically.

Wilson also cites the extraordinary discoveries of John Michell, "who pointed out that the Nineveh number (a vast 15-digit number found inscribed on an Assyrian clay tablet in the ruins of Assurbanipal's library) can be divided by the diameters of the sun and moon, and that a mathematical principle called 'the Canon' seems to lie behind ancient science: the notion that our universe appears to be designed along mathematical lines—the 'code of numbers that structures the universe,' which implies that there is an intelligence behind this design." An example is the sequence of Fibonacci numbers, which play such a basic role in nature, from spiral nebulae to seashells.

For many researchers, it is clear that the history of civilization, as presently taught, has some important missing parts. Possibly a hundred thousand years remain unaccounted for. It seems more than a little important that those missing parts finally be brought to light, which begs the question: If such a great civilization once existed, where might we expect to find its remains? The answer could be coming from planned exploration of the underwater regions located off most of our current coastlines. Before the end of the last ice age twelve thousand years ago, in the period of time known as the Younger Dryas, vast areas of these regions were above water. So we may yet learn what happened then and there. When we do, we will certainly know a great deal more about where our civilization came from than we do now.

Expect the unexpected.

10

Biblical Proportions

Is Plato supported by the Good Book?

The writers of the Hebrew Bible were more literate, and were so sooner, than archaeologists have previously believed. That is the conclusion drawn from handwriting found on seventh-century BCE pottery shards recovered from Arad, a remote garrison far from Jerusalem in Israel.

According to Tel Aviv University biblical scholar Israel Finkelstein, coauthor of a 2016 study, computer analysis of the handwriting reveals that literacy in ancient Judah was widespread, indicating there must have been an educational system of some sort. Scholars have long debated whether or not biblical scribes would have been capable of writing the biblical accounts at such an early date, but the handwritten shards found at the site show that, indeed, even many low-level soldiers were literate, clearly implying education and suggesting that biblical accounts could have been recorded almost in real time. They would not have needed to wait for centuries to be taken down by more literate—if less knowledgeable—writers. The implication is that Bible stories may be considered more historically reliable than some have assumed.*

---

*See Shira Faigenbaum-Golovin, Arie Shaus, Barak Sober, et al., "Algorithmic Handwriting Analysis of Judah's Military Correspondence Sheds Light on Composition of Biblical Texts," *Proceedings of the National Academy of Sciences* 113, no. 17 (2016): 4664–69, https://www.pnas.org/content/113/17/4664. See also Tia Ghose, "The Bible Is Really Old, Handwriting Analysis Shows," LiveScience (online), April 11, 2016, https://www.livescience.com/54368-bible-compiled-early.html.

THE RIVERS OF PARADISE

The Bible says that God planted a garden in the east of a region called Eden. It also says that either four rivers flowed out of it or that one river divided into four: the Tigris, Euphrates, Pishon, and Gihon. There is much debate as to the identity of the last two rivers, but the Tigris and Euphrates are by no means mythical. Indeed, the fertile, well-watered, ancient land of Mesopotamia—literally "between two rivers"—was, and still is, defined by them. Nowhere, though, is there *one* river dividing into even these two, as the Bible appears to suggest.

In *Atlantis Rising* #87 (May/June 2011), in an article titled "The Garden under the Sea," researcher William B. Stoecker tells us that although they flow virtually in parallel for several hundred miles, the Tigris and Euphrates rivers are on opposite sides of a ridge system. Today they join in a delta before emptying into the northern end of the Persian Gulf, but in ancient times they were separate all the way to the gulf.*

Genesis also says that God created the first man, Adam, and then the first woman, Eve, and placed them in the Garden. Soon, though, as we all know, they disobeyed God, eating the fruit of the Tree of Knowledge of Good and Evil. The first couple was then expelled by God from the Garden, and an angel with a fiery sword was stationed at the entrance to prevent their return.

Though the Bible account may seem more like primitive fancy, it could very well be based on fact, even if it is not *literally* true. The Tigris and Euphrates, for example, do not originate as a single river. But in Hebrew, *adam* can mean "mankind," and the word for earth or ground is *adamah,* and Genesis says that God made man from earth or clay. According to this interpretation, the Garden could have been a breeding community of progenitor humans.

In Hebrew, *eden* means "delight," and in Sumerian (the language of early southern Mesopotamia), it means "plain." Southern Mesopotamia (modern Iraq) is still a fairly level plain, and a garden there, as described in Genesis, would certainly be delightful. Could the story of the fall of

---

*For another take on the four rivers, see Rob McRoberts, "Do the Four Rivers Lead Us to the Garden of Eden?," Ancient Origins (online), October 15, 2017, https://www.ancient-origins.net/human-origins-religions/do-four-rivers-lead-us-garden-eden-008971.

Expulsion from the Garden of Eden;
nineteenth-century painting by Thomas Cole

man, due to disobedience to God, be a veiled reference to the transition from a hunter-gatherer culture to an agricultural society, in which people learned to labor for long hours to obtain enough food to survive? The story of the firstborn son of Adam and Eve, the farmer Cain, murdering his brother, the herdsman Abel, is read by some as a reference to ancient conflicts between agriculturalists and pastoralists. Could this be the source of battles, continuing to the present day, between farmers and ranchers? Nobel Prize–winning author John Steinbeck suggested something of the sort in his 1952 novel *East of Eden.*

But was there a real Garden of Eden, and if so, where was it located? Just as people have tried to imagine Atlantis as existing virtually everywhere on Earth except where Plato said it was, some have imagined the Garden of Eden in many scattered parts of the world. But the reference to the Tigris and Euphrates would seem to pinpoint one region.

Some scholars have suggested that the Garden was located in a valley in the Zagros Mountains near the source of the Tigris and Euphrates. The area is part of the Palearctic Tigris–Euphrates ecoregion, which includes Iraq and parts of Turkey, Syria, Iran, Saudi Arabia, Kuwait, and Jordan. During the Holocene Optimum, from about 10,000 BP (before the present) to about 6,000 BP, the Earth was warmer and wetter than at any time since, and the Zagros valley might then very well have resembled a paradise.

Nearby regions in Anatolia (Asiatic Turkey) did support at least some hunter-gatherers, albeit ones capable of erecting large structures of cut and carved stone, like those at Göbekli Tepe, contradicting nearly everything generally believed to be true about such cultures. Archaeologist Klaus Schmidt, for one, thought his discovery at Göbekli Tepe could be the site of the Garden.*

Based on recent discoveries, some researchers have suggested that the Garden of Eden might have been located at the head of, or even *under,* what are now the waters of the Persian Gulf. Sea levels were lower then and much of the gulf was a river valley above sea level. In addition to the Tigris and Euphrates, two other rivers may once have flowed into the northern end of the gulf. Iran's seasonal and presently dammed Karun River might have been one of them, and, during the Holocene Optimum, the Wadi al-Rumah (a.k.a. Wadi al-Batin) flowed from northern Arabia into the upper Gulf.

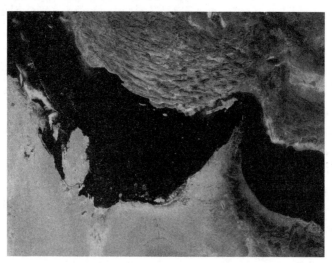

Satellite image of the Persian Gulf

---

*See Andrew Curry, "Gobekli Tepe: The World's First Temple?" *Smithsonian* magazine, November 2008, https://www.smithsonianmag.com/history/gobekli-tepe-the-worlds -first-temple-83613665/.

Ralph Ellis, author of *Jesus, Last of the Pharaohs* (1997) and many other books connecting Hebrew history to Egypt, thinks there is a simpler explanation for the Garden of Eden than the familiar Mesopotamian hypothesis. There is, he points out, only one river in the region that passes through a "garden" and then divides into four branches: the Nile, which runs through the valley oasis of Egypt before branching out at the Delta. The Nile has only two branches today, but in antiquity it had four. For those who argue that the Torah specifically names the Tigris and Euphrates, Ellis counters that the Torah does *not* actually mention these famous rivers at all. In Hebrew, it names the Chiddeqel, said to be another name for the Tigris, and the Parath, believed to be the Euphrates. Some of the biblical references do not readily support the Tigris/Euphrates argument, says Ellis, and, in fact, they point more toward Egypt and the Nile.*

THE STORY OF NOAH

Noah, the 2014 movie starring Russell Crowe, attempted to retell the ancient story of the man who the Bible says built a great ark to enable representatives of all living creatures (two by two) to survive a worldwide flood and to repopulate the Earth. Not only did *Noah* get the full Hollywood treatment, but at about the same time, an ancient cuneiform artifact, apparently offering instructions on how to build a very large boat that could have done the job, surfaced at the British Museum.

In a 2014 press conference, museum curator Irving Finkel displayed an ancient clay tablet that he said explained exactly how one might construct such an ark. Biblical literalists point out that the tablet's instructions refer to a giant round boat, or coracle, whereas the Bible clearly describes a long rectangular affair. Finkel says he is "107 percent" sure that the ark was never built, but still, if it were, the ancient tablet he presents tells how it could have been done.†

---

*Ellis breaks down some of his thoughts on the topic of Egypt being the site of Eden in "Eden in Egypt—Part 1," Ancient Origins (online), July 7, 2014, https://www.ancient-origins.net/opinion-guest-authors/eden-egypt-part-1-001827.
†See Maev Kennedy, "Babylonian tablet shows how Noah's ark could have been constructed," The Guardian, January 24, 2014, https://www.theguardian.com/books/2014/feb/13/ark-before-noah-irving-finkel-review.

Noah and His Ark; nineteenth-century painting by Charles Willson Peale

Most arguments about the ark of Noah seem to revolve around whether or not the biblical story is literally true. Believers, of course, place great stock in the account from the Book of Genesis—usually as it appears in the King James version of the Bible—and therefore are greatly inspired by many as yet unproven allegations, seeming to confirm the Bible story, that such a vessel may have turned up on Turkey's Mount Ararat. There is, though, little or no evidence that the "Ararat" referred to in Genesis is the same place.

For the less literally minded—albeit those who yet respect the veracity of ancient scriptures—the most important inference to be drawn from the story of Noah, it can be argued, is that it is an archetypal account of events surrounding the end of the last ice age, the Younger Dryas. For these, the story—possibly a retelling of the Babylonian epic of Gilgamesh—is but one of the multitude of flood legends, including Plato's story of Atlantis, found worldwide that chronicle the catastrophic end of one age and the birth of another—the end of the prediluvian world and the beginning of the postdiluvian, our own.

Noah's story, however, is not the only reference in the Bible that might point to Atlantis. The Genesis account of the Garden of Eden could refer, as we have seen, to the transition from herding to farming, or it could actually be a veiled reference to a forgotten, albeit enlightened, age when humans communed directly with God, but from which they suffered a catastrophic fall. Read this way, some of the dire prophecies like those in the Book of Revelations for a coming "last judgment" of the "wicked" might actually be vague recollections of a long-forgotten terrible fall of civilization like Atlantis. A similar argument could be made for the Tower of Babel (a.k.a. Babylon).

Researcher Steven Sora thinks the Babel story is not just a cautionary tale but tells us a great deal about our lost history. A Babylonian stele left more than 2,500 years ago by Nebuchadnezzar II points to a now ruined ziggurat named Etemenanki as the Tower of Babel, but the inclusion of floods, droughts, and other catastrophes in some accounts has led some to conclude that the story could be a fact-based reference to the breakup and dispersion of civilization following the end of the last ice age.*

The Tower of Babel;
sixteenth-century painting by Marten van Valckenborch the Elder

---

*The stele is part of the Schøyen Collection, based in London and Oslo. You can see a photo of the stele accompanying the article "The Tower of Babel, King Nebuchadnezzar II and the Schøyen Collection," Archaeology Wiki (online), December 29, 2011, https://www.archaeology.wiki/blog/2011/12/29/the-tower-of-babel-king-nebuchadnezzar-ii-and-the-sch%C3%B8yen-collection/.

JONAH'S JOURNEY

A more direct biblical reference to Atlantis, Sora thinks, may be found in the Book of Jonah. The Bible says that God told Jonah to preach to the city of Nineveh (which today is Mosul in Assyria), a dangerous place both then and now. The Ninevites worshipped Ishtar, and Jonah was told to bring his Hebrew God to the people, something he feared would not be well received. So instead of heading east, the Bible says, he went to Joppa and boarded a ship heading west to a place called Tarshish. The tale of Jonah's voyage, the ensuing storm, and his ultimate ingestion and regurgitation by a "great fish" are universally familiar. What is not so well known is the Tarshish story.

Tarshish is the biblical—likely Aramaic—name for Tartessus. Jonah's story was one of the earliest known references to this lost civilization, but Tartessian ships, it is believed, carried goods from the west to Judah and Israel during the reign of King Solomon, importing silver, gold, and copper as well as Barbary apes. Spain, we know, was rich in silver and Gibraltar is famous for its Barbary apes, so we have clues to the Tartessus location. Some have said that the entire country of Spain was Tartessus, and others believe it is the area known as Andalucia on the southern coast of the Iberian peninsula. Herodotus once described Tartessus as "beyond the Pillars of Hercules," recalling Plato's famed location for Atlantis.

It may be, thinks Sora, that the Tartessians were an offshoot of the Iberian peoples. Both groups are described as having much in common, including a language that, until recently, remained undecipherable. The new translations are based on the incorporation of Phoenician from around 1200 BCE. The Basque, Etruscan, and Tartessian languages are examples of a small group of non-Indo-European tongues found in Europe. The Iberian people were known in Spain from ancient times.* Some believe they arrived there from northern Africa, and linguist Barry Fell claimed these languages shared a writing system. Fell also identified related Basque words, like *arano,* which means "eagle" in both languages. A Gaelic tradition asserts that the Irish were originally from Iberia; the oldest Gaelic name for Ireland is Ibheriu.

---

*For details on the ancient history of the Iberian people, see Carl Zimmer, "A History of the Iberian Peninsula, as Told by Its Skeletons," *New York Times* (online), March 14, 2019, https://www.nytimes.com/2019/03/14/science/iberia-prehistory-dna.html.

Jonah and the "great fish"; nineteenth-century engraving by Gustave Doré

Tartessian merchants were famed for their wealth and were known to sail into the Atlantic, where the "east wind" mentioned in Psalm 48 could drive sailors out into the ocean. The Book of Ezekiel describes them as bringing all sorts of riches to the markets of the east, especially to the port city of Tyrus, including silver, iron, lead, and tin. The tone of Isaiah makes it seem that the Semites regarded their trading partners as a necessary evil. The Phoenicians, they thought, would go after the Tartessian monopoly of metals.

The scholarly consensus on Tyrus is that Ezekiel was referring to the Phoenician city-state of Tyre, the site of which can still be found on the coast of modern-day Lebanon, about fifty miles south of Beirut. But is that the entire story?

According to Dave Hershiser, author of *Beyond the Pillars of Hercules,* H. P. Blavatsky, the founder of the Theosophical Society, in her 1888 book *The Secret Doctrine,* claimed that Ezekiel's account of Tyrus was actually about Atlantis. Many of Ezekiel's descriptions of Tyrus, and those of other biblical prophets, says Hershiser, are of a city far different, both historically and geographically, from the Phoenician Tyre. Although similar in some respects, Ezekiel's Tyrus and the Phoenician Tyre seem entirely different; indeed, Ezekiel's description resembles Plato's Atlantis more than any other place.*

Alterations to the language used in the 1611 King James Bible, now found in many modern translations, Hershiser believes, offer descriptions of Tyrus much different from the one found in the King James version. Consequently, any connections between Tyrus and Atlantis have become obscure, if not completely invisible. Modern translations, he argues, have incorporated current assumptions that Ezekiel's Tyrus must have been the Phoenician Tyre, and the city's description has been made to fit.

In the King James version of Ezekiel 27:3, however, Tyrus is described as "situated at the entry of the sea." This passage is significant for two reasons: first, the sea being mentioned is obviously the Mediterranean, and second, the entrance to the Mediterranean is the Strait of Gibraltar. In other words, the entrance is said to lie on the Atlantic side of the Strait of Gibraltar—at the *western* end of the Mediterranean—matching the location of Atlantis given by Plato in *Critias*. The farthest part of the island of Atlantis, said Plato, reached to just outside the Pillars of Hercules (what the ancient Greeks called the Strait of Gibraltar) and faced the area of southwest Spain, at that time called Gadeira.

The New Interpreter's Bible commentary on the passage paints a different picture, says Hershiser. Ezekiel, it says, was a master of metaphorical language and placed the Phoenician city of Tyre, which is at the *eastern* end of the Mediterranean, on the western side—but in a "literary" way. The King James passage, though, is detailed and not metaphorical in tone. It clearly doesn't match the geographical arrangements of the Phoenician port. The city of Tyre, says the current interpretation, lay on a small island, about a mile in length, and was situated a few hundred yards off the coast of present-day Lebanon, which of course lies on the easternmost shore of the Mediterranean, where it is not really the entrance to anything—making its correlation with ancient Tyrus something with which Madame Blavatsky would surely have disagreed.

---

*Professor Mark Verman of Wright State University in Dayton, Ohio, discusses Ezekiel's depiction of Tyre at great length in "Ezekiel, the Wordsmith, and His Prophecies against Tyre," *Jewish Bible Quarterly* (online), June 26, 2017, https://jbqnew.jewishbible.org /uncategorized/ezekiel-wordsmith-prophecies-tyre/.

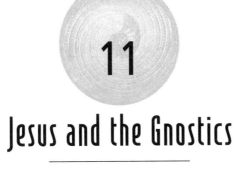

Jesus and the Gnostics

Is there an Atlantis connection to the story?

In November 2018, archaeologists reported discovery, in the Israeli desert, of a 1,500-year-old painting said to be of Jesus as a young man. At about the same time, in the region south of Qumran in Palestine, the neighborhood where the famous Dead Sea Scrolls were found in the 1940s and '50s, new caves with archaeological remains came to light. Though the story drew headlines, no new scrolls have yet turned up, but optimism that they may yet be found was encouraged by the fact that the caves have not been looted. According to archaeologists Randall Price of America's Liberty University and Oren Gutfield of the Hebrew University of Jerusalem, the caves dubbed 53b and 53c contained plenty of well-preserved pottery and cooking ware.* Perhaps by the time you read this, new scrolls and new evidence surrounding the time of Jesus will have been discovered.

Curiously, in an apparently unrelated development, another detail in the traditional story of Jesus also came to light in 2018, when the personal ring of Pontius Pilate was unveiled. Actually found in 1968 in the palace of King Herod near Bethlehem in the West Bank, the small piece of copper alloy jewelry had gone unrecognized for a half century until a proper analysis established its likely historical ownership.† The man who,

---

*Read about the discovery in "Newly Discovered Caves May Hold More Dead Sea Scrolls," *Times of Israel* (online), December 1, 2018, https://www.timesofisrael.com /newly-discovered-caves-may-hold-more-dead-sea-scrolls/.
†See Cnaan Liphshiz, "Israeli Archaeologists Say They Found the Ring of Jesus' Killer," Jewish Telegraphic Agency (online), November 30, 2018, https://www.jta.org /2018/11/30/news-opinion/israeli-archaeologists-say-found-ring-jesus-killer.

according to the Bible, ordered the crucifixion of Jesus has been reviled ever since, but, ironically, by providing tangible evidence of his role in the story Pilate may have inadvertently made a contribution to latter-day debate over the reality of an historical Jesus. Argument over the matter is certainly not new, but recent controversy has put the issue back in the spotlight. That may partly explain why, also in 2018, Pakistani prime minister Imran Khan chose to declare in Lahore, "There is no mention of Jesus in history." In a speech calling for an international convention to ban speech deemed insulting to Muslims, Khan was seen by some as attempting to contrast Jesus unfavorably with Muhammed, whom he described as "Allah's last prophet [and] part of history." Strangely, Khan neglected to mention that Jesus is also revered in Islam.

Debate over the historical reality of Jesus has not been entirely between believers and nonbelievers. Indeed, there are plenty of non-Christian authorities supporting the case for Jesus's existence. In, for instance, *Antiquities of the Jews,* from 93 CE, Flavius Josephus, a Jewish historian, mentioned Jesus and his brother James, as well as John the Baptist. The Roman historian Tacitus recorded the death of Jesus at the hands of Pontius Pilate, and first-century Roman politician Pliny the Younger mentioned knowledge of Jesus gained from interrogating Christians. Other early references, both direct and indirect, have been made in Jewish rabbinical literature, by the Greek philosopher Celsus, and elsewhere.*

Over the past century, archaeology has produced some very interesting evidence that is still far from being fully digested. The much-celebrated Gnostic Gospels—thirteen leather-bound papyrus codices buried in a sealed jar—were discovered in 1945 near Nag Hammadi, Egypt. Comprising fifty-two mostly Gnostic treatises, the codices included three works belonging to the third and fourth centuries. Comparable gnostic texts of the time include numerous references to a special relationship between Jesus and Mary Magdalene. There is even a gospel of Mary Magdalene.

Needless to say, the Roman Catholic Church has not looked kindly

---

*See Zelda Caldwell, "Here's the Historical Evidence from Non-Christian Sources That Jesus Lived and Died," Aleteia (online), April 12, 2018, https://aleteia.org/2018/04/12 /heres-the-historical-evidence-from-non-christian-sources-that-jesus-lived-and-died/. See also Lawrence Mykytiuk, "Did Jesus Exist? Searching for Evidence beyond the Bible," *Bible Archaeology Review,* January/February 2015.

on the Gnostic Gospels or their implications, now or ever. From the church's inception, the early fathers officially proclaimed the teachings of the Gnostics to be heresy. At the time the Nag Hammadi gospels were buried, one could have been tortured and killed just for reading them, which, doubtless, explains why they were hidden.

While a visitor from another planet might expect the two enormous religions contending for worldwide dominance—Christianity and Islam—to differ over the issue of historical authenticity for Jesus, the visitor would be wrong. Both religions agree that Jesus existed. Oddly, some of those most likely to reject the historical case for Jesus consider themselves Christians and align with a more allegorical and mundane explanation of his significance. In a further irony, many of those who fervently believe in a literal interpretation of Bible stories seem to find themselves at odds with evidence now coming to light that points to the real existence of a man called Jesus, but one much different than they may have pictured. For the latter, the best question may not be "Did Jesus exist?" but rather "If he did, what kind of person was he?"

A few years ago, mainstream Christians were shocked to read in the Dan Brown novel *The Da Vinci Code* the claim that not only did Jesus have a flesh-and-blood identity but that he was married and left a bloodline that survives to the present day. Another researcher, *Atlantis Rising* contributor Ralph Ellis (author of *Jesus, Last of Pharaohs*), has argued that Jesus was, in fact, a historical personage in Palestine known as Jesus of Gamala who descended from the Ptolemaic dynasty of Egypt. Popular Egyptian author Ahmed Osman (*Jesus in the Land of the Pharaohs*) thinks Jesus was actually Tutankhamun. Reconciling such widely divergent views might seem impossible, but one thing most alternative researchers agree on is that Jesus was probably connected with the obscure community of ascetics who eventually became known as the Gnostics.

THE APOCALYPSE OF JAMES

New archaeological discoveries help make the point. Only a small number of texts from the Nag Hammadi library had been found in Greek, the language in which they were originally written. But in 2017, religious studies scholars Geoffrey Smith and Brent Landau from the University of Texas at Austin (UTA) added to the list with the discovery of several

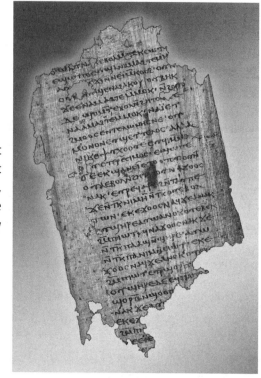

Fragment of a Coptic
translation of the First
Apocalypse of James,
found in the
Nag Hammadi library

fifth- or sixth-century Greek fragments of the Gnostic Gospel known as the First Apocalypse of James, which was previously thought to have been preserved only in its Coptic translations.

According to a UTA press release, this ancient narrative describes how Jesus reveals to his brother knowledge of the heavenly realm and future events, including James's inevitable death. In other words, Jesus initiated James into an esoteric awareness, or special understanding reserved for the initiated, or chosen elect—a recurring theme in Gnostic literature.*

The relationship between Jesus and his brother James has been at the center of much of the debate over the role of first-century Gnostics in the life of Jesus. A tomb discovered in 1980 in Jerusalem's East Talpiot neighborhood, containing several inscribed ossuaries with names corresponding to Jesus and his family members mentioned in the Gospels, including

---

*See the press release from the University of Texas: "UT Austin Professors Discover Copy of Jesus' Secret Revelations to His Brother," UT News (online), November 29, 2017, https://news.utexas.edu/2017/11/29/ut-austin-professors-discover-copy-of-jesus-secret-teaching/.

Geoffrey Smith and
Brent Landau

Mary, has been asserted to be the actual Jesus family tomb. A Discovery Channel documentary and an associated book, *The Jesus Family Tomb,* by Simcha Jacobovici and Charles Pellegrino, were released in 2007.

In 2002, the Discovery Channel and the Biblical Archaeological Society announced discovery of the "James ossuary"—a first-century limestone box said to contain the bones of Jesus's brother. The find was initially greeted with much skepticism, and its discoverer, Oded Golan, was tried for forgery before ultimately being acquitted. In the years since, many scholars have come to think that the ossuary could indeed be the real thing. On the other hand, Robert Eisenman, author of *James the Brother of Jesus* and considered one of the preeminent authorities on early Christians, is on record as very doubtful of the ossuary's authenticity.*

The ossuary is inscribed with Aramaic text declaring the box to be that of James, son of Joseph and brother of Jesus. Until now, it has been impossible to determine exactly where the ossuary originated, but according to Jacobovici, a Canadian-Israeli filmmaker, and Arye Shimron, a geoarchaeologist, it can be directly connected to a purported Jesus family tomb first located in 1980. Jacobovici and Shimron carried out an extensive statistical analysis of the first-century population of Jerusalem and various popular Jewish names of the time and have established the strong likelihood that the inscriptions on both the tomb and the ossuary could

---

*See Robert Eisenman, "'The James Ossuary' and Its Authenticity," *The Jerusalem Post,* January 24, 2011, https://www.jpost.com/blogs/the-eisenman-line/the-james-ossuary -and-its-authenticity-367865.

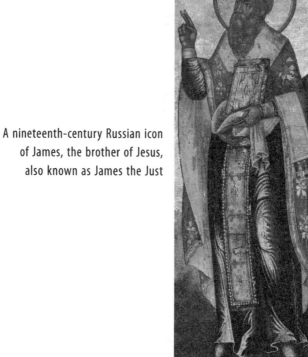

A nineteenth-century Russian icon
of James, the brother of Jesus,
also known as James the Just

The purported ossuary of James

only pertain to the actual Jesus family. Moreover, the researchers claim that a unique chemical signature clearly links the tomb with the ossuary.

While the new research seems to contradict many aspects of the orthodox Gospel narrative concerning the life of Jesus, some scholars, like James Tabor of the University of North Carolina, disagree. Tabor believes the most important thing here is new evidence for the existence of the historical Jesus.*

ESOTERIC CHRISTIANITY

Advocates for a more esoteric kind of Christianity, like that practiced by the Gnostics, point out that the Bible, as presently constituted, is the product of church councils convened to address early controversies. The Council of Nicaea, for instance, was gathered in 325 CE by Constantine I, the newly converted Christian emperor of Byzantium. At the top of the agenda was the so-called Arian heresy. The argument was over the divinity of Jesus—on one side the so-called Gnostics, or Arians, and on the other, the Nicaeans. The Gnostics sought direct personal knowledge of God (gnosis) and took very seriously such statements by Jesus as "Know ye not that ye are gods?" and "The kingdom of heaven is within you." The Nicaeans, on the other hand, saw Jesus as the absolutely essential mediator between God and man. The Gnostics were outvoted and most of their teachings were thereafter forcibly removed from church doctrine.

Some researchers, including Michael Baigent, Richard Leigh, and Henry Lincoln in their book *The Messianic Legacy*, have argued that the fourth-century Gnostics inherited the mantle of the apostle James, brother of Jesus and leader of the first-century church. Few today realize that the church's early years produced many gospels and books purported to have been authored by direct associates of Jesus (i.e., the Gospel of Thomas and the Gospel of Mary Magdalene). Most were destroyed by the church's ruling faction, which wanted no interference with its designs. Some of those once-despised books were rediscovered at Nag Hammadi. Author

---

*Read more in "The Controversial James Ossuary and the Talpiot Tomb," at James Tabor's blog, *TaborBlog*, https://jamestabor.com/the-controversial-james-ossuary-and-the-talpiot-tomb/.

The conversion of Constantine;
painting by Peter Paul Rubens

Elaine Pagels, professor of religion at Princeton University, included many excerpts in her 1989 best seller *The Gnostic Gospels.*

The Gnostic texts appear to fill in gaps exposed by discoveries in the 1940s and '50s of the so-called Dead Sea Scrolls near Qumran in Palestine. Despite bitter resistance from orthodox scholarship, many respected researchers believe the scrolls were created by a sect known as the Essenes, which possibly included Jesus and his followers. Many elements in common to both the Dead Sea Scrolls and his teachings are easily recognized.

Moreover, Norman Golb, author of *Who Wrote the Dead Sea Scrolls?*, says that handwriting analysis shows that at least five hundred scribes were involved. This suggests to many scholars that the texts must have come from a broad movement spread across Palestine and Judaea, not just some tiny isolated sect. This view is supported by Robert Eisenman.

Scroll fragment recently discovered near Qumran

Baigent and Leigh, in their book *The Dead Sea Scrolls Deception,* draw on Eisenman but go further, contending that the Qumranians and early Christians were not only one and the same but nationalist militants, known as Zealots, trying to install their priest-king, Jesus, on the throne of Israel, and possibly his brother James after him. They cite, as does the Gospel of Matthew, Jesus's lineage from King David. He becomes, in their view, someone other than the traditional Jesus, a literal king of the Jews, and perhaps a freedom fighter against the Roman occupation. Ensuing elements of this story line, as it may have impacted European history, were laid out in Baigent, Leigh, and Lincoln's book *Holy Blood, Holy Grail,* and subsequently in Dan Brown's *The Da Vinci Code.*

Such revelations from alternative scholarship have offered compelling new insight into Christian origins. Emerging from the mists of antiquity is a picture of intrigue and treachery in which Jesus's subtle original teachings were codified into a crude set of laws and doctrines enforced by a priestly elite, in collusion with secular princes determined to preserve their authority. The hidden agenda was to distract the people from troublesome notions of personal immortality and to substitute instead the specter of sinful guilt requiring the intercession and vicarious atonement of Jesus. This doctrine mandated the actual worship of Jesus as the wholly unique Son of God and placed the burden of atonement for all human error on his shoulders alone. Thus diverted from accepting responsibility for their own sowings, the people were effectively robbed of the power to challenge their personal oppressors and, ultimately, to transcend their circumstances—prevented, in other words, from endangering their rulers.

THE EGYPTIAN CONNECTION

Among the most interesting alternative interpretations of the meaning of Jesus's life are those that come from comparisons between Christian teaching and that of ancient Egypt.

"The central figure of the ancient Egyptian Religion was Osiris," wrote Egyptologist Sir E. A. Wallis Budge, "and the chief fundamentals of his cult were the belief in his divinity, death, resurrection, and absolute control of the destinies of the bodies and souls of men. The central point of each Osirian's Religion was his hope of resurrection in a transformed body and of immortality, which could only be realized by him through the death and resurrection of Osiris."

Classical writers describe Osiris as a semidivine king who abolished cannibalism, taught men and women to live according to the law of *maat* (divine order), improved their morality, and, filled with love for mankind, set out on a quest to travel the world and bring the benefits of civilization to other cultures. After he is murdered by his jealous brother Seth, Osiris's rebirth is achieved magically by his sister/wife Isis. His second death, caused again by Seth, who dismembers his body and scatters the pieces up and down the Nile, is avenged in an epic battle by Horus, the son of Osiris.

Osiris is believed to have ruled Egypt during the so-called period of Zep Tepi, the First Time, said to be the time of the last ice age, or the Younger Dryas. In other words, the "Egypt" of Osiris was a prediluvian civilization equivalent to Atlantis, as described by the priests of Sais to Plato's ancestor Solon. And in this school of thought, Jesus, as a latter-day inheritor of the legacy of Osiris, would have been the anointed priest-king of Atlantis.

The Egyptian goddess Isis nurses Horus, her son by Osiris, her murdered husband; courtesy of the Museum of Fine Arts of Lyon

Many important symbols of Christianity, including the cross, the shepherd's crook, the special role of Mary, and even the beard of Jesus seem to echo earlier Egyptian practice. Perhaps the link may be explained by Israelite, and ultimately Christian, history. The lawgiver Moses, it must be remembered, was first a prince of Egypt before establishing Judeo-Christian foundations. Some researchers, such as Ralph Ellis, Robert Feather, and Sir Laurence Gardner, have suggested there was a continuous thread from the pharaohs of ancient Egypt and their traditions directly through Old Testament Israelite history to Jesus.

The Egyptians likened the spirit of Osiris to a heavenly bird, much like Christianity portrays the Holy Spirit as a white and shining dove. The Egyptians called the bird Benu, while the Greeks characterized it as a phoenix. According to legend, the creature miraculously appears in the eastern sky at crucial points in history to herald a new world age and then mysteriously sets itself ablaze and is consumed. However, it ultimately arises triumphantly over death, renewed and rejuvenated.

Scholars believe the phoenix was a symbol of Osiris. The attributes

A fourth-century painting from the Commodilla Catacomb in Rome may be the oldest depiction of Jesus as recognizably Jewish, with a beard and long hair. Christian art in Rome had once portrayed him disguised as Orpheus.

of Osiris as phoenix are the same as those of the Christian Messiah. Both appear in the eastern sky (the star of Bethlehem arose in the east). Both rise from the dead. Both symbolize life after death through resurrection. Both signal the start of new ages. Finally, both are associated with prophecies of a second coming.

The Gnostic Christians presented the life and teachings of Jesus primarily as a path of initiation whereby the Christ, acting more as priest than king, guided disciples like his brother James—those with "eyes to see and ears to hear"—through various rituals of purification, culminating in illumination and liberation. In this sense, Jesus's role as anointed revealer of the sacred mysteries harmonizes with the purest and most ancient temple wisdom and practice.

12

The Gods of Atlantis

Where do heroes come from?

No matter how outrageous the final result, there is always some truth to the productions of Hollywood. The titans of Tinseltown like to grab a fact or two for a starting point and then venture into the imaginary, especially where they think there is a market. Mutant powers, as in *X-Men,* are based on actual medical anomalies, cyborgs of the future

Divers find an underwater goddess in this 1985 promotional art
for *The Atlantis Dimension,* a screenplay by Tom Miller and Doug Kenyon
(also see color insert plate 10)

(*Iron Man*) start with current lab experiments, extraterrestrial agendas (*Roswell*) are extrapolated from abduction case histories, and so on.* All of the facts gathered in support of such fiction are intended to serve the purposes of entertainment and to make the willing suspension of disbelief easier to achieve—or that, at least, is the theory.

Hollywood has long known that people will pay to witness great disasters—both real and imagined. From *The Poseidon Adventure* to *The Last Days of Pompeii,* a fascination with spectacular doom may be another symptom of the worldwide amnesia that prevents the waking memory of and confrontation with the suppressed knowledge of ancient catastrophes, like, say, the sinking of the *Titanic* . . . or Atlantis. Our deeply scarred collective psyche, it appears, compulsively seeks a return to the forgotten scenes of a destroyed past.

And there may be something even deeper at work—an innate human ability to recognize greater truth, something that plays a fundamental role in the premises we can intuitively accept in our entertain-

The Last Day of Pompeii, 1830–1833 painting by Karl Bryullov

---

*The list of superhero/mutant powers on the online Superhero Database makes an interesting read; see https://www.superherodb.com/powers/.

ment fare. All of us, after all, experience the same world of dreams that has been with us since the beginning, and that has long been studied by priests and shamans, as well as by wise pioneers like Carl Jung and Joseph Campbell.

Contact with that world of dreams—the universal unconscious mind—puts us in touch with themes and archetypes that we can all understand. George Lucas often said that he consciously worked to incorporate such elements into his *Star Wars* stories, and the same can be said for the makers of many cinematic classics, from *Casablanca* to *Lord Jim, Moby Dick,* and *Apocalypse Now.* Like storytellers for millennia, the best in the business still try to tap the universal fountain of understanding that inspired Homer. Whether or not they succeed is a measure of their storytelling gifts, not the power of the source.

From an ordinary materialist perspective, the human psyche is the conditioned product of a mass culture and simply echoes whatever stimulus is provided to it. We are, in other words, merely expressing in our choices of entertainment the tastes that we have been programmed to appreciate. If that is true, then it really doesn't matter what images are shown to us, because we will obediently react to them in the way we have been trained. Like Pavlov's dogs, we will salivate when the dinner bell is rung. Suppose, though, that within us all, some deeper truth-detection mechanism is at work—some connection with the "absolute" that the fad makers cannot touch. Could there be, within every individual, an unconscious knowledge of the ultimate truth of things, a kind of crystalline geometry, which, though usually dormant—and perhaps somewhat scarred—will, when a particular note is sounded, suddenly begin to sing?

Despite all programming, the distinction between fact and fiction remains a deeply personal experience. That this is true has long been taught by great spiritual teachers from all ages, from East and West, and is regularly experienced by the few who attempt to follow a spiritual path. The reality of such a faculty, or intuition, is, of course, denied by those whose own internal tuning fork has ceased to resonate. Nevertheless, even they, for purposes of controlling others, struggle to re-create the lost effect, even while they deny its existence. Their counterfeit displays may fill the media, but for those who have glimpsed the real thing, the available illusions offer little charm.

THE LEGENDS OF ATLANTIS

In *Atlantis Rising* #124 (July/August 2017), author Steven Sora made the point that the "myth" of Hercules was probably based on some real person who made his heroic mark before the dawn of recorded history as we know it. Sora described a number of elements in the Hercules story that seem to imply a factual basis. Homer's story of Ulysses, for example, has been connected to accounts of the twelve labors of Hercules. Both stories feature special connections to the stars, suggesting that, in some forgotten epoch from before the end of the last ice age—the age of Atlantis, perhaps—Ulysses and Hercules might have been the same person.

The important takeaway is that Greek mythology was based on the stories of people who, though they had *become* gods, were once human like the rest of us. The notion is not unique to the Hercules story. Plato referred

The first labor of Hercules: killing a lion; painting by Peter Paul Rubens

to Zeus, Apollo, and Athena as his "lords and ancestors." Certainly, the practice in modern anthropology of classifying a great reverence for predecessors, like that found in many cultures, as a form of ancestor worship makes more sense given the insight that humans, through numerous incarnations, were believed capable of evolving to higher levels and of becoming virtual immortals, capable of guiding their descendants.

A shrine in a Vietnamese home venerates the ancestors.

Robert Bowie Johnson Jr., author of *The Parthenon Code: Mankind's History in Marble* and *Noah in Ancient Greek Art,* cites the goddess Athena as an example of a human person who became a goddess. She is, says Johnson, a link to the "pre-Flood world"—i.e., the world before the end of the Ice Age. Athena, he believes, was also known by many other names, among them Naamah, who was revered in stories from Babylon and Sumer. The Book of Genesis from the Bible, Johnson says, identifies Athena as "the last person mentioned in the line of Cain: 'And the sister of Tubal-Cain is Naamah' (Genesis 4:22). She was the daughter of Lamech, the last ruler of the Cainites before the Flood."*

---

*For the full text of Johnson's article, see "The Hidden Identity of the Woman Glorified as Athena: Her Link to the Pre-Flood World," Ancient Origins (online), August 24, 2017, https://www.ancient-origins.net/myths-legends-europe/hidden-identity-woman -glorified-athena-her-link-pre-flood-world-008663.

Statue of Athena in the Parthenon of Nashville, Tennessee, a re-creation of the original in Greece

According to writer Julie Loar, later Greek myths say Athena was Zeus's daughter, born as a fully armored adult war goddess. In "Athena or Aphrodite" (*Atlantis Rising* #104, March/April 2014), Loar says earlier myths identify Athena as the principle of wisdom that created the cosmos. Athena is the goddess of wisdom, law and justice, just warfare, mathematics, strategy, the arts, crafts, and skill. Minerva was her Roman counterpart. Metalwork of weapons also fell under her patronage. She is very similar to the Egyptian goddess Neith. Athena used diplomacy and declared war only as a last resort. She then led battles with the disciplined, strategic side of war, in contrast to her brother Ares (Mars), the patron of violence, bloodlust, and slaughter.

The Athenians built their Parthenon on the Acropolis in her honor. Athena's veneration as the patron of Athens seems to have existed from the earliest times, and was so persistent that archaic myths were recast to adapt to cultural changes. The connection between serpents and Athena was explicit in ancient Greece, and, according to Loar, serpents in many traditions were symbols of wisdom. As the stern guardian of the Acropolis, the statue of the goddess showed her accompanied by a great snake that encircled her shield. Herodotus reported that, in Athens, "they have a great snake which guards the Acropolis and to which each month offerings of honey cake are made, and graciously received. By the time of the Persian invasion, the snake refused the offering. When the priestess announced this, the Athenians deserted the city because they believed the Goddess herself had deserted the Acropolis."

Archaic Athena was not a Greek goddess; her name does not have Greek etymology. She was, says Loar, an echo of an ancient goddess, perhaps a bird goddess from ancient Crete, where women had considerable power. Athena's name, which means "Lady of Athens," has survived in Linear B tablets from the Minoan period. In poetry from Homer onward, Athena's most common epithet is *glaukopis,* usually translated "bright-eyed" or "with gleaming eyes." *Glaux,* "owl," has the same root, presumably because of its own distinctive eyes. Another symbol of wisdom, an owl was Athena's constant companion.*

There is even more, though, to the story of Athena than most orthodox historians are willing to admit. Francis Bacon, founder of the secret Rosicrucian society that played a pivotal role in the founding of the United States, dedicated his service to Athena, the Greek goddess of wisdom. According to *The Martyrdom of Francis Bacon* by Alfred Dodd (1945), Pallas Athena was believed to preside over the intellectual and moral side of human life. She was usually shown on Greek temples wearing a helmet, denoting her silent war against sloth and ignorance, and carrying a spear, symbolizing knowledge, poised to strike the serpent—considered by some to represent ignorance—writhing under her foot. According to Dodd, "When the morning rays of the sun glinted on the weapon, causing it apparently to tremble, the common people were in the habit of saying smilingly: 'Athena is shaking her spear again.' She was thus known as 'the Spear Shaker' or the 'Shaker of the Spear.'" This is but one of many

---

*For more on the connection between Athena and the Minoans, see Gregory Nagy, "From Athens to Crete and Back," Classical Inquiries (online), September 10, 2015, https://classical-inquiries.chs.harvard.edu/from-athens-to-crete-and-back/.

reasons that some believe the name Shakespeare was a pseudonym used by Bacon to secretly author the plays attributed to William Shakespeare.

Any who doubt the extent of Athena's hidden influence over the modern world need look no further than the giant statue *Freedom* standing atop the U.S. Capitol. The Capitol building was intended by America's Masonic founders to be a latter-day Greek temple, and many have recognized in the statue a thinly veiled representation of Athena, complete with helmet and (substituting for the spear) a sword. Perhaps they should also consider that gods and goddesses were once human, and that even today, humans still have the potential to become gods and goddesses.

THE BATTLE OF ARCHETYPES

As long as we can remember, assorted prognosticators have floated forecasts of approaching calamity, but so far the "time foretold" has not appeared. Of course, we may be like the man who jumped from the tenth floor and was heard to exclaim as he passed the fifth, "So far, so good."

The main reason, we suspect, for the abundance of negative prophecy is likely more subjective than objective. That is not to say, however, that we should not pay attention to authoritative prophecies, if we can find them. We can all use a good weatherman. The real purpose of true prophecy, it has been said, is to warn. By this reckoning, a prophecy that actually comes to pass is one that has failed.

In the Bible, the prophet Jonah was told to go to Nineveh and warn of the city's coming destruction. When he refused, the story went, he was swallowed by a whale, but after being regurgitated in due time he decided to follow his divine instructions and warn the Ninevites of their imminent destruction, whereupon the people repented of their evil ways and were spared their day of reckoning. The outcome did not please Jonah, who apparently felt that his credibility as a prophet had been damaged. God then rebuked him, pointing out that the result was better than it could have been.

The source of most erroneous prophecy, though, may have more to do with misunderstanding the meaning of the original source, and a determination to read literally material that was never so intended. The biblical Book of Revelations, it can be argued, is not a forecast of world events but an account of contending archetypes vying for dominance within the inner

Freedom, 1863 statue by Thomas Crawford atop the dome of the U.S. Capitol

world of spiritual aspirants. From this perspective, it is probably futile to interpret the words of St. John like we might a newspaper—though, we are told, outer events, even on the world stage, are ultimately a reflection of inner realities and could herald the possibility of greater changes.*

Change is the key word. Everyone wants it, but no one seems too clear on just what it means. Certainly change alone is not the answer to any problem. After all, if things suddenly got much worse, that would be change too, but no one, we assume, wants that. Doubtless, the kind of change people want is for things to get better, but the meaning of that, too, seems obscure. One man's progress is another's degeneration, and so it goes.

---

*For a review of the congruence between apocalyptic archetypes in psychoanalytical work and in religious canon, see Mortimer Ostow, "Archetypes of Apocalypse in Dreams and Fantasies, and in Religious Scripture," *American Imago* 43, no. 4 (Winter 1986): 307–34, https://www.jstor.org/stable/26303943?seq=1#page_scan_tab_contents.

Change that could make an actual difference involves a dramatic episode and what used to be called a metamorphosis, catharsis, transmutation, and other names referring to a transformation more profound than any popular stereotype of change. It is something that must happen to the individual before it can happen to society. It is, apparently, in the nature of all to seek it—either consciously or unconsciously—and its absence creates a powerful force for modifying the status quo. Such change, when thwarted long enough, can lead to explosions and make things far worse, not better. Politicians manipulate these forces at their peril.

The need for such change was well understood by the enlightened ancients, who made it their business to nurture and encourage it. Indeed, the goal of ancient temple practice was liberation from mundane awareness through various rites of passage. Movies today are, to some extent, the inheritors of that tradition, and when they seek catharsis for their audience, they are still part of the ancient temple craft. Part of the magic of drama, even the Hollywood variety, is in the truth that an audience can be led to understand through the presentation of forces—call them archetypes, or gods, or heroes—that shape our consciousness. From the introduction of the hero and the antihero, the conflict, and all of the lesser characters, from the inciting moment to the final climax and resolution, the process can still lead an audience to some measure of catharsis, and, for some, to real change. The formula that worked for the ancient Greeks and Shakespeare still works today, as anyone who has ever been moved by a great flick can testify.

The real argument today is not between those who want change and those who don't. It is between those who celebrate the eternal flowering of the soul, as revealed by dramatic episodes, and those who deny it.

The laws of change that play a role in movies, of course, are a reflection of the principles that bring about change in nature. Caterpillars become butterflies and plants become flowers through the eternal unfolding of subtle geometric processes guided by the same principles that informed the ancient temple practices from which the better modern movies are derived.

At one time, those who consciously experimented with the laws of change in the quest for the liberation of their own soul were called alchemists. Today, they are sometimes called movie producers, even though they may not deserve the credit.

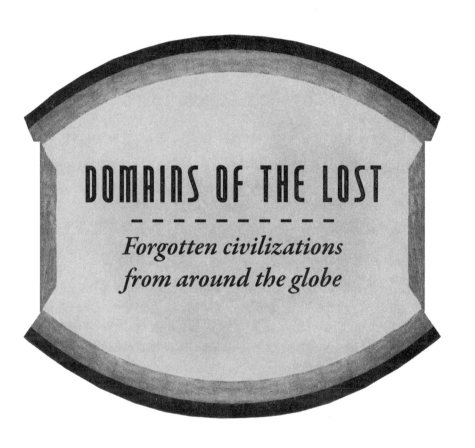

DOMAINS OF THE LOST

*Forgotten civilizations
from around the globe*

13

The Great Atlantis Hunt

Is new research getting us any closer to an actual location?

Ask most self-respecting academics to say out loud whether they think Atlantis could have been a real place, and you get a chuckle for your trouble. Plato's *Critias* and *Timaeus* dialogues, they will tell you, are the only basis for any fantastic legends of a drowned "city." Everything else is derivative and not to be taken seriously. As for a greater prediluvian civilization spread over higher elevations and coastal regions, ultimately to be inundated by floods ending our last ice age, the time period known as the Younger Dryas, the subject seldom comes up, at least in academia. But among those who dare to challenge orthodoxy, there have been many schools of thought since well before Plato. Indeed, even some mainstream academics have begun to suspect that there could be a meaningful correlation between the date ascribed by Plato to the sinking of Atlantis (about 11,500 years ago) and the end of the Younger Dryas. The timing is certainly suspicious.

For those in the alternative research community, it seems clear that some kind of catastrophic event—perhaps a hit from a large meteor or comet—about twelve thousand years ago killed off the woolly mammoths and sent humanity back to the Stone Age. From the Bible to Plato, many ancient sources have described such an ancient catastrophe, but academic science has rejected the notion that anything like that could have happened on Earth for at least millions of years. And while there may be plenty of evidence for a mini ice age, beginning at about the time Plato said Atlantis went down, no one had, until recently, found the actual crater that such a giant impact would have caused.

In November 2018, however, the peer-reviewed journal *Science Advances* published what could be a game changer. Titled "A Large Impact Crater beneath Hiawatha Glacier in Northwest Greenland," the report documented that as recently as twelve thousand years ago, an enormous iron meteorite plunged into Greenland and left a twenty-mile-wide crater beneath what is now known as the Hiawatha Glacier. The mile-wide meteor was one of the twenty-five largest such bolides ever known to have hit our planet. The impact would have had the force of seven hundred million nuclear bombs and caused ripple effects throughout the region and maybe worldwide. In their paper, the researchers admitted that the event could indeed establish the once controversial "Younger Dryas impact hypothesis" as a proven fact. The idea that a large impact of this type in North America some twelve thousand years ago could have caused massive wildfires across much of the Americas and Europe, large mammal extinctions, and disruptions in the weather of the Atlantic Ocean is not new, but the Greenland discovery is the first to identify an actual impact crater.*

The discovery has breathed new life into the perennial campaign to explain Plato's Atlantis story in terms acceptable to mainstream science, even as such efforts often contradict much of what Plato actually said.

ATLANTIS IN THE MEDITERRANEAN

The familiar game of arguing that your own country or its environs was once the site of Atlantis is still afoot. Over the years, nearly every place on Earth has been entered in the Atlantis sweepstakes. From the Sweden of Emanuel Swedenborg and Otto Rudbeck to the British Isles of many Anglophiles, from arguments for South and North America to Europe and the Mediterranean, all have found new and chauvinistic ways to reinterpret Plato. One of the more recent comes from the Italian island of Sardinia, where, not surprisingly, an Italian is making the argument.

---

*For the full report, see K. H. Kjaer, N. K. Larsen, T. Binder, et al., "A Large Impact Crater beneath Hiawatha Glacier in Northwest Greenland," *Science Advances* 4, no. 11 (2014), https://advances.sciencemag.org/content/4/11/eaar8173.

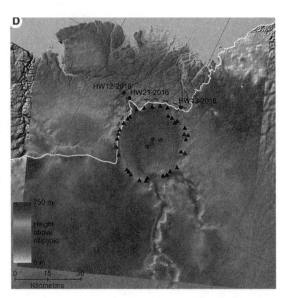

Impact crater beneath Hiawatha Glacier, northwest Greenland; topography based on NASA data (Alfred Wegener Institute [AWI]) (also see color insert plate 12)

In his 2009 book *Le colonne d'Ercole* (The Pillars of Hercules), journalist Sergio Frau stirred up quite a bit of interest in some sectors. UNESCO actually staged a symposium in Paris to promote the idea. Plato was, said Frau, the earliest writer to mention Sardinia, an island destroyed by a natural disaster that some believe was a tsunami sometime in the third or fourth century BCE. Frau's main point was that Alexandrian geographer and librarian Eratosthenes made a mistake in locating the Pillars of Hercules, which became the basis of our modern designation for the spot. Frau says the actual Pillars referenced by Plato were, in fact, on Sicily. If that is true, then Sardinia, he says, becomes the obvious location for Atlantis.*

Frau believes the Bronze Age Nuragic people, whose well-known ruins still exist on Sardinia, were the Atlanteans. The Nuragic civilization is thought to have been wiped out by a tsunami around 1175 BCE.

As with most other Mediterranean-area Atlantis suppositions, such as Santorini, popularized by Jacques Cousteau, Frau's case does not take seriously many of Plato's original Atlantean details. For one thing, the island kingdom's great size—larger than Libya and Asia Minor com-

---

*Read more at "Italian Researcher 'Discovers' Lost Island of Atlantis," *Sputnik*, August 30, 2016, https://sputniknews.com/art_living/201608301044761690-sardinia-atlantis -lost-island/.

Nuragic ruins

bined. And great antiquity, for another—more than nine millennia before Plato. By thus discounting Plato's actual account, Frau seems more interested in making himself acceptable to orthodox scholars, who scoff at any argument taking Plato at his word. The irony is that despite the near universal rejection by mainstream science of Plato's literal Atlantis, the campaign to explain him away continues to the present.

THE CUBAN CONNECTION

Early in the twenty-first century, apparent discoveries on Guanahacabibes, a peninsula at the west end of Cuba, excited many about possible underwater prediluvian ruins. The discovery by Canadian ocean engineer Paulina Zelitsky of what was described as a vast complex of ruins more than two thousand feet below the surface created a brief firestorm of curiosity, not only in the alternative Atlantis research community but with the general public as well. From NPR to the Associated Press, mainstream news media jumped on the story after Manuel Iturralde, a leading Cuban geologist, said he could not explain the site by any standard theory of natural geology. BBC News reported, "The explorers first spotted the underwater city last year, when scanning equipment started to produce images of symmetrically organized stone structures reminiscent of an urban development."* The subsequent public withdrawal of the National Geographic Society

---

*See "'Lost City' Found beneath Cuban Waters," BBC News (online), December 7, 2001, http://news.bbc.co.uk/2/hi/americas/1697038.stm.

Dr. Paulina Zelitsky

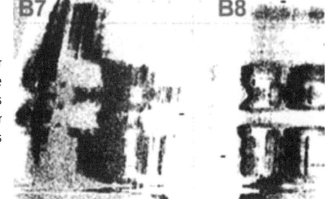

Side-scan sonar survey of the Guanahacabibes underwater structures

from the project proved a virtually fatal blow to the investigation. Even researcher Andrew Collins, who has argued in his widely read books that Cuba was the location of Atlantis, expressed doubt about the human origins of the Guanahacabibes site, stating that things looked pretty natural to him.

Since University of Miami professor J. Manson Valentine's 1969 discovery of the so-called Bimini Road, a linear formation of rectangular limestone blocks submerged in the waters between Florida and the Bahamas, Atlantis seekers from all over the world have swarmed the region looking for clues to ancient civilization. Valentine's discovery, appearing, as it did, to corroborate Edgar Cayce's prophecy—that the beginning of Atlantis's rise from the Caribbean could be expected to begin around 1968 or '69—created a temporary sensation, but when no more major discoveries were immediately forthcoming, interest died down. While some explorers continued to invest time and energy in the area, others threw up their hands and moved on. But did they give up too soon?

According to geologist William Hutton, Cayce predicted that after the Bimini finds, new discoveries would be made in the adjacent land to the southwest. Cayce's actual words: "For this [remains of Atlantis at Bimini] is of the first highest civilization that will be uncovered in some of the adjacent lands to the west and south of the isles, see?" Many have assumed that Cayce meant Yucatán, but could they have been forgetting Cuba?

Submariners from Advanced Digital Communications (ADC), based out of British Columbia, were exploring the area off the west coast of Cuba with sonar equipment when they detected a huge plateau with clear images of urban development. Shapes of silt-covered pyramids, roads, and buildings can be seen from above, claimed Zelitsky. "It is stunning. What we see in our high-resolution sonar images are limitless, rolling, white sand plains and, in the middle of this beautiful white sand, there are clear man-made large-size architectural designs. It looks like when you fly over an urban development in a plane and you see highways, tunnels and buildings," Zelitsky told Reuters.* Most officials knowledgeable about the discoveries were reluctant to speculate publicly, but the site was placed under investigation by the Cuban Academy of Sciences.

Zelitsky proposed that the ruins were perhaps those of a town that existed on a land bridge extending between Cuba and the Yucatán Peninsula of Mexico during the last ice age. The basic idea is that during the ice age, huge amounts of water from the Earth's oceans were stored in the ice sheets that covered vast parts of North America and Eurasia. This caused sea levels to fall, thus exposing land areas that are now underwater, such as the land bridge between Cuba and the Yucatán. Manuel Iturralde, the Cuban geologist, had some thoughts about that. "Iturralde noted," said National Geographic News, "that conclusive proof of man-made structures on the site could reinforce

---

*See "Looking for lost riches in Cuba's seas: Underwater surveyors say they may have found sunken city," *Reuters,* May 14, 2001.

some oral traditions of the Maya and native Yucatecos. These people still retell ancient stories of an island inhabited by their ancestors that vanished beneath the waves."

In 2012, Keith Fitzpatrick-Matthews, who runs the skeptic blog *Bad Archaeology,* said in his report on this case that the depth (over two thousand feet) of the alleged Cuban sunken remains is a big problem. He pointed out that during the last ice age, sea levels dropped a maximum of only about a hundred meters (328 feet)—not enough to expose this particular strip of land.* Not said, though, was the fact that a land bridge such as Zelitsky described did once exist above water in the area, albeit at a much earlier time, when modern humans are not believed to have existed.

Michael Cremo, coauthor with Richard Thompson of the 1999 book *Forbidden Archeology: The Hidden History of the Human Race,* thinks humans have been around much longer than the paleontologists are willing to admit. He rejects the idea that modern humans appeared less than two hundred thousand years ago. Indeed, writing for *Atlantis Rising* #125 in September/October 2017, he said there *is* evidence showing that humans like us existed as far back as hundreds of millions of years ago. The Gulf of Mexico/Caribbean area was indeed a dry basin during the early part of the Jurassic period (145 to 201 million years ago), before being filled with seawater in the Middle Jurassic, according to oceanographer R. M. Darnell in his 2015 book *The American Sea: A Natural History of the Gulf of Mexico.* Cremo points to the Puranas, the historical writings of ancient India, to argue that humans existed at that time, and he believes these early humans created the ruins spotted by Zelitsky and her colleagues.

As for the more recent ice ages, in 2009, a few years after Zelitsky's find, Drs. Greg and Lora Little, both researchers for the Association for Research and Enlightenment (A.R.E.), were investigating the underwater remains of what appeared to be a collapsed multiroom building in the Bahamas, in an area known as Pino Turolla's Column. The building's foundation is clearly man-made, with mitered limestone corners and other debris inside the outer walls. According to an A.R.E. press release, a sample of beach rock from a long, straight foundation wall

---

*See "An Underwater City West of Cuba," *Bad Archaeology* (blog), October 28, 2012, https://badarchaeology.wordpress.com/2012/10/28/an-underwater-city-west-of-cuba/.

Pre–Ice Age structure in the Bahamas near Pino Turolla's Column; photo courtesy of Edgar Cayce's A.R.E.

at the site was carbon-dated to between 21,520 BCE and 20,610 BCE. Conventional archaeological wisdom holds that the oldest dates for humans in the area go back to only about 1000 BCE.*

Even though the beach rock material is obviously older than the building in which it was found, it is still a significant find. "Beachrock forms at the edge of the shoreline," Greg Little explained for *Atlantis Rising* #90, November/December 2011, "where the waves move back and forth across the beach." When this beach rock was formed, sea levels were about three hundred feet below where they are today, and they began to rise at around 15,000 BCE. "We have to assume [the builders] didn't go underwater and pull these slabs up. . . . Around 4,000 BC the

---

*See "Pre–Ice Age Complex Found Off Bahamas Coast," on the website of the Edgar Cayce's A.R.E. organization at https://www.edgarcayce.org/the-readings/ancient-mysteries /atlantis/pre-ice-age-complex-found-off-bahamas-coast/.

sea level was about 15 feet lower than today, so by then this structure would have been essentially at the shoreline. The conclusion is that the structure was built on high ground sometime between 21,000 BC and well before 4,000 BC."

Investigators have been exploring the region since the late 1960s and have located many unusual underwater—apparently man-made—formations, but this was the first site to be carbon-dated, and the results strongly indicate that a highly developed pre–Ice Age culture may once have lived off the coast of the Bahamas.

TAKING PLATO AT HIS WORD

Russian geologist Viatcheslav Koudriavtsev uses recent paleoglaciological and geomorphological data to make the case that Plato should be taken literally. Among other things, Plato's dating for the sinking of Atlantis at roughly 9500 BCE corresponds quite well with the end of the last ice age, a fact that Koudriavtsev believes the ancient Greeks had no way of knowing. The changes in Atlantic sea levels associated

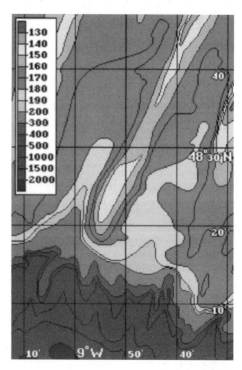

Topology of the Little Sole Bank area, a sand bank in the Atlantic Ocean southwest of Cornwall, U.K. (also see color insert plate 13)

with the rapid melting of the great northern European ice sheets could indeed account for catastrophic events such as Plato described. Koudriavtsev, however, does not think the drowned continent will be found in such previously suspected locations as the Azores, the Canary Islands, Iceland, or the Bahamas, but rather off the coasts of Europe and the British Isles in relatively shallow regions that remain unexplored, especially the area surrounding an underwater hill called Little Sole Bank on Britain's Celtic Sea shelf.* And, curiously, that spot is not the only one in the area that might be Atlantis.

Whether mythical or real, a strange island off the west coast of Ireland, referred to on ancient maps as Hy-Brasil, draws attention to this day, and some argue that it is all that remains above water of the location Plato called Atlantis. The island appears on maps as early as 1325 CE. In "Worlds without End" (*Atlantis Rising* #114, November/December 2015), writer William Stoecker mentioned the island: "There is the old legend of Hy Brasil, an island located a few hundred miles west of Ireland that may or may not have given its name to the country of Brazil, depending on which account you read." And according to a 2015 article in the *Epoch Times,* "The island was included on a 1325 map by the Genoese cartographer Angelino Dulcert where it was identified as 'Bracile.' It later appeared in the Catalan Atlas in 1375, which placed it as two separate islands with the same name, 'Illa de Brasil.' In 1436, it showed up as 'Sola de Brasil' in the Venetian map by cartographer Andrea Bianco."†

Writer Steven Sora, in his article "The Perilous Plight of Rockall Island" (*Atlantis Rising* #90, November/December 2011), suggested that Hy-Brasil might be the very lonely Rockall Island of the Porcupine Bank area. In his 1956 book *Rockall,* British naturalist James Fisher called the island "the most isolated small rock in the oceans of the

---

*For more details, see Viatcheslav Koudriavtsev, "Atlantis: New Hypothesis," Institute of Metahistory (online), November 1, 1997.
†See Bryan Hilliard, "Hy-Brasil: Truth behind the Legendary Phantom Island of Ireland?," *Epoch Times* (online), October 13, 2015 (updated October 19, 2015), https://www.theepochtimes.com/hy-brasil-truth-behind-the-legendary-phantom-island-of-ireland_1755165.html.

Engraving of the first British landing on Rockall Island in 1811

world." In 1997, Greenpeace, in an attempt to save the surrounding area from oil drilling, tried to claim the uninhabited granite island was an independent country and called it Waveland. Today it is again called Rockall and remains within the United Kingdom's exclusive economic zone, but unless you count seabirds—or the ghosts of Atlantis—it is completely uninhabited.

Rockall Island

14

The Polar Continent

What still lies buried beneath miles of ice?

In the quarter century since the discovery of Lake Vostok, the burning—or should we say freezing?—question about the giant subglacial body of liquid water in Antarctica has remained: Will we find life there? Conventional wisdom was that Vostok was probably sterile. It is, after all, very cold and inhospitable down there. But, once again, conventional science seems to have underestimated the capacity of life to exist, and even thrive, in worlds far stranger than previously imagined.

The first ice cores taken from Lake Vostok, almost three miles beneath Antarctica's ice, underwent painstaking analysis, and according to Dr. Scott Rogers of Bowling Green State University in Ohio, the researchers "found much more complexity than anyone thought." In a 2013 paper, Rogers and his colleagues reported that, using genetic sequencing, they had identified no less than 3,500 species from Lake Vostok, including bacteria commonly found in the digestive systems of fish, crustaceans, and annelid worms, in addition to fungi and two species of archaea, or single-celled organisms that tend to live in extreme environments. As might be expected, some of the organisms were ones known to live in extreme cold, but surprisingly, they also found some heat-loving thermophiles. This suggests, the scientists think, the presence of hydrothermal vents deep in the lake. In other words, it may be warm down there. Moreover, claimed Rogers, the presence of both marine and freshwater species indicates that the lake once was connected to the ocean, and that fresh water may have been deposited there by the overriding glacier.*

For many years, *Atlantis Rising Magazine* was among those making the case that there could be a great deal more to the story of Antarctica in general, and Lake Vostok in particular, than conventional science had led us to believe. With the latest evidence for "teeming" life beneath the ice, we thought it worth reconsidering some of the more extraordinary possibilities of the region.

LIQUID WATER BENEATH THE ICE

The largest of Antarctica's nearly four hundred known subglacial lakes, Lake Vostok is located at the so-called southern Pole of Cold, beneath Russia's Vostok Station (site of the coldest temperature ever recorded on Earth, −89°C) on the central East Antarctic Ice Sheet. The Russian research station itself is situated 11,444 feet above sea level. The surface of the lake, however, is approximately 13,100 feet beneath the surface, or approximately 1,600 feet below sea level. One hundred and sixty miles long, and thirty miles across at its widest point, the lake covers an area of about 4,830 square miles, roughly the size of Lake Ontario, but much deeper, averaging 1,417 feet. Lake Vostok's physical characteristics have led NASA scientists to argue that it might serve as an earthbound analog for Europa, the ice-covered moon of Jupiter.

In 1996, by integrating a variety of data, including airborne ice-penetrating radar observations and space-born radar altimetry, both Russian and British scientists confirmed the lake's existence. Over a century earlier, however, Russian scientist Peter Kropotkin had proposed the possibility of fresh unfrozen water under Antarctica's ice sheets, theorizing that the tremendous pressure exerted by the cumulative mass of thousands of vertical feet of ice could increase the temperature at the lowest portions of the ice sheet to the point that the ice would melt. The theory was further developed by I. A. Zotikov, a Russian

---

*For the full paper, see Y. M. Shtarkman, Z. A. Koçer, R. Edgar, R. S. Veerapaneni, T. D'Elia, et al., "Subglacial Lake Vostok (Antarctica) Accretion Ice Contains a Diverse Set of Sequences from Aquatic, Marine and Sediment-Inhabiting Bacteria and Eukarya," *PLoS ONE* 8, no. 7 (2013): e67221, https://journals.plos.org/plosone/article?id=10.1371/journal.pone.0067221.

glaciologist, who in 1967 wrote his doctoral thesis on this subject.

According to a dramatic report released in December 2007 by National Geographic News, Antarctica is not a barren polar desert but a rich, complex environment where "rivers larger than the Amazon link a series of 'lake districts,' which may be heavily populated with mineral-hungry microbes."* By 2008, about 145 lakes had been found. The lakes stay fluid, say scientists, because the ice covers them like blankets, trapping the heat that rises from the Earth's interior. These buried lakes, it is feared, may be contributing to the current rapid melting of Antarctic ice and creating what could be the world's largest wetlands.

The Russians had first discovered Lake Vostok while carrying out a drilling project in 1989. Ever since, speculation on what really might be down there has raged. Some have envisioned a world of perpetual twilight—at least during summer months—warmed by geothermal energy, inhabited with everything from one-celled organisms to giant fish. The lake, we are told, has been sealed by ice for at least four hundred thousand years and likely has a pristine environment, possibly quite different from the world we know. Many have feared that the lake could be contaminated by various proposed exploration attempts, or that some kind of catastrophe could endanger the lives of any explorers, or worse.

LOST CIVILIZATION

Some researchers, like ex-CBS space consultant Richard Hoagland (author of *The Monuments of Mars*), have conjectured that Lake Vostok may contain the ruins of a lost ancient civilization. Indeed, unusual magnetic anomalies have been detected in the neighborhood. Researcher Len Kasten investigated Hoagland's claim and filed the story "Mystery under the Ice" (*Atlantis Rising* #68, March/April 2008).

Hoagland, wrote Kasten, asserted that in early 2001, "a team of scientists from Columbia University, working under the auspices of the National Science Foundation (NSF) . . . began a series of unprecedented low-altitude aerial surveys over Lake Vostok, designed to chart gravitational, magnetic and thermal activity under the ice. In the course of doing

---

*See Christine Dell'Amore, "Antarctica May Contain 'Oasis of Life,'" National Geographic News (online), December 27, 2007.

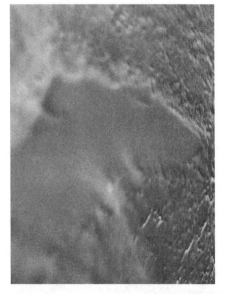

Satellite view of
Lake Vostok

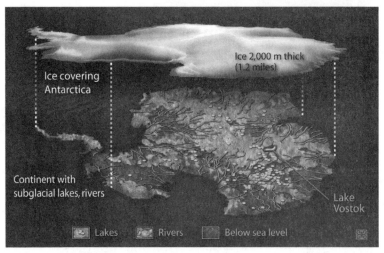

A National Science Foundation chart shows possible waterways
beneath the ice in Antarctica.

so, they made a stunning find. A huge magnetic anomaly was discovered covering the entire southeast portion of the shore of the lake." One possible explanation for the phenomenon, Hoagland theorized, was a large accumulation of metallic structures. This, he argued, could be "the ruins of an ancient, buried city." Immediately after this finding, said Hoagland, the scientists pulled back their Lake Vostok exploration program and

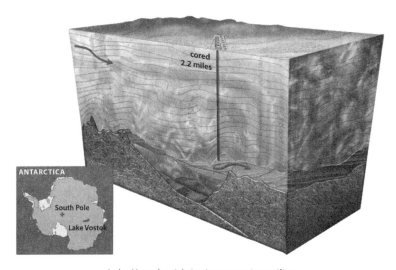

Lake Vostok with its immense ice ceiling;
illustration from the National Science Foundation

A scientist checks on one of Lake Vostok's revealing ice cores;
photo from the National Science Foundation.

turned it over to the NSA. This scenario, he said, is "eerily" reminiscent of the plot of the French novel *Subterranean*, "in which Antarctic scientists discover an inhabited 'Lost City' under the ice."

Over the years, rumors have persisted that in the period preceding and during World War II, the Nazis established a presence in Antarctica and that much UFO activity may have originated from bases maintained beneath the ice after the Nazi defeat. During the war, U.S. admiral Richard Byrd is said to have warned of a threat from the poles. Some say that when, after the war, he visited the polar region with a naval task force, he may have done so to finish off the German bases. Little in the way of convincing evidence to support such assertions has turned up, but one amazing story about Antarctica for which there is plenty of evidence has to do with the cartographer Charles Hapgood.

Hapgood, a professor of anthropology and history at Keene State College in Keene, New Hampshire, was asked by one of his students about Atlantis. Intrigued, he launched a nine-year investigation into ancient geography. Hapgood ultimately developed a theory of periodic displacement of the Earth's sixty-mile-thick crust over the planetary core, which resulted in apparent polar shifts, and in 1958 he published his ideas in the book *Earth's Shifting Crust*. Among those with whom Hapgood corresponded about his theory was president Dwight Eisenhower. The foreword to Hapgood's book, essentially endorsing his thesis, was written by Albert Einstein himself, who died shortly afterward in 1955. "The constantly increasing centrifugal momentum produced in this way," Einstein commented, "will, when it has reached a certain point, produce a movement of the Earth's crust over the rest of the Earth's body, and this will displace the polar regions toward the equator." According to the Scott Polar Research Institute in Cambridge, England, the ice accumulation in Antarctica amounts to two thousand billion tons each year. This, they say, is enough to build a wall ten inches thick and a half mile high from New York to California—every year.

Hapgood's second book, *Maps of the Ancient Sea Kings,* published in 1966, revealed three fully authentic ancient maps (two from the sixteenth century and one from the eighteenth) that clearly contain anomalous knowledge: the continent of Antarctica—configured correctly on all three maps—in an ice-free condition. Since Antarctica was not discovered until 1820, the fact that it should appear in any form on these early maps is perplexing, to say the least. All three mapmakers acknowledged that their information came from much more ancient sources, dating from as far back as 4000 BCE.

The possibility of an ice-free Antarctica only six thousand years ago, as depicted on the ancient maps, caused Canadian researcher Rand

Flem-Ath to consider that the icy continent could have been Atlantis and inspired him to explore the possibility at length. Initially not acquainted with Hapgood's work, he came to conclude that a temperate or tropical Antartica almost perfectly matched Plato's description of Atlantis in *Critias* and *Timaeus*. Flem-Ath was particularly struck by the fact that, when viewed from above the south pole, Antarctica occupies a commanding position at the virtual center of the world's oceans, much as Plato had described the position of Atlantis. Upon discovering Hapgood's crustal displacement theory, Flem-Ath realized that a shift of thirty degrees in the Earth's surface could have placed a large part of Antarctica in an ice-free temperate climate zone. Flem-Ath and his companion researcher, wife Rose, delved deeper into Atlantis and Hapgood's papers, ultimately to synthesize both concepts in their book *Atlantis beneath the Ice: The Fate of the Lost Continent*. Their arguments have been supported by Graham Hancock in his book *Fingerprints of the Gods,* as well as by such well-known, highly respected writers as Colin Wilson and John Anthony West.

NAZI BASES

The aura of mystery surrounding the realm at the bottom of the planet has not abated with the years. It is now covered with a blanket of ice over two miles thick, and it seems natural to wonder what strange secrets might be concealed in its frozen depths. If, indeed, it was Atlantis or some other lost civilization, is it possible that actual artifacts of some kind might yet remain in some warm subterranean cavern or caverns? Apparently the Nazis believed, or at least strongly suspected, something of the sort. It is well documented that in 1938 the Third Reich mounted an elaborate and expensive expedition to the south pole area. When it is recalled that Germany was, at the time, on the brink of launching a world war, with all the related preoccupations and preparations, it seems extraordinary that the mission was found sufficiently important to justify the expenditure of significant resources merely to lay claim to a barren wasteland, with no apparent military significance, halfway around the world. The Nazis, in fact, hired intrepid polar explorer Richard Byrd, then a civilian, to come to Hamburg and brief expedition leaders. That much, at least, can be documented, and according to the apocryphal 1990s-era conspiratorial classic and internet tome *The Omega File,* written by the obscurantist Bruce Alan Walton (a.k.a. Branton), "the Germans discovered vast regions that were surprisingly free of ice, as well as warm water lakes and cave inlets. One vast ice cave within the glacier was reportedly found to extend 30 miles to a large hot-water geothermal lake deep below. Various scientific teams were moved into the area, including hunters, trappers, collectors and zoologists, botanists, agriculturists, plant specialists, mycologists, parasitologists, marine biologists, ornithologists, and many others." One fact, at least, is not disputed: to establish their own rights to the area that had been recently annexed by Norway, the Germans air-dropped hundreds of swastika-adorned flags to mark their claim.

According to British civil servant and WWII historian James Roberts, the Germans succeeded in building an underground base in a massive ice cave, using the inlets they'd discovered for access. Roberts claimed that British soldiers from the secret Antarctic Maudheim Base found the entrance in late 1945 and "followed the tunnel for miles, and eventually they came to a vast underground cavern that was abnormally warm; some of the scientists believed that it was warmed geo-thermally. In the huge cavern were underground lakes; however, the mystery deepened, as the cavern was lit artificially." As Roberts tells it, "The Nazis had constructed a huge base into the caverns and had even built docks for U-boats. . . . [Roberts's source] reported that 'hangars for strange planes and excavations galore' had been documented." This purported British intelligence and other information elicited from former German U-boat captains, it has been alleged, triggered the U.S.-led Operation Highjump in 1946.*

The very real Operation Highjump, officially titled the United States Navy Antarctic Developments Program, was intended to establish the Antarctic research base Little America IV. Consisting of thirteen ships, including the aircraft carrier *Philippine Sea,* and 4,700 soldiers, the mission was in the charge of Richard Byrd, then a navy rear admiral with a distinguished war record. In a November 1946 press release, Byrd benignly claimed, "The purposes of the operation are primarily of a military nature, that is to train naval personnel and to test ships, planes and equipment under frigid zone conditions." However, since it

---

*See James Roberts, "Britain's Secret War in Antarctica," *Nexus* 12, no. 5 (2005), https://nexusmagazine.com/product/britains-secret-war-in-antarctica-part-1-3/?v=7516fd43adaa.

Rear Admiral Richard E. Byrd (center) briefs his officers for Operation Highjump.

was planned by, and under the command of, war hero Admiral Chester W. Nimitz, some believe the real purpose could have been to search for and destroy any Nazi base or bases. Originally scheduled to be a six-month operation, Highjump was mysteriously aborted after only three months. Was its mission accomplished? We may never know.*

Three years later, Admiral Byrd could be found off the Antarctic coast leading an expedition to drill the Ross Sea bottom in places where one of the maps cited by Charles Hapgood, the 1531 Orontius Finaeus world map, had charted various riverbeds. The cores produced by Byrd's group, curiously, contained fine-grained rocks and well-mixed deposits, apparently delivered to the sea by rivers whose headwaters would have been located in the central, and unexplored, regions of the vast continent and seemingly not covered with ice.†

---

*For a series of official documents referencing Operation Highjump, see John Greenewald, "Operation Highjump," Black Vault (online), February 21, 2015, https://www.theblackvault.com/documentarchive/operation-highjump/.
†For more details on Admiral Byrd's second Antarctic expedition, see Paul A. Siple, "The Second Byrd Antarctic Expedition—Botany. I. Ecology and Geographical Distribution," *Annals of the Missouric Botanical Garden* 25, no. 2 (1938): 467–517, https://www.jstor.org/stable/2394231?seq=1#page_scan_tab_contents.

✦

Whether or not future explorations of Antarctica will produce evidence of Nazi technology and/or lost civilizations, it is now clear that, at the very least, life itself has gained a foothold beneath the ice, and has been there for a long time. Who knows what kind of strange history may eventually emerge?

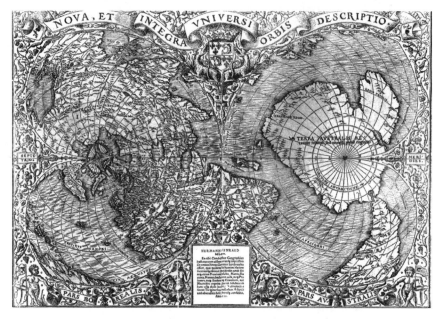

Antarctica, as shown in the Orontius Finaeus world map of 1531

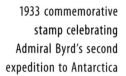

1933 commemorative stamp celebrating Admiral Byrd's second expedition to Antarctica

15

Egypt and Zep Tepi

The search for
monuments of the First Time

In 2013, the world of Egyptian archaeology was ablaze with scandalous allegations that two German archaeologists—students, actually, from Dresden University—had stolen paint material from the famous cartouche of the pharaoh Khufu, which is found in one of the so-called relieving chambers above the King's Chamber in the Great Pyramid of Giza. They had smuggled the paint material out of Egypt and examined it, without permission, in a German lab. The students' intention, apparently, was to demonstrate that the painted symbol was not created in the same time period as the reign of Khufu, and therefore was not authentic. By all reports, they succeeded—of course, their claimed findings have been summarily rejected by Egyptian antiquities authorities, but for other reasons.

The cartouche was first discovered in the nineteenth century by British officer and archaeologist William Richard Howard-Vyse. Since it is the only physical evidence yet found to support the notion that the Great Pyramid was built during the Khufu period, and not—as is believed by many alternative scholars—thousands of years earlier, the importance of such a discovery would be hard to overstate.

The sensitivity of the matter was made clear by the outraged reaction of Egyptian antiquities authorities. Mainstream Egyptology treats the Khufu–Great Pyramid connection as settled science—a virtual article of faith. Though the paint pilferage was represented as an example of entirely reprehensible archaeological theft, it seems possible that there could have been more to the story.*

According to *Al-Ahram,* an Egyptian newspaper, the Egyptian ministry of antiquities saw the theft as "a great violation of Egypt's ancient heritage, and the Great Pyramid in particular—the only surviving monument of the seven wonders of the ancient world." The head of the ministry, Mohamed Abdel Maqsoud, said the ministry would be prohibiting any future archaeological cooperation between itself and Dresden University, as well as the scientific laboratory where the stolen samples were analyzed. Not surprisingly, any suggestion that the Great Pyramid could have been built prior to Khufu was dismissed; Ahmed Saeed, professor of ancient Egyptian civilization at Cairo University, called the findings of the young German archaeologists "totally false and nonsensical." Maqsoud called them "amateurs not expert archaeologists." For their pains, the two Germans were declared criminals and forbidden from doing any further research in Egypt.†

Though cited as irrefutable proof for the standard Khufu pyramid construction doctrine, the cartouche has long been controversial. After Howard-Vyse used gunpowder to blast his way into Campbell's Chamber, topmost of the so-called relieving chambers above the King's Chamber, and announced his discovery of the cartouche, many were immediately skeptical of his claims. The previously discovered Davison Chamber had no such markings. In fact, such markings cannot be found anywhere else in the Great Pyramid. The late best-selling author Zecharia Sitchin was one of those who believed the Great Pyramid is thousands of years older than is officially maintained. In his second book, *The Stairway to Heaven,* Sitchin said that Howard-Vyse faked the marks in the spaces above the King's Chamber. He accused Howard-Vyse (and his assistants Mr. Hill and Mr. Perring) of perpetrating the forgery because of his "determination to obtain a major find as time and money were running out."

In a November 1995 interview with *Atlantis Rising,* Sitchin added

---

*For an example of that outrage, just note the headline of this article: "German Conspiracy Nuts Vandalize Part of Khufu Pyramid," by George Dvorsky, on Gizmodo (online), December 2, 2013, https://io9.gizmodo.com/german-conspiracy-nuts-vandalize-part-of-khufu-pyramid-1475089395.

†See Nevine El-Aref, "Penalties Imposed on Two Amateur German Archaeologists," *Al-Ahram* (online), November 25, 2013, http://english.ahram.org.eg/News/87435.aspx.

William Richard
Howard-Vyse

The Khufu cartouche
in Campbell's
Chamber of the
Great Pyramid;
photo by Robert
Schoch

to his case. Since publication of his book, he said, additional corroboration had come from the great-grandson of the master mason who assisted Howard-Vyse. It seems that on the night in question in 1837, Howard-Vyse was seen entering the pyramid with brush and paint pot in hand and was heard to state that he intended to reinforce some of the marks he had found, ostensibly to render them more legible. Upon failing to dissuade Howard-Vyse from his plan, the mason quit. The story, however, was kept alive and handed down through the family until it eventually came to Sitchin, further reinforcing his unshakable conviction of the true antiquity of the Great Pyramid.

A new line of research has provided further support for the cartouche forgery hypothesis. In "Crime in the Great Pyramid" (*Atlantis Rising* #106, July/August 2014), author/researcher Scott Creighton produced photocopies of pages from Howard-Vyse's personal diaries. Drawings and notes in the diaries reveal that Vyse carefully planned the placement of painted markings in Campbell's Chamber and took some pains to make them look authentic. Creighton spelled out the case in his book *The Secret Chamber of Osiris*.

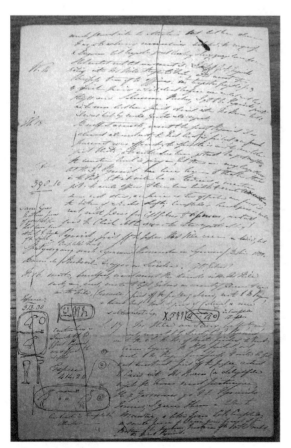

A page from
Howard-Vyse's journal

AN ARTIFACT FROM ZEP TEPI?

A multilevel tomb found in 2015, across the Nile River from the Temple of Seti I at Abydos, has been claimed by Egyptologists to be modeled after the mysterious Osirion, the temple-like structure found behind the Temple of Seti. Called Kampp 327, the miniature structure was uncovered in Thebes in the tomb of Min (Min, it is thought, was a local mayor sometime around the eighth century BCE). In the tomb, a large hall is supported by five pillars, which resembles the structure of the Osirion, and for that reason the tomb was considered its replica.[*]

This led some publications to call Kampp 327 the tomb of Osiris, never mind that the founder god of the ancient Egyptian creation story would have lived many thousands of years earlier. While there is no direct evidence linking the Osirion with Osiris, it might, at least, be an artifact from his time, referred to in the Egyptian creation myth as Zep Tepi, or the First Time. While mainstream Egyptology calls Zep Tepi strictly mythological, there are many serious scholars who recognize that the ancient legend must have been born in historical facts.

Years ago, on a trip to Egypt with the late John Anthony West, this writer toured the Temple of Seti and the Osirion, which, according to many Egyptologists, must also have been built by Seti I around 1300 BCE. If there is one spot in Egypt that clearly shows the disconnect between the preconceived ideas of official Egyptology and the obvious facts, this could be it.

The Temple of Seti is literally covered with hieroglyphs, paintings, and bas reliefs, while the Osirion has *no* such images. The architectural styles of the two structures are also completely different. Like Giza's Valley Temple and Sphinx Temple, the Osirion is made with square columns, while most later Egyptian structures of the period usually have cylindrical columns. Constructed of gigantic red granite blocks weighing as much as a hundred tons each, quarried more than three hundred miles away, the structure is, at the least, a breathtaking engineering achievement, and built at a much lower level than Seti's Temple, so that it would be flooded

---

[*]You can read about the discovery online; see "Ancient Replica of Osireion Unearthed in Egypt," Sci-News.com, January 10, 2015, http://www.sci-news.com/archaeology/science-ancient-replica-osireion-egypt-02396.html.

now by water from the Nile if it were not constantly pumped out. Like the Great Pyramid, such megalithic ruins may very well have been beyond the construction capabilities of the dynastic Egyptians.*

The Osirion at Abydos, in Egypt

John Anthony West, geologist Robert Schoch, and others have cited the astonishing technology on display in these temples as evidence of an advanced civilization that must have existed before the end of last ice age—in other words, in Zep Tepi.

Whether or not the technological mastery of builders from the time of Osiris could have been passed down to the dynastic Egyptians, there can be little doubt that, at the least, the spiritual legacy of that era has survived, even to the present day. The many connections found in modern religions like Judeo-Christianity and Islam to the ancient Egyptian religion of Osiris cannot be logically dismissed.

---

*For a discussion of the true age of the Osirion, see Freddy Silva, "The True Age of the Osirion at Abydos, an Antediluvian Temple," Ancient Origins (online), August 5, 2019, https://www.ancient-origins.net/history/osirion-abydos-0012397.

A VISIT TO THE RED PYRAMID

British-ancient-history writer and information technologist Matthew Sibson operates a popular YouTube channel called *Ancient Architects*. According to his Facebook page, Sibson is "currently re-writing the history of the Stonehenge landscape with new interpretations of Neolithic monuments." He is among those who regularly challenge orthodox Egyptology, but he does so with a level of detail and a command of the facts that make him quite formidable, and not easily dismissed. Among his arguments is that many of the monuments attributed to dynastic Egypt are, in fact, much older. We were especially taken by his June 18, 2018, presentation "The Secret Chamber of the Red Pyramid."

In this piece, Sibson focused on the curious chamber found beneath the Red Pyramid of Dahshur—sometimes called, but without evidence, the "burial chamber." Sibson quotes John Anthony West, who believed the chamber was a remnant from a time even earlier than the Red Pyramid itself, which, incidentally, is conventionally believed to be older than the more famous pyramids of Giza.

In 1999, *Atlantis Rising* sponsored a West-led tour of Egypt, during which this writer noted aloud the odd disparity between the chamber and the pyramid. Several points stood out. The stones in the pit at the bottom of the chamber were clearly of a different type than the structure above. Moreover, while the pyramid had been built with great precision, the pit was chaotic. And even though its stones were doubtlessly cut artificially, their edges had been rounded in a way that, to me, suggested water weathering. I thought the place must be part of a much older site, over which the pyramid had been built, possibly to memorialize a sacred prediluvian place. Whatever weathering had occurred had been arrested by the sheltering pyramid. I thought I was stating the obvious, but West, who overheard me, became excited. "I think you're absolutely right," he exclaimed. "I don't see any other possible explanation."

In *Atlantis Rising* #19 (June 1999), I wrote about our discussion in "Pushing Back the Portals of Civilization": "West referred again and again to what he felt was a truly important discovery, even dubbing the chamber 'Kenyon's Cavern,' adding that he felt the place might help to clinch his case [for a much greater antiquity of ancient Egypt than is believed by mainstream Egyptologists]. . . . 'The opposition is always saying, how can

The "burial" chamber beneath the Red Pyramid of Dahshur, in Egypt

the Sphinx be the only evidence of this earlier civilization? Well it isn't.'"

After seeing Sibson's video, I sent a note to West's colleague Dr. Robert Schoch to ask if he had heard my story. He immediately e-mailed back: "I know the chamber well and yes, John Anthony West told me you observed its seemingly greater antiquity—a really important observation." Schoch also supports the weathering hypothesis for the stones and its explosive dating implications for ancient Egypt.

John West, Sibson believes, must have been close to the truth, but the most important discovery in the place, he thinks, may be yet to come. On the wall opposite the viewing platform, Sibson points to what certainly appears to be a removable block that might lead to some unknown interior void beyond. Moreover, he reveals, there are what seem to be tool marks around the stone's edges that he believes show that someone else may have already attempted, and possibly succeeded in, accessing the Red Pyramid's mystery "void."

THE AGE OF THE GREAT SPHINX

West and Schoch first delivered their seismic shock to Egyptology at the annual conference of the Geological Society of America (GSA) in San Diego in 1991. The idea that the Sphinx could be much older than is officially maintained set off a firestorm of headlines around the world.

The Great Sphinx of Egypt

The argument from West and Schoch was simple but compelling: The Great Sphinx—presently found in desert conditions—has been deeply weathered by rainwater, which has not fallen in the area to any significant extent since very ancient times. Therefore, it must have been carved millennia earlier than previously believed. The inevitable implication is that the official story of the distant past must be rewritten, and our understanding of the level of civilization existing in extreme antiquity must be radically revised. The water weathering of the Sphinx, and the related conclusions, it is clear, could set in motion a scholarly revolution as dramatic and as far-reaching as that provoked by Galileo.

Following the initial GSA presentation, some archaeologists, Egyptologists, and geologists attempted to refute the evidence. But, in turn, their objections were thoroughly answered by Schoch, West, and others.* Moreover, in the intervening years, proponents of the West/

---

*As examples of the great debate between geologists and Egyptologists, see Lee Dye, "Sphinx's New Riddle—Is It Older Than Experts Say? Archeology: Geologists Cite Study of Weathering Patterns. But Egyptologists Say Findings Can't Be Right," *Los Angeles Times,* October 23, 1991; and John Noble Wilford, "Sphinx's Newest Riddle: How Old Is Sphinx," *New York Times,* October 24, 1991. For Schoch's breakdown of the evidence supporting his and West's hypothesis, see "Redating the Great Sphinx of Egypt: The Original 1992 Paper," in R. M. Schoch and R. Bauval, *Origins of the Sphinx,* Inner Traditions, 2017, pp. 337–70.

Schoch argument have continued to gather further supporting evidence from Egypt, much of it first reported in the pages of *Atlantis Rising*.

In 2000, at the GSA conference in Reno, Nevada, the argument was resumed. Before a packed audience of nearly five hundred professional geologists, Dr. Schoch delivered in about fifteen minutes a paper coauthored with West titled "Further Evidence Supporting a Pre-2500 BC Date for the Great Sphinx of Giza, Egypt." Except for two irate Egyptologists who tried to shout down the proceedings, the audience seemed favorably disposed to the ideas presented.

The paper was the Schoch/West response to challenges from the Egyptological establishment to their claims made in 1991. Critics had argued that, no matter what the geological evidence might show, there was no archaeological context to support the greater-age Sphinx thesis. In Reno, Schoch made several points, including a recitation of recently completed studies supporting his work and a list of corroborating facts from a number of Egyptian sites. As stated in the conference abstract: "These include other monuments at Giza and elsewhere exhibiting water-weathering features preserved beneath or within Old Kingdom (ca. 2575–2150 BC) repair campaigns and structures." Sites included the tomb of Queen Khentkaus at Giza, a weathered chamber protected within the Old Kingdom Red Pyramid at Dahshur, deeply weathered shaft tombs adjacent to, or near, much less weathered Third Dynasty structures (ca. 2600 BCE), and more.

The primary argument from the noisy detractors can be paraphrased as this: thousands of Egyptologists have studied the Sphinx for hundreds of years, and it can't possibly be older than the date held by tradition. (In point of fact, however, only a handful of people, including Schoch and West, have actually studied the Sphinx closely.) Other points made by the hecklers were of comparable merit.

Almost no media attended the ensuing press conference, a circumstance that may have been due more to distractions posed by the U.S. presidential election then under way than to a lack of interest in the subject. It certainly was not the first time that discoveries of great importance have been overshadowed by events that ultimately proved to be of considerably less consequence.

16

The Redemption of Rapa Nui

New evidence rules out "ecocide"

For a while now, the politically correct rap on ancient Easter Island has been that its people committed "environmental suicide." But in July 2017, a new paper published in the *American Journal of Physical Anthropology* virtually debunked what has become one of popular science's more cherished memes—the notion that, in an act of "ecocide," the islanders recklessly trashed their own habitat.

The presence of hundreds of enormous carved stone heads, called

The earliest known painting of Easter Island, 1775–1776, by William Hodges

moai, in such a remote location, with virtually no explanatory context, has, of course, intrigued millions for generations, but the inherent contradictions, some argue, have compelled academia to manufacture—with or without adequate evidence—the kind of narrative that would not contradict its standard preconceptions.

"The traditional story," says anthropology professor Carl Lipo of Binghamton State University in New York, "is that over time the people of Rapa Nui [a.k.a. Easter Island] used up their resources and started to run out of food. One of the resources that they supposedly used up was [the forestry] growing on the island. Those trees provided canoes and, as a result of the lack of canoes, they could no longer fish. So they started to rely more and more on land food. As they relied on land food, productivity went down because of soil erosion, which led to crop failures . . . painting the picture of this sort of catastrophe." That, says Lipo, is "the traditional narrative."

In the new paper, titled "Diet of the Prehistoric Population of Rapa Nui (Easter Island, Chile) Shows Environmental Adaptation and Resilience," Lipo and his team analyzed human, faunal, and botanical remains from archaeological sites on Rapa Nui. The team "used bulk carbon and nitrogen isotope analyses and amino acid compound specific isotope analyses of collagen isolated from prehistoric human and faunal bone, to assess the use of marine versus terrestrial resources and to investigate the underlying baseline values." Their findings point to concerted efforts to manipulate agricultural soils and suggest that the prehistoric Rapa Nui population had extensive knowledge of how to overcome poor soil fertility, improve environmental conditions, and create a sustainable food supply. These activities "demonstrate considerable adaptation and resilience to environmental challenges"—a finding that is *not* consistent with an ecocide narrative.*

Earlier in 2017, another paper by Lipo and his team had concluded that, contrary to popular opinion, the Easter Islanders were not warlike, either. The main evidence behind the warrior theory had been a profusion of sharp triangular obsidian objects deemed by European explorers

---

*See "Easter Island Not Victim of 'Ecocide,' Analysis of Remains Show," *BingU News* (the online newsletter of Binghamton University), July 14, 2017, https://www.binghamton .edu/news/story/697/easter-island-not-victim-of-ecocide-analysis-of-remains-show.

Dr. Carl Lipo and *moai*

to be weapons of war. Lipo proved otherwise. After using the latest morphometric techniques to make a thorough analysis of the objects, known as *mata'a,* Lipo concluded that they would have been entirely unsuitable for war. They were *not* spear points. In contradicting the standard belief, Lipo says that the Easter Islanders actually had an "amazing and successful society," and the *mata'a* were probably used for ritual tasks like tattooing or plant processing. "Populations were successful and lived sustainably on the island up until European contact," said Lipo.*

In other words, it is clear that the Easter Islanders, six hundred to nine hundred years ago, knew quite well how to feed themselves, live peacefully, and take care of their world, and that their demise must have been caused by something other than insensitivity to the environment or fear of their fellow humans.

If the ecocide and warrior theories were the only such dubious scenarios promulgated by academia, one could overlook them, but, as it turns out, for almost three centuries the greatest mysteries of Easter Island have been systematically explained away, often in the face of strong evidence to the contrary. In fact, since its discovery on Easter Sunday of 1722 by Dutch explorer Jacob Roggeveen, the remote island

*See the press release from Binghamton University: "Easter Island Not Destroyed by War, Analysis of 'Spear Points' Shows," ScienceDaily (online), February 16, 2016, https://www.sciencedaily.com/releases/2017/12/171220122027.htm.

has posed a clear threat to the consistency of mainstream scholarship. Connecting the known facts to preconceived notions about the history of the world has been, at best, awkward.

On the other hand, for many years "alternative theorists," from James Churchward and Arthur Posnansky to Augustus Le Plongeon and Percy Fawcett, have claimed that there once was an inconceivably ancient, now lost, Pacific-wide civilization. Such claims have been dismissed as, at best, lacking evidence, but ironically, it now appears that a stronger case can be made for the lost-civilization hypotheses than orthodoxy has ever let on. Could the true age of whatever society created the Easter Island's *moai* be older, by millennia, than the relatively recent culture now defended by Professor Lipo?

THE LONGEVITY OF RAPA NUI'S STONE HEADS

The current conventional wisdom—stated as fact by Wikipedia and other mainstream sources—is that Rapa Nui was settled between 700 and 1100 CE. Moreover, declares the online encyclopedia, "ongoing archaeological studies suggest an even *later* date: 'Radiocarbon dates for the earliest stratigraphic layers at Anakena, Easter Island, and analysis of previous radiocarbon dates imply that the island was colonized late, about 1200 CE. Significant ecological impacts and major cultural investments in monumental architecture and statuary thus began soon after initial settlement.'"

In his article "The Astonishing Antiquity of Easter Island," published in *Atlantis Rising* #102 (November/December 2013), researcher/ explorer David Childress counters that conventional Easter Island dating is based on radiocarbon content for wood, bone, and shell found buried in and around the statues and the quarry of Rano Raraku. We do *not* know, Childress points out, just how deeply these objects were buried. Indeed, the dated material might well have been placed there long *after* the statues were carved. While native people may have been near these statues five hundred years ago, leaving all sorts of datable material for later analysis, there is no evidence that these people created the statues. The *moai,* in fact, may have been standing there even then, just as enigmatically as they do today. "Perhaps a fragment of a

Coke bottle from 2013," says Childress, "will be dug up by archaeologists in the future who will similarly misinterpret their find."

The notion that the *moai* may be far older than is generally believed is still derided by academics, and similar claims about advanced stonework found along the western side of South America are also sneered at. Might there be a forgotten link between these two widely separated ancient societies? Although the massive stonework of Sacsayhuamán, near Cuzco in Peru, and many other locations in both Peru and Bolivia is officially credited to the Incans of six centuries ago, temple complexes at Puma Punku and nearby Tiahuanaco boast sophisticated structures that may predate the Incas by millennia.

As noted in chapter 8, the early-twentieth-century director of Bolivia's National Museum, Arthur Posnansky, undertook analysis showing that Tiahuanaco was built seventeen thousand years ago by a people unrelated to the local Aymara Indians. Posnansky also noted architectural similarities between Puma Punku and Easter Island, thousands of miles off the coast of Chile, suggesting that both had been independently influenced by the same earlier high culture.*

Posnansky's observations are consistent with those of James Churchward, whose *Lost Continent of Mu,* and related books, described an advanced civilization, called Mu, that he said flourished in the central Pacific Ocean long before the rise of highly organized societies in Peru or on Easter Island. According to Churchward, before its destruction during a series of natural disasters about twelve thousand years ago, Mu dispatched culture-bearing Naacals, or "serpent priests," throughout Polynesia and to South America, where they laid the foundations for such places as Easter Island and Tiahuanaco.

A partially destroyed wall at Vinapu on Easter Island makes the point. A work of megalithic construction, the wall—consisting of enormous slabs that were very skillfully laid—is unique to the island, but not to the world. Childress was genuinely amazed at the construction, which, he believes, was not only similar but almost identical to that at Cuzco, Machu Picchu, Sacsayhuamán, and Ollantaytambo in the high Andes.

---

*For a brief biographical sketch of Posnansky, a controversial figure in Bolivia's history, see E. J. Marsh, "Arthur Posnansky, the Czar of Tiwanaku Archaeology," *Bulletin of the History of Archaeology* 29, no. 1 (2019): 1; https://doi.org/10.5334/bha-605.

The wall at
Vinapu

Like those constructions, the wall at Vinapu is fitted perfectly with irregularly shaped stones possessing rounded edges, and small triangular stones filling in gaps. One could, Childress says, describe the Andes construction in the same way—polygonal blocks smoothed and rounded, perfectly cut and fitted together, with small keystones placed to help the structure withstand earthquakes. Though practically undatable, the stonemasonry is, he claims, the most sophisticated in the world—essentially unmatched, even today.

Tiahuanaco seems clearly pre-Incan and thousands of years old, but the massive ruins in the vicinity of Cuzco, a still-living city, are usually said to have been built by the Incas just a few centuries ago. Yet, while the ruins at Vinapu on Easter Island are virtually identical in construction with many in Peru, no one is arguing that the Inca made it to Easter Island. A plausible argument can be made that the two sites must have been built by the same lost society, long before the Inca came to town and set up housekeeping in the available ancient structures they found awaiting them.

Aside from the carving of the *moai,* among the most perplexing mysteries of Easter Island is the question of just how primitive people could have moved them for miles from the quarries where they were made, up and down hills and over many obstacles. The go-to explanation is that they could have been "walked" like giant refrigerators by crews pulling ropes. *National Geographic* illustrated the theory on a 2012 cover. However, Childress asks, "why are primitive people even

A 2012 *National Geographic* cover speculates on how the Easter Islanders might have moved their giant statues.

trying to move gigantic statues that weigh at least five tons and are more typically 20 to 40 tons?"

One *moai* that Thor Heyerdahl excavated in 1956 has a masted ship carved on its stomach. It was, Heyerdahl believed, an ancient sailing craft used by explorers from Peru. Others say the image is an early representation of a European ship. The problem with the latter explanation is that the carving was only discovered after Heyerdahl had dug away several feet of soil surrounding it.*

---

*Visit the website of the Kon-Tiki Museum and find your way to the section describing Thor Heyerdahl's expedition to Easter Island. There are many photos here, including one of Heyerdahl with the *moai* on which a sailing boat is inscribed.

Thor Heyerdahl
and one of his 1956
moai excavations

Long before 1000 CE—and no one can prove otherwise—the *moai* may well have been standing just as they are found today, largely buried under many centuries of accumulated dirt. Forty to fifty feet tall for the most part (the largest, still in the quarry, is taller than a seven-story building). The one with a ship on its belly is certainly much older than the surrounding debris.

Among the most dearly held precepts of conventional history is that civilization was born about five thousand years ago in concert with the inventions of the wheel and writing. Before that came primitive farming, and before that hunter-gatherer societies, incapable of any large-scale organized activity. Such was the aftermath of the last major ice age, which concluded about twelve thousand years ago with worldwide floods and chaos (a.k.a. the Deluge). Before that, as far as civilization is concerned, was only darkness. That is the story from mainstream archaeology, and they are sticking to it. The suggestion that civilization of any kind could have preceded the end of the last ice age is scoffed at. Fresh discoveries on many fronts around the world, though, are challenging such assumptions as never before.

Discussed elsewhere in these pages are Göbekli Tepe in Turkey, Gunung Padang in Indonesia, and India's Gulf of Cambay, offering clear evidence of advanced prediluvian culture. Around the world, from the pyramids of Giza to the terraces of Machu Picchu, many ancient structures can now be viewed with fresh eyes, and the idea dawns that much of the great stonework attributed to known societies may have been only their *inheritance,* not their creation. Some of the most interesting evidence for this contention can be found on Easter Island.

Even though the 887 immense and strange statues found there are hard to incorporate into any coherent notion of civilization, as now understood, their moving—let alone carving—clearly required a kind of engineering skill found only in more advanced societies. The same can be said of Göbekli Tepe, Gunung Padang, and many other inexplicable sites.

LITERATE SOCIETY?

Even more strangely, the Rongorongo writing script found on Easter Island offers what some consider clear evidence of a civilized, albeit very ancient, influence. First described by Eugene Eyraud, a French missionary, in 1864, the still untranslated script strongly suggests that, at some point, Easter Island was exposed to a literate culture.[*]

Geologist and archaeologist Dr. Robert Schoch has spent years analyzing the evidence for prediluvian civilization in many places, most notably at the Great Sphinx of Egypt, as described in the preceding chapter. Like Professor Lipo, he believes the conventional scenario for Easter Island's history falls a good deal short of the truth, and he goes considerably further, speculating that not only does Rapa Nui provide evidence of civilization from before the end of the last ice age, but it offers unexpected clues to exactly how that epoch may have come to an end.

---

[*]For an English translation of Eyraud's letter describing this script, see Ann M. Altman (trans.), with Judith Schwartz, "The Sojourn of the First Missionary on Rapa Nui: Eugene Eyraud among the Kanacs, 1864," *Rapa Nui Journal* 17, no. 1 (May 2003), http://islandheritage.org/wordpress/wp-content/uploads/2010/06/RNJ_17_1 _Altman_Schwartz.pdf.

Undeciphered Rongorongo script

The primary trigger for the great glacial melting episode that dramatically raised sea levels all over the world and led to the extinction of many animal species, Schoch believes, was a sudden and unexpected blast of unwelcome energy from our own sun. The argument is made in his 2012 book *Forgotten Civilization: The Role of Solar Outbursts in Our Past and Future*. In fact, says Schoch, the Rongorongo script may contain representations of "plasma" events that could have accompanied solar outbursts, which, he believes, would have terrified people. He cites the work of Dr. Anthony L. Peratt, a specialist in plasma physics at Los Alamos National Laboratory.*

Plasma phenomena, we learn, have many distinctive forms. Some look like intertwining snakes or pieces of rope, and others like stacks of circles. Plasma columns, in fact, can expand in places and form doughnut and cup shapes, or become narrow at other points (due to what are known as "pinch instabilities"), which could have been witnessed in the skies. Peratt and his team have documented many such plasma forms in ancient petroglyphs around the world, and Schoch thinks the

---

*To read more about Peratt's theories on plasma cosmology, read his article "Plasma Cosmology" in *Sky & Telescope* (February 1992), https://plasmauniverse.info/downloads /CosmologyPeratt.pdf.

Rongorongo text might be yet another example. (Read "Easter Island's Rongorongo: Records of a Cataclysm" in *Atlantis Rising* #82, July/August 2010, by Robert Schoch.)

Whether best measured in centuries or millennia; whether the advanced engineering of a long-lost civilization or the primitive handiwork of indigenous local culture; whether literate or not . . . whatever version of Easter Island history eventually prevails, one thing is clear: it will have to exclude the familiar scenario of an insane and warlike people bent on self-destruction, even as they fanatically worshipped their enormous, and weird, idols. That story is, itself, finished. While that narrative might well fit our own society, we now know that it did *not* fit ancient Easter Island.

Modern scholarship, some might conclude, has been projecting its own insecurities onto the ancients. If so, it would not be the first time.

The Pillars of Mu

*What does a hill in Java say
about prediluvian civilization?*

For thousands of years, the vast and strange ruins atop Mount Padang in West Java went unnoticed, but in 1914, Dutch archaeologists realized that the many rows of ancient stone pillars on the spot might be artificial, and they reported the site. In 1979, farmers noticed that the hill where the ruins were found did not fit in with its surroundings. For archaeologist Danny Hilman Natawidjaja of the Indonesian Institute of Sciences, who holds a PhD from Caltech, it was all very curious. Beneath the dense foliage, he suspected, there might be some kind of ancient temple, and in 2012, he launched an investigation to find out.

Known as Gunung Padang, the place is now described as the largest megalithic ruin in Southeast Asia. Carbon-14 dating surveys indicate that at least part of the structure may be more than twenty thousand years old. Standing stones resembling Stonehenge at the structure's summit have been dated to "only" thirty-five hundred years old, but ground-penetrating radar has detected rooms, terraces, and steps buried in the earthen mound beneath the stones. Carbon dating of some of the mortar used in these structures has shown an age of thirteen thousand to twenty-three thousand years, clearly revealing a greater advancement, and at a much earlier time, than anyone had once thought possible for the area, and possibly for the world.

Since the late 1970s, the mountaintop has been a major tourist destination. Some consider it sacred, and before making the "holy" ascent

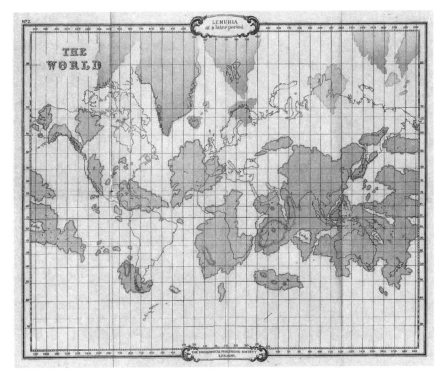

"Lemuria at a later period," based on clairvoyantly drawn maps by theosophist
Charles W. Leadbeater, published by the Theosophical Society in 1904
in *The Lost Lemuria* by William Scott-Elliot

to pound their knuckles and fists on the andesite columns scattered about the site, the devotees, accompanied by a *juru kunci* ("key master" or caretaker), first purify themselves with water from a natural spring at the base of the stairs. Boston University geologist Robert Schoch says the struck stones ring like bells, and they remind him of "musical rocks" at other ancient sites like the obelisk at Karnak in Egypt.

In December 2018, in a paper presented to the American Geophysical Union in Washington, D.C., Dr. Natawidjaja certified that the latest carbon-14 survey "reveals evidences of large underground cavities or chambers" dating to as long as twenty-eight thousand years ago. Dr. Natawidjaja's efforts have been somewhat frustrated by rival Indonesian archaeologists defending the conventional historical time line, and in November 2019 he was still awaiting completion of the peer review process for publication of his paper, but his project has been encouraged by the Indonesian government, and by experts like Robert Schoch.*

In his 2013 book *Plato Never Lied: Atlantis in Indonesia,* Natawidjaja argues that Atlantis is actually the ancient Nusantara civilization, which is still revered in Indonesia. According to Schoch, Natawidjaja is making a case for Atlantis as Sundaland, which, twenty thousand years ago, during the depth of the last ice age, was a fertile land where Java is today.

At that time, sea levels were as much as 130 meters lower than they are now, and the current Java Sea was not a sea at all. Here lay plains and forests bounded by the mountains of Java to the south and Borneo to the north, and from west to east ran a major river system. As sea levels rose following the last ice age, the land was submerged.

"The scientific facts on the natural conditions of Sundaland," says Natawidjaja, writing in *Plato Never Lied,* "in the glacial age give [a] vivid description, illustrating [its] very beautiful nature with a convenient climate and its extraordinary natural supports . . . the low lands in Sundaland which now have been inundated, turning into the Java and Karimata sea, were picturesque lands [fed] by rivers as big as the Nile [and] with temperature of only 25 to 20 centigrade [77 to 68°F], surrounded by mountain ranges with active volcanoes. Furthermore, research on fossils and DNA mitochondrial mapping reveals the colonization of modern human[s] in Nusantara and most parts of the world had begun [by] 60,000–50,000 years ago."

Natawidjaja and his team have been conducting research over several years, and they now believe that Gunung Padang is not a hill but actually a layered series of ancient structures with foundations dating back to the end of the last ice age and earlier.

"Our studies," says Natawidjaja in the abstract to his recent study, "prove that the structure does not cover just the top but also wraps around the slopes covering about 15 hectares area at least." The

---

*For the full paper, see Danny Hilman Natawidjaja, Andang Bachtiar, Bagus Endar, Mudrik Daryono, and Andri Subandrio, "Evidences of Large Pyramid-like Structure Predating 10,000 Year BP at Mount Padang, West Java, Indonesia: Applications of Geological-Geophysical Methods to Explore Buried Large Archeological Site," Earth and Space Open Archive (online), December 12, 2018, https://doi.org/10.1002/essoar.10500119.1.

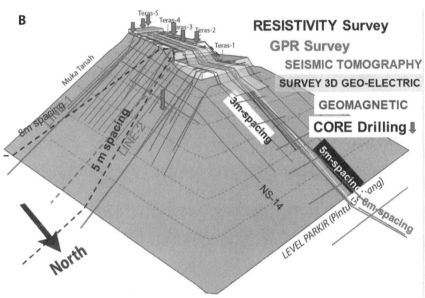

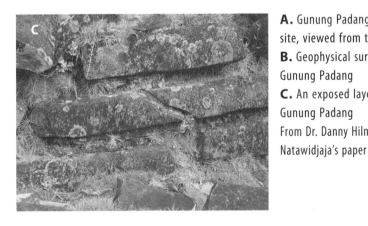

A. Gunung Padang megalithic site, viewed from the south
B. Geophysical survey lines at Gunung Padang
C. An exposed layer of stones at Gunung Padang
From Dr. Danny Hilman Natawidjaja's paper

structures, he adds, "are not only superficial but rooted into greater depth."

The researchers used a combination of survey methods, including ground-penetrating radar, seismic tomography, and archaeological excavations, which show that the site is not just an artificial structure but a series of several layers built over consecutive prehistoric periods. The topmost layer, made up of megalithic rock columns, walls, paths, and spaces, sits above another layer buried some one to three meters below the surface. This second layer, suggests the study, has previously been misinterpreted as a natural rock formation, but it is actually another arrangement of columnar rocks organized in a matrix structure.

Below this is a third layer of arranged rocks—containing large underground cavities or chambers—that extends as much as fifteen meters deep and rests upon a still-lower level. This fourth and lowest layer is made of "lava tongue" basalt rock yet was somehow modified, or carved, by human hands.

According to the researchers, preliminary radiocarbon dating suggests the first layer could be up to approximately 3,500 old years old, the second layer somewhere around 8,000 years old, and the third layer in the vicinity of 9,500 to 28,000 years old.

The purpose of the ancient pyramid, speculates Natawidjaja, could have been religious, but whatever it was, it clearly does not fit the conventional narrative of prehistory. That fact is not going unchallenged by local academics.

According to Wikipedia, thirty-four Indonesian scientists have now signed a petition questioning the motives and methods of the Natawidjaja team. However, in a 2017 interview, Dr. Robert Schoch told *Atlantis Rising Magazine,* "I am convinced it [Gunang Padang] is an 'artificial' structure." Many such claimed sites around the world, he says, are hoaxes or "garbage," but this is "the real thing." Moreover, Schoch made it clear to us that, based on the survey data taken by the Indonesians, he is "convinced, the site goes back to the last ice age."*

Putting together the evidence of Gunang Padang with what he has seen from Göbekli Tepe, the Sphinx of Egypt, and other sites and lines

---

*You can watch the full interview on the *Atlantis Rising Conversations* YouTube channel at https://www.youtube.com/channel/UCgEgzGsc9DOpnLlIP5Q8DAQ.

of data from around the world, Schoch says he believes we are now coming closer to understanding the cataclysmic times and events that took place at the end of the last ice age. Genuine civilizations of a sophisticated nature existed prior to circa 9700 BCE and were devastated by the events that brought the last ice age to a close, very much like the story told by Plato.

THE MU CONNECTION

Interestingly, the story of Gunang Padang is not the only one connecting the islands of the Pacific region with pre–Ice Age civilization. In addition to Easter Island, the Japanese island of Yonaguni, and others, there is another very strange site that is also constructed of thousands of sharply cut volcanic stone "logs" resembling the profusion found at Gunang Padang: Nan Madol, an enormous city, sometimes described as the eighth wonder of the world, on the remote Micronesian island of Pohnpei.*

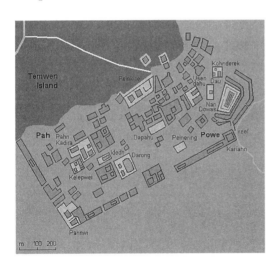

Map of Nan Madol

Constructed from magnetized basalt stones weighing up to fifty tons each, totaling an estimated 250 million tons and stacked to

*For a brief overview of the traditional archaeological and historical understanding of Nan Madol, consult the U.S. National Park Service; just search for "Nan Madol" on the NPS website.

Giant rock structure at Nan Madol

considerable height upon artificial islands spread over an area exceeding eleven square miles, Nan Madol is built on a coral reef, and much of it is underwater. It was built, say the natives, with brute force and magic. While mainstream archaeology has settled on a construction date of around 1000 CE, there is almost no evidence to support that claim. Carbon dating by the Smithsonian Museum of ashes found in 1960 at the bottom of an island fire pit remains about all there is. And there is no evidence directly linking the ashes with Nan Madol's megalithic construction, which remains impossible to date. While conventional archaeologists immediately reject any suggestion of prediluvian civilization in sites such as Gunang Padang, Nan Madol, Easter Island, or even the astonishing structures of Peru or Bolivia, the truth is that it cannot be ruled out. Indeed, say some, the time has come to revisit the work of such forgotten scholars as James Churchward and his associate Augustus Le Plongeon and their controversial hypotheses concerning the lost continent of Mu, also known as Lemuria, which, according to legend, sank somewhere in the Pacific Ocean many thousands of years before Atlantis.

According to researcher Philip Coppens, writing in "New Vindication for Colonel Churchward?" in *Atlantis Rising* #91 (January/February 2012), the first to publish about Mu was Augustus Le Plongeon, a professional archaeologist credited with publishing the first photographs of Chichén Itzá's ruins in Mexico. In his books *Sacred Mysteries Among the Mayas and Quiches* (1886) and *Queen Móo and the Egyptian Sphinx* (1896), Le Plongeon claimed to have deciphered a Mayan document, the Troano Codex, suggesting that the ancestors of the ancient Egyptians were the Maya. The Maya, said Le Plongeon, had arisen from Mu, a lost continent and civilization that he placed on an equal footing with Atlantis. Mu, he said, had been decimated by an enormous volcanic eruption. "Queen Moo"—obviously connected with Mu—had journeyed from America to Egypt and left her mark on history under a new name, Isis. Unfortunately for Le Plongeon, decades later when the Mayan language was fully decoded, it was realized that his interpretation of the codex was erroneous. Some letters that he used, apparently, did not even exist. According to Jack Churchward, the great-grandson and defender of James Churchward, Le Plongeon's problem was his reliance on a translation by C. E. Brasseur de Bourbourg. The younger Churchward claimed that an email from one of Brasseur de Bourbourg's descendants had attributed the botched translation to a channeled spirit.*

Le Plongeon did, however, put the lost civilization of Mu on the map, though it fell to Madame H. P. Blavatsky, founder of the Theosophical Society, to claim it as the birthplace of occult traditions that had been revealed to her. But the man who turned Mu from a legend into a virtual religion was James Churchward, a patented inventor and engineer, who said that in a secret library in India, he had personally observed hard physical evidence for Mu.

Eventually Churchward would write five very popular books on the subject. *The Lost Continent of Mu,* first published privately in 1926, was released in a revised edition in 1931 by New York publisher Ives Washburn, which, after the success of the first Mu book, went on to publish four additional Churchward books: *The Children of Mu* (1931); *The Sacred Symbols of Mu* (1933); *The Cosmic Forces of Mu,* volume one (1934); and *The Cosmic Forces of Mu,* volume two (1935).

---

*You can read more about Jack Churchward's investigations of his great-grandfather's theories at his website, My-Mu.com.

Augustus Le Plongeon

Born in Britain, Churchward eventually settled in the United States. But in years prior, while living in Sri Lanka, he and his wife had owned a tea plantation, from which he traveled to India. There, he said, he had befriended an elderly rishi (priest), who taught him to read the ancient dead language of the "Naacals," who he said were the "sacred brotherhood of Lemuria" (another name for Mu). The priest and two others, said Churchward, were the only people in the world able to read the language, which was recorded on numerous tablets that the priest allowed Churchward to inspect and read. In his books, Churchward suggests that he tricked the priest into showing him the tablets and to teaching him the meanings of the dead language carved upon them. Churchward soon realized that the tablets before him were, by no means, the complete library, but by consulting other resources and scholars, he was still able to piece together a rough but coherent history of the vanished civilization.

The events surrounding Churchward's discovery occurred in the late nineteenth century, but he would not take his Mu material public until 1924, many years after beginning his self-imposed silence. This has led critics to speculate that Churchward was simply responding to a perceived market opportunity and looking to burnish his own credentials by claiming, falsely, that he had studied the matter for many years. That theory, however, is belied by some documented evidence. Churchward, indeed, had been deeply interested in ancient civilizations for many years. His notes reveal that, in the 1890s, he had personally

Colonel James Churchward

discussed the subject of Mu with Le Plongeon and his wife, Alice.

Jack Churchward adds that notes from his great-grandfather—unpublished but referenced in his books—are labeled "Copies of Stone Tablets Found by William Niven at Santiago Ahuizoctla Near Mexico City." Niven, a well-known archaeologist and mineralogist, discovered the first of over a hundred andesite tablets in what is now the northwestern area of Mexico City in 1921. The indecipherable markings on these tablets were the subject of much contention over the last years of Niven's life and were referred to by Churchward as corroborating his original discovery of the Naacal tablets in India. The tablets have been connected by some with Scandinavian petroglyphs cited by Scottish prehistorian Ludovic Mann, and they were also mentioned by Churchward in *The Children of Mu*.

Churchward's nineteenth-century discovery of the Naacal tablets became famous when his claims about Mu were put forward in a major article in the *New York American* newspaper on November 10, 1924. The Mu civilization, or "Empire of the Sun," Churchward said, had sixty-four million inhabitants, known as the Naacals, the priestly brotherhood, keepers of the sacred wisdom, who lived fifty thousand years ago. All known ancient civilizations—India, Egypt, and the Maya—were decayed remnants of Mu's many colonies.

"For seven years, during all my available time," he told a lecture audience at New York's American Society for Psychical Research, "I diligently studied under this old rishi, learning the language of Mu, her symbols, alphabet and writings, with a view of finding out something about ancient man. At that time, I had no idea of publishing my findings. I made the study purely to satisfy my curious self. I was the only one to whom this old rishi ever gave instructions on this subject."

Still, Churchward never produced any hard evidence for his visit to the Naacal library, so unsurprisingly, many have treated his claims with skepticism.

According to Philip Coppens, some aspects of the Mu legend are original to Churchward, and some aren't. It was Le Plongeon who first wrote about the Naacal in 1896, when he identified them as Maya adepts and missionaries, with the word *naacal* meaning "exalted." Thereafter, however, Le Plongeon identified Central America, not Mu in the Pacific Ocean, as their homeland. That idea came from Churchward.

Both Blavatsky and Churchward claimed that in India, they had been exposed to "lost knowledge." Blavatsky's cited source was the Book of Dzyan, which she said was written in Atlantis and was shown to her by the Indian Mahatmas.

Some say that Churchward merely copied from Blavatsky and Le Plongeon for his revelations of Mu, and therefore they must not be true. It could just as easily be said, however, that his story simply confirms the assertions of Blavatsky and Le Plongeon, and possibly all three were telling the truth as they had come to understood it.

18

Tales of the Saraswati

Clues from a lost culture emerge
from the Gulf of Cambay

In 2006, scientists with India's National Institute of Ocean Technology, which had been investigating a possible lost civilization at the bottom of the Gulf of Cambay (or Khambhat, as it is also known) on India's west coast, drew some startling conclusions about the age and advancement of a previously unknown prediluvian society. The report, posted by chief geologist Badrinaryan Badrinaryan, stated that evidence clearly shows that from about thirteen thousand to three thousand years ago, a civilization flourished in the Cambay area, and that there is strong evidence that human habitation there could go back as far as thirty-one thousand years. Badrinaryan went on to say that he believed this "mother culture" was, in fact, the progenitor of the mysterious Harappan civilization, once thought to be *one* of the oldest—if not *the* oldest—in the world.

Based on survey data utilizing the latest high-tech methods, including side-scan sonar, sub-bottom profiling, and multibeam echo sounding, the report makes a case that threatens to overthrow many conventional assumptions about the origins of civilization.*

A previous discovery, announced in 2001, of the apparent remains

---

*To read the report, see Badrinaryan Badrinaryan, "Gulf of Cambay Cradle of Ancient Civilization," posted on GrahamHancock.com, February 1, 2006, http://www.grahamhancock.com/forum/BadrinaryanB1.php.

NASA satellite image of the Indus River Valley near the border of India and Pakistan; the Gulf of Cambay is at the lower left.

A 40- by 19-meter side-scan sonar image of a building with steps in the Gulf of Cambay; photo from the Indian National Institute of Technology

of an ancient city along a six-mile stretch of the Cambay seabed off the Gujarat coast of western India created a worldwide sensation, raising as it did the possibility that highly organized society had once existed where the ocean is now over 130 feet deep. Researchers there said they had detected the structures of a large community resembling major cities of the Indus Valley or Harappan civilization, with the regular geometric patterns of a well-developed culture, some of which were taken to be a granary, a great bath, and a citadel. Canal-like features were also observed. Water in the area, unfortunately, is murky and flowing with very strong currents, making direct visual observation virtually impossible. Still, many small human-made artifacts were dredged up, studied, and cited in the report. Predictably, the reaction from the mainstream archaeological community was skeptical. Many argued that the geometric patterns were caused by the sonar system itself and that the artifacts probably had been washed into the area from well-known civilized regions inland.

Pottery fragment dredged from the Gulf of Cambay; photo from the Indian National Institute of Technology

According to Badrinaryan's 2006 report, though, extensive studies carried out on the evidence produced in the 2001 survey confirmed the original conclusions. The initial side-scan sonar images, for instance, were corroborated by sub-bottom profiling and advanced magnetic methods, which provided even further indications of relatively sophisticated human engineering. Moreover, painstaking geochemical analysis of the artifacts, including pottery, that were brought up has shown them to be made entirely from local materials and not washed in from some other region. As for dating, numerous artifacts were subjected to analysis by radiocarbon, thermoluminescence, optically stimulated luminescence, and other means in some of the most reputable laboratories of the world, including in Oxford, England, and Hanover, Germany. All results have lent further support to the original assertions.

HARAPPAN DAWN

No one knows exactly when the Harappan civilization in the Indus Valley of Pakistan and India was born, but scientists now concede that it is at least two thousand years older than was previously accepted by some academics.* Radiocarbon dates taken in 2012 from Bhirrana, an archaeological site in the state of Haryana in North India, have now pushed the Harappan dawn back to as far as 7380 BCE. It is certainly much older than the recognized civilizations of Egypt and the Fertile Crescent to which it has been compared.

First discovered in the 1920s, the remains of Mohenjo Daro, a prehistoric city in the Indus Valley, have mystified science ever since. Certainly the product of an advanced civilization with sophisticated plumbing and writing, the city was first thought to be about four thousand years old. Even that dating shocked the academic world of the time, suggesting, as it did, that the Indus Valley civilization was a *pioneering* one, and not the result of an invasion from the west—an idea once treated as received wisdom by Western academics.

The Indus Valley civilization, many researchers now believe, was, in fact, much older, and was, in fact, all that remains of the prediluvian civilization surrounding the ancient, but now vanished, Saraswati River mentioned in ancient Hindu texts and extending into what is now the Gulf of Cambay. That culture, it is suggested, may have been the fountainhead of ancient Vedic civilization.

Central to the argument has been a mysterious and, so far, unreadable script found on artifacts, mostly ceramic seals, throughout the region. Hieroglyphs closely resembling the script have been found as far away as Easter Island. The question was: Were the symbols part of a written language or merely the primitive pictographs of a preliterate

---

*To read about the revised dating, see Jason Overdorf, "Archaeologists Confirm Indian Civilization Is 2000 Years Older Than Previously Believed," on the website of *The World* public radio program, November 28, 2012, https://www.pri.org/stories/2012-11-28 /archaeologists-confirm-indian-civilization-2000-years-older-previously-believed.

Ruins at Mohenjo Daro

Statue of an apparent priest-king
found at Mohenjo Daro

people? Now dramatic new research using advanced statistical analysis makes the case that the Indus Valley script was indeed a written language. The research provides powerful support for the proposition that the Indus civilization was much more advanced than has been previously believed.

In 2018, a joint American and Indian study, led by Rajesh Rao,

An Indus Valley
seal depicts written
symbols and someone
in yogic lotus posture.

a researcher from the University of Washington, used computers and mathematics to extract patterns from the script and show that the placement and distribution of the symbols bear the unmistakable characteristics of language. The resulting statistical model reveals the fundamental grammar of a written language. "Such a model," says Rao, "can be valuable for decipherment, because any meaning ascribed to a symbol must make sense in the context of other symbols that precede or follow it." The study was published in the journal *Proceedings of the National Academy of Sciences.**

Artifacts, jewelry, and even children's games have been found, but no weapons of war. As researcher Andrew Robinson put it, "The Indus civilisation seems to have flourished for 700 years without armour,

---

*To read about the study, see Hannah Hickey, "Computers Unlock More Secrets of the Mysterious Indus Valley Script," *UW News* (the online newsletter of the University of Washington), August 3, 2009, https://www.washington.edu/news/2009/08/03/computers -unlock-more-secrets-of-the-mysterious-indus-valley-script/.

weapons, inequality, or royalty."* The Indus people now are given credit for advanced public waterworks—including indoor plumbing and sophisticated irrigation and sanitation schemes—along with many other elements indicating complex urban planning. Multistory brick structures and long, straight streets aligned with a grid are among them.

The Indus Valley "utopia" existed, says orthodox archaeology, from 2600 to 1900 BCE, but that statement also appears in need of updating. A 2016 study cited evidence gathered from state-of-the-art optically stimulated luminescence technology used on pottery in the Mohenjo Daro area, which is now dating that pottery to more than nine thousand years ago, or about 7000 BCE.† That is at least 2,500 years older than once believed. In other words, it is older, by millennia, than the pyramids of Egypt or the megaliths of Stonehenge are currently believed to be (at least by conventional scholars). Researchers from the Archaeological Survey of India (ASI) carried out the study.

Long despised by many Eurocentric historians and scholars, the ancient Vedic wisdom of India now—in the wake of many important recent discoveries—is enjoying a remarkable renaissance not only in India but around the world. There is now reason to revisit the case that Vedic culture, originating in such ancient texts as the Mahabharata and the Upanishads, is much older than previously thought, and that evidence for writing and great architectural and technological achievement from before the end of the last ice age will finally have to be taken seriously. In the process, many orthodox theories of the last century and a half—such as the "Aryan invasion" hypothesis that credits Indian civilization to a mysterious influx of western culture bearers beginning around 1500 BCE—are now upended.

In the eighteenth century, India's British rulers were amazed by the vastness of Puranic time. Before Darwin, British scientists had accepted

---

*See Andrew Robinson, "The Real Utopia: This Ancient Civilisation Thrived without War," *New Scientist* (online), September 14, 2016, https://www.newscientist.com /article/mg23130910-200. Robinson went on to write a book on the state of research into the Indus Valley civilization: *The Indus: Lost Civilizations* (2016).
†See A. Sarkar, A. D. Mukherjee, M. K. Bera, et al., "Oxygen Isotope in Archaeological Bioapatites from India: Implications to Climate Change and Decline of Bronze Age Harappan Civilization," *Scientific Reports,* May 25, 2016, https://doi.org/10.1038 /srep26555.

the common Bishop Ussher biblical chronology, putting the creation of Adam at a little over 4000 BCE. Sir William Jones (1746–1794), a British official and scholar in India, identified Manu (the progenitor of the human race and giver of the religious laws of Manu, according to Hindu mythology) with Adam and put his appearance at 4006 BCE. Ideas like this were promoted in the Indian education system set up by the British.

In the nineteenth century, however, along with the acceptance of Darwinian ideas, British scholarship threw in the towel on such brief biblical chronologies and accepted wholeheartedly the vast time spans of millions and billions of years proposed by geologists like Charles Lyell, which superficially resembled Puranic time scales. But now, instead of placing the first humans at the start of the new time line, science came to believe that humans like us evolved from apes and appeared less than two hundred thousand years ago. Ironically, though, despite India's political independence, the education system set up by the British has continued to operate, and Indian scholars still accept Western scientific views, whatever they happen to be at the time, and to reject Puranic ideas about human origins and antiquity, even though they originate not in Britain but in India.

By contrast, the ancient Sanskrit texts of India should be taken as not only serious history but, perhaps, as prophecy as well, says new research into the Puranas. The Puranas, according to the research, often provide historical detail centuries before actual events. For instance, claims Vedic Sanskrit scholar Dr. Dhulipala Ramakrishna, one Purana foretold the coming of the Gupta dynasty hundreds of years in advance.*

Dr. Ramakrishna cites among other things corroboration of the Puranas to be found in the ancient Buddhist texts known as the Jatakas. The agreement between Vedic and Buddhist text is striking given the wide separation of their sources. Similar support is reported from other historical and archaeological sources.

The historical reliability of India's ancient texts has long been controversial. European scholars have been reluctant to accept the notion

---

*For an article on Ramakrishna's research, see Syed Akbar, "Puranas Are Historical Records," *Deccan Chronicle,* November 30, 2007, https://syedakbarindia.blogspot.com/2007/11/puranas-are-historical-records.html?m=1.

that India's origins predate the West's and have manufactured ideas such as the Aryan invasion hypothesis to account for her beginnings, but now research is revealing that, in fact, civilization in the Indian subcontinent existed long before it arose in the West. Among recent developments reported at the website Archaeology Online and elsewhere, we see the following:

- High-resolution satellite imagery confirms the actual existence of the supposedly mythical Saraswati River, verifying descriptions in the *Rig Veda* of the descent of the mighty ancient river from its source in the Himalayas to the Arabian Sea.
- Linguistic analysis of script found on artifacts provides further evidence. Sites identified as Paniprastha, Sonaprastha, and Indraprastha have yielded pottery and antiquities showing cultural development consistent with the Mahabharata period, and verifying statements recorded in Vedic literature.
- Carbon and thermoluminescence analysis has dated many artifacts to a much greater age than previously believed, providing scientific verification of many scriptural statements. More than thirty-five sites in northern India have yielded archaeological evidence identified with ancient cities mentioned in the Mahabharata. Copper utensils, iron, seals, gold and silver ornaments, terra-cotta disks, and painted grayware pottery have all been found there. Scientific dating of these artifacts corresponds to the non-Aryan-invasion model of Indian antiquity.
- Prediluvian underwater structures have been found, most recently at Mahabalipuram following the 2004 tsunami. And marine archaeological ruins have been found off the coast of Dwarka in Gujarat, the legendary port city of Lord Krishna, including massive walls, piers, wharves, and jetties as described in the Mahabharata and other Vedic literature.

ATLANTIS IN INDIA

A magnificent ancient city and temple complex drowned millennia ago, suddenly brought to the surface by nature's violence. That may sound like another Hollywood Atlantis fable, but this is no fiction. In the wake of the 2004 tsunami, the sudden discovery of massive underwater ruins at Mahabalipuram off the coast of India presented the world of archaeology with a seismic upheaval of its own.*

Extensive offshore diving turned up a giant temple with a great porch and open courtyard, as well as an enormous wall. Scattered throughout a large area of several square miles are square stone blocks. Spokespeople for India's National Institute of Oceanography rushed to declare the ruins were from the Pallava dynasty, dating to the fourth century CE, but that claim was hotly disputed by other experts. Durham University geologist Glenn Milne pointed out in 2002 that there has been very little tectonic movement of the type that could have sunk the temples for at least five thousand years.† Moreover, for centuries, local fishermen have told stories about a great flood that destroyed a city in the area and took several temples into the sea ten thousand years ago.

In his 2002 book *Underworld,* best-selling author Graham Hancock mentions the temple complex off Mahabalipuram as a site that should be explored for evidence of a prediluvian culture. Hancock's own diving explorations had turned up several coastal Indian sites that show evidence of cultural development from a time before when academia says it was possible. Following one such diving expedition in Mahabalipuram, Hancock said, "I have argued for many years that the world's flood myths deserve to be taken seriously, a view that most western academics reject. But here in Mahabalipuram, we have proved the myths right."‡

The emergence of the temple ruins may well prove to be the "smoking gun" long sought by those who believe that world history as presently taught is only the story of civilization since its most recent appearance, and that the original beginnings of advanced human

---

*News of the ruins revealed by the tsunami spread worldwide; see, for example, Tim Sullivan, "Tsunami Revealed Lost Indian City," CBS News (online), March 17, 2005, https://www.cbsnews.com/news/tsunami-revealed-lost-indian-city/.

†Milne gave his assessment directly to Graham Hancock via email; see the transcript at "Dr Glenn Milne dates submergence of Mahabalipuram structures to 6000 BP," GrahamHancock.com, April 10, 2002, https://grahamhancock.com/archive-underworld7/.

‡See James Meek's article about Hancock's explorations: "Divers 'Discover' Ancient Temple," *The Guardian* (online), April 11, 2002, https://www.theguardian.com/uk/2002/apr/11/humanities.highereducation.

activity on Earth will eventually be found buried in lost cultures many millennia older. The resistance to that idea, some feel, is the product of a worldwide cultural amnesia that obscures the truth of human origins and thus blocks spiritual advancement today. Hard proof that advanced prediluvian civilization actually existed could produce an intellectual tsunami capable of exposing many fissures in the current academic paradigm. Not surprisingly, such developments are resisted by the powers that be.

19

Göbekli Tepe and
Stone Age High-Tech

*Could history be due for
some serious rewriting?*

Dramatic recent discoveries at Göbekli Tepe, an out-of-the-way
Turkish archaeological dig a few miles north of the Syrian border
near Urfa, are now challenging conventional history in an unprecedented way. Conclusively dated to several thousand years before its
final burial in 8000 BCE, this vast array of sophisticated carved stone
structures—which are apparently older, by over four millennia, than
Stonehenge or the Great Pyramid—decisively refutes the standard academic myth of prehistory: that humans of the time were strictly primitive hunter-gatherers.

Numerous T-shaped limestone monoliths, profusely and skillfully
decorated with animal carvings and abstract pictograms—some almost
ten feet tall and weighing as much as twenty-five tons—still stand on
Roman-like terrazzo floors. So far, seven major circular enclosures in
the immense 300- by 200-meter site have been excavated, even as radar
and geophysical surveys indicate that as many as twenty more—of similar size and complexity and constructed over 1,500 years prior to the
site's mysterious *intentional* final burial and abandonment—still await
their own investigation.

Though the site was first discovered in 1964, the full significance
of Göbekli Tepe was not recognized until 1994, when the late German

archaeologist Klaus Schmidt began to excavate. Almost immediately, strains began to appear in the mainstream theoretical fabric, perhaps helping to account for the modest publicity first accorded the discoveries. Until his death in 2014, Schmidt insisted that the site, which he believed was the world's first temple, was built by hunter-gatherers, though he acknowledged that the construction would have required the systematic effort of hundreds of workers, at the least, and over many years. Orthodoxy refuses to entertain the notion that civilization, or even agrarian societies, could have existed that far back in time, so conventional scholars like Schmidt are left with little choice but to endorse the idea that the construction must have been by hunter-gatherers. If so, though, Göbekli Tepe falls well outside any currently accepted definition of a "hunter-gatherer" society.*

In the mid-1990s, when John Anthony West and Robert Schoch announced that water weathering proved the Great Sphinx of Egypt was thousands of years older than was traditionally believed, they were met with scorn from the Egyptological establishment. And despite evidence that was widely accepted by professional *geologists,* establishment *Egyptologists,* such as Zahi Hawass and Mark Lehner, continued to deny the very possibility of the Sphinx's greater antiquity.

"Where," they asked, "is the context?" What civilization was up and running at that time and could have done it? Where are the artifacts? In the years following, West and Schoch labored mightily to show that there is actually plenty of evidence in Egypt itself for such ancient achievement (more of that can be found elsewhere in this book). Other, possibly corroborating, material has turned up at many sites around the world, but with Göbekli Tepe came the kind of smoking-gun evidence for prediluvian (meaning before the Great Flood or the end of the last ice age) civilization that many alternative theorists have long believed was there but the amnesia-stricken establishment has persistently and emphatically denied.

Schoch has often mentioned the site in his presentations on Sphinx dating. "Göbekli Tepe is from the same period, or even earlier, than

---

*Journalist Andrew Curry toured the site with Schmidt in 2008. See his report, "Gobleki Tepe: The World's First Temple?," in the November 2008 issue of *Smithsonian Magazine,* https://www.smithsonianmag.com/history/gobekli-tepe-the-worlds-first-temple -83613665/.

what we have at Giza," he told *Atlantis Rising*, "Plus, it is incredibly sophisticated. I do not understand why it has not gotten more publicity. Perhaps because it is so anomalous and just does not fit the conventional paradigm. It sure seems to support what some of us have been arguing for decades."

Interestingly, one of the important discoveries at Göbekli Tepe is the carved figure of a half human, half feline creature—what might best be called a sphinx. Could this, Schoch wonders, have been the model for Egypt's Great Sphinx? And, more importantly, what was the even earlier source of the image at Göbekli Tepe?

Still, even though conventional archaeologists now grudgingly concede there may have been some kind of civilization predating the end of the last ice age, and, at least partially, corroborating Plato's Atlantis account, they remain convinced that whatever anomalous ancient advancements there may have been, they did not include anything that could be called "technology," as has been claimed by some such as Edgar Cayce. Never mind that Göbekli Tepe itself, in its advanced construction details, implies as much.

Schoch, indeed, is one who thinks there is evidence that Göbekli Tepe's builders could write and had a knowledge of astronomy and anatomy well beyond the standard Neolithic model. Another researcher, author Andrew Collins, believes that a tiny bone plaque from Göbekli Tepe in the nearby Sanliurfa museum could be a key, not only to proving an intentional celestial orientation for the complex, but in showing a sophisticated use of three-dimensional perspective for the art itself, many thousands of years before the technique was again mastered by the artists of the Italian and Dutch Renaissance. Collins also believes that there is substantial evidence of advanced astronomical knowledge at Göbekli Tepe.

As remarkable as the case for high prediluvian civilization at Göbekli Tepe may be, however, it is by no means unique. Indeed, there is other credible evidence that well before the end of the last ice age, at least some humans had knowledge of what can only be called technology. In an earlier chapter, we spoke of ancient maps showing an unexplained mastery of geography and cartography, but here are some other examples that also defy easy explanation.

A pillar with carvings from Göbekli Tepe. On the left of the middle level, we see a bird with a sphere, which Andrew Collins believes represents the Cygnus constellation.

A small carved object found at Göbekli Tepe depicts two T-shaped columns, drawn in a sophisticated 3D perspective with a disappearing point.

DENISOVA CAVE

A gorgeous ivory "tiara," made from the tusk of a woolly mammoth some forty-five to fifty thousand years ago, has been found in Siberia's famous Denisova Cave. In the Altai Mountains in the south of western Siberia, the site is the same one where, in 2017, a sophisticated stone bracelet was discovered containing a drill hole that could not have been made without a high-speed drill. The ivory tiara—its large size indicating it was for male, not female, use—was apparently intended to keep hair out of the wearer's eyes. It was found in 2018 along with other advanced artifacts, including ivory needles. According to researcher Alexander Fedorchenko, from the Novosibirsk Institute of Archeology and Ethnography, the existence of such technology in that era contradicts all orthodox theories for the capabilities of Paleolithic man.*

The belief among Russian archaeologists is that the tiara—or diadem—and the stone bracelet were made by Denisovan people. In an interview with the *Siberian Times,* Fedorchenko said, "Finding one of the most ancient tiaras is very rare not just for the Denisova Cave, but for the world. Ancient people used mammoth ivory to make beads, bracelets and pendants, as well as needles and arrow heads."†

The previously discovered stone bracelet had already been declared a game-changing artifact. According to archaeologist Anatoly Derevyanko, the ancient piece is "stunning," and its crafting would have required a very high level of skill, something previously thought impossible for Denisovans. Made of chlorite imported from 125 miles away, the bracelet was held in place with a leather strap passing through a remarkably tiny, finely tooled hole that would have required a high-speed drill to make—a technique thirty thousand years ahead of its time.

Described as a species of hominins from the *Homo* genus, but dis-

---

*Read about the discovery on Live Science (online): "50,000-Year-Old Tiara Made from Woolly Mammoth Ivory Found in Denisova Cave," by Yasemin Saplakogu, December 14, 2018, https://www.livescience.com/64297-ancient-woolly-mammoth-tiara-denisova -cave.html.

†See "50,000 Year Old Tiara Made of Woolly Mammoth Ivory Found in World Famous Denisova Cave . . . ," *Siberian Times,* December 6, 2018, https://siberiantimes.com /science/casestudy/news/50000-year-old-tiara-made-of-woolly-mammoth-ivory-found -in-world-famous-denisova-cave/.

Artist's reimagining of a possible stylized modern use for a forty-thousand-year-old bracelet made from chlorite and found in Denisova Cave in Siberia. The small, precise hole today would require a high-speed drill to duplicate.

tinct from either *Homo sapiens* (humans) or *Homo neanderthalensis* (Neanderthals), the Denisovans have long been considered much less developed than modern humans or even Neanderthals, but the artifacts of Denisova Cave are disrupting all such thinking.

MALTESE ACOUSTICS

Many esoteric and spiritual teachings have long claimed that our very ancient ancestors possessed a science of sound, now lost, that made it possible to do many things that baffle us today. Some researchers, like the late Cambridge-trained scholar John Michell, argued that the ancients were able to use their mastery of chanting and acoustics to levitate heavy objects to build many of the gigantic structures that still stand, and that modern technology would be hard-pressed to duplicate. While no one has been able to prove ancient levitation, new research is demonstrating that the ancients certainly knew a great deal about sound, which we have only recently begun to relearn. On the Mediterranean island of Malta, in the underground mortuary temple known as the Hal Saflieni Hypogeum—ostensibly five thousand years old, but likely very much older—researchers have detected the presence of a strong double resonance frequency inside the Oracle Room, a chamber legendary for exceptional sound behavior.

During testing, a deep male voice in a range of 70 to 130 hertz

Acoustically optimized construction at the Hal Saflieni Hypogeum on Malta

stimulated a resonance phenomenon throughout the hypogeum, creating what was described as a "bone-chilling effect." Sounds continued to echo for up to eight seconds. Archaeologist Fernando Coimbra reported that he "felt the sound crossing his body at high speed, leaving a sensation of relaxation."*

Sound in a basso/baritone range vibrates in a certain way as a natural result of the environment in the hypogeum, just as it does in Ireland's Newgrange passage tomb, megalithic cairns, and any stone cavity of the right dimensions. It is clear that the builders of the Malta temple intentionally used architectural techniques to boost "super-acoustics." Glenn Kreisberg, a radio frequency spectrum engineer with the research group, observed that in the hypogeum, the "Oracle Chamber ceiling, especially near its entrance, and the elongated inner chamber itself, appears to be intentionally carved into the form of a wave guide." Similar design elements are also employed in the building of today's state-of-the-art recording studios.

---

*The quotations and details in this section derive from a press release published by the group researching the hypogeum, which you can find on Science News Wire (online): "Ancient Man Used 'Super-Acoustics' to Alter Consciousness (. . . and Speak with the Dead?)," by Linda Eneix, June 16, 2014, https://sciencex.com/wire-news/164386603 /ancient-man-used-super-acoustics-to-alter-consciousness-and-spe.html.

Project organizer Linda Eneix says, "If we can accept that these developments were not by accident, then it's clear that Hal Saflieni's builders knew how to manipulate a desired human psychological and physiological experience, whether they could explain it or not."

MIOCENE WHEEL RUTS

Anomalous tire and tread tracks of what could be ancient machines, found mostly in Turkey and Spain, but in other places as well, are creating a major archaeological mystery. A respected Russian geologist says he believes the tracks could be twelve million to fourteen million years old.

Dr. Alexander Koltypin, director of the Natural Science Research Center at Moscow's International Independent University of Ecology and Politology, has studied apparent wheels ruts petrified since the middle to late Miocene era. Often intersecting very ancient geological fault lines—which they, thus, must predate—the parallel-track pairs cannot be dismissed as being of recent origin.

Wheel ruts—millions of years old—of petrified stone in Turkey

Koltypin has investigated numerous petrified sites in Malta, Italy, Kazakhstan, France, and even North America. In Turkey, one cluster near Sofia covers an area of about 450 square miles. In Cappadocia are several such areas as large as 300 square miles. Some of the parallel tracks are comparable in gauge to those of modern vehicles with tires about nine inches wide.

The conventional theory, found in the very few references previously devoted to the subject, has been that the tracks were caused by lightweight carts or chariots (though, of course, according to orthodoxy, modern humans and their wheeled vehicles were not around at such early dates). The ruts are far too deep, says Koltypin, to have been made by such small conveyances—even those that could have been drawn by camel. After conducting many field studies in various locations and extensively reviewing scientific literature on the local geology, he speculates that the tracks might have been left by the builders of underground cities found in places like Cappadocia, but he says they are far older than is generally believed and could have been left only by heavy machinery.[*]

THE SCHIST DISK

In Egypt, a Cairo museum has on display a disk known at the Tri-lobed Disk or the Schist Disk. About 61 centimeters in diameter and 10.6 centimeters in height, the disk is made of schist, a very fragile and delicate rock that is said to be almost impossible to carve. Resembling a small dinner plate or concave steering wheel with three identical inwardly folding "lobes," the device has a rimmed hub at its center appearing to be the axis of a wheel.

Recovered in 1936 from the tomb of Sabu in Saqqara, the object looks more like a machine part than any mere decoration. Unanswered questions about it include: What was it for? How was it made? Was it

---

[*]To read about Koltypin's research, visit his website, www.earthbeforeflood.com, or look up his videos on YouTube. See also Liz Leafloor, "Controversial Claim by Geologist: Mysterious Tracks in Turkey Caused by Unknown Civilization Millions of Years Ago," *Ancient Origins* (online), August 18, 2015, https://www.ancient-origins.net/news -mysterious-phenomena/controversial-claim-geologist-mysterious-tracks-turkey-caused -unknown-020489.

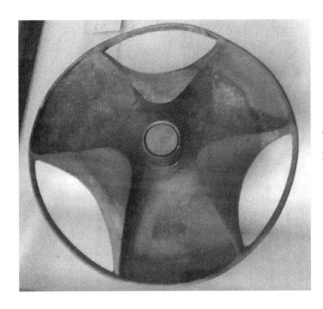

The precisely made Schist Disk—of unknown purpose

some kind of a wheel? Answering any of those question puts a severe strain on conventional archaeology. The disk is conventionally dated to 3000 BCE, even though the Egyptians of that time are believed to have had only stone and copper tools and to have had no knowledge of the wheel. Impossible to reliably date, the Schist Disk is thought by many to be an artifact of predynastic Egypt, possibly dating to before the end of the last ice age—that is, to Zep Tepi, or the First Time.

The Cairo museum also houses many stone vases and containers, from about the same period, carved from extremely hard diorite, with narrow necks but fully hollowed-out interiors beneath relatively thin exterior shells. Even with modern technology, such containers would be almost impossible to duplicate today. Tool design engineer and author Christopher Dunn (*The Giza Power Plant*) sees them as clear evidence of advanced ancient machining.

THE QUARRIES OF BAALBECK

In 2018, a massive megalith was discovered in Lebanon's Baalbek quarry. Weighing an astounding 1,650 tons, the single stone block is 19.6 meters (over 65 feet) long, 6 meters wide, and at least 5.5 meters high, making it significantly larger than either of two other blocks that had been previously discovered in the quarry.

Monolith from the Baalbek quarry, weighing over 1,000 tons;
photo courtesy of Deutsches Archäologisches Institut

On the origin of the enormous megaliths, writer Graham Hancock strongly disagrees with the standard view that they were the work of Roman engineers. Instead, he believes, they are the legacy of a civilization, now lost, that predated the Romans by thousands of years and was probably contemporaneous with Göbekli Tepe. Not only were the Romans incapable of carving—to say nothing of moving—stones of such size, but they were, Hancock believes, in all likelihood unaware even of their existence. The Baalbek monoliths, in fact, may well exceed the lifting capabilities of even our most modern technologies.*

RAMA'S BRIDGE

In 2019, Ramesh Pokhriyal (a.k.a. Nishank), then India's human resource development minister, startled the world by declaring that an

---

*To read more of Hancock's assessment, see his post of November 30, 2014, "Third Giant Megalith, Weighing 1,650 Tons, Confirmed at Baalbek," on his website, GrahamHancock .com, http://www.grahamhancock.com/forum/HancockG11.php.

Ram Setu, an ancient land bridge connecting India and Sri Lanka
(also see color insert plate 14)

eighteen-mile land bridge connecting India with Sri Lanka had been built by ancient Indian engineers. Immediately denounced by India's insecure and self-conscious mainstream press for promoting "pseudo-science," the minister was only echoing recent research suggesting that Ram Setu, as the bridge is called, is made of rocks seven thousand years older than the sandbar on which they rest. The finding, made by a group of American archaeologists, supports ancient accounts from Vedic scripture that Ram Setu was artificially made by Rama, the "mythical" Indian ruler identified in the Ramayana.*

"Rama's Bridge" has long been a source of controversy, and claims of its artificial origin are not new. According to researcher Rita Louise, writing for *Atlantis Rising* #98 ("Rama's Bridge," March/April 2013), "Dr. S. Badrinarayanan, the former director of the Geological Survey of India and member of the National Institute of Ocean Technology (NIOT), performed a survey of the structure and concluded in 2007 that it was manmade. In the course of their study, Dr. Badrinarayanan and his team drilled ten holes along the alignment of Adam's Bridge. About six meters below the surface he found a consistent layer of calcareous sandstone, corals and boulder-like materials. Some 4–5 meters further down, the team discovered a layer of loose sand, and then, below that, formations of hard rock."

According to the Hindu tradition, Rama lived during the Treta Yuga, a period that began 2,165,000 years ago and extended until about 869,000 years ago, many millennia before humans, if they existed at all, were capable of anything other than the most primitive existence.

---

*To read about Minister Pokhriyal's declaration, see "Ram Sethu Was Built by Indian Engineers, Says HRD Minister," *The Hindu* (newspaper), August 28, 2019, https://www.thehindu.com/news/national/ram-sethu-was-built-by-indian-engineers-says-hrd-minister/article29272613.ece.

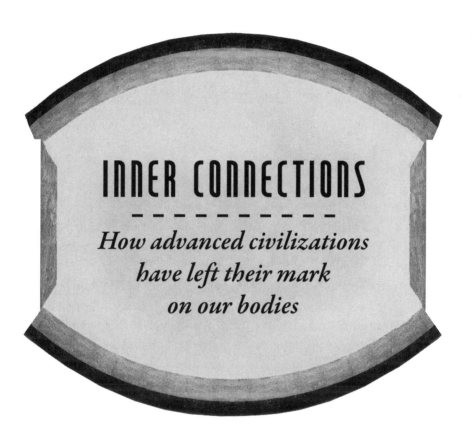

INNER CONNECTIONS

*How advanced civilizations
have left their mark
on our bodies*

20

The DNA Chase

*Have our genes had enough time to
evolve civilization and to lose it, more than once?*

Nonorganic cosmic dust, when held in the form of a plasma, in zero gravity will spontaneously form into double-helix structures, like those in DNA, which, as we know, have the power to reproduce themselves. A report published in the *New Journal of Physics* described experiments on the International Space Station (ISS), two hundred miles above Earth, that produced structures held together by electromagnetic forces that, it was thought, might have the power to reproduce themselves and ultimately to become intelligent competition for life as we know it. The 2007 discovery led a panel of scientists from Germany's Max Planck Institute, the Russian Academy of Sciences, and the University of Sydney to speculate publicly about the possible spontaneous appearance of alien life forms unlike anything we know. The American National Research Council says we should start looking for "weird" life.*

But while materialistic reductionist science perceives such an unexpected appearance of order as leading to random developments that might go scarily awry, many who see the principles of sacred geometry operating universally are unsurprised by the effects discovered in the ISS experiment. For them, life as we know it represents an optimum—

---

*See Stephen Battersby, "Could Alien Life Exist in the Form of DNA-Shaped Dust?," *New Scientist* (online), August 10, 2007, https://www.newscientist.com/article /dn12466-could-alien-life-exist-in-the-form-of-dna-shaped-dust/.

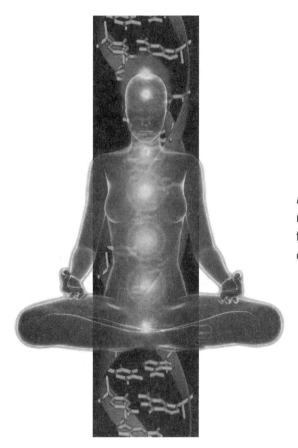

Artist's conception of the morphic field and DNA; art from *Atlantis Rising* (also see color insert plate 19)

rather than random—development of the laws of proportion and harmony that guide the universe, and the great force fields of the abyss display the same unifying principles as those in our little world. In other words, the evidence could be interpreted to mean that alien life, when we find it, may end up being more like what we know than what we don't, though there is certainly room for considerable variation.

The popular explanation for the source of the human mind is DNA. The general view seems to be that most biological characteristics are a function of our genetic molecules and that all answers to questions of mind and body will ultimately be found coded in our DNA. DNA, some would argue, is our identity.

But what if our DNA can be modified by our minds? Wouldn't that indicate that DNA might be more *effect* than *cause*? That is, however, exactly what recent research has shown.

James Watson and Francis Crick, first successful modelers of DNA, in 1953

According to Dr. Linda E. Carlson at the University of Calgary in Alberta, mindfulness therapy adapted from Buddhist meditation has been shown to increase the length of telomeres in DNA. Telomeres are the caps that prevent deterioration of the chromosomes. They are considered essential to DNA health.*

Carlson's study supports the work of researchers like biologists Robert Lanza and Rupert Sheldrake, who have argued in different ways that the mind extends beyond the physical body in some kind of force field that does not depend on physical matter. Such ideas are not suffered gladly by materialistic mainstream academia, but neither were Galileo's.

---

*You can read the full paper from Carlson and her team online: "Mindfulness-based cancer recovery and supportive-expressive therapy maintain telomere length relative to controls in distressed breast cancer survivors," *Cancer* 121, no. 3 (February 1, 2015; first published online November 3, 2014): 476–84, http://onlinelibrary.wiley.com /doi/10.1002/cncr.29063/abstract.

ANCIENT FOOTPRINTS

As we learned in the preceding chapter, a sophisticated ivory "tiara" made from the tusk of a woolly mammoth and dating back an astonishing forty-five to fifty thousand years ago, has given scientists reason to believe that Denisovans and Neanderthals may have preceded humans in many of the developments we now associate with our own march to civilization. New evidence from southwestern France underscores the point.

In 2013, at two archaeological sites, fragments of an advanced tool called a lissoir were found. The artifacts are about fifty thousand years old—so old, in fact, that scientists believe they predate the earliest appearance of humans in Europe. Indeed, it now appears that humans may have learned how to make the tool from Neanderthal predecessors.

A lissoir could be made of bone or wood and is considered a specialized instrument designed to work animal hides to make them softer, tougher, shinier, and more resistant to water. The bone lissoirs found in France by archaeologist Marie Soressi and her team worked just as those used today to create fashionable modern leather goods like handbags.*

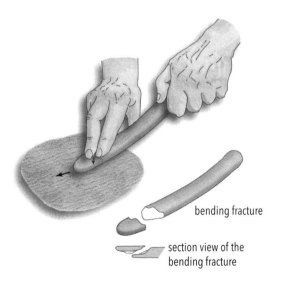

The presumed use of a lissoir; image courtesy of Marie Soressi

bending fracture

section view of the bending fracture

*Read about the discovery in Soressi's paper: "Neandertals Made the First Specialized Bone Tools in Europe," *Proceeding of the National Academy of Sciences* 110, no. 35 (August 2013): 14186–90; https://doi.org/10.1073/pnas.1302730110.

At Jebel Irhoud in Morocco, scientists have found *Homo sapiens* fossils dating to 315,000 years ago, pushing back the official dawn of our species by 100,000 years. The details, reported in the journal *Nature* in June 2017, could threaten the African genesis scenario believed by most paleontologists. It now seems clear that the East African human chapter cited by mainstream scholars was, if anything, a later development, and not the seminal event it has been portrayed to be. The researchers have concluded that humans developed at about the same time all across Africa, many thousands of years before the East African events once believed to represent the dawn of the human saga. According to Jean-Jacques Hublin, author of the study and director of the Max Planck Institute for Evolutionary Anthropology in Leipzig, Germany, "I would say the Garden of Eden in Africa is probably Africa—and it's a big, big garden."* Maybe an even bigger one than Professor Hublin suspected.

According to a study reported in May 2017, an international team of researchers analyzed 7.2-million-year-old fossil remains of hominin creatures classified as *Graecopithecus freybergi* that had been found in Bulgaria and Greece. They determined that these ancient creatures are the ancestors of modern humans, making Europe, *not* Africa, the cradle of humanity. The discovery proves, say the authors, that 200,000 years before the earliest African hominid (not counting the Jebel Irhoud discoveries just described), human ancestors were already starting to evolve in Europe.†

One conclusion that certainly may be drawn from the new research is that, in the long saga of humanity on Earth, there has been time for our forebears to go down many historical rabbit holes, and to follow many time lines, developments, and even civilizations, to a degree as yet unsuspected by orthodox science.

Another recent study now claims there could have been many thou-

---

*Read more about the Hublin team's report in "Oldest Homo sapiens Fossil Claim Rewrites Our Species' History," by Ewen Callaway, *Nature* (online), June 8, 2017, https://www.nature.com/news/oldest-homo-sapiens-fossil-claim-rewrites-our-species -history-1.22114#:~:text=Researchers%20say%20that%20they%20have,to%20about%20 315%2C000%20years%20ago.

†You can read about the findings online; see "Graecopithecus freybergi: Oldest Hominin Lived in Europe, not Africa," Sci-News.com, May 24, 2017, http://www.sci-news .com/othersciences/anthropology/graecopithecus-freybergi-hominin-04888.html.

The archaeological dig in Jebel Irhoud, Morocco. When the site was occupied by early humans, it would have been a cave; the covering rock and much sediment was removed by work in the 1960s.

sands of Neanderthals walking the Earth as long as 744,000 years ago—300,000 years earlier than previously believed. By comparing modern Eurasians, modern Africans, Neanderthals, and Denisovans, scientists at the University of Utah have calculated that there must have been tens of thousands of Neanderthals in Europe alone. Professor Alan Rogers and his team used recently developed DNA techniques to re-create the early history and migration patterns of ancient populations.*

Until recently, one of the primary arguments used to debunk the possible existence of lost civilizations like, say, Atlantis was that there simply had not been enough time for an earlier society to have evolved to anything like our present advanced state. However, given the accepted time line for the development of our own current civilization—about ten

---

*The paper was published in August 2017 in the *Proceedings of the National Academy of Sciences.* You can read a press release about the paper online: "New Look at Archaic DNA Rewrites Human Evolution Story," Phys.org, August 7, 2017, https://phys.org /news/2017-08-archaic-dna-rewrites-human-evolution.html.

thousand years from hunter-gatherer to Silicon Valley entrepreneur—it is easy to see how such advancement could have occurred in the past more than once, and maybe many more times, and then have vanished, leaving scarcely a trace.

MISSING HISTORY

In more recent times, DNA tells many even more surprising stories of forgotten migrations and reveals just how incomplete is the picture we have been presented by orthodoxy. Here are a few examples.

For centuries, if not millennia, both Ireland and Scotland have claimed origins in Egypt. According to one account, Gaythelos, creator of the Goidelic languages and ancestor of the Gaels, went to Egypt at the time of the Exodus, where he married Scota, daughter of the pharaoh, and, after the destruction of the Egyptian army in the Red Sea, fled with her to what would become Portugal, and then later to Ireland. Scota, say the chronicles, arrived in Ireland in about 1700 BCE. Ultimately, she was killed in battle at Tara, but her descendants would go on to become the "high kings of Ireland." The tribe of Danu is reputed to have marked the place of her death with the Lia Fáil, or Stone of Destiny, coronation stone for the kings of Ireland—at least those before 500 CE.

While some may consider much of that story fanciful, researchers from Trinity College Dublin and Queen's University Belfast sequenced the genomes from ancient Irish remains and discovered unmistakable evidence of Middle Eastern ancestry for Ireland's earliest people. DNA extracted from a woman who lived near current-day Belfast some 5,200 years ago showed a majority Middle Eastern genetic heritage, while DNA extracted from three Bronze Age men, from about 4,000 years ago, shows that about one-third of their genetic heritage derived from "ancient sources in the Pontic Steppe"—that is, steppeland running from the Black Sea to the Caspian—and indicates massive migration from western Europe to Ireland. According to Trinity professor Dan Bradley, the study's leader, "There was a great wave of genome change that swept into Europe from above the Black Sea into Bronze Age Europe, and we now know it washed all the way to the shores of its most westerly island." The research indicates that before

The Stone of Destiny on hill in Tara, Ireland

the migration, Ireland's earliest people, who may have come from as far away as the Middle East, were quite different than the Celtic people of today.*

Could another missing piece of biblical history, the Ark of the Covenant, or what's left of it, be sitting on a dusty museum shelf in Harare, Zimbabwe? That is the claim of University of London professor and Indiana Jones wannabe Tudor Parfitt.

It's called the *ngoma lungundu* by its present-day guardians, the Lemba tribe of Zimbabwe, who claim to be descendants of the ancient

---

*The research was published in December 2015 in the *Proceedings of the National Academy of Sciences*. You can read a press release about the paper online: "Scientists Sequence First Ancient Irish Human Genomes," Trinity College Dublin News and Events website, December 28, 2015, https://www.tcd.ie/news_events/articles/scientists-sequence-first -ancient-irish-human-genomes/.

The present-day Lemba tribe greets Tudor Parfitt for a research visit in 1996.

priestly tribe of Levites who guarded the Old Testament Ark. The *ngoma,* they say, came from the "great temple in Jerusalem."*

Parfitt says that DNA studies of the Lemba priests confirm their claim of Hebrew lineage from the time of the original Ark. Moreover, he has carbon-14 dated the wooden drum in the museum, which he says is all that remains of the original Ark, and he says everything checks out. The original gold covering, it is suggested, was stolen by the Babylonians when the Israelites were taken into captivity and the relic disappeared from history. Parfitt's theory contradicts the better-known notion promoted by Graham Hancock that the Ark was taken to Ethiopia. Many other hypotheses have also been advanced for the fate of what is arguably the most important religious artifact in history, involving such well-known guardians of secrets as the Knights Templars, the Rosicrucians, and the Masons.

On another front, the ancient ancestry of America's Cherokee Indians is receiving increased scrutiny. Currently several DNA firms

---

*You can read more about Lemba history and the *ngoma lungundu* in "Lost Jewish Tribe 'Found in Zimbabwe,'" BBC News (online), March 8, 2010, http://news.bbc.co.uk/2 /hi/8550614.stm.

market tests that can be ordered online to determine whether or not one has Cherokee heritage in the family tree. Some of the data derived, it is said, suggests that Cherokees originated in the Middle East or North Africa. Among those who have cited findings, DNA Consultants, Inc., of Longmont, Colorado, reports strong markers indicating Cherokee connections with Berbers, native Egyptians, Turks, Lebanese, Hebrews, and Mesopotamians.*

At other times, some linguists have believed that the Cherokee language (though officially thought to be Southern Iroquoian) is an archaic form of Hebrew, so it is not surprising to learn that some think the Cherokee are one of the lost tribes of Israel. Today, many Americans, including Massachusetts senator Elizabeth Warren, believe they have Cherokees among their ancestors, but it seems unlikely that Cherokee numbers were ever great enough to support a diaspora of such magnitude. It is clear, however, that there was a great deal of interaction and mutual influence between Cherokees and the founders of America, who considered the Cherokee one of five "civilized tribes."

Sequoyah, the inventor of a writing system for the Cherokee language in the 1700s

---

*For an overview of the DNA Consultants Cherokee study, see "Cherokee DNA," posted on the Access Genealogy website, which is part of Richard Thornton's *Appalachian Colonists from the Mediterranean Basin* (2013), https://accessgenealogy.com/native/cherokee -dna.htm.

Many authorities dispute the DNA claims, arguing that there has been so much intermingling of Cherokee blood with other ethnicities that it is virtually impossible to untangle the threads and to draw any significant conclusions. Nevertheless, a quick look at nineteenth-century portraits of Cherokee leaders shows a manner of dress and behavior very much unlike those of any other indigenous American tribe. Though mainstream anthropologists and historians insist that they know where Cherokees come from, they usually concede that such knowledge as they have has many holes.

Charles Darwin was fond of suggesting that organisms often contain leftover parts from earlier stages of development—so-called vestigial remains—that are no longer needed. The human appendix, a small worm-like extension of the lower intestine, is considered an example. Though it is often removed when infected, new Australian research suggests that, in fact, the appendix has many unappreciated functions—and, as in other cases, Darwin was mistaken.

At the Walter and Eliza Hall Institute of Medical Research in Melbourne, Gabrielle Belz and her team have demonstrated that, far from being a throwaway item, the appendix is actually a very important part of the bowel's immune system, providing major protection against gut infections. Researchers at Duke University came to similar conclusions a few years ago.*

Underestimating the full value of natural forms is nothing new, however. In *Atlantis Rising* #116 (March/April 2016), in an article titled "Junk DNA or Not?," science writer Brendan D. Murphy argued that so-called "junk DNA," which was at one time readily dismissed by geneticists, actually contains, as demonstrated by research, what may well be some of the molecule's most vital coding concerning some of the body's most mysterious functions related to consciousness.

The willingness of materialist science to throw away some of nature's most valuable gifts reveals more about the weaknesses of that

---

*See, for reference, "Immune Cells Make Appendix 'Silent Hero' of Digestive Health," on the Walter and Eliza Hall Institute of Medical Research website, December 1, 2015, which offers a synopsis of Dr. Belz's paper, "Complementarity and Redundancy of IL-22-Producing Innate Lymphoid Cells," published in *Natural Immunology* on that same day: https://www.wehi.edu.au/news/immune-cells-make-appendix-silent-hero-digestive -health.

science than it does about any perceived shortcomings in the structures of life itself.

When Michael Drosnin's *The Bible Code* made the best-seller lists in 1997, millions were exposed for the first time to the notion that a previously hidden design in ancient scripture apparently could be unlocked to answer many questions about today's world. Among followers of the esoteric, however, the idea was not new. Stan Tenen, for example, has demonstrated that all the letters in the Hebrew alphabet, of which the original Bible was composed, were created from shadows cast by the hand and contain profound meanings emanating from a higher dimension.*

In 1999, two American doctors published *Healing Codes for the Biological Apocalypse,* in which they claimed to have found codes in the Book of Numbers that could be used to repair damaged DNA. Dr. Joseph Puleo and Dr. Leonard Horowitz say they have found nothing less than an electromagnetic frequency code for "miracles." Using the ancient Pythagorean method to reduce the verse numbers of a particular segment in the Book of Numbers to single-digit integers, Puleo discovered a series of electromagnetic sound frequencies. These, he says—though once known and understood by the Church to have healing properties and used in Gregorian chant—have been lost.

---

*Tenen was interviewed by psychologist and author Dr. Jeffrey Mishlove for Mishlove's *Wisdom Radio* program on March 15, 1999. You can read the transcript ("Interview of Stan Tenen by Dr. Jeffrey Mishlove"), which helps explain some of Tenen's work, online at the website of the Meru Foundation.

21

Mind Fields

Consciousness and reality

Life after death is real and can be proven, claims a world-renowned biologist. According to Robert Lanza from the Wake Forest School of Medicine, the universe is a creation of our consciousness, not the other way around.

The idea is based on quantum physics, as in the famous double-slit experiment, which proves that the behavior of a subatomic particle can be controlled by a person's perception of it. When researchers watch a particle pass through a multi-holed barrier, it travels like a bullet through a single slit. When it is *not* watched, it moves through multiple holes like a wave. The universe exists, says Lanza, only because we are conscious of it, so death, as we conceive it, cannot exist in any real sense. As for life after death, Lanza sees it as a "perennial flower that returns to bloom in the multiverse." He explains these ideas in his 2017 best-selling book *Biocentrism: How Life and Consciousness Are the Keys to Understanding the True Nature of the Universe.*

In the blockbuster *Matrix* films, the idea is put forward that our entire world could be nothing more than a massive computer simulation. Certainly much of the movie's popularity was based on a widely shared intuition that such a thing might be true. The idea has not gone away. In 2016, at the Isaac Asimov Memorial Debate at the American Museum of Natural History in New York City, several experts focused on the possibility. Hayden Planetarium director Neil

Biologist Robert Lanza in his laboratory

Digital simulation of reality from the movie *The Matrix*

deGrasse Tyson went so far as to say he considered the odds of such a thing to be fifty-fifty.*

In 2003, Oxford University philosopher Nick Bostrom speculated that a very advanced civilization with enormous computing power had

---

*You can listen to the debate via the *Science at AMNH* podcast. Look for the episode titled "2016 Isaac Asimov Memorial Debate: Is the Universe a Simulation?" https://www.amnh.org/explore/news-blogs/podcasts/2016-isaac-asimov-memorial-debate-is-the-universe-a-simulation.

decided to run simulations of their ancestors—that is, *us*.* Cosmologist Max Tegmark says the mathematical structure of everything is simply a reflection of the computer code in which the creation was written. The idea, however, that our universe is more information than substance and could be a complete illusion in an entirely synthetic world has been around for a while.

Twenty-five hundred years ago, Plato spoke of just such a thing in his parable of the cave, where prisoners chained in a cave misunderstand the meaning of shadows cast on the wall before them—inferring reality for what was only an illusion created by a fire at the mouth of the cave.

Ironically, most of the computer-simulation notions today seem to originate in the minds of people who reject the possibility of a divine being. Yet arguments that have been made for centuries for the existence of God are now deployed to promote the suggestion that we are all created by some great computer programmer in the sky.

The main difference between the old and the new schools of thought appears to be in the kind of relationship deemed possible with a "creator." Traditional supporters of the God hypothesis, like mystics, generally seem to be expressing a love for the transcendent intelligence they see behind existence, while most of those promoting the computer-simulation hypothesis appear to be envisioning something very disturbing, dystopian, and even alien to human nature. The difference, it seems, is more a state of mind—or spirit—not the plausibility of the conjectures.

For modern positivistic reductionist science, however, the world must seem a scary place. While many of that persuasion may dispute the very existence of consciousness, they now find themselves facing growing opposition from within their own ranks.

A few years ago, Dimitri Krioukov, a professor at the University of California at San Diego, published a study in *Nature's Scientific Reports* suggesting that the universe itself very much resembles a gigantic brain. In an interview, Krioukov said the universe grows like a brain, building its networks as it grows, with the electrical firing between brain cells

---

*You can read more about Bostrom's idea in his paper "Are You Living in a Computer Simulation?," published in *Philosophical Quarterly* 53, no. 211 (2003): 243–55, https://www.simulation-argument.com/simulation.html.

Plato's parable of the cave; 1604 engraving by Jan Saenredam

mirrored in the shape of expanding galaxies. Krioukov was quick to point out, though, that this pattern doesn't mean the universe is thinking. He did concede, however, "for a physicist it's an immediate signal that there is some missing understanding of how nature works." That is, of course, what some might call a "no-brainer."*

And while that may sound like heresy enough for the church of science, the situation is not getting better. Gregory Matloff, a veteran physicist at New York City College of Technology, has now published a paper arguing that humans may be direct extensions of the rest of the universe in both substance and spirit. According to Matloff, a "proto-consciousness field" could extend through all of space. Stars may be thinking entities that deliberately control their paths. Put more bluntly, the entire cosmos may be self-aware. That view is all part of a growing movement called *panpsychism,* and it's the "in" thing in some very exclusive scientific circles. It's kind of like the Gaia hypothesis, which

---

*Krioukov was interviewed by LiveScience. See Tia Ghose, "Universe Grows Like a Giant Brain," LiveScience (online), November 26, 2012, https://www.cbsnews.com /news/universe-grows-like-a-giant-brain/.

postulates that the Earth is a living, breathing, conscious being, but in this case, the concept would apply to entire galaxies, and even the whole universe. Or, as, the ancients might say, "As above, so below."*

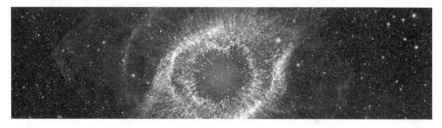

Is the universe conscious?

All of this, of course, has been basic to enlightened spiritual awareness for eons. For science, though, it could be better late than never.

MORPHIC RESONANCE

The prestigious not-for-profit TED Talks organization claims a commitment to informing its patrons about the latest developments in technology, entertainment, and design (TED). Despite charging audiences thousands of dollars to watch speeches, at conferences and streaming live on the web, for which it pays nothing, TED has developed a considerable international following, reaching over a billion viewers so far, but not without taking sides on issues that it finds threatening, like "pseudoscience."

Amid indignant accusations of such heresy, speeches by Rupert Sheldrake and Graham Hancock at the 2013 TEDx Whitechapel in East London were removed from the TED Talks website. After a great deal of ensuing pushback from an outraged public, TED eventually caved and returned the speeches to its site, albeit to a less desirable location—what Hancock called "the naughty corner."

For his celebrated theories of morphic resonance and formative causation, Cambridge-trained biologist Rupert Sheldrake has been roundly

---

*To read more about Matloff's work and panpsychism, see Corey S. Powell, "Is the Universe Conscious?," NBC News *Mach* (online), June 16, 2017, https://www.nbcnews.com/mach/science/universe-conscious-ncna772956.

criticized and, some would say, crucified by the scientific establishment. Sheldrake's well-evidenced suggestion that many of the so-called "laws" of nature would be more properly described as "habits" evolving over time—i.e., "learning" in response to changing needs—has been ridiculed by the academic powers that be. One has even proposed that Sheldrake's books be burned. Now, though, recent research from professor Richard Watson at Britain's University of Southampton postulates that evolution itself may be *intelligent,* and that it can learn from its experience.

Late in 2015, in an opinion paper published in *Trends in Ecology and Evolution,* Professor Watson asked: "Is evolution more intelligent than we thought?" Watson claimed, according to the press release, that new research shows that evolution is able to learn from previous experience, which could provide a better explanation of how natural selection produces such apparently intelligent designs.

By unifying the theory of evolution (which, its adherents believe, shows how random variation and selection is enough to account for incremental adaptation) and learning theory (which believers say can explain how incremental adaptation is sufficient for a system to exhibit intelligent behavior), Watson demonstrates that it is possible for evolution to exhibit some of the same intelligent behaviors as other learning systems (including neural networks).

"A key feature of intelligence," says Watson, "is an ability to anticipate behaviors that will lead to future benefits. Conventionally, evolution, being dependent on random variation, has been considered 'blind' or at least short-sighted—unable to exhibit such anticipation. But showing that evolving systems can learn from past experience means that evolution has the potential to anticipate what is needed to adapt to future environments in the same way that learning systems do."

"If evolution can learn from experience," he continues, "and thus improve its own ability to evolve over time, this can demystify the awesomeness of the designs that evolution produces. Natural selection can accumulate knowledge that enables it to evolve smarter. That's exciting because it explains why biological design appears to be so intelligent."*

---

*You can read the full press release on the university website: "Is Evolution More Intelligent Than We Thought?," University of Southampton News and Events (online), December 18, 2015, http://www.ecs.soton.ac.uk/news/4826.

There are some who would say that Professor Watson is making an argument for God, or an intelligent designer, but with another name. Lawyers might call that a distinction without a difference.

THE BOUNDARIES OF THE BRAIN

Those who have been waiting for science to find the so-called "God spot" in the brain will, apparently, have to wait a while longer. Researchers at the University of Missouri now concede that the human brain doesn't have such a spot, that "spirituality" is a complex phenomenon, and that multiple areas of the brain are responsible.

The researchers say, for example, that spiritual transcendence is associated with decreased right parietal lobe functioning, but that other spiritual functions, like interest in the welfare of others, are related to increased activity in the frontal lobe. According to Brick Johnstone, professor of health psychology, the research shows a neuropsychological basis for spirituality, albeit not in one spot.*

That could be as close to holistic as materialistic science can get, but it is still far from the view held by most of those who consider themselves more spiritual—that the physical brain is merely a receiver or conveyor of thoughts or energy that come from "mind," which exists somewhere other than, or beyond, the physical body.

By the way . . . the special capacity of Einstein's brain—something long asserted by reductionists—has also been thrown out. After studying the great scientist's brain, psychologist Terence Hine of Pace University says it proved to be nothing special, at least in terms of its physical characteristics. According to *Discover* magazine, blind tests with unlabeled slides made from Einstein's brain were no different than slides made from other completely ordinary brains.†

---

*Read the press release about the study from the university: "Distinct 'God Spot' in the Brain Does Not Exist, MU Researcher Says," University of Missouri News Bureau (online), April 18, 2012, https://munewsarchives.missouri.edu/news -releases/2012/0418-distinct-%E2%80%9Cgod-spot%E2%80%9D-in-the-brain-does -not-exist-mu-researcher-says/.

†To read about the study, see "The Myth of Einstein's Brain?," by Neuroskeptic (alias), *Discover* (online), May 24, 2014, https://www.discovermagazine.com/mind/the-myth -of-einsteins-brain.

Albert Einstein

The study may be a major blow to the notion that "mind" or "intelligence" is strictly a function of the physical brain. The unanswered question for science is: If mind or consciousness doesn't come from the brain, where does it come from? The study seems consistent with suggestions from Rupert Sheldrake and others that the mind exists in a kind of force field both within and without the body.* It acts as a receiver of intelligence, very much as a television or radio does for signals that originate elsewhere. Looking for intelligence in the brain is like a primitive human searching for the little people hidden inside a television. (This not to imply, however, that intelligence can be found on television.)

Does size itself matter? The age-old question has gotten some new scientific scrutiny lately, and the answer is: maybe a little bit. We are talking, of course, about the relationship between IQ and brain size. The issue has been hotly debated for at least the last two centuries, with materialists arguing that the size of the brain is the main thing that sets humans apart from animals. Researchers with large crania have apparently been partial to the idea. A 2015 study, however, looked closely at about eight thousand participants and discovered

---

*You can read more about Sheldrake's theories in his article "Extended Mind," published in *The Quest* (July/August 2003), https://www.theosophical.org/files/resources/articles/ExtendedMind.pdf.

that if there is any relationship, it is very small, with a "robust but weak" association between brain size and IQ.*

Still unexplained are well-documented cases of seemingly "normal" subjects who were discovered, after death, to have had virtually no brain at all, as is the fact that developmentally disabled individuals often have very large brains. Three-year-old Chase Britton, for example, who was born completely missing a cerebellum, is provoking astonishment within the world of mainstream medicine. According to news reports, not only is he functioning in a relatively normal way, he seems to be thriving, standing, learning to walk, picking up things, and enjoying life, all things considered impossible for one with his abnormality. The cerebellum, after all, is the part of the brain believed to control motor skills, balance, and emotions.

Doctors at the Children's National Hospital in Washington, D.C., said they do not understand it. In their view, Chase has the MRI of a vegetable. They are, they said, reexamining their theories about brain function.†

THE COMING REFORMATION

In 2013, Dean Keith Simonton, a professor at the University of California at Davis, wrote a commentary in the journal *Nature* pushing the idea that it is unlikely society will ever produce another Einstein or Newton. The reason, he says, is that all the basic principles of how the world works have already been discovered, and little remains to be done, except, perhaps, to write the footnotes.

---

*For the full report, see Jakob Pietschnig, Lars Penke, Jelte M. Wicherts, Michael Zeiler, and Martin Voracek, "Meta-analysis of Associations between Human Brain Volume and Intelligence Differences: How Strong Are They and What Do They Mean?," *Neuroscience and Biobehavioral Reviews* 57 (2015): 411–32; https://doi.org/10.1016/j.neubiorev.2015.09.017.

†To learn more about Chase Britton, see "'He Has Drive Like I Have Never Seen': Boy, 3, Born without Part of His Brain Baffles Doctors after Learning to Walk," *Daily Mail* (online), February 13, 2011, https://www.dailymail.co.uk/news/article-1356516/Chase-Britton-Boy-3-born-brain-baffles-doctors-learning-walk.html. To read about other such cases, see William Herkewitz, "How Much of the Brain Can a Person Do Without?," *Popular Mechanics* (online), September 19, 2014, https://www.popularmechanics.com/science/health/a13017/how-much-of-the-brain-can-a-person-do-without-17223085/.

It is worth remembering that at the turn of the twentieth century there were some who thought we should do away with the patent office, since by then everything worth inventing had already been invented.*

Another point Simonton might have noted is that even if a great discovery were made, there is no guarantee that it would be recognized by the prevailing authorities. If the persecution of Galileo or, more recently, the attempted crushing of Immanuel Velikovsky is any indication, the same hubris that has always blocked our way forward has not disappeared. Ironically, most of those who believe they know genius when they see it are among the first to laugh at developments that do not fit their own particular view of the possible.

Still, in a move intended to remind us of the Copernican revolution of over six centuries ago, a group of respected scientists issued what they called a "Manifesto for a Post-Materialist Science" in 2014. The short paper questioned the standard paradigm of mainstream science that has become a virtual religion to its followers. Manifesto authors are Mario Beauregard, PhD; Gary E. Schwartz, PhD; Lisa Miller, PhD; Larry Dossey, MD; Alexander Moreira-Almeida, MD, PhD; Marilyn Schlitz, PhD; Rupert Sheldrake, PhD; and Charles Tart, PhD. Some scientists, such as former NASA researcher and computational scientist Dave Pruett, writing for the *Huffington Post*, called it a "bombshell."

The abstract proclaims the following:

From its inception, science has continually evolved because of a fundamental reason: the accumulation of empirical evidence that could not be accommodated by entrenched views. The resulting changes have often been minor, but sometimes they have been titanic, as in the quantum-relativistic revolution of the early decades of the twentieth century.

Many scientists believe a similar transition is currently required, because the materialistic focus that has dominated science in the

---

*Read about Simonton's declaration here in "Expert Psychologist Suggests the Era of Genius Scientists Is Over," by Bob Yirka, posted on the Phys.org website, January 31, 2013, https://phys.org/news/2013-01-expert-psychologist-era-genius-scientists.html.

Mario Beauregard, PhD.

modern era cannot account for an ever-increasing body of empirical findings in the domain of consciousness and spirituality.*

Many assumptions made by today's scientists, the manifesto points out, are not supported by evidence and are, in fact, contradicted by a great deal of experimental evidence, most notably in quantum physics. The situation is comparable to that which occurred in the sixteenth century when overwhelming evidence forced the Copernican revolution, culminating in replacement of the outmoded, Earth-centered Ptolemaic model of the solar system. A clear parallel can be seen today in the common belief that the human mind is confined to the brain. Rupert Sheldrake has led the charge in proposing that in the same way that a magnetic field reaches beyond a physical magnet, the mind extends well beyond the brain, and he has the experimental evidence to prove it.

---

*The manifesto was first published in *Explore* 10, no. 5 (September–October 2014). You can read the full document on the website of the Campaign for Open Science, http://opensciences.org/about/manifesto-for-a-post-materialist-science.

22

Return Engagements

Could humans get more than one crack at the challenges of life on Earth?

In the 1993 movie *Groundhog Day,* actor Bill Murray played a TV reporter reliving the same day in Punxsutawney, Pennsylvania, over and over again. In real life, it turns out, many people constantly experience the feeling that they have lived the current moment before, and not only are they overwhelmed by a sense of familiarity with new experiences, but they can provide plausible and complex justifications to support it.

Actor Bill Murray interviews "Punxsutawney Phil" in the 1993 movie *Groundhog Day.*

According to British researchers, some people have such chronic déjà vu that they stop watching TV or movies because they feel like they always know what is coming next. Such feelings, said the psychologists, could lead to other more serious problems like depression. The condition afflicts many, said Dr. Chris Moulin, who expressed hope that ways could be found to relieve the problem.*

In *Groundhog Day,* Murray's character was forced to keep refining his behavior until eventually he stopped reliving the day. Many who believe in reincarnation see a lesson for life in the tale, believing humans are required to continue repeating the experience of life on Earth until they get it right, or else, as Yogi Berra famously observed, "it's déjà vu all over again."

A mantra of the pro-life movement has been that life begins at conception. But could it actually begin before conception? A 2014 study from Boston University showed that until about the age of seven, children have a strong sense that their own existence goes back to well before their mother bore them. The researchers, Natalie Emmons and Deborah Kelemen, examined children in Ecuador from two cultures: rural indigenous Shuar and urban Ecuadorian. Most children from both groups indicated that they felt they had existed or had feelings and desires before their own conception. At about the age of seven or eight, however, such ideas were dropped.†

Tracking evidence for reincarnation is the subject of continuing scientific study at the University of Virginia in Charlottesville, where Dr. Jim Tucker is currently carrying on the research of the late Dr. Ian Stevenson, who pioneered the academic investigation of reincarnation. One key focus of the research involves marks on the body that connect successive incarnations. Considerable evidence links traumatic injury in one life with birthmarks in the next. Stevenson himself documented 210 such cases.

---

*For the full report, see C. Wells, C. Moulin, P. Ethridge, et al., "Persistent Psychogenic Déjà Vu: A Case Report," *Journal of Medical Case Reports* 8, no. 1 (December 2014): 414, https://www.researchgate.net/publication/269281426_Persistent_psychogenic _deja_vu_A_case_report.

†See Natalie A. Emmons and Deborah Kelemen, "The Development of Children's Prelife Reasoning: Evidence from Two Cultures," *Child Development* 85, no. 4 (July–August 2014): 1617–33, https://www.bu.edu/cdl/files/2014/01/EmmonsKelemen _prelife_withsuppmat.pdf.

Plate 1. Artist Tom Miller's conception of the end of Atlantis

Plate 2. Movie poster for *Atlantis, the Lost Continent,* directed by George Pal

Plate 3. Artist Tom Miller's conception of a Giza hall of records

Plate 4. Inside Naica Mountain's Crystal Cave

Plate 5. The Roselli map, a typical thirteenth-century portolan navigational chart

Plate 6. This full map is made from a mosaic of many portolans apparently copied from older sources. Portolan shorelines are in blue. Actual shorelines are in red. In the resulting composite, the Mediterranean is displayed with much more accuracy than the common sailing knowledge of the time would have permitted, suggesting that the source maps contained more advanced geographic knowledge than the map copiers possessed.

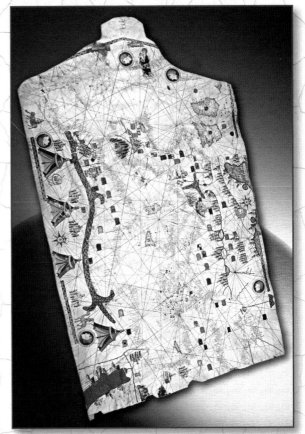

Plate 7. An artist's conception of a terraformed Mars

Image courtesy of Ittiz

Plate 8. Emergency retaining ponds at the Gold King Mine spill site near Silverton, Colorado

Plate 9. Researcher in Spain's El Sidrón Cave

Photo courtesy of CSIC Comunicación

Plate 10. Divers find an underwater goddess in this 1985 promotional art for *The Atlantis Dimension,* a screenplay by Tom Miller and Doug Kenyon.

Plate 11. An artist's depiction of an ancient nuclear explosion on Mars

Art by Randy Haragan for the cover of *Atlantis Rising* (September/October 2014)

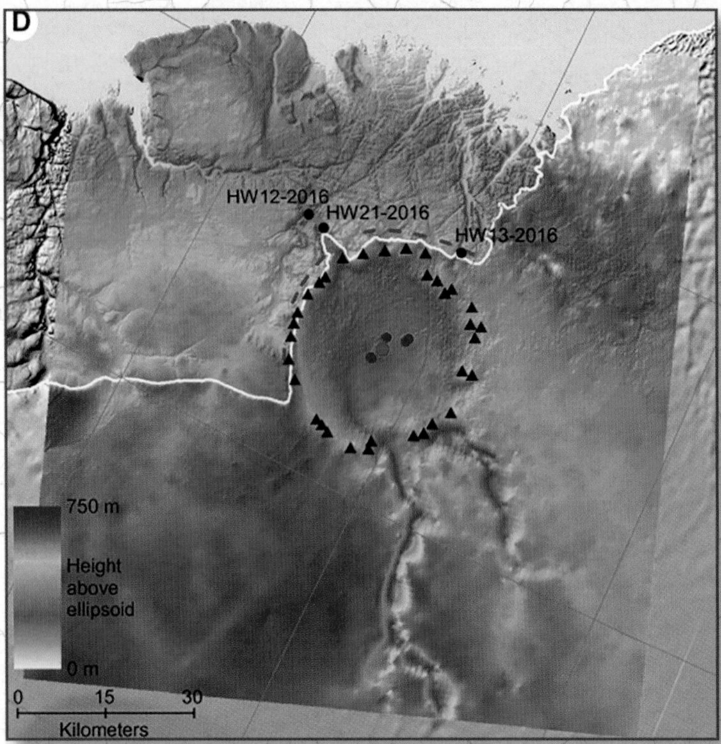

Plate 12. Impact crater beneath Hiawatha Glacier, northwest Greenland; topography based on NASA data

Alfred Wegener Institute (AWI)

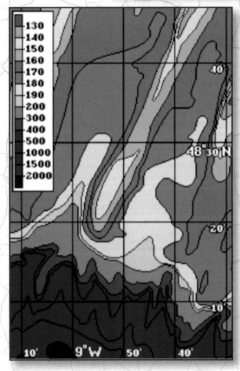

Plate 13. Topology of Little Sole Bank, a sand bank in the Atlantic Ocean southwest of Cornwall, U.K.

Plate 14. Rama Setu, an ancient land bridge connecting India and Sri Lanka

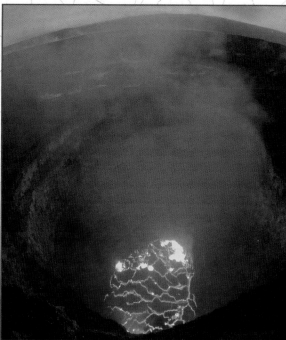

Plate 15. The aurora borealis (northern lights) is caused by charged particles from the sun.

Plate 16. Northern portion of the Kilauea caldera during the 2018 eruption

Plate 17. A chamber in the vast underground city beneath Derinkuyu, Turkey

Plate 18. The brooch of Tutankhamun

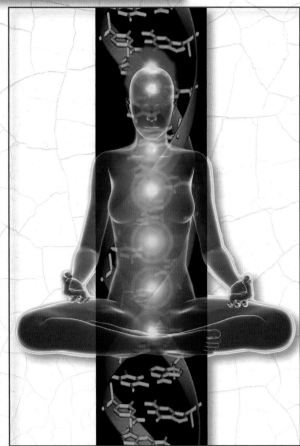

Plate 19. Artist's conception of the morphic field and DNA
Art from *Atlantis Rising*

Dr. Jim Tucker

The marks can, apparently, also be intentional. Tucker recounts the story of an aged woman in Thailand who expressed the desire to reincarnate as a boy. Her daughter marked the back of her neck in white paste. Soon after her mother's death, the daughter gave birth to a boy with a virtually identical white mark on the back of his neck. When he was old enough to talk, the boy claimed possession of his grandmother's things.*

Despite significant resistance to the idea in the West, the Stevenson lab has accumulated documentation for over 2,500 cases supporting the reincarnation hypothesis.

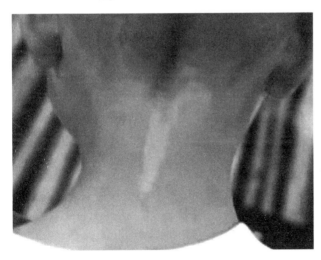

A birthmark on the neck of a boy in Thailand mirrors one made on his grandmother's neck before her death and his subsequent birth; image from YouTube.

---

*For more detail on this case and others, read "Are Birthmarks Connected to Violent Death in Past Life?," by Tara MacIsaac, *Epoch Times* (online), November 6, 2013, updated February 11, 2016, https://www.theepochtimes.com/are-birthmarks-connected -to-violent-death-in-past-life_347860.html.

The idea that the development of the human story requires more than one chapter may be one of the most ancient on Earth, but despite enormous implications, it is yet to be fully investigated, the UVA research notwithstanding. Yet despite nearly total ignorance of the topic, materialistically minded scientists have not hesitated to attack the belief as illogical, impossible, lacking evidence, and essentially preposterous—rank superstition only. But could there be more to the concept than they suppose?

For nearly fifteen years, Tucker, professor of psychiatry and neurobehavioral sciences and director of the UVA Health System's Division of Perceptual Studies, has been investigating many claims—not just unexplained body marks—made by children, usually between the ages of two and six, who say they've had past lives. The children are sometimes able to provide enough detail about those lives that their stories can be traced back to an actual person—rarely famous and often entirely unknown to the family—who died years before.

Tucker says the strength of the cases he encounters varies. Some can be easily discounted—for instance, when it becomes clear that a child's innocuous statements come within a family that desperately misses a loved one. But in a number of the cases, Tucker says, the most logical, scientific explanation for a claim is as simple as it is astounding: somehow, the child recalls memories from another life.

"I understand the leap it takes to conclude there is something beyond what we can see and touch," Tucker told *Virginia Magazine* reporter Sean Lyons. "But there is this evidence here that needs to be accounted for, and when we look at these cases carefully, some sort of carry-over of memories often makes the most sense."*

In his 2015 book *Return to Life,* Tucker details some of the more compelling cases he's researched and outlines his argument that discoveries within quantum mechanics, the mind-bending science of how nature's smallest particles behave, provide clues to reincarnation's existence. "Quantum physics indicates that our physical world may grow

---

*The article in which Lyons interviewed Tucker, titled "The Science of Reincarnation," was published in the Winter 2013 issue of *Virginia Magazine,* a publication of the University of Virginia, https://uvamagazine.org/articles/the_science_of_reincarnation.

out of our consciousness," Tucker writes. "That's a view held not just by me, but by a number of physicists as well."

The belief in reincarnation, taught for thousands of years in many religions East and West, is that a nonphysical yet more permanent human form is—in the ongoing development of a greater identity—at the moment of birth simply starting a new life in a new physical body. At death, the worn-out physical body is merely discarded. In India, the idea is a part of the doctrine of cyclic existence, fundamental to teachings like Jainism, Buddhism, Sikhism, and Hinduism. Ancient Greek philosophers like Pythagoras, Socrates, and Plato held a similar belief in "metempsychosis." Reincarnation has been part of many spiritual teachings, both ancient and modern, exoteric and esoteric, like Gnosticism or Theosophy, and many streams of orthodox Judaism. It is also found in the beliefs of numerous indigenous peoples throughout the world. It is also more widely believed in America than is generally thought.

According to a 2009 poll from the Pew Research Center's Forum

A typical series of incarnations; art from *Atlantis Rising*

on Religion & Public Life, Eastern and New Age beliefs are widespread in America, where religious beliefs and practices do not fit neatly into conventional categories. Large numbers of Americans engage in multiple religious practices, mixing elements of diverse traditions. Many also blend Christianity with Eastern or New Age beliefs such as reincarnation. When polled, 24 percent of the public overall and 22 percent of Christians said they believed in reincarnation.*

Though many orthodox Christians insist that reincarnation is not part of the Bible, they must contend with at least two prominent instances that make clear references to the notion: In John 9:1–2, when Jesus saw a man blind from birth, "His disciples asked him, 'Rabbi, who sinned, this man or his parents, that he was born blind?'" If the man's blindness could have resulted from his own sin, he would have had to have lived a prior life where he could have acted somehow to cause his current affliction. The implication of the possibility of a previous life—i.e., reincarnation—was not questioned by Jesus, at least not according to the Book of John.

Another example involves the ninth-century BCE prophet Elijah. According to the Old Testament (II Kings 2:11), Elijah was taken into heaven in a fiery chariot. Four centuries later, in the final line of the Old Testament, the prophet Malachi says that before the coming of the "great and terrible day of the Lord" (Malachi 4:5), God would again send Elijah. Consequently, Jewish tradition looked for Elijah to herald the coming of the Messiah. The disciples of Jesus, believing that Jesus was the Messiah, wondered where Elijah was. Jesus's answer (appearing first in Mathew 11) was that Elijah has already returned as John the Baptist—again, clearly validating the ancient belief in reincarnation.

If, even before the Bible was written, there was—as in the story of Noah or Atlantis—a great fountainhead of civilization that came to a catastrophic end, what influence might it still have on our world today? Is some kind of unconscious genetic or race memory at work, as Immanuel Velikovsky envisioned? Or does the ancient notion of reincarnation provide a better explanation?

---

*The poll asked many more interesting questions, of course. To read the results, see "Many Americans Mix Multiple Faiths," posted on December 9, 2009, on the website of the Pew Research Center, https://www.pewforum.org/2009/12/09/many-americans-mix-multiple-faiths/.

Elijah and the prophets of Baal; 1658 painting by Juan de Valdés Leal

Popular Atlantis researcher Frank Joseph (author of *Before Atlantis, Atlantis and the Coming Ice Age,* and *Survivors of Atlantis,* among other titles) has carefully investigated evidence of reincarnation and its significance for the story of Atlantis in the work of Edgar Cayce, widely known in the last century as the "Sleeping Prophet." In the 1920s, '30s, and '40s, Cayce gave thousands of readings on thousands of subjects. Among the famous and influential people to seek his guidance were Woodrow Wilson, Thomas Edison, Irving Berlin, and George Gershwin. Of the sixteen hundred people for whom he conducted "life readings," about seven hundred were told of conditions in Atlantis, which he said was the vanished homeland of civilization. In "Plato or Cayce," a March/April 2009 article for *Atlantis Rising Magazine,* Frank Joseph described Cayce's amazing credentials as a genuine seer into the ancient past, with very deep insight into the reincarnation question. He cited two important examples. One concerned the Essenes, the tiny second-century BCE Jewish sect now credited with leaving the world the Dead Sea Scrolls. The Essenes, who lived an austere monastic life, focused on prophesied divine retribution and an impending "last judgment" by God to be visited upon sinful humanity. Cayce mentioned the Essenes in 1936, when he described a female client's incarnation near Jerusalem:

> The entity was what would now, in some organizations, determined a sister superior or an officer of the Essenes. . . . For the entity was associated with the school on the road above Emmaus near the road that goes down toward Jericho and towards the northernmost coast of Jerusalem.*

At the time of this life reading, scholarly opinion held that all Essene groups were exclusively male. But fifteen years later, the remains of Khirbet Qumran, the site of an Essene community like Cayce had described, were excavated just where he said they would be. Graves in the area yielded female as well as male skeletons, thus establishing that the religious community was *not* exclusively male after all.

Cayce's belief in the doctrine of reincarnation is self-evident in the account. A lifetime of such readings had convinced him of the human soul's immortality, its survival after physical death, and its inevitable rebirth in a new body. He regarded reincarnation as no pointless recycling of the spirit but part of the great moral order of the cosmos, in which each material manifestation of life on Earth was conditioned by a previous life—to gain knowledge through experience, to resolve ongoing problems, or simply to serve. In any case, it reaffirmed each individual's sense of purpose and destiny.

---

*This is Cayce Record 1391-1, no. 35–36, from *The Essenes: A Compilation of Extracts from the Edgar Cayce Readings* (Edgar Cayce Foundation, 2006), pages 44–45, https://www.scribd.com/document/326876539/Cayce-Edgar-Evans-Cayce-Edgar-on-Atlantis-pdf.

One of the Qumran caves where the Dead Sea Scrolls—believed to have been hidden by members of an ancient Essene community—were found

The reincarnation theme appears again in another remarkable Cayce life reading from May 6, 1939:

> For the entity was among those spoken of as a 'holy woman,' first the entity coming in contact with those activities at the death and raising of Lazarus and later with Mary, Elizabeth, Mary Magdalene,

Martha; all of these were a part of the experience of the entity as Salome.*

The only mention of Salome in the New Testament describes her as a witness to the Crucifixion, but *not* at the raising of Lazarus. In 1960, however, Dr. Morton Smith, an associate professor of history at Columbia University, discovered a copy of a letter written by Saint Mark. Scholars at the Society of Biblical Literature and Exegesis established its authenticity and ascertained that the document had originally belonged to Clement of Alexandria, who lived in the third century and was one of the Christian Church's most important founding fathers. The copy attributes the story of Lazarus to Mark, though the account had previously been found only in the Gospel of John. Saint Mark's version is virtually the same as Saint John's, save for a minor detail coinciding with Cayce's life reading: Clement of Alexandria's copy states that a woman witness to the miracle was called Salome.

In its present state of deep amnesia, the human race struggles to answer such basic questions as: Who are we? The answers, we are told, will be found in our DNA. Identity, it is argued, is all about our group—race, gender, sexual orientation, and so on—and if DNA is not conclusive, then it is all just a matter of personal choice. We are free to identify with whatever group we choose. Of course, those who have spent a lifetime in that group, and whose dues are paid up, can't be blamed for questioning the credentials of Johnny-come-latelies who would ignore DNA and decide, for political or other reasons, to appropriate membership in another tribe. Not even DNA, though, is good enough for admission to some clubs.

In chapter 20 we reported on controversy surrounding the belief of many Americans that they have Cherokee Indian heritage, but the issue of identity goes far deeper than DNA. Some scientists, such as Rupert Sheldrake, suggest that the most important factor in shaping human identity is morphic fields. Many researchers agree, arguing that beyond the physical body, "biofields" of some kind go further than DNA in accounting for human complexities.

---

*This is Cayce Record 1874-1. You can find it, with explanation, in *Edgar Cayce on Atlantis,* by Edgar Cayce, edited by Hugh Lynn Case (Warner Books, 1968), page 44.

To explain such mysteries these days, the much more ancient, widespread, albeit related notion of reincarnation is regaining lost standing. Strong evidence for the phenomenon is accumulating rapidly, especially in past-life studies of children, as chronicled in Tucker's book.

Moreover, it can be argued that the reincarnation hypothesis goes far beyond explaining extraordinary coincidences, marks on the body, unusual memories, and so on. Viewed through the lens of reincarnation and karma (that is, cause and effect—"you reap what you sow"), human injustice becomes easier to understand, if not to forgive. Even racial hatred takes on a different meaning when one realizes that individuals may be part of an oppressor race in one particular life, but in a subsequent embodiment, they may belong to a victim class—perhaps on the opposite side of some ancient conflict?

The American Civil War, Edgar Cayce said, was a reenactment, with reincarnated characters, from the ancient conflict that destroyed Atlantis. Is it implausible, we wonder, to believe that today's great conflicts are but the latest replay of some very ancient, yet unresolved drama in which the same actors are once again upon the stage?

23

The Battle of Light and Darkness

*Tracking the ancient struggle for
control of the self*

While many of the secular materialists who dominate Western culture and science have applauded the left-leaning policies of Pope Francis I, they have, nonetheless, been dismayed by his emphasis on the role of evil in the world, his frequent mentions of the Devil, and his open advocacy of exorcism. Those who believe that reality can be explained entirely by the effects of ordinary physical laws are much threatened by the notion that invisible and undiscovered forces could underlie visible events, and they seek to dismiss and discredit such ideas as superstition—the unfortunate legacy, they might say, of the very dark history of the human race—or what Carl Sagan called the "demon-haunted world" in his book of that same title.

The Catholic Church, we have been told, still takes evil very seriously, and some of its leaders, including Pope Francis, want the church to be much more aggressive in confronting it. Those suspecting that measures stronger than garden-variety psychotherapy may be needed to deal with the kind of persistent personal evil abroad in today's very dark world may be surprised to learn that in 2016 the Vatican gave a new green light to the practice of exorcism. With formal recognition of the International Association of Exorcists, the Holy See signed off on the practice made familiar to millions in the 1973 film *The Exorcist*—the ancient ceremonial procedure for driving demons out of those possessed by them. Priests desiring to try it, however, were

A ferryman takes souls across the river Styx—in ancient Greece,
the frontier between life and death; engraving by Gustave Doré

told they needed permission from their bishop and that their client
would require examination by medical specialists to rule out psychological issues that might be treatable by other means. Press reports in
September 2016 cited calls from church scholars to increase the number
of qualified exorcists. Psychologist Valter Casciola, a consultant to the
International Association of Exorcists, declared that the lack of priests
capable of fighting the forces of evil was an "emergency."*

---

*Read more about modern-day exorcism in "Exorcism and Demonic Possession Are Now
Tools in the Culture Wars," by Chris Roberts, in *The Observer* (online), January 3, 2019,
https://observer.com/2019/01/pope-francis-exorcism-demonic-possession-culture-wars/.

Among those putting exorcism in the spotlight was the late Father Gabriele Amorth, known as the "Exorcist of Rome," who died in 2016; he claimed to have performed more than 160,000 of the rituals.* The late Benedictine priest Father Pellegrino Maria Ernetti, who died in 1994, at one time was a world-famous practitioner of the craft in the Venice area of Italy.

Recognition of the existence of an ancient warfare between good and evil is certainly not unique to the Catholic or other Christian churches. Moreover, mystics and scholars of many esoteric traditions, from Theosophist to Sufi, Gnostic, and Zoroastrian, have long asserted the need to align with the forces of "light" and to seek to overcome "darkness." The church, with some cause, blames the proliferation of occult and satanic practices through the internet for an upsurge in the number of people falling into the clutches of sheer evil. The case can be made, however, that a failure to educate the next generation to the intense nature of what has also been called by the religiously persuaded the "battle of Armageddon" may be part of the problem.

For centuries, initiates in all schools were carefully and arduously trained in an understanding of and respect for the invisible forces of life, but today, millions are left to stumble upon the truth by accident and, more often than not, to find themselves unprepared for the challenge and unaware that they can and should call for assistance from higher dimensions. Missing for most is any insight into the existence, just beyond the tangible world we live in, of a vast yet invisible sewer—called hell in many traditions, and the astral plane in others—where lurk throngs of lost earthbound entities of every imaginable form and description. Most of these, we learn from various wisdom traditions, are simply parasites who, like mosquitoes, seek any energy they can steal from those fortunate enough to operate in actual physical bodies. Some, however, are much more malevolent. Indeed, say the more illumined teachers, ancient fallen angels, driven by an intense hatred for the natural order, against which—long before Atlantis—they have rebelled, are

---

*Learn more about Father Amorth, and the documentary about his life, from "New Film Documents Famous Exorcist Fr. Gabriele Amorth," by Sr. Rose Pacatte, *New Catholic Reporter* (online), April 19, 2018, https://www.ncronline.org/news/media/new-film -documents-famous-exorcist-fr-gabriele-amorth.

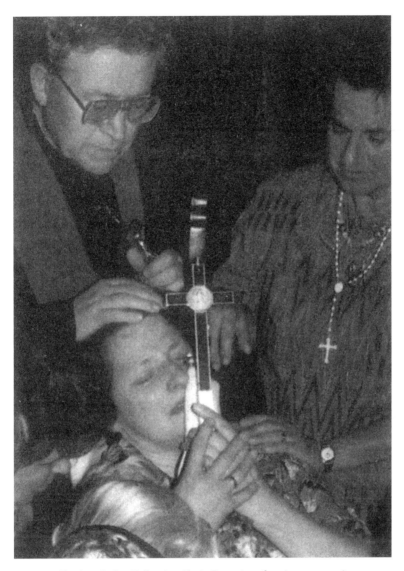

The late Father Pellegrino Maria Ernetti performing an exorcism

still on the prowl. According to this school, the world is in the mess it is primarily because many of these dark spirits have made it into physical bodies like ours, where they collude with their disembodied brethren and, as the King James Bible puts it, are "seeking whom [they] may devour." The blindness of potential victims to the dangers is an important asset for the dark beings, who, according to some accounts, do all they can—through distraction, temptation, outright lies, or anything else that works—to spread the darkness.

The history of the world, poet Ishmael Reed is often credited with saying, is the history of a war between secret societies.* Religion, as we know it, is just the public tip of a very secret "iceberg" by which human activity can, in large measure, be manipulated for good or ill. And just as the real designs of its leaders may have been obscure, so too may the true intent of many religions have been hidden. As with the wind, however, the absence of visibility doesn't mean an absence of force, direction, or intensity. And to the observant, straws in the wind can reveal an ultimate goal. Just as there may be socially approved religions that advance the secret purposes of powers that be, there are also forbidden religions that do not, whose followers must meet in virtual secrecy.

If religion can be defined as a set of beliefs and practices, preserved by its faithful, that proclaim the nature of divinity and his (or her, or its) relationship to the human race, then many people are actually "religious" who do not know it. Even those who deny that a deity exists are themselves religious in that they profess a belief in the nature of deity— namely, that it does *not* exist, a fact they cannot prove, but which they maintain with something very much like faith.

Many thus have come to the opinion that behind the curtain, strings are being pulled, and that preachers of every persuasion, including the secular, the scientific, and the political, proclaim visions claimed to have been revealed to them, even as an ancient and invisible chess match among secret elites has shaped the history of our world and continues to do so.

Today, as never before, the great struggle is focused on the true dimensions of the inner being, and at stake could be the survival of the human soul itself.

THE DWELLER ON THE THRESHOLD

For many esoteric traditions (i.e., for the "initiated"), a key to understanding the ancient warfare of good and evil on both the personal

---

*For a discussion of this attributed quote, see http://www.rawillumination.net/2013/09/reeds-mumbo-jumbo-and-illuminatus.html.

and planetary level is a mysterious phantom called the Dweller (or the Guardian) on the Threshold. According to esoteric scholar Manly P. Hall, "The first great step in the initiations of the ancients was the passing of the strange monster that dwelt on the line between the physical and spiritual worlds." Speaking in 1924, Hall, author of *The Secret Teaching of All Ages,* explained, "The Children of Light were told that they could never go forth into distant lands or earn the wages of Master Builders until they faced with courage and resolve the demon that dwelt ever with them but was invisible until they sought to awaken within themselves the subtle forces of which he was composed." This fearful specter, said Hall, was the sum total of all the sins of each individual, which must eventually be confronted before one can be free of the limitations of mortality.*

The term *Dweller* is usually credited to the nineteenth-century British novelist Edward Bulwer-Lytton. In his novel *Zanoni,* published in 1842, he used the name to refer to a malevolent entity embodying all the darkness accumulated by an individual through all of his incarnations. Bulwer-Lytton described himself as a Rosicrucian, but the Dweller on the Threshold is a concept familiar not only to many spiritual traditions but in psychology and literature as well, especially in the romantic novels of the nineteenth century. Stories like *Dr. Jekyll and Mr. Hyde, The Picture of Dorian Gray,* and even *Moby Dick* draw heavily on the idea that humans are bound by an adversary that they carry about within themselves, which must ultimately be conquered if they are not to be destroyed themselves.

In the *Kung Fu* TV series of the 1970s, Kwai Chang Caine, the lead character, played by David Carradine, remarked at one point (paraphrasing) that if one confronts his Dweller, he does so on his own terms, but if one fails to do that, he must still meet the Dweller, but on the Dweller's terms.

In the Bulwer-Lytton novel, the character of Clarence Glyndon—an English artist aspiring to "the secret knowledge"—is assisting a master alchemist, the adept Zanoni, when he secretly, and disobediently, enters

---

*You can read Hall's original lectures, which he compiled into manuscript form, online at www.manlyphall.info. The quotation here comes from number 29, "Children of the Elements, Part 6: The Dweller on the Threshold," https://manlyphall.info/manuscript-lectures/29-children-elements-6/29-children-elements-6.pdf.

Nineteenth-century author Edward Bulwer-Lytton, who is credited with coining the term *Dweller on the Threshold* in his novel *Zanoni;* 1831 portrait by Henry William Pickersgill

In the 1970s, actor David Carradine played the kung fu master Kwai Chang Caine in pursuit of a spiritual quest.

his master's laboratory and samples a forbidden elixir. The terrifying result is the appearance before him of a hideous female phantom, to whom he finds himself inextricably attached for the rest of his life. The only way Glyndon can relieve himself of the presence of this apparition is by gratifying his lower appetites and reveling in sensual pleasures, essentially squandering his life energy—effectively killing himself by degrees. When he gives in to the phantom's demands, she seems to go away. When he tries to rise above them, she reappears to drag him down again.

"The Dweller of the Threshold," wrote Franz Hartmann, MD, "meets us in many shapes." In *The Theosophist* magazine in 1889,

St. George and the Dragon, taken from
a World War II British military recruitment poster

Hartmann wrote, "The Dweller is the *Cerberus* guarding the entrance to Hades; the Dragon which *St. Michael* [or St. George] is going to kill; the *Snake* which tempted Eve, and whose head will be crushed by the heel of the woman; the *Hobgoblin* watching the place where the treasure is buried, etc. He is the king of evil, who will not permit that within his kingdom a child should grow up, which might surpass him in power; the *Herod* before whose wrath the divine child *Christ* has to flee into a foreign country, and is not permitted to return to his home until the king is dethroned or dead."*

---

*Hartmann's piece was originally published as "The Dweller of the Threshold" in *The Theosophist,* volume 11, in 1889. The article was republished in 1920 by the Theosophical Publishing House in India as pamphlet number 115 of the Adyar Pamphlets series. See https://cdn.website-editor.net/e4d6563c50794969b714ab70457d9761/files /uploaded/AdyarPamphlet_No115.pdf.

On one level, the encounter with the Dweller can be as mundane as trying to overcome a bad habit and replace it with a new one. Making any such change involves a conflict between the object of desire or aspiration and some kind of "dragon." In old folktales, says historian Hugh Shearman, "the hidden treasure, the sleeping beauty, the imprisoned princess was represented as guarded by a dragon or some other fearsome creature. Or if there was no living guardian, there was at least an obstacle of very formidable character."

"In our personal lives, this works at every level," Shearman adds. "Once we have followed for a while a certain course of living, we have acquired a momentum which carries us along, the momentum of habit. A great part of this is unconscious. We are not aware of all the forces in our natures which we have mobilized by our pattern of repeated daily habit in thought, feeling and action. Then for some reason we decide to change direction, to abandon old habits and adopt new ones, to direct our life in some new way. At once we find that we are up against the accumulated momentum or our past, which we had hitherto been hardly aware of."*

THE ADDICTION SYNDROME

In today's world, probably nothing captures the dilemma of the Dweller more than drug addiction and alcoholism. The embrace of toxic self-destructive behavior by a codependent victim in search of some empty reward provided by some abused substance is a familiar pattern. Chemical abuse, though, is far from being the only example of such behavior. Indeed, almost every evil abroad in the world, it seems, can be traced to a hopeless and self-destructive quest for some worthless reward.

The most pervasive substance abuse of the Western world may well be materialism—a great emotional attachment to junk. A deep confusion over the nature of reality, it can be argued, has produced a near universal trance state in which the visible world seems to be made of very solid (i.e., "real") stuff. That illusion of solid boundaries to our existence is, in fact, so strong and so pervasive that any suggestion that

---

*See Hugh Shearman, "The Dweller on the Threshold," *The Theosophist* (April 1977), http://www.katinkahesselink.net/other/shearman43.html.

it might be otherwise, is—if not completely ignored—greeted with derision by fellow inmates. This is true despite the certain scientific knowledge that all material is made up almost entirely of empty space, in which are only dancing force fields of spinning particles and/or waves that our collective senses have agreed to interpret as "solidity." Illusions notwithstanding, everyone dances madly to the music—and very loud music it is. Almost completely drowned out are more subtle signals—the "still small voices"—that speak, not from outside, but from inside of us, attempting to turn our fractured and fevered attention toward freedom and away from the common slavery to crude phenomena, and to cause us to reach for more important, if less noisy, stuff.

An auto junkyard, monument to materialistic addiction

The loss of appreciation for more subtle things like spiritual freedom, we suspect, is at the heart of most of society's ills. Whether it be a reductionist "scientist" insisting that the human brain is the sole source of consciousness, a preacher declaring the Earth is only six thousand years old, or a stickup man relieving us of our wallet, we are left violated—our true worth and depth uncomprehended. Such tyrannies of aggressive salesmanship or just plain brute force would not be possible in a world where the faculties of all were sufficiently developed to free us from the dense yoke of materialism.

Like slavery, materialism can take many forms. In politics, it is fundamental to the strategies of both right and left. On the one hand, personal gain (read that as material wealth) is pursued with little regard for the rights of those unfortunate enough to get in the way. On the other hand, the needs and rights of the individual are sacrificed to some blind ideal of collective good (sold as material prosperity for all). In the mass culture, we see the addiction to consumer goods. In religion, it comes as a hopeless attempt to follow holy writ literally. For reductionist science, it comes as the complete rejection of ideas falling outside the prevailing materialist paradigm.

With so many ways to shackle our minds, it's no wonder that few can summon the strength or the wit to break free and to challenge the collective Dweller on the Threshold. And, lest we forget, the Dweller (or guardian) is not simply an individual phenomenon. According to Manly P. Hall, the Dweller "is really the *sin* body of all creatures who have individual intelligence."

In the twenty-first century, could the ghost of Atlantis be, in fact, the Dweller on the Threshold for the entire enterprise of civilization? If so, we will not move forward until we have faced it.

OTHER WORLDS

Lost civilizations
from outer space

24

The Nukes of Mars

Is there an ancient connection with Earth?

In 2014, Mars One—the European nonprofit organization that aims to send a team of four on a *one-way* trip to Mars in 2024—announced the selection of 705 candidates chosen for the daring mission from a pool of 200,000 applicants. The chance to be one of first humans to set foot on the Red Planet was apparently irresistible to many, even with no chance of return to the home planet. If the Mars One project ever comes off, its intrepid voyagers will have fulfilled an ancient quest, but they might not be the first intelligent beings to set foot on Martian soil.*

Since at least the nineteenth century, the possibility of life on Mars has been one of the great preoccupations of life on Earth. Ever since telescopes have been able to provide enough resolution to identify surface features, there have been those convinced that Mars, like Earth, could be inhabited. In 1877, Italian astronomer Giovanni Schiaparelli made maps of apparently long straight lines on Mars, which he called *canali*, "channels," and named after rivers on Earth. His Italian term was transliterated to English as "canal" and led to the popular notion of a civilized Mars. The idea later became a staple of science fiction, most notably in H. G. Wells's *War of the Worlds* (1897), which featured an invasion from Mars.

About a century later, the idea took a dramatic new turn with the

---

*To check on the current status of the Mars One mission, visit the program's website: https://mars-one.com.

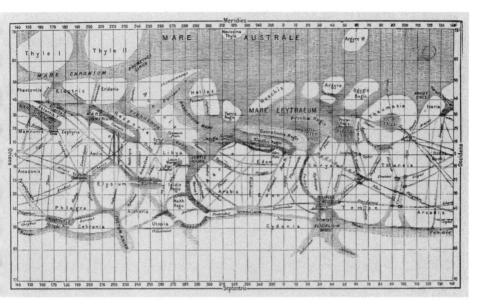

An 1877 map of Mars drawn by Italian astronomer Giovanni Schiaparelli
based on his telescopic observations

2002 publication of *The Monuments of Mars,* by Richard Hoagland. NASA's Viking 1 orbiter had photographed a gigantic and enigmatic humanlike face gazing up from the Cydonia plain, along with the apparent ruins of a city nearby. Controversy over the meaning of that discovery has raged ever since. Dismissed as a trick of light and shadow by NASA, the monuments of Cydonia have yet refused to be fully dismissed, and now some scientists have argued that not only did Mars host ancient civilized life, something like what we find on Earth, but it may also have been a place of death, also like what we have seen on Earth.

Dr. John Brandenburg, a senior propulsion scientist at Orbital Technologies and author of the 2013 book *Life and Death on Mars: The New Mars Synthesis,* assembled compelling evidence that, about 180 million years ago, Mars was the site of a nuclear explosion—one that wiped out much of what existed on the surface, leaving the red-colored desert planet we find today. While many scientists, including geological expert and astronaut Harrison Schmitt, agree that an ancient nuclear event could have occurred, most think it would have had natural causes. Brandenburg, though, thinks the evidence defies natural explanation.

A 1976 satellite image of the Cydonia plain of Mars. The formation at the upper left is the "face" discussed by Richard Hoagland in his book *The Monuments of Mars.*

Dr. David Beaty, NASA's Mars program science advisor, told Fox News that he finds Brandenburg's evidence "intriguing and fascinating," but he wants a Mars probe to investigate the possible site.*

The evidence for a Martian nuclear event appears to radiate from a hot spot over the northern Mare Acidalium region, an area that includes Cydonia. "The spectrum of krypton and xenon isotopes found in the Mars atmosphere, particularly xenon-129 and krypton-80," Brandenburg told *Atlantis Rising* in a recent interview, "are both produced by nuclear explosions, the xenon-129 directly from fission of uranium-238, and thorium by high energy fusion neutrons, and the krypton-80 by intense neutron bombardment of the soil." Mars meteorites found on Earth come from subsurface rock and, relative to Earth rocks, are depleted in uranium, thorium, and potassium, all radioactive

---

*Read the article at John Brandon, "Was There a Natural Nuclear Blast on Mars?," *Fox News*, April 1, 2011, https://www.foxnews.com/science/was-there-a-natural-nuclear-blast-on-mars.

Nuclear physicist
Dr. John Brandenburg,"

elements. However, gamma rays from the Martian surface, as measured by both Russian and American spacecraft, show much higher levels of radiation from two particular hot spots. This adds up to the signature of two possible nuclear events. The data has been confirmed and in May 2013 was published in *Science Magazine.**

Mars at that time, believes Brandenburg—before being attacked— was in something like Earth's Bronze Age. He has no idea who the attacker may have been. That is one of the reasons he believes we need to travel to Mars and see if any records may have been left.

For years, the possibility that nuclear explosions took place on Earth in ancient times has been a subject of much speculation. Evidence of intense heat and high radiation from more than five thousand years ago has been found in the Mohenjo Daro region of Pakistan. Unexplained deposits of glass in the Egyptian Sahara have inspired similar conjecture. In India, the ancient Sanskrit epic poem *Mahabharata* included accounts of events that sound very much like ancient nuclear warfare. Such possibilities were taken very seriously by Robert Oppenheimer, father of the modern atomic bomb.

Strangely, the evidence for nuclear destruction on Mars at least partially corroborates accounts coming from many once derided sources. According to the late Zecharia Sitchin, ancient Sumerian

---

*For a quick breakdown of Brandenburg's theories and others, see Nathan Falde, "Evidence of Major Cataclysm on Mars Which Would Have Destroyed Any Life," Ancient Origins (online), June 22, 2019, https://www.ancient-origins.net/news-science-space /evidence-major-cataclysm-mars-which-would-have-destroyed-any-life-00670.

An artist's depiction of an ancient nuclear explosion on Mars; art by Randy Haragan for the cover of *Atlantis Rising* (September/October 2014) (also see color insert plate 11)

records tell of the destruction of a planet known as Tiamat by a rogue planet called Nibiru. In his 1988 book *Catastrophism and the Old Testament,* Donald W. Patten theorized that a planet called Astra collided with Mars after breaking into pieces, much as Comet Shoemaker-Levy 9 did before hitting Jupiter in 1994. Many esoteric traditions, such as Theosophy, have long held that the asteroid belt between Mars and Jupiter is the aftermath of a collision between a planet known as Maldek and Mars. Whether this might have led to some kind of nuclear event on Mars is unclear, but many intuitive sources have long held that Maldek was destroyed by the nuclear weaponry of a civilization gone mad. Such assertions are easily found on the internet.

Usually known by the name Phaeton, this hypothetical fifth planet—fifth from the sun, that is—was originally proposed by

German astronomer Johann Elert Bode after the discovery of Ceres, largest of the asteroids, in 1801. The notion that the asteroid belt resulted from a planetary collision is known as the disruption theory. Though it has been summarily rejected by mainstream science, new evidence is forcing many to reconsider ideas once dismissed as fringe.

ANCIENT LIFE ON MARS

In 1986, longtime Mars researcher Brandenburg, who coauthored, with Monica Rix Paxson, the book *Dead Mars, Dying Earth,* became the first scientist to stand before a scientific conference and announce the hypothesis that a paleo-ocean once existed on Mars. At the time, the idea seemed absurd to the mainstream planetary science. However, recent visual evidence from the Mars Global Surveyor—of sites where water flowed in the past, and of an ocean shoreline—supports his claim. Perhaps the most telling evidence of the paleo-ocean was from recent images from the Mars Orbiter Laser Altimeter (MOLA), which showed a huge topographical depression in the northern Martian hemisphere where an ocean, covering approximately one-third of the surface of Mars, was located.

The presence of this large body of water on the surface of Mars, claimed Brandenburg, tells us a great deal about the planet's history. For example, the presence of liquid water reveals that temperatures on Mars, currently ranging from –137° to +16°F, were at one time above freezing. This is a remarkable fact. Here is a planet, about half the size of Earth and much further away from the sun (a minimum of 56 million miles further away), that was at one time warm enough for abundant water to flow.

The presence of flowing water and warmer temperatures also reveal that Mars once had an atmospheric greenhouse and much higher atmospheric pressures than it does today. (The atmosphere on Mars today is a mere 1 percent of Earth's.) This atmosphere was probably primarily carbon dioxide, which is, as we all know, a very effective gas for retaining solar energy and warming a planet. However, the red color of the Martian "soil" tells us that there was abundant oxygen on Mars as well. The reddish color is caused by oxidized iron in the Martian terrain, like rust, and is very similar to landscapes seen in the desert southwest in North America and the cracked deserts left by the destruction of Amazon rain forests.

Suddenly we know that the warm, wet circumstance needed for life to emerge was at one time present in our neighborhood—on Mars. But was there life on Mars? The answer is growing in certainty daily: yes. To begin with, although we have never collected and brought back sample rocks from Mars, Mars has actually sent a few to Earth for us to examine.

"Mars sent Earth a love note sixteen million years ago," wrote Paxson in *Dead Mars, Dying Earth.* "Inscribed on a stone, toward the starry ether thrown, it took millions of years to be captured by gravity to take a flaming plunge through the currents of our planet's atmosphere. Fallen and alone, it lay on ancient ice unread for thirteen thousand years. But when its code was broken and its legend read, the message that was etched in stone told humans we are not alone. 'I too have life.'"

It is difficult to imagine how a rock from the surface of Mars could land on our own planet. In fact, it wasn't until we discovered meteorites that we could clearly identify as lunar (because we had collected samples on the moon to compare them with) that we were able to conceive of any solid material arriving here from another body in our solar system. However, although we'd never brought back a sample from Mars, we had run tests on the surface during the Viking mission that allowed us to read the unique signature of oxygen isotopes in meteorites from Mars. So when researchers discovered meteorite ALH84001 lying on the ice in Antarctica, they were able to determine that it was of Martian origin. They subsequently found that it contained microfossils of Martian bacteria, a finding that was strongly bolstered by the discovery of a form of magnetite—produced only by living processes—in ALH84001.*

In October 2011, isotopic analysis indicated that the carbonates in ALH84001 were precipitated at a temperature of 64°F with water and carbon dioxide from the Martian atmosphere. According to Wikipedia, the carbonate carbon and oxygen isotope ratios imply deposition of the carbonates from a gradually evaporating subsurface body of water, prob-

---

*You can see a photo of the meteorite, and read NASA's perspective on it, on the NASA website at https://www.nasa.gov/mission_pages/mars/multimedia/pia00289.html.

ably a shallow aquifer meters or tens of meters below the surface.

It is a little-known fact that the meteorite that was the basis of the NASA announcement of Martian microfossils is just one chapter in an expanding story of exobiology from Mars. For example, John Brandenburg has identified a second category of meteorites, known as carbonaceous chondrites, as Martian, and they contain microfossils in far greater abundance than ALH84001, more like what we'd expect to find at the bottom of a pond on Earth. And that doesn't even begin to illuminate the discoveries of microfossils in other rocks from "out there somewhere."

At the turn of the twentieth century, scientist Svante August Arrhenius advanced the theory of panspermia, which holds that the universe is throbbing with life and this life travels from one cosmic body to another as spores driven by solar pressure. Though Arrhenius won a Nobel Prize in Chemistry in 1903 for his work on electrolysis, the scientific community did not adopt his notion of panspermia. In fact, they ridiculed it. Nevertheless, our understanding that life can survive under very extreme conditions has changed much in recent years. We now know that, on Earth, it is possible for life to thrive deep within hot water vents at the bottom of the ocean, deep under Antarctic ice, in volcanic lava, and even inside nuclear reactors. Does it remain inconceivable that life could survive in the frigid cold of outer space?

A TALE OF TWO PLANETS

As described in a recent paper by Richard C. Hoagland, Martian history can be uncovered in other parts of the solar system.* While most people think of the solar system as stable and predictable, evidence to the contrary streaks through our atmosphere daily as meteors— shattered planetary remains rich in inner core materials. Mars has been nearly destroyed by them.

Mars emerged five billion years ago, we are told, as an independent planet, considerably less dense than Earth, but abundant in water and all

---

*See Richard C. Hoagland, "A New Model of Mars as a Former Captured Satellite: Bimodal Distribution of Key Features Due to Ancient Tidal Stress?," *Semantic Scholar,* 2001, https://www.semanticscholar.org/paper/A-NEW-MODEL-OF-MARS-AS-A -FORMER-CAPTURED-SATELLITE-Hoagland/5569be7a00ab3679ef98192fa09646 89f5ab84f3.

the necessities for life. Described in the Hoagland paper as a "Garden of Eden" planet, Mars had an Earth-like environment then and laid down vast sedimentary formations, as documented by the Mars Global Surveyor. This lasted through 450 million years of relative planetary peace, until, roughly 500 million years ago, a bully arrived and took over the neighborhood—the empty space between Mars and Jupiter. The bully was what some researchers, among them the late national astronomer Tom Van Flandern, call Planet V. It too was part of the original solar system, had its own moons, and was wandering about. There was a "fight" (a clash of energies and momenta). "Blood" was spilled. But when it was all done, Mars had become just another moon of Planet V.*

Dr. Tom Van Flandern's Mars anomalies press conference at the National Press Club in 2001; photo by Paul Nahay

The gravitational pull from the bully planet progressively slowed Mars from twelve hours per rotation to about twenty-four hours, caused tidal bulges to develop at the equator, and put immense stress upon the Martian crust and interior. The tides, of a power and size dwarfing anything ever seen on Earth, scoured great trenches on Mars.

Things continued thus until some sixty-five million years ago, when catastrophe struck. The liberation of Mars came again, but with a devastating carpet bombing that all but destroyed the planet and other parts of the solar system—and coincided with the death of the dinosaurs.

In the Hoagland model, perturbations of another former member

---

*You can read more about Van Flandern's argument in his paper, "The Challenge of the Exploded Planet Hypothesis," *International Journal of Astrobiology* 6, no. 3 (July 2007): 185–97, https://www.cambridge.org/core/journals/international-journal-of-astrobiology/article/challenge-of-the-exploded-planet-hypothesis/3EE7D6DA4F83A9B9F25500F46081AC50.

of the solar system, designated Planet K, around sixty-five million years ago caused it to wander right across the path of Mars, upsetting Mars's spin axis and leaning it over some sixty degrees, before Planet K smashed headlong into Planet V and unleashed an explosion that reduced both to giant bits four to five times the mass of Earth. Mars was squarely in the path of this explosion and received on its exposed side not only a shotgunning of smaller, more energetic debris but soon thereafter the huge, slower pieces, which smashed into the surface with tremendous force, excavating many of the enormous craters we see today. According to Hoagland, this is why Mars is both lopsided and so weird in terms of geological age measurements. The protected side is the crust as it was, which is accordingly thin, but the exposed side has an enormous accretion of Planet V's guts slathered across it. Consequently, it is much thicker than its relatively undamaged counterpart, as well as being of an entirely different composition. This interaction of Mars with Planet K, just prior to the cataclysmic collision of Planet K with Planet V, is also why the heavy southern hemisphere cratering on Mars does not straddle the planet's current equator.

But long before the big chunks arrived, the real damage had been done. The initial withering barrage of millions of half-mile-diameter rocks blew away much of the Martian atmosphere, sending it forever into space. And when Planet V was destroyed, the instant release from that planet's strong gravity freed the Martian oceans, which snapped back to their former global extent, unleashing tidal waves beyond description, which widened and deepened the already existing Valles Marineris (initially begun when Mars was captured a half billion years before) to over three miles deep and three thousand miles long—the largest known canyon in the entire solar system.

A nuclear-winter-like phenomenon then occurred, with a massive drop in temperature leading to the formation of the well-known Martian polar ice caps and the disappearance of the remainder of Mars's water beneath the outer crust, driven by the inexorable demands of spin, pressure, and temperature.

Nor was all well in the rest of the solar system. Venus, according to Hoagland, impacted by the spreading wave of interplanetary debris from the collision, took such a pounding that its surface was totally re-melted, removing all the old craters, superheating and contaminating the atmosphere, and literally knocking the planet into its baffling retrograde spin.

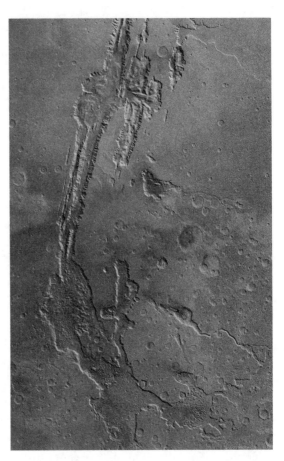

The Valles Marineris formation on Mars, the deepest and longest known canyon in the solar system

Iapetus, one of Saturn's icy moons in the outer solar system, was also plastered by the wave of carbon-rich debris heading outward from the sun, emerging with one light half and one dark—as the most asymmetric colored natural object in the solar system. Earth, too, had an asteroid drop in, which blasted the Yucatán peninsula, taking with it the dinosaurs. Van Flandern thought, and Hoagland agrees, that the deadly planetary collision also accounted for the existence now of both asteroids and comets. The accelerating discovery of more and more asteroid satellites, pooh-poohed only a few years ago by planetary scientists as "dynamically impossible," is fundamental evidence of their formation in this recent planetary cataclysm.

Certainly any future colonizers from Earth will have plenty to investigate when they arrive on Mars. Some of what they find may provide a cautionary tale for their home planet.

25

Searching for ET

New research aims to find an elusive quarry

For years, Hollywood has romanticized the search for life on planets other than Earth—especially the intelligent kind. Since 1960, when astronomer Frank Drake first attempted to deploy a radio telescope to listen for alien radio signals, the search for extraterrestrial intelligence (SETI) has been a key element in many a cinematic story line. Films like *Contact, Independence Day,* and *ET* have offered variations on the theme of earnest, if lonely, researchers striving to lead the world to a new interstellar awareness. The reality, however, has been somewhat less inspiring. The maverick—if not entirely mad—scientist heroes of contemporary mythology have, more often than not, been forced to struggle for respect and funding, while their more conventional brethren have raked in the big bucks.

Dr. Frank Drake

277

Actress Jodie Foster listens for ET in the 1997 movie *Contact.*

Ironically, even those with more exotic notions of ET life have had their differences with SETI. That includes Richard Hoagland, who, in his 1987 book *The Monuments of Mars,* cited as evidence for an advanced ancient alien civilization the giant, seemingly humanoid face on the red planet's Cydonia plain. In an interview with *Atlantis Rising* ("Artifacts on the Moon," *Atlantis Rising* #2, February 1995), Hoagland derided SETI as a "false-front Western town"—ignoring real evidence in order to preserve an entrenched, more Earth-centric way of thinking.

Life for SETI enthusiasts, however, is now changing, and maybe in a big way.

In 2015, at a press conference of the Royal Society in London, the late world-renowned British cosmologist Stephen Hawking announced that he had joined forces with Russian billionaire Yuri Milner to launch a new initiative to search for life amid the stars, on a scale never before attempted. Christened "Breakthrough Listen," the new radio astronomy project is intended to dramatically accelerate efforts already underway. Where earlier researchers have scratched for scraps from a few wealthy patrons, like Microsoft cofounder Paul Allen, in order to fund their efforts, the new plan will lavish a hundred million dollars on the enterprise, and, perhaps, bring a new prestige—maybe even glamor—to the field. Whether that will result in actual discoveries, recognized as such by mainstream science, remains to be seen.

As Hawking sees it, "Life arose spontaneously on Earth, so in an infinite universe, there must be other occurrences of life." In particular, he is excited by recent discoveries of so-called exoplanets in faraway star systems that, at least superficially, resemble Earth. According to Geoffrey Marcy, an astronomer at the University of California at Berkeley, who is given credit for discovering the first exoplanet, "The universe is apparently bulging at the seams with the ingredients of biology." Still, no predictions about how soon ET may be smoked out are being offered, though the program is certainly expected to track him down eventually. Nevertheless, the campaigners believe, the redoubling of effort will increase exponentially the chances of making contact sooner rather than later. Previous efforts, they believe, have been, at best, anemic.

Milner is one of the fifty richest men in the world, says *Fortune Magazine*. His money comes primarily from investments in internet technology, including Facebook. In 2012, he established the Breakthrough Prize to recognize important discoveries in science and math, and while he is making an enormous startup investment, the long-term funding for Breakthrough Listen is expected to come

Stephen Hawking at Cambridge in 2008

Yuri Milner

from crowdfunding on the internet. The enthusiastic public will also be invited to lend the computing power of their smartphones to the project. The Green Bank Telescope in West Virginia and the Parkes Observatory telescope in New South Wales, Australia, are also participating. According to the National Science Foundation, Breakthrough Listen will scan the nearest million stars, both in our own galaxy and in a hundred others that are nearby. The Green Bank Telescope, in fact, is expected to devote a full 20 percent of its observation time to the search for telltale radio signals from another civilization.

Breakthrough Listen, it is said, will generate vast amounts of data, all of which will be available for public analysis, likely constituting the largest amount of scientific data ever made so widely available. The team will use and develop what is expected to be the most powerful software ever for sifting and searching the flood of data. All software will be open source. Both the software and the hardware used in the Breakthrough Listen project will be compatible with those of other telescopes around the world, so any can join the search. Besides using the Breakthrough Listen software, scientists and the interested public will be able to contribute to it and to develop their own applications to analyze the data.*

---

*See the press release about the project: "Green Bank Telescope Joins 'Breakthrough Listen,'" National Radio Astronomy Observatory (online), July 20, 2015, https://public .nrao.edu/news/pressreleases/gbt-breakthrough-listen.

The Green Bank Telescope

IS ET CALLING?

The new project comes on the heels of other recent developments that have also excited the SETI community. Some might argue, in fact, that ET is already calling. While most scientists won't go there yet, they do acknowledge that they have a major puzzle on their hands. An intense burst of unexplained radio activity, it seems, has now been picked up by two major radio telescopes on opposite sides of the globe.

First detected in recordings made at Australia's Parkes Observatory in 2007 by astronomer Duncan Lorimer and his team at West Virginia University, the signal was very distinct and appeared to be emanating from beyond the Milky Way. Later, when similar signals came in from much closer but were not confirmed by any other receivers, they were written off as some kind of fluke. And so the matter rested. In 2014, however, the Arecibo Observatory radio telescope in Puerto Rico reported detection of the same signal.

The big question is, what is it? So far there are several schools of thought. Some think the signal may be caused by pulses from the collapse of supermassive stars. Others believe it may be generated by solar flares from nearby stars. Arguments have been made that it could be some kind of signature for the long-sought dark matter. And yes, some scientists have even begun to speculate about extraterrestrial civilizations. That kind of talk clearly causes heartburn among the scientific elite, but nobody has yet ruled it out.*

In August 1977, Jerry R. Ehman was working on a SETI project for Ohio State University when he picked up an unexplained signal with an apparently intelligent origin. Ehman famously wrote "Wow!" on the computer printout, and ever since it has been called the Wow! signal. The event never recurred and was also written off as a fluke, but it has never been satisfactorily explained to orthodox astrophysicists.

Physicist Paul LaViolette, however, has speculated that the Wow! signal was indeed the work of an extraterrestrial civilization. In his 2006 book, *Decoding the Message of the Pulsars,* LaViolette notes that since 1967, astronomers have been analyzing very precisely timed signals coming from radio-emitting beacons called pulsars. Pulsars, believes LaViolette, are immense navigational beacons created by an ancient spacefaring civilization.†

LaViolette is not the only scientist who thinks the unmistakable signs of ET civilization may be already available to us. In fact, they could be hidden in plain sight in our own backyard.

---

*NPR ran a story on the Arecibo reports and responses to it, and you can listen to it online; see Joe Palca, "Close Encounters of the Radio Kind? Mystery Bursts Baffle Astronomers," on NPR's *Weekend Edition Saturday* (online), July 26, 2014, http://www.npr.org/2014/07/26/335335653/close-encounters-of-the-radio-kind-mystery-bursts-baffle-astronomers?ft=1&f=1007.

†For more on LaViolette's research, see "The Pulsar Mystery" by Len Kasten in *Atlantis Rising* #24, August 2000.

CROP CIRCLES AND OTHER DIMENSIONS

As a case in point, a 2009 study of British crop circles by researchers in England and America pointed to some kind of plasma discharge behind the phenomenon.

BLT Research, a team formed by New York businessman John Burke, Michigan biophysicist William C. Levengood, and British crop circle researcher Nancy Talbott, has analyzed the microscopic changes made in the stalks of crop circle plants and has demonstrated that something very unusual is at work.

In the 1990s, multiple plant abnormalities—including the elongation and stretching of plant nodes, holes blown in the nodes, the distinct bending of nodes, and inhibited seed-head development—in crop circles had been documented at various laboratories in both the United States and Great Britain. Such commonly reported effects, however, accompanied only "genuine" crop circles and were not found in the mechanically flattened creations of various hoaxers.

"We were curious to know," said Talbott in the team's report, "if some of the recent British formations continued to exhibit these same visible plant changes."

After careful comparison between affected plants and controls taken in similar conditions outside the circles, the BLT team concluded that the only known method that could possibly produce the observed effects would be a plasma discharge of some kind.*

A pair of British pub frequenters, Doug Bower and Dave Chorley, famously claimed in the 1990s to be the creators of all crop circles. Like roosters claiming credit for the sunrise, however, they also had their doubters, and the question of who or what—terrestrial or otherwise—is generating the many immense and astonishing images appearing regularly in fields throughout the world, and especially in Wiltshire County of the U.K., remains a mystery, Doug and Dave notwithstanding.

Then, of course, there is the notion that extraterrestrials may inhabit other dimensions, on other planets as well as this one, and

---

*To read BLT's full report, see Nancy Talbott, "Plant Abnormalities Indicate Plasma Discharge in 2009 UK Crop Circles," BLT Research Team Inc. (online), 2009, http://www.bltresearch.com/fieldreports/uk2009.php.

Appearing after a single rainy night in August 2001 at Milk Hill, Wiltshire, England, this giant 900-foot-diameter crop circle captured enormous worldwide interest but has never been satisfactorily explained. It is composed of 409 circles in a pattern called a double, or six-sided, triskelion.

may be able to navigate in nonphysical ways that we do not presently understand.

The eighteenth-century Swedish polymath Emanuel Swedenborg wrote a great deal about ETs that he said he had personally encountered. His first experience with a "nonhuman" personage, he claimed, came in 1744, when he was the head of the Swedish Board of Mines.

One of the most advanced thinkers of his time (or any other time, for that matter), Swedenborg wrote on virtually every area of scientific investigation, including physiology, invention, and brain neurons, about which he made some of the earliest known observations. He was friends with Immanuel Kant and other celebrated thinkers. William Blake, Arthur Conan Doyle, Carl Jung, Honoré de Balzac, Helen Keller, William Butler Yeats, and many others noted that they were deeply influenced by him. The author of more than twenty books, Swedenborg served in many official capacities and, despite his claims of having personally communicated with extraterrestrials, was much celebrated throughout his life.

In his books, Swedenborg described in detail beings from Jupiter, Mars, Mercury, Saturn, Venus, and the moon, as well as from planets beyond our solar system. From his many encounters, Swedenborg concluded that the planets of our solar system are inhabited, and that such an enormous undertaking as the universe would not have been for just one race, nor could only one "heaven" be derived from it.

Beings from other worlds, he wrote, were in contact with him for over a decade and had appeared physically before him. Coming at many times and places, they provided many details about the universe that later became part of conventional thinking. Swedenborg's nebular hypothesis is still widely accepted, and it is believed that in developing the theory, he preceded Immanuel Kant, considered the originator of the hypothesis, by many years. In *Earths in the Universe* (1758), he wrote that the majority of planets in the universe were inhabited. Gradually he came to realize that those beings he met resided spiritually on other planets but could become instantly present on Earth if they chose.

Swedenborg's works were immensely popular in his own time and have been subject to much discussion and study ever since.

EXTRATERRESTRIAL INTERVENTION ON EARTH

Even on the mundane material plane, though, strange new evidence might indicate a previously unappreciated link between this world and others. Consider the case of a minute metallic sphere recently captured by a high-altitude balloon in the U.K. Scientists say it has led them to reconsider the possibility of intelligent intervention in the life of Earth. In fact, astrobiologist Milton Wainwright at the University of Buckingham thinks his team may have found concrete evidence indicating what they call "directed panspermia."

First proposed by DNA pioneer and Nobel Prize winner Francis Crick over forty years ago, directed panspermia suggests that some highly advanced galactic civilization could have seeded life on Earth. If Wainwright is right, the process may still be going on. The original nineteenth-century panspermia theory, as mentioned earlier, holds that the seeds of life could have been carried in a random manner from planet to planet by spores, radiation, comets, meteorites, and so on. Crick, however, thought that the transmission of life from one world to another would have required civilized intelligent intervention.

The Buckingham scientists launched balloons nearly seventeen miles into the stratosphere. When material from one was collected and examined, a small crash mark was found, indicating the spherical object didn't simply land softly. About the width of a human hair, the ball had filamentous life on the outside and a "gooey" biological material oozing from its center.

The possibility of ET origins, Wainright concedes, would be impossible to prove unless "we can find details of the civilization that is supposed to have sent it." In the meantime, there are still those who are willing to speculate.*

CALLING ET

Since its beginnings, the privately funded SETI program has been content to train its radio telescopes toward space and simply to listen for anything unusual—keeping an ear out just in case some other civilization, not unlike our own, might want to strike up a conversation. By all conventional accounts, though—except, possibly, for the Wow! signal—our number has yet to be dialed. For some, though, that is not good enough, and they are determined somehow to break the ice with whatever cosmic lonely hearts may yet be out there.

A group of scientists and investors have now created what they call a continuous message beacon to initiate a conversation with whatever extraterrestrial civilization might be willing to talk. For a small fee, you can include your own message in the nonstop transmission. To carry

---

*See Lee Spiegel, "UK Scientists: Aliens May Have Sent Space Seeds to Create Life on Earth," *Huffington Post* (online), February 13, 2015, updated December 6, 2017, http://www.huffingtonpost.com/2015/02/03/aliens-send-space-seed-to-earth_n_6608582.html.

out their intergalactic hailing plan or courting dance, Dr. Jacob Haqq-Misra and his colleagues have taken over the Jamesburg Earth Station radio dish in Carmel, California.

The project has its critics. Canadian bioethicist, transhumanist, and futurist George Dvorsky views the idea as "both useless and potentially reckless." After all, there is no guarantee that whatever advanced civilizations may be out there are friendly. They could well prove quite nasty. Indeed, who is to say they won't react to our beacon in the way some of us would to the annoying buzz of a fly—by squashing the source? Maybe not, but do we really want to take the chance?*

At least one government on Earth, Russia, admits that an ET invasion would be too much to handle. According to a report from *RIA Novisti,* carried by the *Huffington Post,* the Russian defenses are self-admittedly not capable of defending against an extraterrestrial threat. That may seem obvious, given the advanced technology any interplanetary invader would require just to get here, but the question came up in a recent press conference at the Titov Main Test and Space Systems Control Center near Moscow.

While declaring that his country's defenses were sufficient to handle any earthbound threat, center deputy chief Sergey Berezhnoy noted, quite seriously, that the vast array of available weapons would be inadequate for an extraterrestrial attack.† The Russians are not alone in that regard. Notwithstanding Hollywood speculations, as in *Independence Day,* the military capacities of no country on Earth, including the United States, seem in any way capable of meeting such a threat.

Understandably, military agencies, like the U.S. Air Force, remain reluctant to concede any reality to the alien threat. That might help explain, some feel, the stonewalling of events like the 1947 Roswell affair.

It is equally clear that inviting communication from unknown worlds with unknown agendas could be unwise, if not foolhardy.

Stephen Hawking said for years that he dreaded what an alien

---

*Read Dvorsky's full response online: "New Project to Message Aliens Is Both Useless and Potentially Reckless," Gizmodo, June 12, 2013, http://io9.com/new-project-to-message-aliens-is-both-useless-and-poten-512863567.

†See Lee Spiegel, "Could Earth Defend Itself from an ET Invasion?," *Huffington Post* (online), October 8, 2013.

civilization could do to Earth, perhaps wiping out humans the way we would an ant colony. Hawking's curiosity, however, apparently got the better of him, since he was eager to get on with his Breakthrough Listen initiative anyway.

Oh, by the way, forget about easily identifiable little green men. The aliens may look a lot like us, says a Cambridge University evolution expert. Extraterrestrials that resemble human beings, says professor Simon Conway Morris, should have evolved on at least some of the many Earth-like planets that have been discovered by astronomers in recent years. In his new book *The Runes of Evolution,* Conway builds on the principle of convergent evolution—the idea that different species will independently evolve similar features.*

Who can say the aliens are not here already? After all, how would we know?

Run that through your data processor, SETI geeks.

---

*For a review of Morris's book, see Paul Gallagher, "Forget Little Green Men—Aliens Will Look Like Humans, Says Cambridge University Evolution Expert," *The Independent* (online), July 2, 2015, http://www.independent.co.uk/news/science/forget-little-green -men-aliens-will-look-like-humans-says-cambridge-university-evolution-expert -10358164.html.

26

The Planet X Conjecture

Are we close to finding Nibiru?

In 2016 came credible new claims for the discovery of a long-sought ninth planet in the solar system (with Pluto now excluded, eight remain, officially speaking). The existence of the legendary body, often referred to as Planet X, has been long dismissed as strictly imaginary, but detractors, it turns out, may have spoken too soon.

In his 1976 best-selling book *The Twelfth Planet,* and its many sequels, the late researcher Zecharia Sitchin claimed he had decoded from the ancient cuneiform tablets of Sumeria the story of a mysterious rogue planet that periodically (every 3,600 years) approached the vicinity of Earth. Named Nibiru, the planet was populated, said Sitchin, by a powerful, technologically advanced race of giants known as the Anunnaki, which intervened forcefully in the affairs of Earth, accounting—Sitchin believed—for many of the anomalies of our ancient history. Ever since publication of *The Twelfth Planet,* legions of Sitchin acolytes have searched in vain for scientific evidence for the existence of Planet X.

Arguments over the possibility of another planet beyond the orbit of Neptune have raged since long before Sitchin, but nothing conclusive had ever appeared. Then, in December 2015, fresh scientific news on the subject emerged with the submission of two Swedish papers to the journal *Astronomy & Astrophysics.* The new findings soon rekindled the long-simmering debate and generated headlines around the world. The Swedes claimed to have spotted a new, relatively large body

Planet X as visualized by a NASA artist; the glowing orb in the distance represents our sun.

out in the neighborhood of Pluto. Astronomer Wouter Vlemmings at Chalmers University of Technology, coauthor of both studies, reported observation of an object moving against background stars, which the team dubbed Gna, after a swift Nordic deity who delivers messages for Frigg, the goddess of wisdom.*

Unfortunately, or so it seemed at the time, for Planet X believers, both papers were immediately dismissed by the astronomical establishment. The object reported, it was thought, might possibly be a large asteroid. Nevertheless, further analysis remained to be done, so the file—at

---

*See Ellie Zolfagharifard, "Is There a Super Earth on the Edge of Our Solar System? Controversial Study Says There May Be a Mega-planet Orbiting Our Sun," *Daily Mail* (online), December 11, 2015, https://www.dailymail.co.uk/sciencetech/article-3356577 /Is-SUPER-EARTH-edge-solar-Scientists-say-mega-planet-orbiting-sun.html.

least in theory—stayed open. The big news came in January 2016. "The solar system appears to have a new ninth planet," trumpeted the prestigious magazine *Science*. A new study from two "respected planetary scientists" was making the case this time. According to Konstantin Batygin and Mike Brown of the California Institute of Technology (Caltech) in Pasadena, as published in the *Astronomical Journal*, this discovery is different from all the previously claimed Planet X findings. "We believe it enough," says Brown, "where we're willing to write a paper and stand up and say, 'Yes. For the past century everybody who said there was a Planet X is crazy. And they were all wrong. But we're right.'"*

Astrophysicists Konstantin Batygin and Mike Brown of Caltech

Brown got the first clue to his current conclusions in 2003, when he led a team that found Sedna, an object slightly smaller than both Eris and Pluto. Sedna's odd, far-flung orbit made it, then, the most distant known object in the solar system. Its perihelion, or closest point to the

---

*To read about the discovery, see Eric Hand, "Astronomers Say a Neptune-Sized Planet Lurks beyond Pluto," *Science* (online), January 20, 2016, http://www.sciencemag.org /news/2016/01/feature-astronomers-say-neptune-sized-planet-lurks-unseen-solar-system, and also Jesse Emspak, "A Brief History of the Hunt for Planet X," *Smithsonian Magazine* (online), December 15, 2015, http://www.smithsonianmag.com/science-nature /brief-history-hunt-planet-x-180957551/?no-ist.

sun, lay at 76 astronomical units (an astronomical unit is the distance from the Earth to the sun), beyond the Kuiper Belt and far outside the influence of Neptune's gravity. The implication was clear: something massive, well beyond Neptune, must have pulled Sedna into its distant orbit.

Not everyone is convinced that a new planet has been found. Writing for *Atlantic* magazine in January 2016, science writer Thomas Levenson says, "There aren't any obvious errors in Batygin and Brown's gravitational argument, but nature has plenty of ways to fool astronomers into seeing planets where there are none. Any mass exerts (as Newton saw it) a pull on everything else, and Newton's universal law of gravitation describes how strong that tug will be, and what motion would result. In the case of Neptune and, presumptively, Planet Nine, undiscovered objects reveal themselves in the unexplained residues of motion of what's already been observed, once all the known gravitational influences have been tallied up."*

As for the folks at NASA . . . though they admit they're excited by the possibility of a new planetary discovery, caution still reigns. "The idea of a new planet is certainly an exciting one," NASA's director of planetary science, Jim Green, told the *Christian Science Monitor,* but he qualified, "It's too early to say with certainty that there is a so-called 'Planet X' out there."

Other astronomers have argued that there could be an unseen planet much closer to Earth. Perturbations in Mercury's orbit have led to speculation about a planet in that area, dubbed Vulcan.

BEYOND NEPTUNE

As early as 1906, astronomer Percival Lowell was looking for his own version of Planet X, which he believed was indicated by perturbations observed in the orbit of Neptune. Over the years, there have been several reports of large objects in the Kuiper Belt (i.e., Pluto and Eris), but until now, none has been heavy enough to make a serious claim to the

---

*See Thomas Levenson, "A New Planet or a Red Herring?," *The Atlantic,* January 25, 2016, http://www.theatlantic.com/science/archive/2016/01/a-new-planet-or-a-red -herring/426810/.

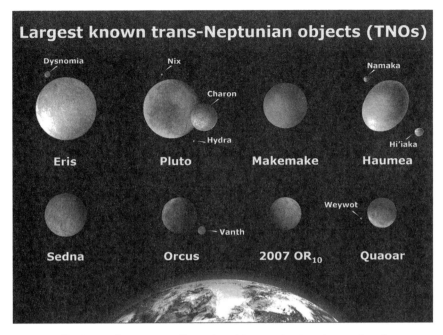

The largest known trans-Neptunian objects—that is, minor or dwarf
planets that orbit the sun beyond Neptune

title of Planet X. The newly discovered body, however, is said to be
nearly as big as the planet Neptune. Though no one has seen it yet, its
presence has been confidently proposed, and other experts have agreed
that the numbers add up.

"The scientists inferred the planet's presence," says *Science,* "from
the peculiar clustering of six previously known objects that orbit
beyond Neptune. They say there's only a 0.007% chance, or about one
in 15,000, that the clustering could be a coincidence. Instead, they say,
a planet with the mass of ten Earths has shepherded the six objects into
their strange elliptical orbits, tilted out of the plane of the solar system." The new ninth planet's orbit around the sun is estimated to take
around fifteen thousand years.*

Neptune itself was discovered in 1846, after the French mathematician Urbain Le Verrier had predicted the existence of a giant planet

---

*Again, see Eric Hand, "Astronomers Say a Neptune-Sized Planet Lurks beyond Pluto," *Science*
(online), January 20, 2016, https://www.sciencemag.org/news/2016/01/astronomers
-say-neptune-sized-planet-lurks-beyond-pluto.

based on irregularities in the orbit of Uranus, and at the time, many observers suspected another planet might be orbiting beyond. Then, after the turn of the twentieth century, Lowell began to argue that discrepancies in the orbits of Uranus and Neptune could be explained by the gravity of an unseen planet. When Pluto was discovered in 1930, many thought it validated Lowell's hypothesis, and consequently it was initially dubbed the ninth planet. In 1978, it was determined that Pluto had too little mass to have produced the observed effects on the orbits of Neptune and Uranus. After further research, including measurements by the Voyager spacecraft, it was decided that Pluto would be better classified as a dwarf planet, leaving the "ninth planet" title vacant.

When Zecharia Sitchin wrote *The Twelfth Planet,* he followed ancient practice and included the moon and the sun on his solar system list. A lifelong student of Sumerian cuneiform text, as well as Hebrew and Egyptian hieroglyphics, Sitchin always insisted that the ancient texts should be read not as myths but, quite literally, essentially as journalism. Forget about Jungian archetypes and metaphysical/symbolic analysis. "If somebody says a group of 50 splashed down in the Persian Gulf, under the leadership of Enki," he told *Atlantis Rising* in a November 1995 interview (#5, "Visitors from Beyond"), "and waded ashore and established a settlement, why should I say that this never happened, and this is a metaphor, and this is a myth, and this is imagination, and somebody just made it all up, and not say [instead] this tells us what happened." Sitchin elaborated his unique explanation of the ancient texts into a vast and detailed history of what he believed were the actual events surrounding mankind's origins. He presented in his books extensive six-thousand-year-old evidence that there is one more planet in the solar system, from which "astronauts"—the biblical Nephilim (giants)—came to Earth in antiquity.

The extra planet, he said, was called Nibiru, or Marduk in Babylonian. This planet, Sitchin argued, had a very eccentric orbit, traveling from far beyond Pluto, cutting across the orbits of the rest of the planets, and then half-circling the sun between Mars and Jupiter, taking 3,600 Earth years in the process. On its closest orbital approach, about 450,000 years ago, a band of Nibiruans known as the Anunnaki landed on Earth in southern Mesopotamia and proceeded to mine gold, evidently needed for their planet's survival. Early efforts in the Persian

Gulf proved inadequate, so underground mining in South Africa was begun.

Unused to such backbreaking toil, the workers ultimately rebelled, precipitating a visit to Earth by Anu, Lord of Nibiru. At a meeting convened to resolve the problem, it was decided to genetically engineer a race of slave workers by crossing the ape-like creatures then inhabiting Earth with the Anunnaki. About 300,000 years ago, after a period of trial and error, the "perfect model" of a primitive worker was achieved by implanting the engineered embryo into the womb of a "birth goddess." Mass production quickly followed. The rest, according to Sitchin, was history.

The late Zecharia Sitchin

ET INTERVENTION

Of course, the idea that our planet has hosted visitors from other worlds who have played an important yet secret role in our history—and, perhaps, the fall of Atlantis—has become very popular in recent years. The research of best-selling authors like Sitchin and Erich Von Däniken (*Chariots of the Gods*) has been spotlighted by the History Channel's *Ancient Aliens* show. The idea of alien intervention in the affairs of

Earth in both the past and the future could be deemed more plausible if the home planet of the visitors is within our own solar neighborhood, and not light-years away. Certainly many of those who believe that the mysteries of advanced ancient technology on Earth are best explained by alien intervention see support for their viewpoint in the recent planetary discoveries. The same is also true for fans of science fiction who have witnessed many developments first described in their favorite reading material.

Science fiction, after all, has been right about many amazing things, and some have even speculated, over the years, that SF writers must have had access to secret and authoritative sources of information. As researcher William B. Stoecker explained in "Foreseeing the Past" (*Atlantis Rising* #94, July/August 2012), some writers of the genre do "seem to have had knowledge of our own mysterious past, as well as knowledge of the present, unavailable to most people." He cites Jonathan Swift's famous satire *Gulliver's Travels,* seen by some as early science fiction, which in 1726, over a century before their discovery, mentioned the two moons of Mars. Swift said they orbited at three and five diameters of Mars in orbital periods of 10 and 21.5 hours. The actual moons orbit at 1.4 and 3.5 Martian diameters from the red planet, in 7.6 and 30.3 hours. While not exact, this is pretty close for a coincidence.*

In their 1966 book *Intelligent Life in the Universe,* astrophysicists I. S. Shklovskii and Carl Sagan devoted a chapter to arguments that scientists and historians should seriously consider the possibility that extraterrestrial contact occurred during recorded history. Though Shklovskii and Sagan stressed that these ideas were speculative and unproven, the authors argued that sub-light-speed interstellar travel by extraterrestrial life was a certainty when considering technologies that were established or feasible in the late 1960s; that repeated instances of extraterrestrial visitation to Earth were plausible; and that prescientific narratives can offer a potentially reliable means of describing contact with aliens.

Sagan illustrated this hypothesis by citing the 1786 expedition of French explorer Jean-François de Galaup, comte de La Pérouse, which

---

*For more details on Jonathan Swift's predictive capacities, see Steven Novella's post "Jonathan Swift Predicted the Moons of Mars," *Neurologica* (blog), July 11, 2008, https://theness.com/neurologicablog/index.php/jonathan-swift-predicted-the-moons-of-mars/.

The late Carl Sagan

made the earliest first contact between European and Tlingit cultures in the American Northwest. Record of that contact was preserved as an oral story by the preliterate Tlingit. Over a century after its occurrence, it was then recorded on paper by anthropologist George T. Emmons. Although it is framed in a Tlingit cultural and spiritual paradigm, the story remained an accurate telling of the 1786 encounter. According to Sagan, this proved how "under certain circumstances, a brief contact with an alien civilization will be recorded in a re-constructible manner." He further states that "the reconstruction will be greatly aided if (1) the account is committed to written record soon after the event; (2) a major change is effected in the contacted society; and (3) no attempt is made by the contacting civilization to disguise its exogenous nature."*

Additionally, Shklovskii and Sagan cited tales of Oannes—a fishlike being attributed with teaching agriculture, mathematics, and the arts to early Sumerians—as deserving closer scrutiny as a possible instance of paleocontact due to its consistency and detail.

---

*See I. S Shklovskii and Carl Sagan, *Intelligent Life in the Universe* (San Fransisco: Holden-Day, 1966).

During World War II, natives on numerous Pacific Islands, exposed to the technologies of advanced civilization for the first time, became dependent on the supplies brought by cargo flights and subsequently formed what became known as "cargo cults." Foreign soldiers were deified and worshipped for the bounty they delivered, and continued to be long after they had left.* Many believe the experience of the islanders is equivalent to that of ancient people encountering extraterrestrial visitors. Richard Hoagland, author of *The Monuments of Mars,* claims that NASA, which had studied the cargo cult phenomena, from the time of its inception, made it policy to withhold any evidence of extraterrestrial civilization from the public, precisely because of the fear that we might be destructively influenced by contact with any advanced off-planet society.

There are others who argue that ET influence in our past may not consist entirely of the kind of crude physical events envisioned by materialist scientists who dominate today's culture. Indeed, some, like Swedish polymath Emanuel Swedenborg, have claimed that intercommunication between this world and others has been going on for millennia, but in subtle spiritual ways well beyond the capacity of most earthlings to fully appreciate.

Whatever the nature of any new ninth planet, or any potential life thereon, it seems unlikely that it will to be able to interface with Earth anytime soon. Like other objects in its Kuiper Belt neighborhood, it is a very long way from Earth. Its closest approach to the sun, in fact, is seven times farther than that of Neptune, and in its outward journey it may well travel far beyond any of the frozen worlds we have identified so far. In the meantime, scientists are continuing to scan the skies, mostly from an observatory in Hawaii, in hope of eventually laying eyes on our elusive distant neighbor. But don't look for any emissaries to drop by.

---

*For more details on the cargo cults, see Peter M. Worsley, "50 Years Ago: Cargo Cults of Melanesia," *Scientific American,* May 1, 2009; originally published May 1959, https://www.scientificamerican.com/article/1959-cargo-cults-melanesia/.

27

Ancient Astronaut Theory

Reality or science fiction?

In the wake of the success of the History Channel's *Ancient Aliens,* it should come as no surprise that the original idea of extraterrestrials influencing the development of civilization on Earth is now attributed to many. According to Dr. Gregory Little—researcher, publisher of the online magazine *Alternate Perceptions,* and regular contributor to *Atlantis Rising*—who has studied the matter extensively, the ancient astronaut hypothesis has been attributed to everyone from horror writer H. P. Lovecraft to popular astronomer Carl Sagan, but few contemporary researchers really understand the true origins of the concept.[*]

For today's followers of UFO-ology, Erich Von Däniken's 1968 blockbuster best seller *Chariots of the Gods* provided an introduction to the subject, and Zecharia Sitchin's 1976 best seller *The Twelfth Planet,* with its extensive account drawn from ancient Sumerian cuneiform texts, filled in the details. Both books led to many sequels, which remain massively popular and inspired the History Channel series. Many documentaries, books from like-minded writers, and virtually religious fervor from true believers have ensued. For mainstream

---

[*]See Gregory Little, "The True Origins of the Ancient Astronaut Idea," *Alternate Perceptions Magazine,* September 2014, http://www.apmagazine.info/index.php?option=com _content&view=article&id=570:archaeotrek-august-2033&catid=2&Itemid=44, and its followup, "The Origin of the Ancient Astronaut Idea: Archaeology Textbook Reveals That Everyone Is Wrong," December 2014, http://www.apmagazine.info/index.php?option=com _content&view=article&id=598:archaeotrek-august-2047&catid=2&Itemid=44).

Erich Von Däniken

academic scholars, however, the very suggestion that there could have been intelligent intervention in human history from other worlds has always been taboo, if not outright anathema.

Clearly threatened by the immense popularity of the notion, orthodoxy seems more than willing to trash any heroes of ancient astronaut lore. "Skeptics," says Little, "will seemingly go to great lengths to demean the Ancient Aliens idea." The very idea, they will say, was plagiarized from science fiction. However, even if science fiction could be shown to have contributed some inspiration for the hypothesis, that is not the same thing as disproving it, and Little goes into considerable detail in debunking such arguments.

SCIENCE FICTION AND SPIRITUALISM

Seeming connections between science fiction and what might be called "ancient astronaut theory" can be found well into the past, and certainly long before Sagan or Lovecraft. *The War of the Worlds* by H. G. Wells, for example, first published in 1897, described an invasion from Mars, but it was by no means the first book to make us worry about ET intervention. Three years earlier, French astronomer and science fiction writer Camille Flammarion had published *Omega: The Last Days of the World,* imagining how telepathic communication from other worlds could alter the course of history on Earth. Years later, prolific science fiction writer Edgar Rice Burroughs would speculate on telepathic links and out-of-the-body travel between Earth and Mars.

The so-called Flammarion wood engraving, by an unknown artist, which first appeared in Camille Flammarion's 1888 book *L'Atmosphère: Météorologie Populaire.*

Other vintage science fiction books that made ancient astronauts their central theme include William Windsor's *Loma, a Citizen of Venus,* published in 1897, in which Loma comes to Earth specifically to influence a young girl and a physician in order to advance civilization. In *Aleriel, a Voyage to Other Worlds,* by W. S. Lach-Szyrma, published in 1885, ETs influence the formation of Christianity. Another novel, *Two Planets,* published in Germany by Kurd Lasswitz in 1897, tells of a Martian outpost at the North Pole; the advanced Martians take some earthlings back to Mars.

As early as 1871, novelist Edward Bulwer-Lytton, in *Vril: The Coming Race,* envisioned a technologically advanced civilization secretly surviving beneath the surface of the Earth in vast spaces connected by long tunnels. Years later, the book would become very popular with Nazis. Though the inhabitants of this subterranean world were said to be descendants of a prediluvian surface civilization, their great advancement sharply distinguished them from the ordinary surface humans, whom they ultimately attempted to conquer. The underground world, it was said, was highly telepathic.

Another book published around the turn of the twentieth century was *A Dweller on Two Planets,* by Frederick Spencer Oliver, which detailed the forgotten yet highly advanced world of Atlantis before its final destruction in about 10,000 BCE, and the continuing hidden and subtle relationship between Earth and a higher civilization on Venus, also known as Hesper. For the initiated, Venus is understood to be much more than the seemingly hellish and uninhabitable world observed by conventional astronomy today. Life can be established, it is argued, and can successfully evolve in many dimensions that cannot be detected by garden-variety consciousness on Earth. According to this line of thinking, when modern science examines Venus, it sees only that which corresponds to frequencies to which life on Earth is presently linked. Meanwhile, life existing on bands unfamiliar to observers on Earth cannot be detected. The same, it follows, would hold true with other extraterrestrial worlds. Such notions have gained some academic scientific support in recent years under the heading of multiverse theory.*

Oliver finished writing *Dweller* in 1897 and published it in 1905. It is said to be an account of the life of the "true" author, identified as "Phylos the Thibetan." The story deals with deep esoteric material, including karma and reincarnation. It also describes technology attributed to Atlantis, including flying craft called vailx. Though similar technology may be familiar today, Oliver wrote about it well before the invention of the airplane and even included illustrations depicting the craft. Just as some in the critical establishment have claimed that Erich Von Däniken's work was plagiarized, so have some attempted to suggest that Edgar Cayce, the famed sleeping prophet of Virginia Beach, borrowed much of his own story of Atlantis from Oliver's account.

But while skeptics may have difficulty explaining—without resort to accusations of collusion—how such widely separated accounts could share so many details, a simpler answer might be that the stories are

---

*Read more about multiverses in "Parallel Universes: Theories & Evidence," by Elizabeth Howell, on Space.com, May 10, 2018, https://www.space.com/32728-parallel-universes.html.

Vailx dream; art by Randy Haragan for the cover of *Atlantis Rising* (January/February 2015)

Vailx illustration from *A Dweller on Two Planets*

Elizabeth Clare Prophet

based on shared experience of dimly recalled yet subconsciously significant events, preserved through either race memory or reincarnation. Certainly the Spiritualist movement—very influential in the late nineteenth and early twentieth centuries—had an impact on all of these writers. Many of them were self-described spiritualists or were followers of the Theosophy movement founded in the 1870s by H. P. Blavatsky and Henry Steel Olcott. Madame Blavatsky wrote at length about life on other worlds, and her views were later preserved and perpetuated by other theosophical teachers like Annie Besant, Rudolph Steiner, and Alice Bailey. The tradition continues today in related activities like the "I AM" movement, led by Guy and Edna Ballard, and the Summit Lighthouse, founded by Mark and Elizabeth Clare Prophet. All share a belief that human consciousness is capable of interdimensional navigation and that it is possible, by inner faculties alone, to journey to other worlds and to communicate directly with the inhabitants.

THE OAHSPE

One of the most striking examples of the Spiritualist influence in the 1880s, according to Dr. Little, was *Oahspe*. Even today, investigators continue to sift through claims made in this immense, nine-hundred-page volume published in 1882. John Ballou Newbrough (1828–1891), a New York dentist, reportedly produced the book through "automatic writing." Touted as a history of the past twenty-four thousand years, it was widely read and was popular in Spiritualist circles. Ostensibly the

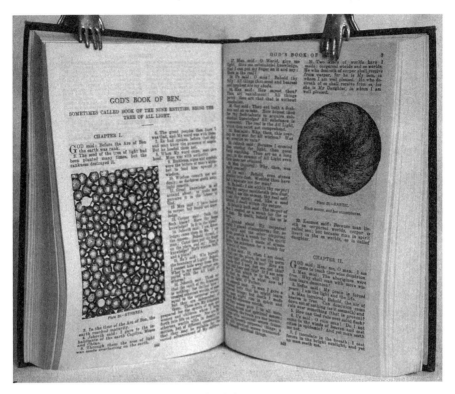

The *Oahspe*

secret history of Earth, the book offered details of extraterrestrial powers said to have influenced the development of humanity. *Oahspe* sometimes calls the extraterrestrials "angels" but makes it clear that they are physical beings performing the work of their leaders (called "gods"). In essence, the *Oahspe* is another version of ancient astronaut theory.

The *Oahspe* describes literally legions of flying ships coming to Earth in ancient times from other worlds to teach mankind. Several hundred pages are devoted to descriptions of the craft that travel between planets and star systems—and to their many inhabitants. The book makes it clear that there are "hundreds of millions" of these extraterrestrials.

According to Dr. Little:

From the contents of the *Oahspe,* there can be no doubt, the gods and their legions of angels are flying around the universe. . . . [Their craft] are called fire-ships, star-ships, and dozens of other names. There are many inhabited worlds throughout the universe but the fire-ships are said to be the vehicles of god and angels. . . . The *Oahspe* reveals that just as we need ships to cross our oceans that the gods and their angels [physical beings] need ships to cross the 'atmospherean' oceans between planets. The ships usually remain invisible because man would fear them if he were able to see them.

According to the *Oahspe,* "Early in man's development the angels descended from the heavens in their fire-ships to teach man. They first raised man upright and then taught him to dwell together in cities and nations."

EMMANUEL SWEDENBORG

Little believes that the individual who deserves the most credit for the ancient astronaut hypothesis is the eighteenth-century Swedish polymath Emmanuel Swedenborg. World famous in his own time, Swedenborg was a confidant of kings, queens, inventors, physicians, and theologians. He wrote more than twenty books, served in many official capacities, and continued to be well respected even after his ideas about life on other planets were made public. Details of Swedenborg's story have been previously discussed in chapter 25.

In 1758, Swedenborg devoted an entire book, *Earths in the Universe,* to life on other worlds. Beings from those worlds, he explained, had

Emanuel Swedenborg

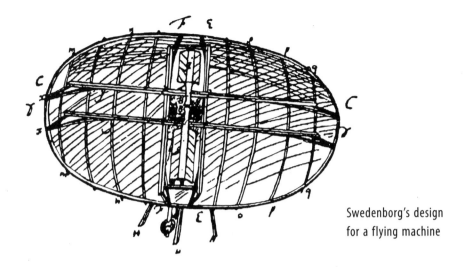

Swedenborg's design
for a flying machine

been in contact with him for over a decade and had physically mani-
fested in front of him. He related that these beings came to him in several places and provided information about the universe, and that the
majority of planets in the universe were inhabited. Gradually, he said,
he had come to realize that those which he had seen resided spiritually on other planets, but that they could become physically real if they
chose. He spoke of beings on Mars, Venus, the moon, Saturn, Mercury,
and Jupiter. He also wrote of many other inhabited planets outside our
solar system. Swedenborg's works were immensely popular in his time
and have been subject to much "interpretation" ever since. Some have
taken his reports more as depictions of human "spiritual states" as they
would exist on various planets. In some ways, says Little, this is similar
to what Edgar Cayce later called "planetary sojourns."

While a few modern writers want to give the credit to others for
depicting life on other planets and wondering how it might influence
Earth, the fact is, Little believes, Swedenborg was the first, and most
detailed. Moreover, he was the one likely most responsible for the birth
of the Spiritualist movement and its many subsequent variations.

EXPLAINING EARTH'S MYSTERIES

Some have cited the Hindu Vedic scriptures as evidence of extraterrestrial intervention in Earth's ancient past. The late Dr. V. Raghavan, a

Sanskrit scholar at the University of Madras, was convinced that the many references to flying machines, ray weapons, advanced chemistry, and other science-fiction-like technology in the scriptures are clear evidence that at least four thousand years ago, India was host to ETs. Dr. Little doesn't rule out such claims but underscores that such evidence is irrelevant to his claims about the origins of ancient astronaut theory: "[Vedic India] did have a lot of flying ships and death rays, but claims that their origins were from 'elsewhere' [i.e., extraterrestrial in origin] aren't so clear. If there is anything in the ancient literature mentioning that the opposing sides in the battles came from other worlds, I don't know about it."

Accounting for the mysterious advancement of ancient civilization on Earth certainly does not require a belief in extraterrestrial intervention—not the physical kind, anyway. In fact, the entire controversy serves to highlight a split in human thinking that can also be found in other debates: the materialist versus the mystical.

The materialists believe that the primary reality of all things is physical. Their ranks would include, but are not limited to, most mainstream scientists. On the other side is what might be called the metaphysicalists, including, but not limited to, mystics and most New Agers. Most ancient astronaut proponents appear, just as with orthodox science, to be motivated by a desire to find a physical explanation for the otherwise virtually unexplainable. Giorgio A. Tsoukalos, heir apparent to the Erich Von Däniken empire and primary commentator on the History Channel's *Ancient Aliens,* recently said, regarding the hypothesis that angels could actually have been physical beings and not merely spiritual, "At last, an explanation that makes sense."

What makes sense to a materialist, though, is not necessarily the only possible explanation for much that we know to be true. And even though that possibility could be very threatening to mainstream—or fundamentalist—science, discoveries in quantum physics, including ideas like nonlocality and entanglement, make it clear that ultimate truth could be more friendly to mysticism than to materialism. Typical of the new kind of thinking is the concept of biocentrism. Its chief proponent, renowned biologist Dr. Robert Lanza, says life after death is real and can be proven.

"The universe only exists," he says, "because we are *conscious* of it." In such a world, interplanetary travel might, it seems, be feasible without resort to any of the physical apparatus (i.e., spacecraft) that we now consider essential.*

Were the spectacular achievements of our ancient predecessors the result of ET intervention? But if aliens helped us, then who helped the aliens? Could there be explanations other than the popular ones? Writer William Stoecker believes we should not rule out the influence of a benign guiding spirit. In "Ancient Astronauts or Guiding Spirit? The Mysterious Origins of Ancient Technology" (*Atlantis Rising* #89, September/October 2011), he points out that benevolent spirits may be behind many of our greatest achievements. A case in point is that of German chemist Friedrich August Kekule, who figured out the structure of the benzene ring in 1865 after a kind of waking dream of serpents seizing their own tails.

Could the nature of reality actually be fully comprehensible to us all if it were not improperly perceived through superstitious belief systems like materialism? In chapter 21, we examined Plato's parable of the cave, in which prisoners chained in a cave and watching shadows on the opposite wall mistakenly conclude that the shadows are the source of the voices they can hear. Ultimately the prisoners are freed and discover the fire at the mouth of their cave, and they learn that it was their jailers who were casting the shadows and doing the talking. At first the newly enlightened prisoners must struggle to comprehend the unfamiliar world they now see, but eventually their eyes and their imagination adjust to the light, and reality becomes clear.

Could pinpointing the source of ancient mysteries depend more on the quickening of our own *inner* vision than on any conquest of *outer* space? Someday, perhaps, when we have mastered the challenges of Earth, we will simply open our eyes and behold the glowing truth directly.

---

*You can learn more about biocentrism in Lanza's 2009 book, *Biocentrism: How Life and Consciousness Are the Keys to Understanding the True Nature of the Universe.*

SIGNS OF A CRIME

----

*Cover-ups and conspiracies
to bury the truth*

Once and Future Psychos

Considering the pathological factor

When the first millennium CE rolled over, civilization, such as it was, we are told, went nearly mad with fear for the world's impending end. A thousand years later, the same fears reappeared. Once more, the times were said to be those foretold by prophets of both good and ill.

Could the anticipation of dreadful events have been overrated, or were they simply premature? Twenty years into the new millennium, even after the hysteria of 2012, at a time when most economic news seems positive, and most of us have embraced the high-tech possibilities—from smartphones to smart cars—of the digital age, we still face technological nightmares of dystopian proportions, not unlike *1984, Brave New World,* or worse.

Not a few Americans, indeed, have begun to worry about the dangers of artificial intelligence, and alarm bells have begun to sound in some unexpected quarters. From the late astrophysicist Stephen Hawking to Bill Gates, Elon Musk, and Steve Wozniak, many at the cutting edge of science and technology appear quite frightened at the prospect of out-of-control robots turning on their makers.

The possible dangers once reserved to science fiction, such as HAL 9000, the out-of-control computer in *2001,* now, with the rise of drone technology and remote killing machines of all sorts, seem very possible. Do we really have to worry that AI could soon surpass human intelligence and take control of our world? Maybe not, but what if the "benign" artificial intelligence now emerging turned psychotic?

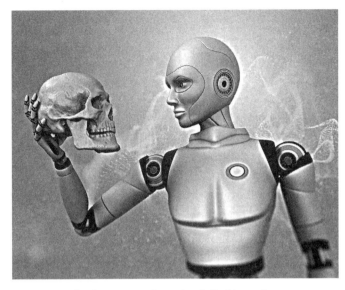

A robot contemplates the skull of its maker

HAL 9000 as a psychopath; art from *Atlantis Rising*

Scientists at MIT—intentionally, to make that very point—claim to have created the first "AI psychopath." Dubbed Norman after the title character in Alfred Hitchcock's notorious film *Psycho,* the computer was fed a steady diet of horrifying pictures by its programmers and then presented with a series of seemingly innocuous ink blot tests.

Sure enough, the computer read the images as scenes of terror and horror. The lesson to be drawn: unscrupulous programmers can turn computers into psychopaths, capable of immense evil without remorse, and which, incidentally, can be made to replicate themselves.*

Hawking, who very much feared AI, once commented, "If people design computer viruses, someone will design AI that improves and replicates itself. . . . This will be a new form of life that outperforms humans."

While such nightmarish possibilities might not seem an immediate threat, it is worth remembering that, for decades, entire generations of computer-literate children have been fed—in both their news and their entertainment—a steady diet of destructive and horrifying imagery. Could the fruit of that process be a tech-savvy and self-loathing population bent on destroying itself and its own machines?

A 2019 report from the Center for the Governance of AI (CGAI) at Oxford University suggests that many people are concerned about where artificial intelligence might lead next, contradicting the view held in some quarters that the threat has been exaggerated to lend weight to the claims of techies touting the power of their own industry. The prospect of unrestrained "advances" in AI, and many other disturbing technologies—from genetic engineering to warfare in space—is worrisome to many in the extreme.†

GOOD INTENTIONS?

The Pentagon's Defense Advanced Research Projects Agency (better known as DARPA) is exploring the possibility of using genetic engineering to create organisms that could, in theory, make Mars habitable for humans.‡ The idea would be to assemble the DNA of plants that could

---

*To learn more about the MIT project, see "Meet Norman—the World's First 'Psychopathic Artificial Intelligence' Unveiled by MIT," Sky News (online), June 12, 2018, https://news.sky.com/story/meet-norman-the-worlds-first-psychopathic-artificial-intelligence-unveiled-by-mit-11402216.

†The CGAI report was based on a 2019 survey of two thousand U.S. adults. See Baobao Zhang and Allan Dafoe, *Artificial Intelligence: American Attitudes and Trends* (Center for the Governance of AI, Future of Humanity Institute, University of Oxford, January 2019), https://www.fhi.ox.ac.uk/aipublic2019/.

‡For more on the story, see Jason Koebler, "DARPA: We Are Engineering the Organisms That Will Terraform Mars," *Vice* (online), June 24, 2015, https://www.vice.com/en/article/ae3pee/darpa-we-are-engineering-the-organisms-that-will-terraform-mars.

An artist's conception of a terraformed Mars;
image courtesy of Ittiz (also see color plate 7)

not only survive but thrive, and could build up the atmosphere to something in which humans could live—i.e., to turn the red planet green.

While not explicitly admitting to the pursuit of such a project, the deputy director of DARPA's Biological Technologies Office, Alicia Jackson, told a biotech conference in 2013, "For the first time, we have the technological toolkit to transform not just hostile places here on Earth, but to go into space not just to visit, but to stay."

According to Jackson, DARPA has already developed software, called DTA GView, that maps genomes in fine detail and gives scientists a new way to mine the huge genetic library that has been amassed. The long-term plan is to pick and choose preferred genes from a number of species, combine them, and create new organisms. The agency will start with simple bacteria and microorganisms. More complex organisms will come later.

It is all part of a long-term plan for terraforming, which would seek to seed on Mars plants that use photosynthesis to generate gases that would transform the atmosphere ultimately into something that humans could breathe.

For those who worry over whether or not humanity is qualified to take on such godlike responsibilities, proponents argue that because the target planet, Mars, is virtually dead anyway, science should be given a pass. However, the idea is first to "rehabilitate" tracts of land that have been devastated by natural or man-made disasters here on Mother Earth.

Some, alarmed by the prospect of that kind of experimentation, point out that the U.S. Environmental Protection Agency (EPA), whose job it is to shield us from such devastation, is now reaping the unforeseen consequences of its own unforced errors. A massive spill of three million gallons of contaminated wastewater from an abandoned Colorado gold mine in 2013 is a good example. The cost of cleaning up the EPA's mistake will run into billions of dollars.*

The road to environmental hell, it seems, may well be paved with good intentions.

In 2016, fear generated by an epidemic of babies born with micro-cephaly (an abnormally small and deformed head) spread worldwide. Commonly believed to be caused by a mosquito-born virus known as Zika, the situation led to a wave of intense countermeasures, and then suspicion arose that the real cause of the birth defects was not Zika but, instead, pyriproxyfen, a larvicide manufactured by a Japanese subsidiary of the Monsanto chemical company, which was, ironically, intended to destroy the Zika-bearing mosquitoes.

Monsanto denies the claim. However, a group of doctors in Argentina came forward to argue the point. Calling themselves Physicians in the Crop-Sprayed Towns, the doctors pointed out that there had been previous Zika outbreaks, infecting as much as 75 percent of a population, without resulting birth defects. In 2014, though, as part of a massive state-run mosquito control program, pyriproxyfen

---

*See Matthew Brown, "Interior Finds EPA Caused Mine Spill It Hoped to Avoid," *Washington Post* (online), October 22, 2015, https://www.washingtonpost.com/politics/epa -faulted-for-3-million-gallon-spill-of-wastewater-from-gold-mine/2015/10/22 /d2a30b70-78fe-11e5-bc80-9091021aeb69_story.html.

Emergency retaining ponds at the Gold King Mine spill site near Silverton, Colorado
(also see color insert plate 8)

had been introduced into drinking water supplies in the affected areas. Its intended effect was to produce malformations in the mosquitoes. Colombian president Juan Manuel Santos stated publicly that he saw no evidence linking microcephaly with Zika, and many communities began to rethink their mosquito control strategies, fearing that they could be contributing more to the problem than the solution.*

If, indeed, pyriproxyfen was the cause of the birth defects, it would not have been the first time that chemical pesticides had proven worse than the conditions they were intended to cure. Previous culprits have included DDT, Agent Orange, and malathion.

THE STANDARDS OF EVIL

Whether or not the chances of catastrophe are increasing, the expectations of such eventualities certainly are, and if human consciousness has anything to do with shaping the world around us, we must conclude that, by that factor alone, the possibilities for evil have been augmented and an old-fashioned reductionism/materialism at the heart of

---

*See Reed Johnson and Rogerio Jelmayer, "Brazil State Bans Pesticide after Zika Claim," *Wall Street Journal* (online), February 15, 2016, https://www.wsj.com/articles/brazil -state-bans-pesticide-after-zika-claim-1455584596.

politically correct thinking could be leading to growing acceptance of some things once considered evil.

University of California professors Jan Stets and Michael Carter, who have studied the issue, think we have good reason to be concerned. Convinced that life is really nothing more than chemical reactions brought about by the interplay of random forces, modern intellectuals have always had something of a problem with concepts like morality and ethics. After all, what rational basis can there be—in an entirely impersonal universe—for anything but looking out for number one? For Stets and Carter, the answer is to be found in a socially sensitive self-image, where a kind of "moral identity" standard prevails. When the standard is set low, as they suggest it is with bankers, stockbrokers, mortgage lenders, gangsters, and so on, shame and guilt are not sufficient to impede bad behavior. When it is set high, as, we infer, it is with saints and politically correct role models, the impulse to do socially unacceptable things is impeded. And that, the professors suggest, is how we get "good guys" and "bad guys." Forget about John Wayne, noble ideals, and all that. It is all a matter of behavioral conditioning.*

The irony is that such arguments are actually popular with both ends of the political spectrum. The right, as epitomized by someone like writer Ayn Rand (founder of objectivism and author of *Atlas Shrugged*), sees the unrestrained pursuit of self-interest as the only rational course for society, since the best and the brightest will naturally prevail, and the rest of us will benefit from their achievement and resulting wealth. For the left (as represented by activists like Saul Alinsky, author of *Rules for Radicals*), the ostensibly unjust wealth acquired by the "privileged classes" must be redistributed in a more equitable manner, by force, if necessary. Both sides see the world in essentially materialistic terms and believe that the most important issues revolve around who gets the goodies—what some consider junk—and how they get them. Each offers a radically different approach for awarding the highly prized stuff called wealth, and

---

*See Jan E. Stets and Michael J. Carter, "A Theory of the Self for the Sociology of Morality," *American Sociological Review* 77, no. 1 (2012), https://journals.sagepub.com/doi/abs/10.1177/0003122411433762?journalCode=asra.

contradictory visions of what constitutes freedom and what makes tyranny. We'll leave the debate on which works best to others, but it is clear that neither offers much of real value to the more spiritually inclined, though a lot can be said for "freedom."

Both schools, indeed, reject, or at least disregard, the notion of an intelligent creator and of any obligation on the part of the human race to honor and respect the source of its own existence. Thus, in ignoring one of the most deep-seated and powerful of human desires— to reunite with one's source—the eventual result of such reasoning, whether originating with left or right, will, we suspect, prove anything but desirable.

Richard Weikart, a professor of history at California State University in Stanislaus, is the author of *From Darwin to Hitler: Evolutionary Ethics, Eugenics, and Racism in Germany*. In "Dehumanizing," an article published in *Atlantis Rising* #93, May/ June 2012, Weikart blamed Charles Darwin, Karl Marx, and Frederich Nietzsche for the dehumanizing effects of much of today's materialistic culture. Such thinking, he argued, prepared the way for

Doomed children in a Nazi concentration camp

the Nazi atrocities of World War II. The idea that humans are simply biological machines—products strictly of instinct, heredity, and environment—opened the door for the gas chambers of Auschwitz and worse.

Ironically, what is called "humanism"—theoretically a celebration of uniquely human virtues—has become a virulent attack on individual uniqueness and a justification for the wholesale practice of such dark notions as eugenics, racism, political violence, and all the abuses of a heartless fascist tribalism bent on crushing and silencing its challengers. In its crosshairs is any suggestion that humans could be, at their core, divine, and deserving of freedom and dignity. From the slaveholders of the Civil War to the Reds of the Russian Revolution, the "Reign of Terror" in the French Revolution, and the Holocaust of World War II, dark elites equipped with such soulless power-seeking rationales have felt empowered to bend others to their will and to subject them to whatever demonic cruelties they might choose—all while claiming, with a straight face, some kind of humanitarian (i.e., "scientifically based") authority for their policies and to justify their total control over the hearts and minds of the people.*

The concentration camps of World War II may be gone, but, sadly, the dark beings that inspired them, and upon which they depended, live on. Could their continued existence be but the most recent echo of voices far more ancient than most dare to consider? "Those who do not learn from history are doomed to repeat it," said the philosopher George Santayana. Is it possible that the failure to remember consciously what may once have transpired on Earth increases the likelihood that we will actually have to relive it?

---

*You can read Weikart's condemnation online; see "The Dehumanizing Impact of Modern Thought: Darwin, Marx, Nietzsche, and Their Followers," a post on the Discovery Institute website, July 18, 2008, https://www.discovery.org/a/6301/.

29

Dark Genetics and the Nazis

Has ancient evil come back to haunt us?

In 2015, when South Korean and Russian scientists announced plans to clone a woolly mammoth, the idea was to combine genetic material taken from a mammoth—quick-frozen at the end of the last ice age—with modern elephant DNA and produce a hybrid. Whether the result would be an actual mammoth was a subject of some debate.

Unfortunately for the credibility of the budding science of cloning, the leader of the Korean-Russian project was Dr. Hwang Woo-Suk, a veterinarian and stem cell researcher who, in 2006, after claiming that he had cloned a human embryo and extracted stem cells, was targeted by one of the largest investigations of scientific fraud in history. Hwang was subsequently convicted and sentenced by a South Korean criminal court for using fraudulent data, and according to *Nature* magazine, "The revelation has destroyed the best evidence so far that stem cells can be extracted from a clone and matched to a specific patient. With Hwang discredited, both the field of therapeutic cloning and the public's trust in science have suffered a serious setback."*

Undeterred by the fiasco, however, researchers from South Korea's Sooam Biotech Research Foundation announced that they, along with Dr. Hwang, were actively working on cloning a woolly mammoth, and that they intended to take full advantage of dramatic recent discoveries

---

*See "Woo Suk Hwang," *Nature* News (online), January 11, 2006, https://www.nature.com/collections/szlcbykgyl.

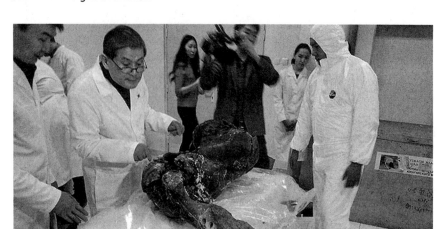

Dr. Hwang Woo-Suk collects samples of mammoth tissue; photo courtesy of YSIA.

in genetic research to achieve their peculiar goal. The experimenters planned to work with DNA taken in 2013 from "Buttercup," a well-preserved mammoth calf found in the permafrost on Maly Lyakhovsky, a Siberian island. The group believed they had the best-preserved genetic material ever recovered from an extinct species. When excavated, Buttercup had produced a thick red fluid from its abdomen. As of this writing, however, it remains unclear whether the experiment has succeeded.*

In the movie *Jurassic Park,* scientists extracted a minute amount of DNA from the blood of a mosquito that had been preserved in amber since the Jurassic era 175 million years ago. In real life, DNA quickly breaks down after the cell dies, making the possibility of finding an intact strand of DNA in Jurassic blood virtually nonexistent. So far, successful cloning has been done only with DNA harvested from living cells with intact genetic material. Astonishingly, though, in 2017,

---

*For more details on the mammoth project, see Nick Stockton, "This Bad-Boy Geneticist Wants to Clone a Mammoth," *Wired* (online), March 23, 2015, https://www.wired.com/2015/03/bad-boy-geneticist-wants-clone-mammoth/, and also Tia Ghose, "Can the Long-Extinct Woolly Mammoth Be Cloned?," Live Science (online), November 16, 2014, https://www.livescience.com/48769-woolly-mammoth-cloning.html.

Will we someday be able to photograph woolly mammoths, cloned back into existence? Art by Randy Haragan for the cover of *Atlantis Rising Magazine* (July/August 2015).

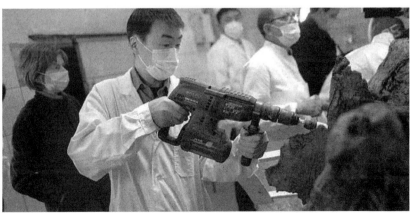

A technician extracts DNA-bearing material from Buttercup the mammoth calf; photo courtesy of YSIA.

research from scientists at the University of Toronto, China, and Taiwan provided the first evidence of actual proteins preserved within the 195-million-year-old rib of a *Lufengosaurus* dinosaur.*

Moreover, in 2013, researchers reported that the fossil of a blood-filled mosquito had, in fact, been found, not in amber, but in shale. While possessing no DNA that might be used for cloning, the ostensibly 46-million-year-old bug still contained the blood molecules of some unidentified prehistoric animal. The female parasite was discovered in Montana by a team from the U.S. Museum of Natural History led by Dr. Dale Greenwalt.†

On another front of the DNA frontier, scientists say they are nearing the point where, if they wanted to, they could clone a Neanderthal person. At the least, they say, they expect to be able to make body parts for it. Recent advances in sequencing the DNA of a Neanderthal woman who died in a cave in Croatia thirty thousand years ago have brought the Neanderthal cloning possibility near to fruition.‡

Paleoanthropologists claim that very soon they will understand Neanderthal biology as well as our own, which, for some, begs the question: How well do we understand our own biology? Such concerns, however, have not slowed the relentless march of rudderless science passing for progress, and any resemblance between the popular current narrative and Mary Shelley's horror story *Frankenstein* seldom comes up in the conversation.

While scientists may not currently embrace—at least publicly—the

---

*See the press release about the research from the University of Toronto: "Good Ribbance: U of T Researcher Finds Dino Rib Bones Reveal Remnants of 195-Million-Year-Old Protein," by Nicolle Wahl, U of T News (online), February 1, 2017, https://www.utoronto.ca/news/good-ribbance-u-t-researcher-finds-dino-rib-bones-reveal-remnants-195-million-year-old-protein.

†See Dale E. Greenwalt, Yulia S. Goreva, Sandra M. Siljeström, Tim Rose, and Ralph E. Harbach, "Hemoglobin-Derived Porphyrins Preserved in a Middle Eocene Blood-Engorged Mosquito," *Proceedings of the National Academy of Sciences* 110, no. 46 (2013): 18496–500, https://www.nature.com/news/blood-filled-mosquito-is-a-fossil-first-1.13946.

‡Read about the DNA sequencing of Neanderthals (and Denisovans) here: Kay Prüfer, Cesare de Filippo, Steffi Grote, et al., "A High-Coverage Neandertal Genome from Vindija Cave in Croatia," *Science* 358, no. 6363 (November 3, 2017): 655–58, https://science.sciencemag.org/content/358/6363/655.

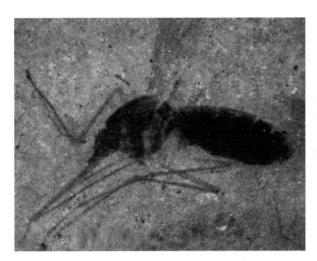

Female mosquito fossil containing chemical traces of its last blood meal; photo courtesy of the Smithsonian National Museum of Natural History, Washington, D.C.

radical cloning agenda, the temptation is certainly there, and if history is any guide, where there is temptation, there are also those who can rationalize giving in to it. Some who believe that current society is a rerun of lost ancient civilization see great danger in contemporary DNA experimentation, which they believe mirrors abuse that contributed directly to the cataclysmic destruction of a prior advanced world.

ANCIENT DARK SCIENCE

Among serious proponents for the existence of Atlantis are many who also suspect that forgotten ancient civilization fell because of great evils that flourished there. One of the worst, it is said, was an advanced and unscrupulous science of genetic engineering that produced many monstrosities. Mythological creatures like centaurs, satyrs, chimeras, and maybe even the Great Sphinx of Egypt are, it is believed, but subconscious reconstructions of the horrors of an otherwise mercifully forgotten time.

Edgar Cayce was one who spoke of such nightmares, and in the 1920s, he said that, through reincarnation, many who played key roles in the catastrophic destruction of Atlantis would soon return to resume their ancient agendas. Cayce told of strange creatures produced through the genetic science of that time. In fact, he said, the battle over what to do with such creatures led to warfare that eventuated in the complete destruction of the empire. The sheer horror of much that may

Chiron the centaur teaches Achilles to play the lyre in a Roman fresco from Herculaneum; photo courtesy of the National Archaeological Museum of Naples.

have transpired could go far in explaining the deep amnesia that may frustrate attempts to uncover reliable records of that lost world—one in which many intuitively sense that they may once have actually participated. Perhaps one of the most compelling, if least understood, reasons that so many people share a visceral objection to research in areas such as stem cell science has to do with our partial recollection of nightmarish encounters with the actual result of unchecked genetic experimentation.

Today, under the guise of a science intended to create life-saving replacement organs, researchers all over the world have actually begun to try uniting the genes of distinct animal species, creating what are called hybrid chimeras. In vitro fertilizations of human genes in animal wombs—pigs, for example—would be used. New attempts to plant human stem cells aimed at producing specific organs are already underway. Janet Rossant at the Hospital for Sick Children (SickKids) in Toronto is a leader in the field. In 1980, she was one of the first to combine the genes of two species of mice. Now techniques that she developed are being used by researchers in an effort to create organs for transplant. The journal *Nature* is already on record defending the practice.*

Fictional movies like *Frankenstein* and the *Island of Dr. Moreau* may already seem passé as the facts on the ground become even more strange—not unlike, perhaps, what happened with that "lost civilization" of Atlantis.

The 1996 horror film *The Island of Doctor Moreau* is based upon H. G. Well's 1896 novel of the same title. In it, Wells described an

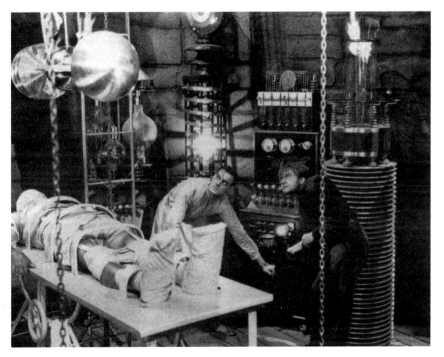

The creation of Frankenstein, from the 1931 movie

---

*Read more at Jane Janet Rossant, *Nature Reviews Genetics* 8 (2007): 330, https://www .nature.com/articles/nrg2108.

isolated island visited by a shipwrecked man, where the mad Dr. Moreau created, via vivisection, human-like beings from animals. In the twentieth century, such evil science became terrifyingly real in the Nazi concentration camps of the Third Reich during the Holocaust. Experiments carried out by Dr. Josef Mengele, a.k.a. the "Angel of Death," on living human beings in his laboratory at Auschwitz made him a real-life equivalent of Dr. Moreau.

Scientists now no longer need to rely on such primitive methods as vivisection (the practice of performing operations on live animals for the purpose of experimentation or scientific research). State-of-the-art genetic engineering can do a great deal worse by manipulating the genome, and there is evidence that once again science may be running amok.

In 2013, Dr. Eugene McCarthy, a Georgia-based geneticist, proposed that humans first arose from an ancient hybrid cross between pigs and chimpanzees. He wanted to do some experiments, he said, to test his thesis, but he said he wouldn't actually produce any creatures.[*]

No scientific consensus has yet emerged that he should be allowed to proceed, but not all researchers in the field are quite so squeamish. According to Britain's *Independent* newspaper, "Scientists have created genetically-engineered mice with artificial human chromosomes in every cell of their bodies, as part of a series of studies showing that it may be possible to treat genetic diseases with a radically new form of gene therapy."[†]

Recent reports that stem cells taken from aborted human fetuses have been used to test what kind of flavors might be successful in artificial foods reveal the surprising extent of what may be coming into play as the science develops. As science blogger Michael Snyder warned in 2013, "Over the past decade, there have been some absolutely stun

---

[*]See "Leading Geneticist Dr. Eugene McCarthy Claims Humans Descended from Sex between a Chimp and a Pig," News.com.au (an online news site in Australia), December 28, 2013, https://www.news.com.au/technology/science/leading-geneticist-dr -eugene-mccarthy-claims-humans-descended-from-sex-between-chimp-and-pig/news -story/4ce8ab13db14897d0a8ea1b81e6b09ab.

[†]See Steve Connor, "Exclusive: Mice with human chromosomes—the genetic breakthrough that could revolutionise medicine," *The Independent,* July 11, 2013, https:// www.independent.co.uk/news/science/exclusive-mice-human-chromosomes-genetic -breakthrough-could-revolutionise-medicine-8701357.html.

ning advances in the field of genetic modification. Today, it is literally possible for college students to create new lifeforms in their basements. Unfortunately, laws have not kept pace with these advancements, and in many countries there are very few limits on what scientists are allowed to do."*

Many of those who would like to see a recovery of the advanced sciences that possibly went down with Atlantis may yet get their chance. Unfortunately, that is not necessarily good news. Could some of that science have been reawakened in the laboratories of the Third Reich?

HITLER'S BIOENGINEERS

New research is now raising the question: Did Hitler plan biological warfare against the Allies? Recently uncovered concentration camp records indicate that the Nazis were indeed investigating such offensive weaponry.

According to records from Dachau, plans were made to release malaria-bearing mosquitoes from airplanes. Such plans, it has been reported, were developed by both the Germans and the Japanese, but most experts doubt they were ever set in motion. Hitler issued edicts against such things, but some have argued that Nazi biological research was not simply defensive. That is the view of Klaus Reinhardt of Germany's University of Tübingen, as reported in the December 2013 issue of the journal *Endeavor*. Reinhardt believes that insect researcher Eduard May, who died in 1956, guided such a program.†

While malaria-bearing mosquitoes would not have been very useful in northern Europe, the suggestion is that they might have been deployed in the marshes of southern Italy. The Japanese might have had more use for such a thing, but, like most biological strategies of this type, they would have been as much a danger to the "targeter" as the "targetee."

Hitler's biological experiments were not reserved for humans only.

---

*See Michael Snyder, "Human-Animal Hybrids: Sick and Twisted Chimeras Are Being Created in Labs All Over the Planet," *The Truth Wins* (blog), July 11, 2013, http://thetruthwins.com/archives/human-animal-hybrids-sick-and-twisted-chimeras-are-being-created-in-labs-all-over-the-planet.
†See Dan Vergano, "Nazi Scientists May Have Plotted Malaria Mosquito Warfare," *National Geographic* (online), January 29, 2014, https://www.nationalgeographic.com/news/2014/1/140130-nazi-biological-weapons-biowarfare-mosquito-malaria-history/.

A recent National Geographic documentary revealed that the Nazis planned to bring back animal species that had been extinct for nine thousand years. *Hitler's Jurassic Monsters,* which first aired in 2014, showed how Hermann Göring, Hitler's second in command, led a secret effort to employ a technique called back-breeding to reinstate giant aurochs and other species.

Though not actually Jurassic, the now-extinct aurochs (considered the ancestors of modern cattle) were, nonetheless, monstrous creatures that stood seven feet tall at the shoulders. They were also said to have had very nasty dispositions. The plan, as detailed in Nazi diaries found near fossilized auroch bones, was to breed the animals in zoos and then establish them in captured Polish forests, where they could be hunted at leisure by elite officers looking for more challenging quarry.

Apparently the Nazis believed that the strategy could earn them more street credit with the German people, associating themselves with legendary primeval hunters involved in blood sport. Since they themselves had arrived so recently on the stage of history, the Nazis wanted to fabricate a longer and stronger narrative for themselves.

Göring, himself a fanatical hunter, looked to redeem his manhood with something more challenging than foxes, hares, and the occasional deer. He certainly was not afraid to dispose of inconvenient humans, such as the Jews who occupied the Białowieża forest where he dreamed of hunting aurochs.*

CONTROLLED MINDS

The world of dystopian—if not paranoid—science fiction has contemplated an even greater danger than genetic manipulation. Fears of a new science of mind control have now reached beyond the tin-foil-hat crowd, but the idea is not a new one. From George Orwell's *1984* to the Richard Condon's *Manchurian Candidate,* the nightmare of a totalitarian state determined to manipulate the innermost thoughts of its citizenry has

---

*See Laura Cox, "Revealed: Hitler's Twisted Plan to Bring Back Giant Historic Beasts from the Dead . . . So That Top Nazis Could Hunt Them," *Daily Mail* (online), June 13, 2014, https://www.dailymail.co.uk/news/article-2657396/Hitler-wanted-bring -prehistoric-wild-Auroch-cows-dead.html.

Giant auroch bulls painted on the wall of Lascaux Cave

been a familiar, but very chilling, theme. And now, it appears that an important barrier between nightmare and reality may have been breached.

A neuroscientist at the Boston Children's Hospital has experimented with a crude technique that not only allows him to predict decisions before a subject is conscious of making them, but to change those decisions even before they are made. Working with electrodes originally planted in the brains of epilepsy patients to identify the source of seizures, Dr. Kreiman demonstrated that he can know before the patient whether or not the patient will choose to press a particular button. And now he has moved to the next stage, flashing a stop sign before the patient himself knows what he is going to do. The patient is startled, feeling his mind has been read, but his choice to press the button is effectively reversed.*

Kreiman's experiment was presented to the British Neuroscience Association with the expressed hope that it might help with the treatment of Parkinson's disease. Does it, however, open the door to hidden agendas and manipulating minds for other purposes—political correctness, perhaps? Many feel that before the doctor's next experiment, maybe another kind of "stop sign" should be flashed.

---

*See David Talbot, "Searching for the 'Free Will' Neuron," *MIT Technology Review* (online), June 17, 2014, https://www.technologyreview.com/s/528136/searching-for -the-free-will-neuron/.

30

The Trouble with Peer Review

Are the authorities of science to be trusted?

If you thought that important archaeological discoveries were being hidden from the public, and that laws intended to preserve the public's right to know were being routinely violated, you could expect to be sneered at by the science-and-media establishment, but you would, nevertheless, be right. That is the view of professor Keith Kintigh of the Arizona State University School of Human Evolution and Social Change. Kintigh sits on the board of directors of the Center for Digital Antiquity.

"Today, nearly all archaeological field work in the U.S.," he says, "is executed by private firms in response to legal mandates for historic preservation, at a cost of about a billion dollars annually. However, only a minuscule fraction of the data from these projects is made accessible or preserved for future research, despite agencies' clear legal obligations to do so. Severe loss of these data is not unusual—it's the norm."

In a column for *The Conversation,* an independent, not-for-profit media outlet featuring important articles by the top authorities in many fields, Kintigh explains that the primary data from many important archaeological investigations is being lost, and the federal agencies that are legally required to protect it are not doing so. The loss of such hard-won information about our past, Kintigh thinks, is probably attributable to misfeasance, rather than malfeasance, but to

Scene from an Inquisition, by Spanish painter Francisco Goya, circa 1812

more skeptical observers, serious disturbances in the force have long been clear.*

Atlantis Rising columnist Michael Cremo wrote often about what he called a knowledge filter that automatically screens out data that does not fit the prevailing knowledge paradigm. In his books, *Forbidden Archaeology* and *The Hidden History of the Human Race,* Cremo cited many highly respected and rigorous studies documenting evidence that challenged the standard time line of human development—research that was generally completely ignored or hardly mentioned at all by the establishment.†

The truth is, serious researchers on many controversies have seen their work routinely dismissed as "pseudoscience" because it violates the

---

*See Keith Kintigh, "America's Archaeology Data Keeps Disappearing—Even Though the Law Says the Government Is Supposed to Preserve It," *The Conversation* (online), October 17, 2018, https://theconversation.com/americas-archaeology-data-keeps -disappearing-even-though-the-law-says-the-government-is-supposed-to-preserve-it -104674.

†For presentations and interviews from Michael Cremo, see "Michael Cremo Speaks Bluntly about the Institutional 'knowledge filter' and Who We Really Are," *Ronmamita* (blog), April 9, 2015, https://ronmamita.wordpress.com/2015/04/09/michael-cremo -speaks-bluntly-about-the-institutional-knowledge-filter-and-who-we-really-are/.

accepted paradigm. Rupert Sheldrake, for example, despite rigorous training at Cambridge and years of the most advanced work in his field, finds his research banished from Wikipedia and his TED Talks removed from mainstream circulation simply because, it appears, he has produced evidence of nonphysical fields influencing human and animal behavior, thus contradicting the materialistic assumptions of mainstream science.

Late in 2009, the Climatic Research Unit (CRU) at the University of East Anglia in Norwich, England, was hacked, and over three thousand pages of email and computer code were soon disseminated across the internet. The documents soon led climate warming skeptics to declare proof of scientific fraud and deceit of enormous significance. Dubbed "Climategate," the controversy was to derail much of the climate change agenda at the time, including the 2009 United Nations Climate Change Conference in Copenhagen.

The CRU had become, along with NASA, one of the most influential organizations in the ongoing debate over man-made global warming. Its studies and numbers provided the primary basis for most of the pronouncements of the United Nations Intergovernmental Panel on Climate Change (IPCC), which has led the charge for sweeping changes in world economies, all aimed at countering the perceived threat from so-called anthropocentric global warming.

In the hacked files was advice on how the scientists could avoid complying with Freedom of Information Act (FOIA) requirements for release of temperature data supporting their conclusions (Britain's FOIA—more stringent than America's—made it a crime to deny a legitimate request for the data underlying a decision from a government-funded agency). Included were discussions of how to manipulate the peer review process to exclude skeptics. Included also was the admission of a "travesty"—the failure of CRU's computer models to account for an apparent worldwide decline in temperatures since 1998, which had inconveniently defied all predictions of the climate change lobby.

While most of the focus was on the emails, potentially more incriminating were other elements that slowly came to light. Computer code included with the stolen documents revealed the underlying flaws in models that had triggered the climate-warming alarm bells. While the revelations may not directly disprove the hypothesis of man-made global warming, they certainly cast considerable doubt on the integrity of the

The Hubert Lamb Building at the University of East Anglia where the Climatic Research Unit (CRU) is housed

Controversial climate scientist Phil Jones

science involved, including the iconic and widely publicized "hockey stick" graph created by Penn State climatologist Michael Mann, which purported to show a steep and unprecedented rise in world temperatures. (Mann was one of the authorities whose motives were thrown into sharp question by the CRU exposures.)

Within days of the revelations, CRU director Phil Jones was forced to step down and make way for a University of East Anglia investigation of professional misconduct, but the process did not end there. After all, vast sums of money were at stake, if not the very survival of many of the world's largest economies. Draconian measures that might have been proposed to help stave off a "looming planetary eco-catastrophe" could hardly be justified if the underlying science itself was in doubt. Major investigations of the central arguments for and against man-made global warming were demanded.*

The details of the entire affair were widely available on the internet, and it seemed only a matter of time until the facts became common knowledge. The reaction in print media and the internet blogosphere was scathing. *Atlantic* magazine's widely respected blogger Clive Crook—though his initial writing was that nothing in the CRU dump surprised him much—soon changed his tune. Within days he was writing, "The closed-mindedness of these supposed men of science, their willingness to go to any lengths to defend a preconceived message, is surprising even to me. The stink of intellectual corruption is overpowering."†

British columnist George Monbiot, who had previously been one of the most outspoken defenders of the warming hypothesis, wrote, "It's no use pretending that this isn't a major blow. The e-mails . . . could scarcely be more damaging. . . . I'm dismayed and deeply shaken by them. . . . I was too trusting of some of those who provided the evidence I championed. I would have been a better journalist if I had investigated their claims more closely."‡

ALTERNATIVE SCIENCE

For those in the alternative science community, the implications of Climategate were even more profound. One of the most troubling

---

*For details on the story of the CRU scandal, see Jonathan Petre, "Climategate U-turn as Scientist at Centre of Row Admits: There Has Been No Global Warming since 1995," *Daily Mail* (online), February 14, 2010, https://www.dailymail.co.uk/news/article-1250872/Climategate-U-turn-Astonishment-scientist-centre-global-warming-email-row-admits-data-organised.html?ITO=1490.

†See Clive Crook, "Climategate and the Big Green Lie," *The Atlantic,* July 14, 2010, https://www.theatlantic.com/politics/archive/2010/07/climategate-and-the-big-green-lie/59709/

‡See George Monbiot, "Climate Change Email Scandal Shames the University and Requires Resignations," *The Guardian* (online), February 2, 2010, https://www.theguardian.com/environment/georgemonbiot/2010/feb/02/climate-change-hacked-emails.

aspects of the case has to do with the peer review system itself, on which the big science establishment bases its legitimacy.

In theory the idea sounds fine: Scientists look at a particular phenomenon, come up with some kind of explanation (hopefully a convincing one), do experiments to test their hypothesis, and then submit their work to other scientists (their peers) to see if they can obtain the same results. If the hypothesis holds up, everything is published and then other scientists get to take a crack at the idea. To keep favoritism and politics out of it, the process is supposed to be anonymous so that no one need fear retribution or expect any particular reward. That is the way the system is supposed work, but does it?

As columnist Mark Steyn wrote in 2009, "The trouble with outsourcing your marbles to the peer-reviewed set is that, if you take away one single thing from the leaked (CRU) documents, it's that the global warm-mongers have wholly corrupted the 'peer-review' process."*

The "peer review process," however, was in trouble long before Climategate.

When Richard Sternberg, editor of the scientific journal *Proceedings of the Biological Society of Washington,* decided in 2004 to publish a paper making the case for intelligent design, he had no idea what he was in for. Despite scrupulous attention to correct peer review procedures, Sternberg, who holds two PhDs in biology, was accused of being a shoddy scientist and a Bible thumper and of taking money under the table from fundamentalists. "I was basically run out of here," he recalls. The U.S. Office of Special Counsel, an independent agency whose job it is to protect federal officials from reprisals, found that senior scientists with the Smithsonian's National Museum of Natural History did indeed retaliate against Sternberg for running the article.†

According to the *Washington Post,* the Special Counsel investigators

---

*See Mark Steyn, "CRU's Tree-Ring Circus," *National Review* (online), November 28, 2009, https://www.nationalreview.com/2009/11/crus-tree-ring-circus-mark-steyn/.

†Sternberg himself notes that he accepted the paper for publication, even though he was not a proponent of intelligent design, in the name of the objective pursuit of science. For the full story from an organization that does support the idea of intelligent design and seeks to free science from its bias against it, see Sarah Chaffee, "A Biologist and Journal Editor: Richard Sternberg," Free Science (online), November 30, 2017, https://freescience.today/story/richard-sternberg/.

Richard Sternberg,
journal editor

examined email traffic from the scientists and noted that "retaliation came in many forms . . . misinformation was disseminated through the Smithsonian Institution and to outside sources. The allegations against [Sternberg] were later determined to be false." James McVay, the principal legal adviser in the Office of Special Counsel, wrote to Sternberg, "The rumor mill became so infected that one of your colleagues had to circulate [your résumé] simply to dispel the rumor that you were not a scientist."*

The Sternberg controversy publicly exposed a common tactic of the mainstream science camp (epitomized by organizations like CSICOP)—the use of ad hominem attacks that have nothing to do with the merits of the arguments presented. Frequently heard is the accusation that intelligent design advocates are closet creationists masquerading as scientists.

A similar tactic used by global warming activists is to call those who question the validity of their arguments "deniers," thus equating them with Holocaust "deniers." Of course, the first use of the word involves an unproven theory and the other a thoroughly documented historical event (the murder of six million Jews in World War II), but the distinction gets lost in the fray.

---

*See Michael Powel, "Editor Explains Reasons for 'Intelligent Design' Article," *The Washington Post,* August 19, 2005, https://www.washingtonpost.com/archive/politics /2005/08/19/editor-explains-reasons-for-intelligent-design-article/6700e62d-d1de -40b3-a756-1da6469ff4bd/.

The usual claim made by the establishment in such disputes is that the matter is already settled, which is another way of saying, "Don't argue with us, we know best." In the global warming debate, such is emphatically not the case. Richard S. Lindzen, professor of meteorology at the Massachusetts Institute of Technology, for one, said in a piece for the *Wall Street Journal,* "Climate science isn't settled. Confident predictions of catastrophe are unwarranted." Even the BBC recently expressed doubt over whether the facts can support the main contentions of the global warming alarmists. Is the sunspot cycle, for example, the real source of much of the warming we might have experienced? Such authoritative views have done little, though, to stem the widespread clamor that the debate is *over,* global warming is accelerating, human activity is the primary cause, and any questioning of the merits of those claims is at the planet's peril.*

Another area where the conventional scientific consensus has been challenged is over whether advanced civilization on Earth could have existed before the last ice age, something that orthodox archaeology adamantly deputes and keeps out of its debates. But recent dramatic discoveries at Göbekli Tepe in Turkey are now widely acknowledged to be a challenge to conventional history, and that characterization could well prove to be a major understatement. Carbon-dated at twelve thousand years old, Göbekli Tepe offers incontrovertible evidence for advanced human activity at a time when our ancestors are said to have been still at the hunter-gatherer stage—thousands of years earlier than we had been told was possible. (See chapter 19 for more details.)

As another example, when maverick Egyptologist John Anthony West and Boston University geologist Robert Schoch announced in the mid-1990s that water weathering proved the Great Sphinx of Egypt was thousands of years older than traditionally believed, they were greeted with derision from conventional Egyptology. And despite evidence widely accepted by professional geologists, the orthodox archaeologists have continued to deny the possibility of the Sphinx's greater antiquity. (See chapter 15 for more details.)

---

*See Richard S. Lindzen, "The Climate Science Isn't Settled," *Wall Street Journal* (online), November 30, 2009, https://www.wsj.com/articles/SB1000142405274870393 9404574567423917025400.

Among the many other underreported stories has been the work of Rupert Sheldrake. In fact, his book *A New Science of Life,* containing his theory of morphic resonance, was declared by John Maddox, editor of the prestigious peer-reviewed journal *Nature,* to be one "that should be burned." Phillip Stevens, while at London's Imperial College, based his master's dissertation on Sheldrake's treatment at the hands of the science establishment. Though personally skeptical of Sheldrake's theories, Stevens found, to his surprise, that despite an unblemished academic record and a research fellowship at the Royal Society, Sheldrake had been unfairly subjected to scorn from colleagues for publishing his theory. Stevens also found that skeptics like Dr. Richard Wiseman had failed to use the normal scientific procedures that scientists usually follow when collaborating and reporting their results. Wiseman had actually duplicated many of Sheldrake's experimental results, a fact that he conveniently omitted in his published condemnation of Sheldrake's work.*

Similarly hostile receptions have greeted the work of Sam Parnia on near-death experience, Dean Radin on psi phenomena, and others.

So much for the way big science expresses its *disapproval,* but how is it doing when it comes to those who win its *approval*? Not very well there either, it seems.

Take the case of Jan Hendrik Schön, a young German scientist whose star, reportedly, had already risen. After being credited with a number of amazing discoveries—including plastic transistors, new superconductors, microscopic molecular switches, and more—the then thirty-two-year-old researcher at Bell Labs was the toast of big science around the world and considered one of the hottest researchers on the planet. But he was, it turns out, a fake. His peers and the scientific journals (including *Science*) who published his bogus work had been completely fooled.†

---

*Stevens discussed his findings in an interview with Alex Tsakiris for the *Skeptiko* podcast; see "Scientific Community Unfair to Dr. Rupert Sheldrake, Imperial College London Dissertation Asserts," *Skeptiko* (podcast) no. 88, December 1, 2009. To read more about Sheldrake and his treatment by the mainstream scientific community, see Tim Adams, "Rupert Sheldrake: The 'Heretic' at Odds with Scientific Dogma," *The Guardian* (online), February 4, 2012, https://www.theguardian.com/science/2012/feb/05/rupert-sheldrake-interview-science-delusion.

†You can read the full story in "Physicist Found Guilty of Misconduct," *Nature* (online), September 26, 2002, https://www.nature.com/news/2002/020923/full/news020923-9.html.

Science fraudster
Jan Hendrik Schön

The Schön case, we learn though, is not that unusual. South Korean cloning pioneer Hwang Woo-Suk, for example, recently made international headlines when it was discovered that he was faking data (see chapter 29). Now, according to the journal *Public Library of Science,* in a review of twenty-one scientific misconduct surveys of the period from 1986 to 2005, more than two-thirds of researchers said they knew of colleagues who had committed "questionable" practices and one in seven said that included inventing findings. Of course, very few scientists, just 2 percent, admitted to having faked results themselves. The most common area of fraud appears to be in medical research, which is seen as evidence for the effect of commercial pressure.

It is not, however, just the gross violations such as falsification, plagiarism, and fabrication that are of concern. According to a study authored by Raymond De Vries, an associate professor of medical education and a member of the bioethics program at the University of Michigan in Ann Arbor, scientific misbehavior seems to be endemic. De Vries says that intense competition between scientists is causing them to worry about things they shouldn't be thinking about, like how their data will be interpreted, not just its integrity. In other words, they are thinking about whether their research will lead to conclusions their peers might not like. Other issues also mentioned by the study include the increasing number of rules that scientists are supposed to follow and questions of how to deal with the growing competition for the rewards in a shrinking pie.

De Vries's study collected its data primarily from six focus groups comprising a total of fifty-one researchers gathered from top U.S. research universities. The groups were asked to discuss misconduct that the participants had either practiced or witnessed. "After the focus groups," said De Vries, "we felt like we had been at a confessional. We didn't intend this, but the focus groups became a place where people could unburden themselves."*

From the intelligent design of Richard Sternberg to West and Schoch's greater antiquity of the Sphinx to the morphic resonance of Rupert Sheldrake, the same conflict, it seems, plays out over and over in scientific debate. Witness the heliocentric solar system of Galileo or the catastrophism of Immanuel Velikovsky. Some, like writer Thomas Kuhn (*The Structure of Scientific Revolutions*), have perceived a recurring pattern in which the ideas that are unthinkable to one generation become the orthodoxy of the next.

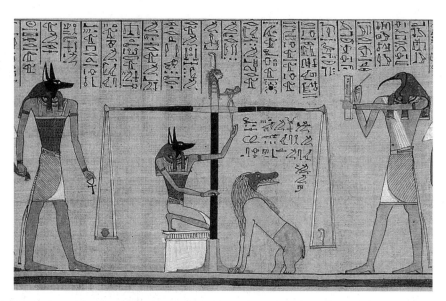

A soul is weighed in the balance at the final judgment of Osiris.

---

*See Raymond De Vries, Melissa S. Anderson, and Brian C. Martinson, "Normal Misbehavior: Scientists Talk about the Ethics of Research," *Journal of Empirical Research on Human Research Ethics* 1, no. 1 (2006): 43–50, https://www.ncbi.nlm.nih.gov/pmc/articles/PMC1483899/.

The first step in regaining our understanding may be to remember that many who claim to *know* what they are talking about may, in fact, only *believe* they do. And although they may feel quite passionate on the matter, the rest of us will need to hear something much better than their preachments before converting to their faith.

In the trial of the soul described in the afterworld of the ancient Egyptians, the heart of the deceased—symbolic of his virtue, moral character, and earthly deeds—was laid before Osiris on a set of scales and weighed against a single feather representing *maat,* the divine law. If the scales balanced, the deceased was allowed to pass into heaven.

Will today's big science make the cut? You be the judge.

31

Twisting Wikipedia

Slanting the facts on the online encyclopedia

In the age of the internet, everyone has access to facts and information as never before. Or do they? While it is true that a diligent researcher can uncover vast quantities of information on just about any subject, just how reliable is it? Now, it turns out, one of the most relied-upon sources of internet information could be something quite different from its billing.

Wikipedia's logo, with a twist

Wikipedia, the free "crowdsourced" online encyclopedia, was founded in 2001 by web entrepreneur Jimmy Wales and encyclopedist Larry Sanger. It prides itself on providing a free and collective exchange of information while covering all sides of many controversial topics. Though frequently consulted by almost all web users, Wikipedia has been accused of secret bias toward favored groups—and worse. At the same time, alternative points of view, like those advanced in *Atlantis Rising Magazine,* have been presented in a manner that is often distorted, dismissive, or downright insulting. Could the same entrenched materialistic-paradigm protectors who have, for centuries, successfully blocked the dissemination of much important knowledge on many worthy topics now be applying their systematic suppression techniques to the world's leading online encyclopedia?

ALTERNATIVE SCIENCE

One prominent example of an obviously materialistic bias at Wikipedia is the entry on homeopathy. Proponents of homeopathy have argued that Wikipedia does not accurately define or represent this natural system of medicine. In many places the entry provides incorrect information, uses biased references, and gives negative thoughts and feelings rather than scientific evidence of the effectiveness of homeopathy.

"Homeopathy," declared Wikipedia in its entry on the subject in 2015, "lacks biological plausibility, and the axioms of homeopathy have been refuted for some time. The postulated mechanisms of action of homeopathic remedies are both scientifically implausible and not physically possible." Dismissed out of hand is the 1988 paper by French immunologist Jacques Benveniste, published in the journal *Nature,* which clearly showed a demonstrable effect for very high homeopathic dilutions of an antibody on human basophils, a kind of white blood cell.* Wikipedia has recently expanded its homeopathy coverage with an immense article including hundreds of references obviously intended to discredit the practice. Cited

---

*See E. Davenas, F. Beauvais, J. Amara, et al., "Human Basophil Degranulation Triggered by Very Dilute Antiserum against IgE," *Nature* 333 (1988): 816–18, https://www.nature.com/articles/333816a0.

Luc Montagnier, winner of the 2008 Nobel Prize in Medicine

in opposition to homeopathy is the notorious debunker and stage magician James Randi, even as strong support for homeopathy by Dr. Luc Montagnier, winner of the 2008 Nobel Prize (for discovery of the AIDS virus), is entirely ignored in the homeopathy entry, though it is mentioned in Wikipedia's entry for Montagnier himself.

Another area where Wikipedia displays an obvious bias against alternative science is in its treatment of the influence of electromagnetic forces on large-scale phenomena in the universe. Regarding the related plasma cosmology—proposed by such influential scientists as Nobel Prize–winning Hannes Alfvén, and constituting a major part of the "electric universe" hypothesis advanced by astrophysicists like Wal Thornhill and others—Wikipedia cluelessly declares, "[Plasma cosmology] is contrary to the general consensus by cosmologists and astrophysicists which strongly supports that astronomical bodies and structures in the universe are mostly influenced by gravity, Einstein's theory of general relativity, and quantum mechanics." Hotly disputing that contention is Henry Bauer, emeritus professor of chemistry and science at Virginia Polytechnic Institute, who charges that Wikipedia's editing process "takes only one dedicated fanatic to dominate any given Wikipedia entry or topic." Furthermore, he complains, "arbitration on

Hannes Alfvén, 1970 winner of
the Nobel Prize in Physics

Wikipedia is controlled by sometimes anonymous individuals whose credentials are thereby unknown."*

Concerning intelligent design theory, which Wikipedia equates with "neo-creationism" and a disbelief in evolution, the website says, "The neo-creationist movement is motivated by the fear that religion is under attack by the study of evolution." On the contrary, intelligent design theorists do *not* disbelieve in evolution. They simply differ with Darwinists over what the evidence shows to be its guiding processes.

Biologist and author Rupert Sheldrake is best known for his hypothesis of morphic fields and morphic resonance, which, he says, "leads to a vision of a living, developing universe with its own inherent memory." A fellow of Clare College at the University of Cambridge in the 1960s, Sheldrake did important research in developmental biology. Later he became the principal plant physiologist at the International Crops Research Institute for the Semi-Arid Tropics (ICRISAT) in Hyderabad, India. More recently, he was director of the Perrott-Warrick Project, administered by Trinity College at the University of Cambridge. In its entry on Sheldrake, Wikipedia goes out of its way to state that his morphic resonance theory "is not accepted by the scientific community as a real phenomenon and Sheldrake's proposals relating to it have been characterized as pseudoscience." The brief biography

---

*See Henry Bauer, "The Fairy-Tale Cult of Wikipedia," blog post for the Thunderbolts Project (online), January 22, 2010, http://www.thunderbolts.info/thunderblogs/guest1 .htm.

concludes mockingly, "Despite the negative reception Sheldrake's ideas have received from the scientific community, they have found support in the New Age movement, such as from Deepak Chopra. Sheldrake argues that science should incorporate alternative medicine, psychic phenomena, and a greater focus on holistic thinking." Notwithstanding Wikipedia's disrespect, writing for *Scientific American* in 2014, influential science writer John Horgan says, "[Sheldrake] possesses a deep knowledge of science, including its history and philosophy (which he studied at Harvard in the 1960s). This knowledge—along with his ability to cite detailed experimental evidence for his claims—make Sheldrake a formidable defender of his outlook."*

On another major scientific front, the famous hypothesis re-dating the Great Sphinx based on water weathering data, as advanced by Robert Schoch and John Anthony West, Wikipedia says, "Egyptologists, geologists and others have rejected the water erosion hypothesis and the idea of an older Sphinx, offering various alternative explanations for the cause and date of the erosion." But as Dr. Schoch has pointed out in *Atlantis Rising Magazine* and elsewhere, while his thesis may be questioned by some Egyptologists, it is widely accepted throughout the community of academic and professional geologists.

Complaints of significant Wikipedia bias can be found in many places on the web. Perhaps the loudest come from Christians and political conservatives (who have, in response, erected their own online encyclopedia, Conservapedia, with an entire entry devoted to "examples of bias in Wikipedia"). The practice causing the greatest alarm, though, is manipulation of Wikipedia's editorial process by corporate interests in ways that, it can be argued, are threatening public health and welfare.

ASTROTURFING

Investigative journalist Sharyl Attkisson has warned about a widespread public relations strategy called "astroturfing" and sees Wikipedia as a key part of the technique. She worked as a correspondent for CBS News

---

*See John Horgan, "Scientific Heretic Rupert Sheldrake on Morphic Fields, Psychic Dogs and Other Mysteries," *Cross-Check* (a blog for *Scientific American*), July 14, 2014, http://blogs.scientificamerican.com/cross-check/2014/07/14/scientific-heretic-rupert -sheldrake-on-morphic-fields-psychic-dogs-and-other-mysteries/.

for twenty years and has received multiple Emmy Awards for her work. In her 2013 book *Stonewalled,* she addresses the unseen influences of corporations and special interests on the information and images the public receives every day in the news and elsewhere.

In a 2015 TEDx event in Nevada, Attkisson explained what she means.* Astroturf—the artificial turf used on playing fields—is a "perversion of grass roots—as in fake grass roots," she noted. In terms of public relations, astroturfing happens "when political or corporate or other special interests disguise themselves and publish blogs, start Facebook and Twitter accounts, publish ads, letters to the editor, or simply post comments online to try to fool you into thinking an independent or grassroots

The intersection of science and money; composite art for the cover of *Atlantis Rising* by Randy Haragan

---

*You can watch Attkisson's complete TEDx talk, "Astroturf and Manipulation of Media Messages" (February 6, 2015, at the University of Nevada) on YouTube, https://www.youtube.com/watch?v=-bYAQ-ZZtEU.

Sharyl Attkisson,
Emmy-winning
investigative journalist

movement is speaking. The whole point of astroturf is to give the impression there is widespread support for, or against, an agenda when there's not. Astroturf seeks to manipulate you into changing your opinion by making you feel as though you are an outlier when you are not."

Astroturfers, Attkisson says, seek to "controversialize" those who disagree with them. "They attack news organizations that publish stories they don't like, whistle blowers who tell the truth, politicians who dare to ask the tough questions, and journalists who have the audacity to report on all of it. Sometimes astroturfers simply shove so much conflicting and confusing information into the mix that you are left to throw up your hands and disregard all of it—including the truth. [They] drown out a link between a medicine and a harmful side effect—say vaccines and autism—by throwing a bunch of conflicting, paid-for studies, surveys, and experts into the mix, confusing the truth beyond recognition."

Wikipedia, Attkisson says, is "astroturf's dream come true." Though it is billed as the free encyclopedia that anyone can edit, "the reality," she says, "can't be more different."

"Anonymous Wikipedia editors," she argues, "control and co-opt pages on behalf of special interests. They forbid and reverse edits that go against their agenda, they skew and delete information, in blatant violation of Wikipedia's own established policies, with impunity, always superior to the poor schlubs who actually believe anyone could edit

Wikipedia, only to discover they are barred from correcting even the simplest factual inaccuracies."

"Try adding a footnoted fact or correcting a fact error on one of these monitored Wikipedia pages," she complains, "and poof, you will find—sometimes in a matter of seconds—your edit is reversed." She describes the case of celebrated author Philip Roth, who in 2012 tried to correct a major factual error about the inspiration behind one of his book characters on a Wikipedia page. No matter how hard he tried, though, Wikipedia's editors wouldn't allow it. The entry kept undoing the edits and reverting back to the false information. When Roth finally reached a person at Wikipedia—which was no easy task—and tried to find out what was going wrong, they told him he was simply not considered a credible source on "himself."

Attkisson also cited a 2014 medical study that looked at medical conditions described on Wikipedia's pages and compared them to actual peer-reviewed published research. Wikipedia, it turns out, contradicted medical research 90 percent of the time.* "You may never fully trust what you read on Wikipedia again," says Attkisson, "nor should you."

In theory, Wikipedia articles are written by disinterested volunteers and are based on reliable secondary sources. However, when a person searches for an article's title, Google will rank a Wikipedia article as the first result. The consequence is that public relations firms and "reputation management" companies work hard to remove any negative or controversial facts relating to their clients from Wikipedia articles. And, according to Conservapedia.com, although such paid editing is explicitly forbidden, Wikipedia does little to enforce the rules against paid editing and there are numerous examples of such editors introducing biased content on behalf of their clients. Moreover, when large Wikipedia donors are involved, says Conservapedia, Wikipedia selectively fails to enforce its ban on paid editing. Many organizations that visit the Wikimedia Foundation Headquarters also engage in undisclosed paid editing to promote themselves.

---

*See Robert T. Hasty, DO; Ryan C. Garbalosa, DO; Vincenzo A. Barbato, et al., "Wikipedia vs Peer-Reviewed Medical Literature for Information about the 10 Most Costly Medical Conditions," *Journal of the American Osteopathic Association* 114 (May 2014): 368–73, https://jaoa.org/article.aspx?articleid=2094721.

In 2013, the *International Business Times* reported that companies were willing to pay top dollar to PR firms willing to "fix" their entries. Wikipedia, wrote technology reporter Thomas Halleck, "is facing an onslaught of editors paid by private interests to edit and create articles, while its volunteer ranks are dwindling."

Wikipedia, after all, is free of advertising, and readers can also use it for free. The idea is that tens of thousands of independent editors motivated only by a desire to spread the truth can edit the material and keep it up to par. But even in 2013, the number of active editors was down nearly 40% from prior years. The result is that existing editors have more influence over what gets to stay in, says Halleck, but that is not the whole story.

Halleck spoke of one particular editor, Mike Wood, who is paid by companies and individuals to create and maintain articles that present them in the best light. "Sometimes," says Halleck, "[Wood] is even asked to remove negative information from a client's page. Wood likens himself to an attorney in court, advising a client on what course of action they can and cannot take. He charges as little as $50 for a small Wikipedia edit, up to $2,000 for the creation of a new article. Wood says that Wikipedia is his main source of income, and he makes more editing for hire on his site, LegalMorning.com, than from any other work he has pursued."*

The result of Wood's effort, and that of others like him, is that, at a minimum, the public gets an unreliable picture of the truth. And as Sharyl Attkisson has argued, for someone trying to use Wikipedia to decide what kind of drug might be safe, the results could be disastrous.

THE BATTLE FOR THE INTERNET

While the risks of putting a thumb on the scales of pharmaceutical information may be clear to all, some believe that possibly even more serious are the dangers to our entire society from distorting the meaning of important new scientific knowledge. Among these is Craig Weiler,

---

*See Thomas Halleck, "Wikipedia and Paid Edits: Companies Pay Top Dollar to Firms Willing to 'Fix' Their Entries," *International Business Times* (online), November 8, 2013, http://www.ibtimes.com/wikipedia-paid-edits-companies-pay-top-dollar-firms-willing -fix-their-entries-1449172.

author of the 2013 book *Psi Wars: TED, Wikipedia and the Battle for the Internet.* On his blog, *The Weiler Psi,* he argues that Wikipedia's treatment of Rupert Sheldrake is particularly egregious. A group of skeptical ideologues, Weiler says, has taken control of Rupert Sheldrake's biography page. Their ultimate goal, he believes, is no less than to control all available information across the collaborative encyclopedia.*

In March 2013, Sheldrake was involved in a controversy following his speech "The Science Delusion" at TEDx Whitechapel in London. Like Wikipedia, the prestigious not-for-profit TED Talks organization claims a commitment to keeping its patrons informed—in this case, about the latest developments in technology, entertainment, and design (TED). TED has achieved a sizable following for its brand, estimated in the billions. Now another kind of distinction can be added to its collection: censorship.

After hearing Sheldrake challenge the materialistic assumptions of contemporary science, the skeptical movement rose up as one, mad as hell, and the TED people soon fell in line, pulling Sheldrake's

Biologist Rupert Sheldrake at TEDx

---

*See Craig Weiler, "Wikipedia Cyberbullying: A Case Study," *The Weiler Psi* (blog), December 30, 2013, https://weilerpsiblog.wordpress.com/2013/12/30/wikipedia -cyberbullying-a-case-study/.

speech from their web lineup. They also removed a speech by Graham Hancock. However, despite publicly citing an unnamed science board for its decision, TED, in the wake of the ensuing and overwhelming public backlash, again retreated and restored both speeches to its site, but to a less favorable location or, as Hancock famously called it, "the naughty corner."

Later Sheldrake, in his newsletter, exposed an organized group called Guerrilla Skepticism for its determined efforts to modify Wikipedia entries on behalf of its agenda. Clearly threatened by someone with such a large—and approving—public following, the militant skeptical community, nevertheless, doubled down and renewed its unrelenting campaign to modify Wikipedia entries to reflect its own perspective on what it calls pseudoscience—that is, paranormal phenomena and the like. Now fully aroused, the group went after the Sheldrake threat, hammer and tong.* Weiler also was savaged after he reported on the attacks on Sheldrake's page.

The assault on Sheldrake is not an isolated problem, Weiler says. There are many aggressive ideologues who want to control Wikipedia, especially over so-called fringe topics, but these aggressors, he says, do not so much express their own point of view as viciously attack that of those with whom they disagree.

According to Weiler, one Wikipedia editor known as "Tumbleman," who seemed knowledgeable about parapsychology, tried to defend the notion of having an objective discussion about Sheldrake and his reputation. Attempting to take a more neutral stance toward Sheldrake and his scientific theories, Tumbleman challenged the biases of the skeptics. The result was a concerted attack on Tumbleman himself. A campaign to have him banned followed, and ultimately succeeded.†

One of Wikipedia's talk pages carried comments by an administrator who sided with the Guerrilla Skeptics. For Weiler, that was clear

---

*See Greg Taylor, "Maverick Biologist Rupert Sheldrake Criticizes Attacks by 'Guerilla Skeptics' on Wikipedia," *Daily Grail* (blog), October 10, 2013, https://www.dailygrail.com/2013/10/maverick-biologist-rupert-sheldrake-criticizes-attacks-by-guerilla-skeptics-on-wikipedia/.

†See Craig Weiler, "Wikipedia: The Trial of Tumbleman," *The Weiler Psi* (blog), October 18, 2013, https://weilerpsiblog.wordpress.com/2013/10/18/wikipedia-the-trial-of-tumbleman/.

evidence that Wikipedia not only is aware of the actions of the skeptical organization but has made no effort to stop them.

Anyone interested in subjects like astrology, the paranormal, metaphysics, faith/spirituality, alternative medicine, or even atheism or skepticism—what Wikipedia terms "fringe" topics—will soon learn that the "free" online encyclopedia has little interest in their views. They will also find, according to many reports, that they are dealing with a virtually secret cabal, dominated by a small group of editors, supported by at least two full-time supervising "experts" who zealously patrol, editing and deleting pages while claiming authority as strictly unbiased referees. Making, reportedly, up to ten thousand edits per year under the cloak of anonymity, they ensure, say critics, that their favored doctrine of scientism triumphs, bad science is white-washed, and inconvenient evidence is suppressed. At the same time, editors who dare to challenge the powers that be are ridiculed, intimidated, and banned in virtual tribunals.

Many critics, like Craig Weiler, marvel at just how the skeptics have been able to carry out such devious strategies so effectively. Galileo, we suspect, may have had similar questions about the Roman inquisition almost four centuries ago, but he didn't have Wikipedia to contend with.

ANCIENT DOOM

- - - - - - - - - -

*The end of civilizations
past and present*

32

Cosmic Collisions

Science takes a new look at threats from space

On the morning of February 15, 2013, the city of Chelyabinsk in the southern Ural mountains of Siberia got a taste of what the last days of Atlantis may have been like.

Traveling at close to forty thousand miles per hour, a meteor flashed through the heavens and exploded with an estimated force of about five hundred kilotons of TNT (or about twenty to thirty times the force of the atomic blasts at Hiroshima and Nagasaki, in Japan, that ended World War II). The explosion occurred about ten to fifteen miles above the ground, but still, the resulting shock wave blew out windows in over three thousand buildings in six cities of the sparsely populated region. The dazzling flash was witnessed by thousands (more than 1,200 were injured by flying glass), and soon the multitude of photos taken by many digital cameras were going viral on the internet.

The astrological sign
for comet

358

In October 2013, divers fished a large chunk of the meteor, weighing more than half a ton, from nearby Lake Chebarkul. Scientists reported finding pieces of the meteor across the area, but this one was, by far, the largest, measuring over five feet in length.*

In February 2013, an exploding meteor left a double contrail in the skies over Chelyabinsk in Siberia.

The meteor recovery from Lake Chebarkul drew a crowd.

---

*The recovery of the meteor from the lake was carried live on Russian television. You can watch some of the coverage online; see "Russia: Huge Chunk of Chelyabinsk Meteor Recovered from Lake," YouTube, October 17, 2013, https://www.youtube.com/watch?v=n1TL_jaVijY.

As newsworthy as the event certainly was, its full significance was slow to be fully appreciated. Though entirely unforeseen by astronomers and astrophysicists, the Chelyabinsk meteor served as both an unwelcome reminder of an historic precedent and a herald of coming attractions. Few could fail to note similarities to the still unexplained 1908 explosion at Tunguska (also in Siberia), which is thought to be the strongest impact event in modern history, leveling over 1,500 square miles. The Chelyabinsk meteor also marked the beginning of what was already being called "the year of the comet." Understandably, many religious devotees saw the heavens of those days as full of long-prophesied "signs and wonders."

The devastated Siberian forest following the 1908 Tunguska explosion

On the very day of the Chelyabinsk explosion came a long-promised close encounter of the physical kind with Asteroid 2012 DA14, a 150-foot-wide space rock, which passed just 17,200 miles above Earth's southern hemisphere—closer than the orbits of many weather satellites.*

---

*For details on Asteroid 2012 DA14, see "Asteroid 2012 DA14—Earth Flyby Reality Check," NASA (online), February 15, 2013, https://www.nasa.gov/topics/solarsystem /features/asteroidflyby.html

Scientists who publicly touted their prowess at being able to find and track the asteroid with such accuracy openly admitted that if it struck Southern California, it would wipe out everything from Los Angeles to San Diego. "Experts" were quick to point out that Earth and this asteroid were *not* on a collision course—something due more to luck than to any wisdom on their part. The Siberia meteor was certainly large enough to have destroyed most of any major city that it might have hit, yet no one saw it coming. That much, at least, is not in dispute.

A few years earlier, in July 1999, a meteor estimated to be as large as a railroad locomotive descending at a forty-five-degree angle exploded in the skies over New Zealand with a brilliance that eyewitnesses said matched the sun. Visible from as far north as Auckland and to the south as far as Christchurch, the explosion produced a long fiery tail reported by airline pilots and picked up on radar. Buildings shook and panicked observers flooded emergency switchboards. According to some reports, the blast produced a bright blue cloud of smoke that covered the nearby town of Napier and its sixty thousand inhabitants for more than an hour. Debris from the explosion was blamed for at least one forest fire.*

THE RETURN OF THE CATASTROPHISTS

In the Enlightenment of the seventeenth and eighteenth centuries, when modern science first emerged in Europe, those who studied rocks, landforms, and fossils—work that would ultimately become the primary earth sciences of geology and paleontology—believed that Earth's past had been shaped by sudden and violent catastrophes, primarily the flood of Noah. For those early scientists, it was all about the Bible. But then, with the rise of Darwinism, Christianity fell into disfavor among intellectual elites, and the catastrophism associated with biblical flood doctrine was rejected and replaced with uniformitarianism, the view that the past was shaped by processes we can see still at work today. We were told to consider as the norm the very slow changes of the climate,

---

*See Jennie McCormick, "Fireballs: The Taranaki Daylight Fireball, 1999 July 7," *WGN, Journal of the International Meteor Organization* 34, no. 5 (2006): 135–42, https://ui.adsabs.harvard.edu/abs/2006JIMO...34..135M/abstract.

the gradual advance and retreat of glaciers, the almost imperceptible rising of mountain ranges, and the equally slow processes of erosion.

By the late eighteenth century, the advocates of uniformitarianism, led primarily by James Hutton and Charles Lyell, dominated earth sciences. A brief rebellion led by Georges Cuvier in the early nineteenth century was crushed. Although he had not relied on any biblical accounts, Cuvier still believed that there had been truly catastrophic floods and earthquakes in the distant past. Nevertheless, his challenge to the uniformitarians failed, and their doctrines were no longer to be questioned. The matter was settled.

Today, however, the great danger that Earth faces from unexpected space projectiles is finding new credence in circles where previously scant attention was given to such risks. "Vindication for Entrepreneurs Watching Sky: Yes, It Can Fall," proclaimed a *New York Times* headline reporting on Chelyabinsk. "For decades, scientists have been on the lookout for killer objects from outer space that could devastate the planet," noted William J. Broad. "Warnings that they lacked the tools to detect the most serious threats were largely ignored, even as skeptics mocked the worriers as Chicken Littles." Overnight, though, the opinion climate has dramatically changed. From Silicon Valley to Washington, D.C., many soon flocked to the cause. "Wouldn't it be silly if we got wiped out because we weren't looking?" asked Edward Lu, a former NASA astronaut and Google executive who leads a major detection effort.* In the meantime, congressman Dana Rohrabacher of California, then vice chairman of the House Committee on Science, Space, and Technology, responded to the Russian fireball by telling Space.com, "The event should serve as a wakeup call."† Indeed.

As early as 1996, however, *Atlantis Rising* had published a cover story, "Cosmic Collisions," by Joseph Jochmans that made the very point. "Rocky or iron asteroids 2,000 feet or more in diameter and icy

---

*See William J. Broad, "Vindication for Entrepreneurs Watching Sky: Yes, It Can Fall," *New York Times* (online), February 16, 2013, https://www.nytimes.com/2013/02/17/science/space/dismissed-as-doomsayers-advocates-for-meteor-detection-feel-vindicated.html.

†See Leonard David, "Russian Fireball Highlights Asteroid Threat, Lawmaker Says," Space.com (online), February 16, 2013, https://www.space.com/19833-russia-meteor-asteroid-threat.html.

cometary bodies of 4,000 feet or more in size," Jochmans wrote, "would be able to penetrate the atmosphere and hit the surface with forces of 10 to 100 megatons of TNT respectively." The possibility that such a strike could have destroyed Ice Age civilizations such as Atlantis may have stimulated interest.

Generally the notion that Earth's long history has been punctuated by immense catastrophic events has been sneered at by mainstream academic science committed to the gradualist view of history. As has been previously noted, though, there have been a few, like Immanuel Velikovsky, who have gone against the tide. Now events that might have passed unnoticed a few years ago are drawing new scrutiny.

In 2016, Comet Pan-STARRS passed by Earth only about a hundred million miles away, and many were able to see it. Later that year, Comet ISON—trumpeted as the "comet of the century"—appeared. Long feared as omens of disaster, comets, with their long fiery tails, have for millennia been identified as celestial dragons and bringers of trouble.

Sunday, April 15, 2018, was a good day, but it could have been otherwise. That was the day when a 150-foot asteroid came within a whisker (astronomically speaking) of hitting Earth, and with virtually no warning. Within hours of its discovery, said NASA scientists in Arizona, Asteroid 2018 GE3 passed within 119,500 miles of us—or about half the distance to the moon. Probably six times bigger than the Chelyabinsk meteorite, GE3 could have caused a far greater disaster somewhere on Earth.*

Once one of millions of space rocks forming the "asteroid belt"—a giant band of rocky debris between the orbits of Mars and Jupiter—GE3 had never before been seen by Earth's astronomers. The real possibility that such an unexpected, and unwelcome, visitor from space could strike our planet is not to be ignored these days. New research has made it clear that catastrophic collisions with objects from space have happened in even recent history—not just many millions of years ago, when they are widely credited with destroying the dinosaurs. The Younger Dryas mini ice age event, which some think caused the destruction of Atlantis, now

---

*For more on Asteroid 2018 GE3, see Kate Samuelson, "A 150-Foot Asteroid Flew Alarmingly Close to Earth Just Hours After Being Spotted," *Time* (online), April 16, 2018, https://time.com/5241352/asteroid-earth-ge3/.

appears to have been caused by a collision with the remains of a shattered comet. (See the next chapter for a discussion of this possibility.)

According to some researchers, the big threat to Earth may come from "dark" comets—those that are virtually unseen and undetected by us. Of the three thousand comets that have entered our solar system, the whereabouts of only about twenty-five are known, and astronomers Bill Napier in the U.K. and David Asher in Northern Ireland say they think that is because once its ice and gases have burned away, the underlying crust of a comet reflects only a fraction of the light and that makes it hard to see.* For example, when Comet IRAS-Araki-Alcock passed Earth in 1983 at only three million miles away—the closest in two hundred years—it was detected only two weeks before it passed because most of its gases were gone and the surface was extremely dark.†

According to a report from scientists at the Universidad Nacional Autónoma de México, the end of the world as we know it could have happened in 1883, when a comet eight times the size of Haley's came within 120 miles of Earth. If it had actually struck the planet, the destruction, it is estimated, could have been as great as the event said to have killed the dinosaurs millions of years ago.

Hector Javier Durand-Manterola, lead author of the report, says the conclusion is based on a photo and research by Mexican astronomer José Bonilla, which was published in the magazine L'Astronomie in 1886. At the time, the picture was called the first photo of a UFO. It showed an array of 447 misty-looking objects followed by a misty tail. According to Manterola's team, Bonilla had observed a highly fragmented comet, which new calculations show was in an approach almost parallel with the Earth's surface. The objects are estimated to have been between three hundred and five thousand miles away, and between forty and seven hundred yards in diameter.‡

---

*See Paul Parsons, "'Dark' Comets May Pose Threat to Earth," New Scientist (online), February 11, 2009, https://www.newscientist.com/article/mg20126954-800-dark-comets -may-pose-threat-to-earth/.

†See John Noble Wilford, "A New Comet to Approach Close to Earth," New York Times (online), May 6, 1983, https://www.nytimes.com/1983/05/06/us/a-new-comet -to-approach-close-to-earth.html.

‡See Hector Javier Durand-Manterola, Maria de la Paz Ramos Lara, and Guadalupe Cordero, "Interpretation of the Observations Made in 1883 in Zacatecas (Mexico): A Fragmented Comet That Nearly Hits the Earth," October 12, 2011: arXiv:1110.2798.

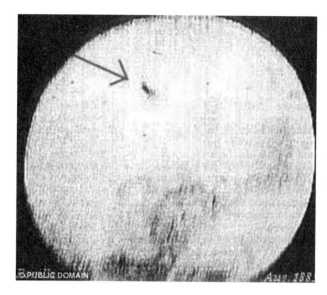

Astronomer
José Bonilla's
1883 photo of a
threatening comet

Some scientists question the findings, pointing out that such a comet breakup would have filled the sky with meteors, and that such an event was never reported. In fact, the regular Perseid meteor shower that followed shortly after the sighting was in no way unusual.

NASA has recently reported that the risk to Earth from planet-killing asteroids or comets is less than originally thought. It only takes one, though, to ruin your entire day.

Cosmic collision;
cover art from the
February 1996 issue of
Atlantis Rising

MEETING WITH OUMUAMUA

Has our solar system just been visited by an interstellar intruder car-rying greetings from ancient life on some alien world light-years away? That is a question that interests not only UFO researchers but many mainstream scientists. In late November 2017, a mysterious interstel-lar object named Oumuamua (Hawaiian for "messenger") suddenly appeared on a path bending sharply around our sun. The giant, cigar-shaped, almost black object was first spotted by the Pan-STARRS observatory in Hawaii. It has many qualities that are very much *un*like a typical asteroid or comet, and though it was not something astrono-mers had seen before, it did closely resemble a particular form that some scientists have speculated would be ideal for an interstellar mission.

An artist's conjecture of Oumuamua; image courtesy of NASA

Immediately, many began to wonder whether the object might be some kind of probe dispatched by some advanced civilization elsewhere in the universe. Plans soon formed to take as thorough a look as pos-sible while the fast-moving object was still within range of Earth's sensors. One of the first to take on the challenge was Russian billionaire Yuri Milner and his Breakthrough Listen project (see chapter 25).

Guided by Avi Loeb (Harvard's astronomy department chair), Stephen Hawking, and others, Milner's group set out to use the Green Bank radio telescope in West Virginia to listen very carefully for any signals emanating from the object. In an email to Milner, Loeb said, "The more I study this object, the more unusual it appears, making me wonder whether it might be an artificially made probe which was sent by an alien civilization."*

In the meantime, astronomer Alan Fitzsimmons from Queen's University Belfast, the lead author of another major new study already published on the object, reported that Oumuamua was wrapped in a strange "organic coat," which might be some kind of insulation for an unknown but presumably icy core.†

With the aid of new technology, astronomers have begun to scan the skies with growing intensity and now report a dramatic increase in the rate of discovery of potential killer asteroids. Such objects could create damage comparable to that envisioned in Hollywood features like *Deep Impact* and *Armageddon.*

According to the BBC, newly published research argues that the course of human evolution could have been influenced by frequent cosmic catastrophes. Dr. Benny Peiser, a social anthropologist at Liverpool John Moores University in the U.K., and Michael Paine, an impact researcher from the Planetary Society in Australia, now argue that the most likely cause of hominid extinctions may be more than twenty globally devastating catastrophes that occurred over the last five million years.

The researchers performed a computer simulation of cosmic impacts throughout the period to give an indication of the environmental disruption that may have occurred during the evolution of our species.

---

*See Marina Koren, "Astronomers to Check Mysterious Interstellar Object for Signs of Technology," *The Atlantic* (online), December 11, 2017, https://www.theatlantic.com /science/archive/2017/12/yuri-milner-oumuamua-interstellar-asteroid/547985/.
†See Queen's University Belfast, "Alien object 'Oumuama was a natural body visiting from another solar system." *ScienceDaily*, December 18, 2017, https://www.sciencedaily .com/releases/2017/12/171218120141.htm.

368 ✦ Ancient Doom

The simulation looked at the worst event in each of the preceding five thousand millennia. They found that over the period of the simulation, some 57 percent of millennia suffered an impact that would potentially have had consequences for land-dwelling creatures.*

The research reignites the long-standing debate between the so-called gradualist and catastrophist schools of history. On one side, the orthodox academics view, inspired by Darwin, attempts to explain natural history as the product of a slow process of survival and mutation, while the other side sees external forces at work. The latter includes so-called "biblical creationists" but is by no means limited to them. In recent years, many established scientists, including Dr. Robert Schoch, have begun to challenge the ruling viewpoint with the hardest of scientific evidence. Schoch himself thinks the greatest extraterrestrial threat could be from massive plasma discharges from the sun, but the role that collisions with objects from space may have played is being examined more closely, and a growing body of scientific opinion is now coming to recognize that there may be more threats from space than has been previously considered.

"The reason that *Homo sapiens* has survived in spite of these global disasters," Dr. Peiser told the BBC, "has little to do with the traditional explanations given by Neo-Darwinists. It is sobering to realise that we are alive due to cosmic luck rather than our genetic make-up."

---

*See David Whitehouse, "Asteroids Affected Human Evolution," BBC News (online), April 12, 2001, http://news.bbc.co.uk/2/hi/science/nature/1272368.stm.

33

Extinction Event

New light on the mystery of the Younger Dryas

In his book *Secret of Atlantis* (published posthumously, in German in 1976 and in English in 1978), renowned German scientist-engineer Otto Muck said that about twelve thousand years ago an asteroid streaked in over North America from the northwest. Before crashing into the Caribbean and destroying much of what Muck said was then Atlantis, the asteroid broke up and left more than three thousand shallow craters across what are now the Carolinas and several other states, including Maryland, Virginia, and Georgia and reaching as far west as Kansas and Nebraska. Known today as the Carolina bays, the elliptical crater-like shapes, though a common feature of many landscapes, are virtually unknown to the public. Any possibility, though, that they may have played a role in the great North American animal extinction event now known as the Younger Dryas is completely rejected by mainstream science, if not by Otto Muck.

The name of the 12,800 BP (before the present) event comes from a flowering tundra plant, *Dryas octopetala*. Its presence signals a colder climate. Two less extreme colder periods were known as the Older Dryas and the Oldest Dryas. The drop in temperature before the last major glaciation occurred virtually overnight, requiring only decades to spread over most of the northern hemisphere. Glaciation would take centuries to reach its maximum extent.

Dire scenarios envisioned by Otto Muck and other catastrophists have often involved strikes by large bolides from space, which in about

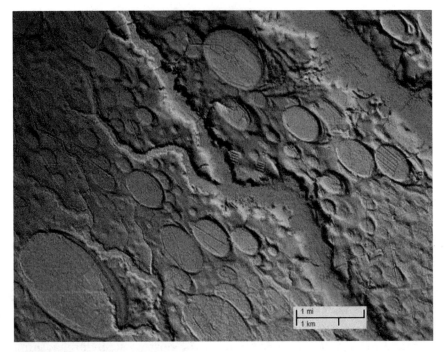

Satellite image of Carolina bay
formations; image courtesy of NASA

Dryas octopetala
flowers

10,000 BCE, they speculate, caused the destruction of an advanced civilization, killed off the woolly mammoths, and hurled our ancestors back to the Stone Age. But even though ancient sources, from the Bible to Plato, are filled with tales of such immense calamities, the prevailing academic paradigm has always discarded theories that any such thing could have happened on Earth for millions of years at the least.

If you had asked, you would have been told that while we may have evidence for a mini ice age called the Younger Dryas, beginning about the time Plato said Atlantis sank, any kind of giant hit from space as proposed by catastrophists would have caused an enormous impact crater, which has never been found. As for the Carolina bays, the go-to explanation was that centuries of high winds were the cause, and any suggestion that they might have had a role in the Younger Dryas was dismissed out of hand. For many years, that has been the state of the debate, but a recent discovery may have changed that. From Greenland has come evidence for exactly the kind of projectile impact that could have triggered the Younger Dryas and been the death knell for any advanced civilization that might have been up and running at the time.

In a study entitled "A Large Impact Crater beneath Hiawatha Glacier in Northwest Greenland," the peer reviewed journal *Science Advances* published the startling news in 2018. Just twelve thousand years ago, said the authors, an enormous iron meteorite crashed into Greenland, and where today we find a glacier, there is beneath the ice a twenty-mile-wide crater that can be precisely dated. The mile-wide meteor, said the study, was among the largest such objects ever known to have struck Earth. The impact, it is calculated, would have had the force of seven hundred million nuclear bombs. Geologists concede it could have caused ripple effects not only throughout the region but maybe worldwide. Many experts have already accepted that the event could indeed establish as recognized scientific fact the once controversial Younger Dryas impact hypothesis.*

Computer-rendered image representing the giant impact crater
beneath Greenland's Hiawatha Glacier

---

*For the full report, see K. H. Kjaer, N. K. Larsen, T. Binder, et al., "A Large Impact Crater beneath Hiawatha Glacier in Northwest Greenland," *Science Advances* 4, no. 11 (2014), https://advances.sciencemag.org/content/4/11/eaar8173.

While that theory has been controversial in the past, there are many who have long believed that a large impact in North America eleven thousand to thirteen thousand years ago could have been the cause of massive wildfires across much of the Americas and Europe, large animal extinctions, and disruptions in the weather of the Atlantic Ocean. The new Greenland discovery is the first to identify an actual impact crater of sufficient size to support the theory.

In "What Ended the Ice Age?" the cover story for *Atlantis Rising* #113 (September/October 2015), writer Cynthia Logan laid out independent researcher Randall Carlson's extensive case that the so-called Younger Dryas mini ice age was brought on by a comet impact. A leading alternative science researcher, Carlson says that ancient myths of floods and lost civilization tell a real story of life on Earth punctuated by a cosmic impact, and he has deployed a small army of volunteers to pursue some large-scale field research, mostly in America's Pacific Northwest. In his 2015 book on lost civilizations, *Magicians of the Gods,* best-selling author Graham Hancock relied extensively on Carlson's research.

Recent discoveries, like those at Göbekli Tepe in Turkey, at Gunung Padang in Indonesia, and in the re-dating of the Sphinx in Egypt, make it clear that advanced civilization of some kind predated the end of the last ice age. Reinforcing the Greenland discovery, a report from another major study is providing even more evidence that not very long ago—geologically speaking—life on Earth was violently interrupted and our last ice age began. Titled "Extraordinary Biomass-Burning Episode and Impact Winter Triggered by the Younger Dryas Cosmic Impact—12,800 Years Ago," the report offers a hair-raising tale of enormous firestorms—worse than those that killed the dinosaurs many millions of years earlier—that ravaged as much as a tenth of Earth's surface. The ensuing mini ice age, set in motion by immense dust clouds that smothered the planet, lasted for a thousand years.

The researchers say that the firestorms were caused by hits from comet fragments as large as sixty-two miles across. "The hypothesis is that a large comet fragmented and that chunks impacted the Earth, causing this disaster," says Adrian Melott from the University of Kansas, one of the authors. "A number of different chemical signatures—carbon dioxide, nitrate, ammonia and others—all seem to indicate that an astonishing 10 percent of Earth's land surface—or about 3.86 million square miles—was consumed by fires."*

One analysis carried out on patterns in pollen levels suggested that pine forests were suddenly burned off and replaced by poplar trees—a species specializing in covering barren ground, as might be expected when the planet has been hit with a series of massive fireballs.

The widespread impact of the comet fragments and the ensuing firestorm are blamed by the team for the Younger Dryas event, itself a relatively brief blip in the planet's temperature history that has been popularly attributed to changing ocean currents.

Though the largest to date, the University of Kansas–led study is not the first to blame a cosmic impact for the Younger Dryas. In January 2009, a team of researchers, led by University of Oregon archaeologist Douglas Kennett, reported finding abundant tiny particles of diamond dust in sediments dating to 12,900 years ago at six North American sites—powerful evidence for a cosmic impact effect. Their report, published in the journal *Science*, proposed that an impact event, possibly involving multiple comet airbursts, set off the Younger Dryas, leading to many extinctions across North America, including that of the indigenous Clovis culture and a large range of animals, including mammoths.†

For many years, fashionable conventional wisdom regarding massive extinctions of megafauna (large animals like woolly mammoths) in North America at the beginning of the Younger Dryas has had it that human hunters, battling the effects of climate change, like starvation, were the cause. That theory, it is now clear, no longer holds water. Most anthropologists now recognize that human hunters were in America much earlier than once thought, having come by both land and sea, and if they could have destroyed wildlife here, the question becomes: Why did they not do it in Eurasia, Africa, and elsewhere before that time? Such mass extinctions of both plant and animal species, however, might

---

*See David Nield, "A Recent Ice Age Was Triggered by a Firestorm Bigger Than The One That Killed The Dinosaurs," ScienceAlert (online), February 4, 2018, https://www.sciencealert.com/13000-years-ago-gigantic-fires-consumed-the-world-causing-ice-age.
†See the press release from the University of Oregon: "Six North American Sites Hold 12,900-Year-Old Nanodiamond-Rich Soil," University of Oregon media relations office (online), January 2, 2009, https://uonews.uoregon.edu/archive/news-release/2009/1/six-north-american-sites-hold-12900-year-old-nanodiamond-rich-soil.

Nanometer-sized diamonds occur at the base of a layer of sediment directly above the remains of extinct animals (mammoths, dire wolves, et cetera) and artifacts from the Clovis culture at a research site in Murray Springs, Arizona; image courtesy of the University of Oregon.

be brought on by rapid climate change, and/or by truly catastrophic events, such as volcano eruptions or major comet or asteroid impacts that might, in turn, also trigger severe climate change.

Not everyone yet agrees that a comet impact kicked off the Younger Dryas event, but recent studies are making a very strong case for it, and vindicating at least one aspect of the long-derided catastrophist view of history.

TROUBLE FROM THE SUN

One committed catastrophist who does not look to some kind of cosmic bolide strike to explain the Younger Dryas is Dr. Robert Schoch. Though the Boston University geologist concedes that he was once of that mind, he now says that to explain the events at the beginning of the last age, we should look no further than the sun. In his 2012 book *Forgotten Civilization: The Role of Solar Outbursts in Our Past and Future,* Schoch says that despite popular misconceptions, the sun is not

Some of the megafauna brought to extinction by the Younger Dryas event;
art by Mauricio Antón

a stable, unchanging, eternal ball of fire in the sky. Indeed, from an astrophysical and geological perspective, the sun is quite the opposite. "It is," he says, "unstable, continually seething and churning, in disequilibrium, discharging not only visible light, but also a large energy array across the electromagnetic spectrum, and belting out charged particles as well." While the sun may have little hiccups from time to time, it can also suffer from major bouts of coughing, spewing massive "solar storms" toward Earth. Such storms, thousands of times more powerful than anything recorded in modern times, have left their marks in prehistoric records. Indeed, Schoch believes, many of the mysterious cataclysmic episodes of human history are best understood as plasma events resulting from major solar outbursts.

Sometimes referred to as the fourth state of matter, plasma consists of electrically charged particles. Familiar plasma phenomena on Earth today include lightning and auroras, the northern and southern lights, as well as large-scale upper atmospheric phenomena known as sprites. In the past, much more powerful plasma events sometimes took place, due to major solar outbursts (including what are known as coronal mass ejections). Los Alamos plasma physicist Dr. Anthony L. Peratt and his associates have argued that ancient petroglyphs (carvings on rocks) found worldwide record an intense plasma event (or events) in prehistory.

In his 2009 book *The Sun Kings,* British author Stuart Clark tells us that, in 1859, "around the world telegraph systems crashed, machines burst into flames, and electric shocks rendered operators unconscious. . . . Compasses and other sensitive instruments reeled as if struck by a massive magnetic fist." Occurring simultaneously all across the northern hemisphere, the disruptions completely bewildered the scientists of the day, save one, an English amateur astronomer who looked to the skies for an explanation. At the exact moment of the event, Richard Carrington, at the telescope of London's Kew Observatory, witnessed a large solar flare, which he soon connected to the effects then blasting the world.

The storm on the sun would continue for eight days, during which time "the entire Earth was engulfed in a gigantic cloud of seething gas, and a blood-red aurora erupted across the planet from the poles to the tropics," reported Clark. Observers in the Caribbean, as far south as Trinidad, were treated to spectacular aurora borealis displays. In the

The aurora borealis (northern lights) is caused by charged particles from the sun (also see color insert plate 15).

Rocky Mountains, the nighttime northern lights were so brilliant that gold miners thought morning had come, and roosters prematurely crowed the dawn. Enormous quantities of negatively charged ions, Carrington concluded, had been released into the Earth's magnetosphere by the solar flare that he had witnessed. The event not only caused spectacular northern lights but also shorted out the world's telegraph systems.

At first scientists were reluctant to believe that a storm on the sun, ninety-three million miles away, could have caused the calamity, but eventually they came around and named geomagnetic solar storms Carrington events, after their discoverer. Two successors to the first incident have been identified so far. And while the effects on Earth of a storm on the sun may have been relatively harmless in the time of the telegraph, the effects of such an event in the age of the internet and smart electronics would certainly be much more consequential.

THE POLE SHIFT QUESTION

And then, of course, there are volcanoes. Enormous eruptions of the Kilauea volcano on Hawaii's large island in 2018 transfixed the world with spectacular images of towering lava fountains and vast flows of molten rock, rendering much of the famed tropical paradise uninhabitable. Going almost unnoticed, however, was a related effect, which could portend future consequences more dire. As visitors approached the volcano, their magnetic compasses suddenly reversed, switching north and south poles and going into uncontrollable spins. The effect has caused some of those who worry about global warming to add another concern to their list—the possibility of a magnetic pole shift.

Cartographer Charles Hapgood wrote in the 1950s that an advanced prediluvian civilization, possibly Atlantis, was destroyed by a relatively sudden shift in the angle of Earth's polar axis, and some fear we may be approaching a recurrence—if not the full physical axial kind, at least a magnetic polar swap of the Kilauea type. Any of these possibilities could be catastrophic, and all have precedent in relatively recent natural history.

Any civilization on Earth at the time of such an event could very well have been destroyed. Indeed, an impact event on the scale of the one suspected of causing the Younger Dryas might itself have led to a

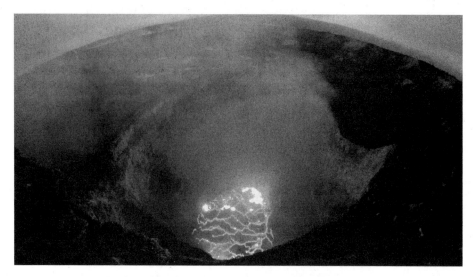

Northern portion of the Kilauea caldera during the 2018 eruption
(also see color insert plate 16)

pole shift of some kind. In 2009, NASA researchers made the case that global warming could actually cause a small pole shift, suggesting that sudden warming and the consequent melting of polar ice caps could cause a small shift in the poles, which, over time, could be significant.*

Whether that kind of shift is imminent or not, there is considerable evidence locked in volcanic rocks from around the world that the magnetic poles of Earth have indeed shifted many times and could be overdue for a replay. The last one occurred, scientists think, about 780,000 years ago.

According to a 2008 study published in the journal *Science,* massive swirls in volcanic rocks far beneath the surface can cause Earth's magnetic poles to shift, and recent satellite studies by the European Space Agency confirm that the planet's magnetic poles are indeed shifting, and, moreover, that the shift is speeding up.†

---

*See Rachel Courtland, "Global warming could change Earth's tilt," *NewsScientist,* August 20, 2009, https://www.newscientist.com/article/dn17657-global-warming -could-change-earths-tilt/.

†See the press release about the study from the University of Wisconsin at Madison: "Earth's Magnetic Field Reversals Illuminated by Lava Flows Study," ScienceDaily (online), September 26, 2008, https://www.sciencedaily.com/releases/2008/09/080926105021 .htm.

Could the greatest cause of climate change be not human activity, as we have been led to believe, but, in fact, the tilt of Earth's axis? The idea is not new, but now a respected Harvard researcher says he has proven it. If he is right, climate scientists everywhere may need, inconveniently, to go back to their computer models.

Professor Peter Huybers has used state-of-the-art computer models to prove that tiny shifts in Earth's axis cause glaciers to either advance or retreat in cycles lasting either ten thousand or forty thousand years. In a 2011 paper published in the journal *Nature,* Huybers explained that there are two cycles of tilt change, known as obliquity and precession. When they align correctly, ice melts. When they oppose each other, glaciers advance. In past periods of deglaciation, sea levels have risen by 130 meters, and temperatures by 5 degrees Celsius. Moreover, atmospheric carbon dioxide in such periods increased by over 40 percent.*

Serbian geophysicist Milutin Milankovitch first argued for such a thing a century ago. In his theory, according to Wikipedia, the Earth's axis completes one full cycle of precession approximately every twenty-six thousand years. At the same time, the elliptical orbit rotates more slowly. Milankovitch believed the combined effect of the two precessions leads to a twenty-one-thousand-year period between the astronomical seasons and the orbit. In addition, the angle between Earth's rotational axis and the normal to the plane of its orbit (obliquity) oscillates between 22.1 and 24.5 degrees on a forty-one-thousand-year cycle. It is currently 23.44 degrees and decreasing.†

Precession is the cycle behind the so-called astronomical ages, where the constellation seen at sunrise during the spring equinox appears to slowly move backward (precess) through the zodiac at a rate of about one sign every 2,150 years (we are now entering the age of Aquarius). Many modern alternative science scholars, as well as ancient sages, have suggested that this precession of the equinoxes tracks the rise and fall of civilizations.

---

*See Peter Huybers, "Combined Obliquity and Precession Pacing of Late Pleistocene Deglaciations," *Nature* 480 (2011): 229–32, https://www.nature.com/articles /nature10626?proof=true.

†For a simplified explanation of Milankovitch cycles, as they're known, see Steve Graham, "Milutin Milankovitch (1879–1958)," on the Earth Observatory website (part of NASA), March 24, 2000, https://earthobservatory.nasa.gov/features/Milankovitch.

34

Fires of the Underworld

What history can be found beneath the surface?

Almost seven thousand years ago, primitive hunters in the Himalayan territory of Kashmir witnessed the explosion of a distant star and memorialized their impressions in a petroglyph. That, at least, is the story told in 2017 in the *Indian Journal of History of Science* to explain an ancient carving that appears to depict twin suns in a tableau with two hunters and a bull.

For years, archaeologists examining the petroglyph thought they were looking at two suns, but a team of scientists in India and Germany reasoned that there cannot be two suns, so something else must be going on. By tracking known supernovas in astronomical records, the researchers settled on an event known as Supernova HB9, a star that exploded around 4600 BCE near the Orion constellation, just above the Taurus (bull) constellation.*

Extraterrestrial explosions have a long history of influencing life on Earth in ironic ways. In 1572 CE, a great supernova in the Milky Way, visible to the naked eye, caused a public sensation and provided the great Danish-Czech astronomer Tycho Brahe an opportunity to introduce his controversial new theory that stars existed far beyond the distance to the moon.

---

*See Michael Safi, "Two Suns? No, It's a Supernova Drawn 6,000 Years Ago, Say Scientists," *The Guardian* (online), January 10, 2018, https://www.theguardian.com /world/2018/jan/10/two-suns-no-its-a-supernova-drawn-6000-years-ago-say-indian -scientists.

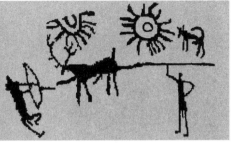

A seven-thousand-year-old Kashmir petroglyph depicts two suns; image courtesy of the *Indian Journal of History of Science.*

More recently King Tut's "brooch," a perfectly preserved arti-fact taken from his tomb, may have memorialized an ancient comet exploding upon collision with Earth. The royal chest covering is part of the treasure discovered in 1922 by Howard Carter and Lord Carnarvon when they famously opened the tomb of the boy pharaoh Tutankhamun in Egypt's Valley of the Kings. Scientists now believe the carved yellow stone at the center of the royal ornament was formed by a comet hitting Earth twenty-eight million years ago. Ground zero for the cataclysmic comet hit, it is said, was a four-thousand-square-mile area in the Sahara desert, where melted sand provided significant quantities of rare yellow silica glass, from which King Tut's brooch was carved. Researchers have now come up with a mysterious black pebble from the same area, which they believe is meteorite debris from the comet's nucleus.*

The exploding-comet hypothesis is one effort to explain anomalous glass deposits found on Earth, but it is not the only one. In recent years, some have argued that the ancient silica glass in Egypt resulted from a nuclear explosion, one of the few things that could have produced the necessary heat—about 3,600 degrees Fahrenheit. Similarly melted artifacts found near Mohenjo Daro in modern-day Pakistan have also been attributed by some to ancient atomic warfare that was seemingly described in vivid detail by ancient Hindu scriptures.

---

*See "Pectoral of Tutankhamun Holds Evidence of Ancient Comet," Archaeology Wiki (online), October 9, 2013, https://www.archaeology.wiki/blog/2013/10/09/brooch-of-tutankhamun-holds-evidence-of-ancient-comet/.

The brooch of
Tutankhamun (also see
color insert plate 18)

Consider this passage from the *Mahabharata,* the Sanskrit epic believed by academia to have been written in the eighth century, but by others to be much older:

> A single projectile charged with all the power in the Universe. . . . An incandescent column of smoke and flame as bright as 10,000 suns, rose in all its splendor. . . . It was an unknown weapon, an iron thunderbolt, a gigantic messenger of death which reduced to ashes an entire race. . . . The corpses were so burned as to be unrecognizable. Their hair and nails fell out, pottery broke without any apparent cause, and the birds turned white. . . . After a few hours, all foodstuffs were infected. To escape from this fire, the soldiers threw themselves into the river.

Ancient skeletons unearthed in 1927 from Mohenjo Daro were reported by some sources to show high levels of radiation and to lack the decay that might normally be expected. Victims, furthermore, appear to

Unexplained skeletons found in a 1927 archaeological dig at Mohenjo Daro, Pakistan

have dropped where they stood, suggesting, perhaps, a massacre or some terrible weapon of mass destruction.*

FORTS OF GLASS

Egypt and Pakistan are not the only places, however, to provide unexplained clues to the possibility of superheated ancient warfare. In Scotland and parts of Europe, many large ancient hill forts have been melted to virtual glass. *Vitrification* is the official term used to describe the phenomenon. A 2018 study by Forest Enterprise Scotland and the University of Stirling was the most recent of many attempts to prove

---

*For details on the nuclear destruction hypothesis, see "Powerful Evidence of Nuclear Wars in Ancient Times," Gaia (online), November 20, 2019; "Nuclear Events in Ancient India?," Biblioteca Pleyades (online), n.d. (accessed September 16, 2020); and "Nuclear Event in Ancient India," in the "Tracking Ancient Man" section of the Ancient Hebrew Research Center (online), 2016. The orthodox explanation for the skeletons unearthed from Mohenjo Daro is also available on online; see George F. Dales, "The Mythical Massacre at Mohenjo-Daro," *Expedition Magazine* 6, no. 3 (1964), on the website of the Penn Museum.

Vitrified Iron Age
Scottish fort

that, despite doubts you may have had, burning wood in the forts could, in fact, have been enough to cause the vitrification:

> A timber superstructure, which included ramparts and towers, was set alight and the resulting blaze heated the stones. The fire was so intense that it was able to melt stones because of the anaerobic environment that developed, as the flames burned down into the stones. The absence of oxygen in the anaerobic conditions made the fire much more intense, and allowed it to reach the temperatures that would have burned the slabs until they melted and fused.*

In the opinion of other researchers, though, the Stirling study failed to answer the many basic questions raised. In "The Heat of Battle— Who Turned Ancient Hill Forts to Glass?" published in *Atlantis Rising* #132 (November/December 2018), Frank Joseph recalled his own investigation at the Craig Phadrig ruins near Inverness and threw cold water on the new study. "The University of Stirling experiment failed to vitrify anything more than a tiny handful of rubble, far short of the vitrification covering even the smallest of Scotland's six dozen forts," wrote Joseph. "The archaeologists were simply unable to keep their fires burning long enough to sustain the necessary temperatures." The study, he added, was simply a rerun of work done by University of

---

*See "Archaeologists Solve Ancient Mystery of 'Melted' Iron Age Fort," *Scotsman* (online), April 30, 2018, https://www.scotsman.com/lifestyle-2-15039/archaeologists -solve-ancient-mystery-of-melted-iron-age-fort-1-4732710.

Edinburgh archaeologist Vere Gordon Childe eighty-four years earlier.

Neither study, said Joseph, could provide more than a few melted droplets to show for many tons of burning brushwood and extra timber. Clearly, a concentrated, far more powerful, longer-lasting heat source had vitrified Craig Phadrig and its associated fortresses.

In 1980—building on the Childe effort—Dr. Ian Ralston of Edinburgh University's department of archaeology undertook an even more ambitious project in northeast Scotland, building a twenty-five-foot-long partial replica of a stone fort. Described on the *Arthur C. Clarke's Mysterious World* television show, the attempt to re-create a vitrification event required a tremendous amount of work on the part of the archaeologists:

> Professional dry-stone wallers toiled for days to build the wall of rocks laced with timber [which was then set alight]. . . . After several hours and many tons of wood, a load of old furniture has to be commandeered from the local dustman, as the only way to keep the temperature up. Later, yet another consignment of wood, the sixth of the day, arrives to keep the fires burning. As night falls over Aberdeen, weary helpers begin to realize the true extent of the mystery of the vitrified forts, to wonder not only how the fort builders could achieve the searing temperatures needed to melt the rock, but how they managed to drag vast quantities of wood up to the hilltops with only primitive transport. The morning after . . . twenty-two hours after the first fire was lit . . . at first sight, the result looks disappointing. There are no ramparts of fused stone.*

SHELTER FROM THE STORM

Many ancient extinction-level events, it now appears, could have threatened humanity, both before and after the last ice age. As discussed earlier in this book, we have evidence of human civilization before

---

*The experiment was included in episode 3 of *Arthur C. Clarke's Mysterious World*, which aired on September 16, 1980. You can watch parts of the episode online; see "Scotlands Vitrified Hill Forts—Arthur C. Clarkes Biggest Unsolved Mystery," posted by lucylastik60 on YouTube, May 10, 2011, https://www.youtube.com/watch?v =PIoYZLZySzl, *Arthur C. Clarke's Mysterious World*.

the end of the last ice age (10,000 BCE or earlier) at Göbekli Tepe in Turkey, the Gulf of Cambay in India, and elsewhere. When that evidence is coupled with DNA research establishing the sophisticated domestication of plant and animal species (once thought to go back only five thousand to ten thousand years, but now reliably traced back at least thirty-two thousand years, and maybe much further), the time interval in which civilization could have *evolved* to a high level is expanded significantly—perhaps many times.* And, as the priest of Sais told Plato's ancestor Solon, it could also have been *destroyed* many times. In fact, the time available for such developments, as established by conventional science, has now been expanded sufficiently that, it could be argued, high ancient civilization now seems more likely than not. We just haven't found it yet.

Or have we?

Officials in Turkey's Cappadocia region now believe the exploration of vast and complex underground cities found in their region is going to lead to the rewriting of human history on Earth. Under intense investigation since their discovery in 2012, the astonishing sites have drawn the attention of archaeologists from around the world. So far, over two hundred underground cities are reported; most have not been adequately explored, and it seems likely that many more wait to be discovered.†

To this day, nobody really knows the true extent of these or other underground cities of the area, but they are substantial. In "The Ancient Subterranean Shelters of Cappadocia" (*Atlantis Rising* #95, September/ October 2012), Robert Schoch described two of the cities:

> Kaymakli consists of at least eight floors or underground stories (only four of which are currently accessible), each extending in a labyrinthine manner over a vast area. The city may have supported a

---

*See, as an example, the story of the domestication of wolves in Brian Handwerk, "How Accurate is *Alpha*'s Theory of Dog Domestication?," *Smithsonian Magazine* (online), August 15, 2018, https://www.smithsonianmag.com/science-nature/how-wolves-really -became-dogs-180970014/.

†See Jennifer Pinkowski, "Massive Underground City Found in Cappadocia Region of Turkey," *National Geographic* (online), March 26, 2015, https://www.nationalgeographic .com/news/2015/03/150325-underground-city-cappadocia-turkey-archaeology/.

population of 3,000 to 4,000 people plus farm animals and supplies, all housed underground.

Derinkuyu, with an estimated twenty floors and extending an estimated 85 meters (280 feet) below the surface may have supported anywhere from a few thousand to 10,000 people plus their livestock and goods. And the underground cities may not have been entirely isolated from one another. Kaymakli and Derinkuyu are less than a dozen kilometers (seven and a half miles) from each other and there are reports of a tunnel that may connect them.

A chamber in the vast underground city beneath Derinkuyu, Turkey
(also see color insert plate 17)

Cappadocia's astonishing underground cities, Schoch believes, though occupied, in all probability, many times since, were *originally* built around the end of the last ice age about twelve to thirteen thousand years ago.

So far, the archaeological establishment has not claimed to be able to definitively date the new discoveries, though the conventional wisdom has been that they were built during the time of Greek and Roman control. There is indeed evidence that they were occupied at that time, but that does not explain when the structures were *first* excavated. That issue remains very much open to debate.

THE WORLD BENEATH OUR FEET

The Greeks and Romans believed in Hades, the underworld of the dead—but not as a place of punishment, though it was not thought to be particularly pleasant. The idea of a vengeful God condemning sinners to an eternity of fiery torment developed much later, as a way to keep followers in line. The Egyptians believed in an underworld called the Duat. The Mayan underworld was Xibalba.

Mayan civilization was concentrated in the Yucatán Peninsula, which is honeycombed with caves and underground rivers and dotted with cenotes, places where cave roofs have collapsed, providing access to the water inside. In other cultures, people traditionally believed that fairies, elves, gnomes, and the like lived underground, often in hollowed-out hills, or in a kind of parallel universe that could be accessed through tunnels or caves.

In India, high in the cliffs above the Waghora River, are twenty-nine vast and complex underground chambers known as the Ajanta Caves. In the nearby Ellora Caves, thirty-four highly advanced structures, similar to those at Ajanta, have been carved from basalt bedrock. But as Schoch pointed out in "The Sacred Caves of India" (*Atlantis Rising* #125, September/October 2017), "the basalts of Ajanta and Ellora are even harder and more difficult to carve than the volcanic bedrock, consisting of congealed volcanic ash (tuff) that was primarily used for the underground structures of Cappadocia." Ajanta and Ellora "are said to be primarily the work of [Buddhist] monks, but when have monks ever been connected to such amazing feats of construction? Where are the records or remnants of their technology? These 'caves' were not cut into the bedrock using just simple tools and the 'chip-chip' method; this is mind-boggling engineering. Monks are typically known for possessing nothing other than their faith."

German archaeologist Heinrich Kusch says that the remains of a vast network of tunnels beneath hundreds of Neolithic settlements from Europe to Scotland to Turkey has been found and partially mapped.

The cliffs of Ajanta, India, with caves cut into the rock face;
photograph courtesy of Robert Schoch and his wife, Catherine Ulissey

In his book *Secrets of the Underground—Door to an Ancient World,*
Kusch argues for the existence of an enormous network of such tunnels.
Parts of the ancient catacombs still exist today, over twelve thousand
years later. Some sites go back over thirty thousand years. Seven hun-
dred meters of tunnel have been exposed in Germany's state of Bavaria.
Three hundred and fifty meters' worth have been unearthed in Styria,
Austria. But that, Kusch claims, is just the tip of the proverbial iceberg.*

The networks, some believe, were intended to protect humans from
predators. Others think some of the linked tunnels were used like highways are today, making it possible to travel safely even in times of war or
dangerous weather. Much of what remains today is quite small, barely
capable of accommodating modern human explorers, but some examples have more room and even seating space for visitors. Many of the
tunnels had been sealed off by the medieval church, possibly concerned

---

*See April Holloway, "Extensive Ancient Underground Networks Discovered through-
out Europe," Ancient Origins (online), June 11, 2013, https://www.ancient-origins.net
/news-history-archaeology/extensive-ancient-underground-networks-discovered
-throughout-europe-00540.

about heathen influence. Not all tunnels link up, but many do, and the existence of a massive pre–Ice Age network seems clear.

As William B. Stoecker points out in "The Long Lost World Beneath Our Feet" (*Atlantis Rising* #128, March/April 2018), it is hard to see how ancient caves could have been intended only as a strategic refuge against attack. Invaders, it seems clear, could have taken the land above and left the people beneath to starve or suffocate, their ventilation shafts blocked.

As is the case for many spectacular ruins around the world, no one can say with certainty just when, how, or for what reason these underground cities were originally built. They could well be thousands of years older than the peoples who ultimately used them and who have been erroneously credited with the original constructions. Such seems to be the case in Peru, where the Inca civilization of recent centuries is given credit for the vast and sophisticated stone constructions of megalithic times.

Many questions remain unanswered: Why did ancient people go to such trouble and expense to live underground? Did they face some threat from the sky—perhaps a nuclear war, as ancient Hindu texts appear to describe, or a supermassive solar outburst, as theorized by Robert Schoch? While caves might be able to shelter survivors until a danger was past, how could the people know in advance that such dangers were coming to allow for the required long-term building project of enormous underground cities? Clearly, the builders must have had great knowledge, and perhaps technology, that we don't have today.

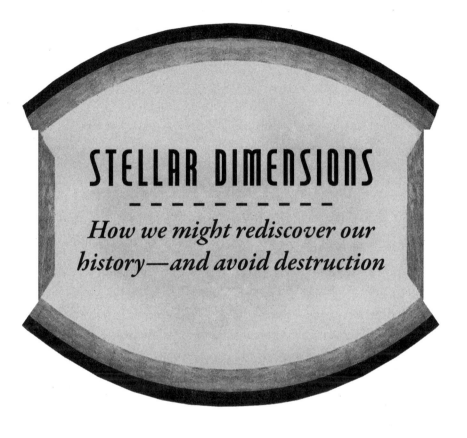

STELLAR DIMENSIONS

----

*How we might rediscover our
history—and avoid destruction*

Archaeology from Space

Could satellite imagery fill in the blanks of the Atlantis story?

According to Jimmy Bright, producer of a popular YouTube channel called *Bright Insight,* Plato's Atlantis may have been hiding all along in plain sight. Bright points to a previously unexplained feature in the Mauritanian portion of the Sahara desert near the northwestern coast of Africa. Formally known as the Richat Structure, and sometimes called the "Eye of the Sahara," it is composed of immense concentric circles of raised ground—once, perhaps, interspersed by waterways. The circumference of the Richat Structure is very close to the exact dimensions listed by Plato, about 23 kilometers, and it is bordered by mountains to the north and has what looks like an opening to the sea on the south, just as Plato described.

The Richat Structure was discovered in 1965 by NASA astronauts of the Gemini IV mission.* At first it was thought to be an impact crater, but that hypothesis has since been ruled out by the absence of melted rock, which would be present in any large impact crater. The prevailing view, currently, is that the Richat is the remains of what once were domed layers of Earth's crust. That theory, however, has never been fully investigated, much less proven.

---

*You can download the original report from the Gemini IV mission, with photos of the Richat Structure, from the NASA website. See "Terrain Photography on the Gemini IV Mission—Preliminary Report," published June 1, 1967, and digitized and posted on September 2, 2013, at https://ntrs.nasa.gov/archive/nasa/casi.ntrs.nasa.gov/19670017945 .pdf.

Spanish illustrator Rocío Espín Piñar's rendering of Atlantis as described by Plato

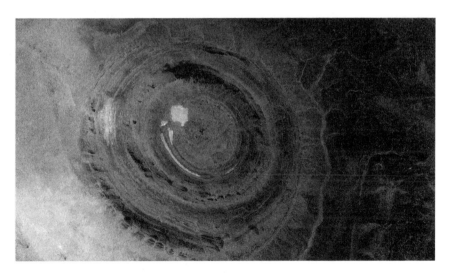

The Richat Structure; image from Google Earth

Bright argues that before the time of the last ice age—the so-called Younger Dryas, which began with an event occurring at about the same time that Plato says Atlantis went down, circa 9500 BCE—the Richat must have been at sea level, with seawater then filling all of its channels. Indeed, there are many archaeologists who believe the Younger Dryas mini ice age was triggered about then by the impact of some kind of massive bolide from space that might have rearranged a great deal of Earth's geography.

Bright's argument for Atlantis in the Sahara is a recent example of what has become a recurring theme for alternative archaeology—the use of imagery recovered from outer space to support research into areas once considered out-of-bounds by earthbound archaeologists.

For those who think Atlantis-in-the-Sahara may be a bridge too far, other satellite photography suggests that maybe southern Spain should be considered as a possible Atlantis location. That, at least, is the view of Dr. Rainer Kuehne of the University of Wuppertal in Germany. Kuehne believes Plato's celebrated island was simply a region of the Spanish coast destroyed by flood between 800 and 500 BCE.

Kuehne points to satellite photos he found in 2004 showing features seemingly matching those described by Plato. A salt marsh area known as Marisma de Hinojos near the city of Cadiz contains two rectangular structures in the mud and parts of concentric rings that may once have surrounded them. Kuehne believes the rectangular feature could be the remains of the "silver" temple devoted to the sea god Poseidon and a "golden" temple devoted to Cleito and Poseidon.

Like the Thera scenario popularized by the late Jacques Cousteau, which placed Atlantis in the Bronze Age Mediterranean, the Spanish theory seems to require some special arithmetic to account for Plato's dimensions. Though most conventional academics have tried to argue that Plato's numbers were exaggerated, Kuehne's giant circles would suggest that, if anything, Plato may have understated the city's dimensions.*

ANCIENT TRAILS AND CANALS

In "Atlantis of the Sands" (*Atlantis Rising* #70, July/August 2008), Frank Joseph told of how satellite imagery was used to locate the lost city of Ubar (a.k.a. "Ubar of the High Towers") on the Arabian peninsula. For many years, archaeologists had scoured the sands of Arabia for any physical trace of the ancient city. The towers were

---

*See Paul Rincon, "Satellite Images 'Show Atlantis,'" BBC News (online), June 6, 2004, http://news.bbc.co.uk/2/hi/science/nature/3766863.stm.

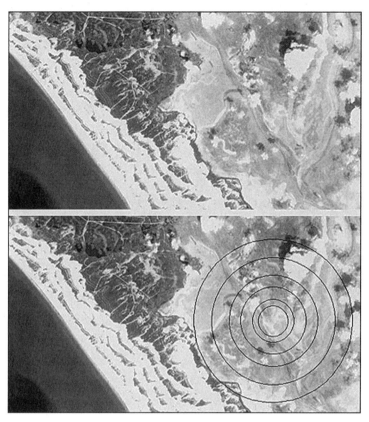

A satellite picture of Marisma de Hinojos, with Plato's rings superimposed

its most notable features; this ancient urban commercial hub had needed to defend its great wealth from the likes of Sarru-kinu, king of Sumeria, and Mursili II, king of the Hittites. Inscriptions at Ebla, one of the earliest kingdoms of Syria, referred to Ubar as a cult capital where all the profane arts of black magic and thaumaturgy flourished, which matches the city's portrayal in Bedouin myth, but it seemed to have forever disappeared, just as prophesied in the Koran. Then, in 1984, an orbiting satellite tracing medieval routes used by spice traders followed faint outlines into a far older network of roads in south Oman's Dhofar province. As Dr. Bob Curran relates in his 2007 book *Lost Lands, Forgotten Realms,* "Further investigation using x-ray scanning revealed the surrounding area was the roof of a large, underground, limestone cavern, filled with a huge,

The ruins of Ubar

Ancient trails in
the Ubar area;
Landsat image
courtesy of NASA

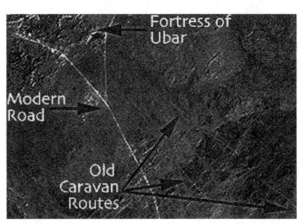

subterranean lake that had formed a water-table for a city built above it."

More recently, on the other side of the Arabian Sea, satellite imagery demonstrated to the satisfaction of many scholars that the legendary Saraswati River mentioned in ancient Vedic scripture was, in all likelihood, a real river. The river's banks once teemed, many believe, with prehistoric peoples. Until recently, conventional science had taken the position that the Saraswati was entirely mythical, but a 2011 study of satellite images of western India and eastern Pakistan strongly supported claims that eight thousand to ten thousand years ago, the Saraswati flowed through what is now a virtual desert there.*

Elsewhere in India, satellite images of a submerged land bridge connecting the continent with Sri Lanka have been proposed as confirmation of accounts in the Ramayana of just such a bridge, called Ram Setu and said to have been built 1.7 million years ago by the god Rama, assisted by a band of monkeys. (See chapter 19 for more on the land bridge.) Such assertions have, of course, been ridiculed by orthodox scholars. D. N. Jha, professor of history at Delhi University, said that what had been captured by NASA's cameras was a geological formation. "To link that with Rama or Ramayana is ridiculous," he said.

In Jha's view, the Ramayana itself cannot be older than 2,500 years. Such academic dogmas, though, seem threatened by recent satellite photos of the Saraswati and other evidence revealing an apparently pre-Harrapan, prediluvian culture that once thrived where the murky seas of the Gulf of Cambay now roll. And whether Ram Setu was man-made or not, remote sensing satellite imagery makes it clear that before the end of the last ice age, when sea levels were much lower than they are now, it certainly could have united India and Sri Lanka.

THE NEW ARCHAEOLOGISTS

According to *Popular Science* magazine, the "new archaeologists" are carrying out their research without getting their hands dirty, learning more from above the atmosphere than from the bottom of any dig. Archaeologists Damian Evans and Bill Saturno, for example, have used radar imaging satellites to detect many previously undiscovered details in Cambodia's great temple complex at Angkor Wat.† Thanks to such

---

*See A. K. Gupta, J. R. Sharma, and G. Sreenivasan, "Using Satellite Imagery to Reveal the Course of an Extinct River below the Thar Desert in the Indo-Pak Region," *International Journal of Remote Sensing* 32, no. 18 (2011): 5197–216, https://www.researchgate .net/publication/233169848.

†See Mara Hvistendahl, "The Space Archaeologists," *Popular Science* (online), May 22, 2008, https://www.popsci.com/scitech/article/2008-05/space-archaeologists/.

techniques, scientists are unearthing whole civilizations and rewriting history books.

In 2016, images found on Google Earth appeared to show two immense and previously unknown artificial pyramids in Egypt. According to the website Ancient Code, the location contains a 620-foot-wide triangular plateau and two nearby pyramids. Larger than any other known structures in Egypt, including the Great Pyramid, the potential pyramids attracted considerable attention at the time. At first they were dismissed as natural formations, but the hypothesis that these pyramids are manmade, proposed by American researcher Angela Micol, is said to be corroborated by a number of antique maps of the region. Indeed, thirty-four old maps (including three made by the engineers of Napoleon) and twelve old documents, mostly from scientists and senior irrigation officials, in the possession of an Egyptian couple (one of whom is a former Egyptian ambassador to Oman) clearly label the formations as pyramids.

For years, Micol and her website, Satellite Discoveries & Google Earth Anomalies, have been using publicly available satellite imagery to locate lost ancient sites around the world. At one point Micol found a Landsat image of a region in the Bahamas, to the east of Cay Sal Bank, showing a large gridded pattern that defies any natural explanation.

For those who secretly yearn to be an archaeologist but are daunted by the prospect of years of academic study, the long-sought opportunity may have now arrived. Sarah Parcak is an actual space archaeologist who teaches at the University of Alabama in Birmingham. Instead of digging through the mud and debris of centuries, however, to find clues to Earth's past, she pores over high-resolution satellite imagery for all kinds of out-of-the-way places, looking for anomalies and other clues to buried archaeological sites. The problem is that there is far more unexplored territory than any one person can possibly investigate. She needs help, and plenty of it. Her solution is a website.

Parcak has launched the website GlobalXplorer, which offers to teach anyone with a computer and an internet connection how to recognize archaeological targets. The idea is to use crowdsourcing, a new version of the old saw "Many hands make light work"—or in this case, many eyes. No special training is required. The site promises to tell you what you need to know.

Unexplained pyramidal formations in Egypt;
images from Google Earth

We live, it has been speculated, in the ruins of a vast structure that is too great to be seen with unaided earthbound eyes. By climbing to higher altitudes (or even outer space), we can get beyond—a "bird's-eye" perspective—and can discover designs invisible at ground level. Powerful tools once unavailable even to an academic elite can now be accessed by anyone.

In the American Southeast, imagery from outer space provided by Google Earth has revealed hundreds of miles of coastline on both the Atlantic and Gulf coasts of Florida, as well as in other states, that are seemingly strewn with the ancient remains of an enormous water-wise culture. Astonishing evidence of this population, which would have existed before the end of the last ice age, when sea levels rose an average of five to twenty-five feet, or more, to their present levels, can be seen in thousands of satellite photos, discovered by John Jenson, a retired paper manufacturing specialist living in central Florida. Though admittedly he is not an archaeological professional, Jenson's impressive research and assembled case is not, as some might believe, easily dismissed and now clearly demands much further research.*

According to Jenson, the mysterious lost civilization that he found on Google Earth built "extremely sophisticated and precisely-engineered channels" for purposes of agriculture, navigation, and habitat. Some double canals are three hundred to five hundred feet wide and continue for many miles in exactly straight lines. The structures, suggesting hydraulic, aquatic, industrial, and mechanical engineering on a massive scale, he believes to be as sophisticated as those found in current technology.

Much of the evidence is now under water, but based on the well-documented water table rises over the past ten thousand years, Jenson estimates the canal builders' habitation to be sometime postglacial, but, he believes, it was segmented into two different time frames—one about 3,500 years ago, and the other about 8,500 years ago. Visible remains in marshes and wetlands, he says, imply a population in excess of thirty million, and possibly much more. These figures are based on the visible

Two dock- or quay-like channels just east of Flagler Beach, Florida.
According to John Jenson, the north or top channel is about 1,750 feet.
The south channel is about 2,100 feet. Each outlet has an opening feature
that includes a narrowing at the entry.

---

*The photos can be examined and Jenson's online paper can be read online at https://www.academia.edu/3779666/Ancient_Canal_Builders_Overview.

A complete canal system at Grassy Key was not built for modern use, says Jenson, because there is no outlet to open water. Yet open water is less than four hundred feet away. Several other channels and canals can be found aboveground and on the tidal shelf.

Artificial harbors at North Palm Beach are cut into the tidal plain at about the same depth as all the harbors and canals along this section of the Intracoastal Waterway. Most of these do not meet the current tidal shoulder and appear to have been cut out when the current tidal plain was above water.

areas left intact following modern urbanization and the farming of habitable land on the Atlantic Coast.

In 2009, *Atlantis Rising* reader Paul Kristofek, while studying satellite images supplied by Google Earth, made another startling discovery: Beneath the Atlantic Ocean, about forty-five miles east of Harkers Island, North Carolina, is a giant right angle with perfectly straight arms and, nearby, a long, straight rectangular feature with precisely parallel sides. Both distinctly visible figures appear to be of artificial origin. The location, Kristofek tells us, is at latitude 34.5° and longitude 76°. The sides of the right triangle are about seven miles long and the rectangle appears to be about 12.5 miles. Kristofek had no knowledge of what the source of the feature might be, and neither did we at *Atlantis Rising*. Nevertheless, we found them certainly worth further investigation.

In Peru, a gigantic network of earthworks could have been created in the image of birds, snakes, and other animals, arranged as geoglyphs by ancient Peruvians. That is the contention of researcher Amelia Carolina Sparavigna, who discovered the animals in satellite imagery. If true, it suggests that the ancient Peruvians had some way of making observations from great heights. That capability, some argue, is already evident on Peru's famed Nazca plain, where animals are depicted on the ground in figures so large, they can be observed only from the air.*

Sparavigna used Google satellite maps and an astronomical image-processing program that she developed to identify the images. So far there is no consensus over their authenticity. Some say they are just agricultural artifacts.

As to whether the ancients were capable of aerial observation, the question has led some, like Erich Von Däniken and Zecharia Sitchin, to speculate that indigenous populations were visited by extraterrestrials traveling in spacecraft, while others speculate that, to obtain the needed higher perspective, ancient shamans were able to exit their bodies and take flight. Now all we may need to get the same effect are Google Maps.

---

*See Amelia Carolina Sparavigna, "Symbolic Landforms Created by Ancient Earthworks Near Lake Titicaca," submitted September 12, 2010; revised September 16, 2010: arXiv:1009.2231.

A pond is the eye of this seeming giant bird.

At issue here are not the bona fides of some academic study, but visible evidence of lost civilization.

THE CRYPTOZOOLOGICAL CONNECTION

Could the sheer investigative potential of satellite imagery exceed even archaeology? Consider the following: Apple Maps, the satellite photography service of Apple Inc., may have taken the first actual picture of the Loch Ness monster, also known as Nessie. According to Andrew Dixon, a Scottish social worker, he accidentally discovered the photo as he explored satellite imagery of the mysterious lake on his computer. Dixon supplied the photo to a local Nessie research club and to the British *Independent* newspaper.

In the photo, the hundred-foot-long floating creature appears to be paddling toward the south. Some have speculated that the picture is actually of a boat's wake (boats can be seen in the area); however, no boat is visible leading the wake.*

---

*See Kashmira Gander, "Loch Ness Monster Found on Apple Maps?," *The Independent* (online), April 19, 2014, https://www.independent.co.uk/news/uk/this-britain/loch-ness-monster-found-on-apple-maps-9271075.html.

Previously, purported photographs of the legendary animal have been largely dismissed as hoaxes. Thought by some to be a representative of the extinct plesiosaur species, Nessie has proved elusive prey for the millions who have tried to authenticate her existence with photography and other methods, such as sonar. Some cryptozoologists claim that the satellite photo could be a game changer, but more study is required.

36

Paranormal Portals

The role of special senses in the quest for lost knowledge

The 2013 film *Secret Life of Uri Geller—Psychic Spy?* documented the famous spoon-bender's secret life as a Mossad and CIA agent. According to reporter Geoffrey Macnab, as early as the 1960s, Geller was involved in global espionage, and he was secretly reactivated after 9/11. The story is consistent with news reports that appeared in the 1990s confirming the military use of remote viewing in the project code-named Stargate. In the years since, substantial detail has surfaced on techniques used in Stargate, which had been developed under Drs. Harold Puthoff and Russell Targ at the Stanford Research Institute in the 1960s and '70s. The out-of-body experiences of Geller and another celebrated psychic, Ingo Swann, were reported to be central to the original research.*

Though publicly ridiculed at the time by academic scientists, mainstream media, and professional debunkers, the project—though abandoned amid controversy—was, nevertheless, very real. Substantial evidence that the work was reopened to help a related project, called Prism, to fight the war on terror, is reported in the film.†

---

*A listing of CIA research papers by Puthoff and Targ is available online at https://www.cia.gov/library/readingroom/search/site/Russell%20targ?page=14.

†For a review of the documentary, see Geoffrey Macnab, "Uri Geller Psychic Spy? The Spoon-Bender's Secret Life as a Mossad and CIA Agent Revealed," *The Guardian,* June 14, 2013, https://www.theguardian.com/media/2013/jun/13/nsa-uri-geller-psychic-spy.

Uri Geller on a 2013 book tour in Moscow; photo courtesy of D. Rozhkov

Now, as many wonder whether or not it is possible to learn the real history of planet Earth and the role of lost ancient civilizations, one group of researchers is proposing that advanced remote viewing methods be harnessed. It is not our intention to endorse or reject such a strategy here, but since recent experiments in the area seem to threaten established concepts of time, space, physics, and consciousness itself, the idea certainly deserves some thought.

One of the leaders in the field is Courtney Brown, PhD, director and founder of the Farsight Institute, a nonprofit research and educational organization dedicated to the study of the phenomenon of nonlocal consciousness, usually called remote viewing. Brown's 2005 book, *Remove Viewing: The Science and Theory of Nonphysical Perception,* posits that the remote-viewing phenomenon is a consequence of superposition formation on the quantum level.

The Farsight Institute works in collaboration with several of the best-known remote viewers, including the Hawaii Remote Viewers' Guild, led by Glenn Wheaton, a Special Forces veteran, and people who have trained in the Controlled Remote Viewing technique designed by Lyn Buchanan, formerly of Army Intelligence. One area of great interest to the institute involves unsolved mysteries of the past.

In 2014, for example, in a video called *The Great Pyramid of Giza: The Mystery Solved,* the institute took on the mining of the largest rocks used in the construction of the Great Pyramid. Remote viewers were asked to look into mining operations, processes, and construction of the Great Pyramid, and in particular, how the largest rocks were moved into position during construction. They also looked into the pyramid's purposes. The viewers, moreover, were requested to provide the date and time of the events they were viewing. To see what they learned, you can watch the video and others from Farsight Institute on the institute's website (www.farsight.org).

Remote viewing, however, is not the only, nor the first, technique to call on intuition and inner awareness to pursue the answers to ancient riddles.

In his 2009 book *A Needle in the Right Hand of God,* Yale University professor R. Howard Bloch wrote: "In the summer of 1937, Mrs. Edith A. Pretty, a widow living on her estate in Suffolk, East Anglia, recounted to Vincent Redstone, a local historian and Fellow of the Society of Antiquaries, her dream of the previous night. She had seen 'a large white horse with a helmeted rider, then the burial of a man and the flashing of gold objects as they were placed in the grave beside him.'" Bloch added, "Her nephew came with a dowser's rod and assured her there was gold buried under the largest barrow."

Redstone arranged for Mrs. Pretty to meet with him and Guy Maynard, curator of the Ipswich Corporation Museum. They decided they should get Basil Brown, a local amateur archaeologist, to excavate the mounds. Brown took up residence at what would later become the celebrated archaeological dig of Sutton Hoo and began work, assisted by two farm workers. There were eighteen mounds on the property. At Mrs. Pretty's suggestion, Brown began excavating the first mound but found nothing significant. He moved on to other mounds. Mrs. Pretty then insisted that he go back to the first mound. Brown's further excavations revealed that a Viking-type ship was buried there.

A team of professional academic archaeologists replaced Basil Brown. On July 21, 1939, the new team found their first gold object, a piece of jewelry. Many other gold and silver objects, including the famous helmet and face mask, soon followed. It was obviously the burial site of an elite person. But no skeleton was found. An inquest granted possession of the Sutton Hoo treasures to Mrs. Pretty, who soon thereafter donated them to the British Museum. Within a few days, World War II began, and for safekeeping the Sutton Hoo treasures were buried in an old Underground tunnel in London. After the war, they were placed on permanent display in the British Museum.*

Another well-known example of paranormal archaeology comes from Glastonbury in England, where Bligh Bond, a well-known

Replica of the helmet from Sutton Hoo

British architect and archaeologist, claimed that he had been guided by long-dead monks to the lost ruins of the abbey. Appointed in 1908 by the Church of England as Glastonbury's director of excavation, Bond reported that in his historic locating of the ruins, he was led by the spirits of abbey monks. Bond's account, though well established, was virtually ignored by authorities of church and state. Bond's unorthodox sources were revealed in his 1918 book, *The Gate of Remembrance*. Ever afterward, he was scorned by the church and his professional colleagues.

---

*See Veronica Walker, "The Ghostly Treasure Ship of Sutton Hoo," *National Geographic* (online), January 17, 2017, https://www.nationalgeographic.com/history/magazine /2017/01-02/sutton-hoo-england-anglo-saxon-treasure-ship/.

The ruins of Glastonbury Abbey; photo courtesy of Reruntuhan Biara

ESP AND THE SKEPTICS

Today, new evidence has emerged clearly establishing the seriousness with which U.S. intelligence agencies once took evidence based on paranormal sources. Despite attempts by so-called skeptics like Michael Shermer and James Randi to dismiss reports that U.S. military and intelligence services used remote viewing to gather clues about enemy actions, a newly declassified document shows that the CIA, in an effort under the auspices of Project Sun Streak—successor to the controversial Project Stargate—employed the technique to pursue terrorists behind the Lockerbie bombing plot that destroyed Pan Am Flight 103 on December 21, 1988, killing 270 people (259 on board and 11 on the ground).

According to a memo from June 7, 1990, a "psychic" at an undisclosed location was asked to offer more details on a photo of the reconstructed baggage carrier holding the bomb. The document also referred to "psychoenergetics," apparently meaning psychokinesis—where

The wreckage of Pan Am Flight 103 in December 1988

physical actions are performed using mental powers alone. Included with the document were copies of notes and sketches.*

Project Stargate was a secret U.S. Army unit established in 1978 at Fort Meade, Maryland, by the Defense Intelligence Agency (DIA) and the Stanford Research Institute (SRI) to investigate the military and domestic potential for psychic phenomena in intelligence applications. After it became public in 1995, the project was said to have been abandoned.†

For many years now, the so-called skeptical community, spearheaded by stage magician James Randi, has insisted that if any claims of the paranormal (i.e., telepathy, psychokinesis, miracles) can be proved, the prover can win a million dollars. So far no one has been able to claim

---

*See "The 'STARGATE Project': The CIA Psychic Spies," *Intel Today* (blog), January 29, 2017, https://gosint.wordpress.com/2017/01/29/the-stargate-project-the-cia-psychic -spies/, and also Judith Duffy, "CIA Files on Stargate Paranormal Project Reveal Scottish Locations Used for Training 'Psychic Spies,'" *The Herald* (of Scotland; online), January 21, 2017, https://www.heraldscotland.com/news/15039661.cia-files-on-stargate -paranormal-project-reveal-scottish-locations-used-for-training-psychic-spies/.
†Read more about Project Stargate in "Stargate [Controlled Remote Viewing]," by John Pike, Federation of American Scientists (online), December 29, 2005, https://fas.org /irp/program/collect/stargate.htm.

the prize, and some have inferred, therefore, that such things must be impossible, or else surely someone would have won. Few, however, have read the fine print in the "amazing" Randi offer, which makes collecting the money even more difficult than actually manifesting paranormal powers. One who read Randi's fine print and elected not to compete was Dr. Rupert Sheldrake, Cambridge-trained biologist and author of the best seller *Science Set Free* (published as *The Science Delusion* in the U.K.) and many other books.

Sheldrake has demonstrated with a great deal of evidence that so-called paranormal abilities such as telepathy are, in fact, common in both humans and animals. He has little use for Randi and his ilk, pointing out in a letter to *The Skeptic* magazine that "Randi may have done a useful job in exposing fraudulent showmen, but he has no scientific credentials, and has made fraudulent claims himself." Randi and his fellow militant debunkers, Sheldrake notes, have made what is an essentially theological argument for the ultimate supremacy of the material world but, as is the case for most religions, have offered no proof. In what might be called the "first church of reductionist materialism," their narrow worldview is held to be a fundamental doctrine that must not be questioned.*

The parallel between so-called skepticism and religious-like intolerance and persecution has long been clear. In criticizing Rupert Sheldrake's 1983 book *A New Science of Life,* John Maddox, editor of the journal *Nature,* called it "a book for burning." Sheldrake described being on the receiving end of such a prescription as exactly like being excommunicated by the pope. He knew, he says, that he had become dangerous for other scientists to know. In the inquisitions of the Middle Ages, forbidden books and their authors were often consigned to the flames. Modern offenders like Sheldrake may not be burned at the stake, but they are, nevertheless, subjected to ostracism, rejection, and academic sanction.†

For those who long for a more enlightened era in which new ideas that could benefit the world can be examined on their merits, without

---

*Sheldrake's letter was published in volume 22, issue 2 of *The Skeptic.* At the time of this writing, you can read it online by searching for "Volume 22 Issue 2 Letters: Rupert Sheldrake on James Randi," or at https://www.skeptic.org.uk/magazine/features/letters/.

†See Rupert Sheldrake, "Nature Editor Sir John Maddox Cries Heretic," in the "Reactions" section of Sheldrake's personal website, https://www.sheldrake.org/reactions /sir-john-maddox-book-for-burning.

subjugation to narrow doctrinal agendas, it is worth remembering that defensiveness of this sort is a sign of weakness, not strength. In their standard tactics, the current materialist establishment reveals an insecurity, doubtless born in the unconscious dread that nature itself, thus disrespected, could ultimately return the favor and render them powerless and as naked as the legendary emperor with new clothes.

THE GREATER POTENTIAL
OF HUMANS AND ANIMALS

You may actually be able to tell the future without consciously knowing it. That is the conclusion of a 2012 study supporting the idea of precognition—the ability to anticipate near-future events without any actual evidence foreshadowing the event. Examples could include when you know the car beside you is about to turn into your lane, or when you know your boss is coming down the hall. So says Julia Mossbridge, lead author of the study, who is still at pains to argue that it is all biology—just processes we don't understand yet. Her study uses brain scan MRIs to demonstrate that our bodies often know before we become actually conscious of a fact.*

All of this lends weight to the arguments of scientists like Sheldrake who have proven the existence of similar phenomena, like our ability to know when the phone is about to ring, or to know when someone is staring at us.

For those who have experienced it, the existence of extrasensory perception (ESP) is indisputable, but still, they may be pleased to learn, by way of the usual methods of communication, that even hard science could be coming around. As an example, in a peer-reviewed study, researchers at the University of Bucharest in Romania have shown that when the brain of a close friend is electrically stimulated, there is a corresponding neural spike in the electrocardiogram of the subject.†

---

*See Julia Mossbridge, Patrizio Tressoldi, and Jessica Utts, "Predictive Physiological Anticipation Preceding Seemingly Unpredictable Stimuli: A Meta-analysis," *Frontiers in Psychology* 3 (2012): 390, https://www.frontiersin.org/articles/10.3389/fpsyg.2012.00390/full.

†See W. Giroldini, L. Pederzoli, M. Bilucaglia, et al., "EEG Correlates of Social Interaction at a Distance," F1000Research 4 (2015): 457; https://doi.org/10.12688/f1000research .6755.3.

In another example, this one from his book *The Sense of Being Stared At,* Sheldrake argues that the human sensitivity to the gaze of other humans is significant evidence of extrasensory perception. A 2009 study published in *Current Biology* presents evidence that even birds are sensitive to what people are looking at. It seems that jackdaws, a member of the crow family, know whether people are looking at food they are interested in and will wait until the humans look away before trying to get it. For the writers of the study, researchers at the University of Cambridge and Queen Mary University of London, this can only mean that the birds are watching the eyes of humans and calculating what they are looking at and what they are not.* Sheldrake, we suspect, would argue that the birds are reacting to the field of human awareness. He has also produced considerable evidence that many domestic animals react to their masters' thoughts at a distance and thus know such things as when their owners are coming home. Such ideas, while still considered impossible by mainstream science, are yet gaining wider acceptance.

And speaking of birds: Many birds migrate for thousands of miles, but the question of how they manage to navigate so well and on such tight seasonal schedules has baffled science for generations. In recent years, studies have indicated that the secret may lie in a special sensitivity to Earth's magnetic field. It has not been entirely clear, however, just how birds are able to read that field, though it has been speculated that it may work for them something like a compass works for humans, but no one has really explained it.

Now a pair of European studies are claiming that there is a strange protein in the birds' eyes that makes it possible for them to actually see, at some other level of their vision, the planet's magnetic field. Biologists at Sweden's Lund University, who studied zebra finches, and at Germany's Carl von Ossietzky University in Oldenburg, who studied robins, found that a protein called cryptochrome, linked to circadian rhythms, can facilitate something called magnetoreception.†

---

*See "Birds Can 'Read' Human Gaze," Phys.org (online), April 2, 2009, https://phys.org/news/2009-04-bird-human.html.

†For a briefing on both studies, see Michelle Starr, "Birds Can See Earth's Magnetic Fields, and Now We Know How That's Possible," ScienceAlert (online), September 1, 2018, https://www.sciencealert.com/birds-see-magnetic-fields-cryptochrome-cry4-photoreceptor-2018

A German robin

Alternative science researchers of one school of thought have long believed that magnetoreception is a faculty available to many species, including humans. Some have even theorized that ESP is related to magnetic sensitivity. The research of Rupert Sheldrake, however, suggests that to explain ESP, something deeper may be needed.

Bumblebees not only can learn to use tools but can teach the trick to their colleagues. That was the finding of a 2016 study in which Lars Chittka at Queen Mary University in London showed that the bees can learn to pull a string to release sugar water, and that other bees who merely watched the first ones would also pick up the trick.*

For materialistic scientists, it all shows how powerful the tiny bee brain must be, but anyone reading William B. Stoecker's article "Animal Technologies" in *Atlantis Rising* #120 (November/December

*See Sylvain Alem, Clint J. Perry, Xingfu Zhu, et al., "Associative Mechanisms Allow for Social Learning and Cultural Transmission of String Pulling in an Insect," *PLOS Biology* 14, no. 10 (2016): e1002564, https://journals.plos.org/plosbiology/article?id=10.1371/journal.pbio.1002564.

The buff-tailed bumblebee (*Bombus terrestris*); photo by Alvesgaspar

2016) knows there are other, indeed more credible explanations. As Sheldrake has argued, the brains of animals, from bees to humans, are not the *source* of intelligence but rather—like radios or televisions—are mere *receivers*. In fact, argues Sheldrake, a trick successfully learned by any creature increases—through what he calls morphic resonance—the speed with which its entire species can acquire a new skill or habit.

Something like that certainly appears to be at work among research scientists, who can quickly learn—and more quickly than ever—just which kind of studies will benefit their careers and which will not.

37

Tunneling through Time

Could visitors from the past and future be here after all?

A few years ago, an HBO/BBC film comedy, *Frequently Asked Questions About Time Travel,* explored the humor potential in the possibility of a time warp in the men's room of your favorite pub. Even serious people, however, think about time travel. In his best-selling book *Physics of the Future,* popular physicist Michio Kaku explored to what extent the technologies and devices of science fiction, including time travel, that are deemed impossible today might well become commonplace in the future, just as lasers, televisions, atom bombs, and other familiar technologies of contemporary life were once deemed impossible. Kaku says a time machine is consistent with the known laws of quantum physics, although he thinks it would take an unbelievably advanced civilization to actually build one.*

The late British cosmologist Stephen Hawking suggested that the absence of tourists from the future could be taken as evidence that time travel, at least to a designated time in the past, is not going to be achieved, though Carl Sagan once argued that such tourists might actually be here but just not talking. If they were talking, they might have difficulty staying out of trouble. In fact, not a few homeless

---

*See J. R. Minkel, "Borrowed Time: Interview with Michio Kaku," *Scientific American* (online), November 24, 2003, https://www.scientificamerican.com/article/borrowed-time-interview-w/.

people have reported being visitors from the future. How do we know they are not?

TIME-TRAVELING PHOTONS

Could time travel, as in the movie *Back to the Future,* be more than a science fiction fantasy? A group of physicists at the University of Queensland in Australia are convinced that it is indeed possible in some way based on their model of how time-traveling photons might behave. At the quantum level, at least, they argue, the so-called grandfather paradox could be resolved.

In the grandfather paradox, a person who travels to the past and kills his own grandfather would block the existence of his father or mother and therefore himself. The time-traveling character played by Michael J. Fox faced similar challenges but, thanks to movie magic, was able to overcome them.

In their investigation, the Australian researchers studied the behavior of a photon traveling through time and interacting with its older self. They employed a closely related case in which the photon would travel through normal space-time and interact with another photon stuck in a time-traveling loop through a wormhole, known as a closed timelike curve. Simulating the behavior of the second photon, the researchers were able to study the behavior of the first. The results showed that when the second photon is prepared in just the right way, consistent evolutions can be achieved.*

In other words, it is possible that the murdered grandfather's existence could both continue and not continue. To avoid headaches, don't meditate for too long on this theory.

"Time travel is not only possible, we may be doing it by the end of this century." That is the astounding notion currently proposed by at least one respected college professor. Using Einstein's equations, Ronald Mallett, a physicist at the University of Connecticut for thirty years,

---

*See Jonathan O'Callaghan, "Could Time Travel Soon Become a Reality? Physicists Simulate Sending Quantum Light Particles into the Past," *Daily Mail* (online), June 23, 2014, https://www.dailymail.co.uk/sciencetech/article-2665781/Could-time-travel -soon-reality-Physicists-simulate-quantum-light-particles-travelling-past-time.html.

has designed an actual time machine that he plans to build and test in the near future. Whether we can actually time travel will depend upon the outcome of experiments he is now pursuing.

According to Mallett, who published his first research on time travel in the journal *Physics Letters* in 2000, all other proposals for warping space/time involve gigantic quantities of mass, but his concept is different. He explains, "Einstein showed that mass and energy are the same thing. The time machine we've designed uses light in the form of circulating lasers to warp or loop time instead of using massive objects."*

Mallett was inspired as a child to investigate time travel. After he had seen the movie of H. G. Wells's story *The Time Machine*, he wanted to travel into the past to warn his deceased father of the dangers of smoking. Now, however, he subscribes to the parallel universe concept of alternative realities and does not believe the present moment can be changed by manipulating past events. Instead, he believes any time traveler's action would generate a separate reality independent of the present.†

In the *Terminator* movies, a robot from a future, robotically controlled civilization returns to our time in an attempt to destroy a young hero destined to overthrow the robots. It makes pretty exciting science fiction, but could such a thing really happen, and might it account for the uncommonly bad luck that for years surrounded—not to say haunted—startup efforts for the Large Hadron Collider (LHC) in Cern, Switzerland?

In 2009, the *New York Times* reported that two highly respected physicists, Holger Bech Nielsen of the Niels Bohr Institute in Copenhagen, Denmark, and Masao Ninomiya of the Yukawa Institute for Theoretical Physics in Kyoto, Japan, had publicly suggested and supported with rigorous mathematics the proposition that the so-

---

*See "'We Can Build a Real Time Machine,'" BBC News (online), July 11, 2018, https://www.bbc.com/news/science-environment-44771942, and also Lisa Zyga, "Professor Predicts Human Time Travel This Century," Phys.org (online), April 4, 2006, http://www.physorg.com/news63371210.html.

†See Dennis Overbye, "The Collider, the Particle and a Theory About Fate," *New York Times* (online), October 12, 2009, https://www.nytimes.com/2009/10/13/science/space/13lhc.html?_r=1&ref=science&mtrref=undefined&gwh=5AEE435DE36BCC E3DF5C8FB3C39C1714&gwt=pay&assetType=REGIWALL.

called Higgs boson particle—which the LHC particle accelerator was intended to produce and, by all reports, actually did so in 2013—might be "abhorrent to nature." It might, said the scientists, be acting somehow in the future in a way that would ripple back through time to prevent its manifestation—in other words, sabotaging itself from the future, sort of like murdering its grandfather. If so, the plot apparently failed, as the Higgs was, we have been told, discovered in 2013, with a Nobel Prize subsequently awarded.

So much for time travel . . . or maybe not. There are still some who say that not only is time travel possible, but the U.S. military already has time travel technology.

THE TRUMP COINCIDENCE

In 2003, Andrew Basiago, a Washington State attorney, declared himself a whistleblower for a top-secret government program dubbed Project Pegasus that, he says, in the 1960s and '70s, under the auspices of the Defense Advanced Research Projects Agency (DARPA), not only perfected time travel but had actually sent human subjects to explore the past. At the age of eleven, as one of those subjects, Basiago says, he personally witnessed the Gettysburg Address in 1863. He claims that an old magazine photograph actually shows him on the spot wearing a Union Army parka and shoes far too big for his feet.

While there are few who have taken Basiago's story seriously, in 2009, Dr. David Lewis Anderson, a physicist who claimed to have personal knowledge of time control research by the U.S. Air Force, also came forward. Anderson was interviewed by the late Art Bell on the *Coast to Coast AM* radio program in 2010. According to Anderson, time travel technology has been successfully pursued, not only by the U.S. but by other countries as well.*

Strangely, the ranks of apparently credible people claiming personally to have journeyed back in time have also included a high ranking and widely respected Benedictine priest, Pellegrino Maria Ernetti, who died of cancer in 1994. A world-class musicologist and

---

*You can listen to the interview online on the *Coast to Coast AM* website; see https://www.coasttocoastam.com/show/2010/01/31.

a proficient scientist, Ernetti's views on religious, scientific, and other matters were sought out from all over Europe by those as eminent as French president François Mitterand. Ernetti stated publicly that—with the help of a team of high-ranking scientists, including Enrico Fermi—he had in the 1950s melded quantum physics with ancient astral lore to create a time-traveling device that he called the "chronovisor." It had enabled him, he said, to see back in time and to witness Christ dying on the cross. The device had also permitted him to peer back to ancient Rome in 169 BCE and to watch a performance of *Thyestes,* a drama by the father of Latin poetry, Quintus Ennius, now lost. Ernetti's chronovisor produced a widely circulated picture that he said was of Christ dying on the cross.

While such possible evidence of time travel may be widely questioned, it has not always been for lack media attention. One extraordinary case recently drawing considerable interest involves the work of Ingersoll Lockwood, a late nineteenth-century American political writer, lawyer, and novelist who produced a unique blend of science fiction and fantasy. At one time a professional diplomat, Lockwood was

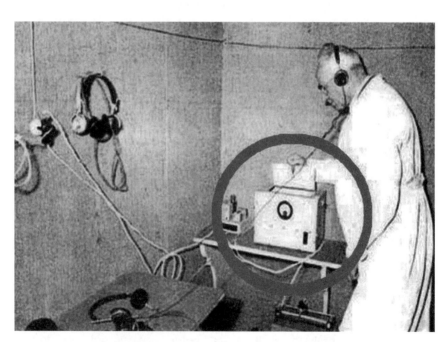

Father Ernetti operating his chronovisor in the 1950s

Ingersoll Lockwood

appointed consul to the Kingdom of Hanover by Abraham Lincoln. At the time the youngest member of the U.S. consular force, he served in the post for four years. Two of his most popular works were illustrated children's stories, focusing on a fictional character with a now-familiar name: Baron Trump. The following shortened and paraphrased account from *Newsweek* in July 2017 is typical of reports on the Lockwood/Trump story:

> A wealthy young man, Baron, lived in Castle Trump, and was the lead character in Lockwood's first two fictional novels, *The Travels and Adventures of Little Baron Trump and His Wonderful Dog Bulgar* and *Baron Trump's Marvelous Underground Journey*. The little boy, who had an unending imagination and "a very active brain," was bored by the luxurious lifestyle to which he was accustomed. In a twist of fate, Trump visited Russia to embark on an extraordinary adventure that would shape the rest of his life.
>
> Lockwood's final novel, titled *1900; or, The Last President*, was published in 1896.
>
> Some astonishing connections can be made between the Lockwood nineteenth-century characters and the current first family of the United States. The main character's name, for example, was the same as President Donald Trump's son, even though it was

spelled differently. Young Trump's adventures began in Russia and were directed by "the master of all masters," a man named Don.

Before leaving for his voyage through the unknown, Trump was told of his family's motto: "The pathway to glory is strewn with pitfalls and dangers."

Illustrations from the novels showed young Trump dressed in lavish, old-fashioned clothing and jewelry as he departed from Castle Trump and began his voyage to Russia to locate an entrance into alternate dimensions.

But by Lockwood's third novel, *The Last President,* things became even more strangely linked to the present day.

The story began with a scene from a panicked New York City in early November, after the election of an enormously opposed outsider candidate.

"The entire East Side is in a state of uproar," police officers shouted through the streets, warning city folk to stay indoors for the night. "Mobs of vast size are organizing under the lead of anarchists and socialists and threaten to plunder and despoil the houses of the rich who have wronged and oppressed them for so many years."

"The Fifth Avenue Hotel will be the first to feel the fury of the mob," the novel continues, citing an address in New York City where Trump Tower now stands. "Would the troops be in time to save it?"

Lockwood's creations have resurfaced online. Some claim the Trump family possesses a time machine that has allowed them to remain powerful to this day.

The Last President doesn't follow the same fictional narrative of Lockwood's previous novels, though the links to Trump were once again abundantly clear. In this book, also titled *1900,* the president's hometown of New York City feared the collapse of the republic in the wake of the transition of presidential power. Some Americans began forming a resistance, protesting what was seen as a corrupt and unethical election process.*

---

*For the original *Newsweek* version, see Chris Riotta, "Did an Author From the 1800s Predict the Trumps, Russia and America's Downfall?," *Newsweek* (online), July 31, 2017, https://www.newsweek.com/donald-trump-predicted-ingersoll-lockwood-adventures -barron-melania-last-644284.

From the frontispiece of
*Baron Trump's Marvelous
Underground Journey*

Barron Trump,
at age twelve

THE ESOTERIC CONNECTION

Among many factors not mentioned by *Newsweek* are connections between Lockwood and the deep occult. In fact, a note on the title page of *1900; or, the Last President* states, "This is a work of memetic occultism." Memetics, says Wikipedia, is an approach to evolutionary models of cultural information transfer; critics regard it as a pseudoscience. The term *meme,* coined by Richard Dawkins in his 1976 book *The Selfish Gene,* is based on so-called memetics.

Other books of Lockwood's time can also be said to be part of a mystical tradition some have called the "underground stream." Included would be those of Edward Bulwer-Lytton, a British official, member of Parliament, and occultist. As a novelist, he is known for several novels, including the previously noted *Zanoni, The Last Days of Pompei,* and *Vril: The Coming Race* (1871), which drew heavily on his interest in the occult and contributed to the early growth of the science fiction genre. The book, which told the story of a subterranean race waiting to reclaim the surface of the Earth, popularized the hollow Earth theory. Adopted by theosophists and occultists since the 1870s, Vril would develop into a major esoteric topic and eventually become closely associated with other widespread, albeit esoteric, themes following World War II. Another book in this category, *Etidorhpa, or the End of the Earth: The Strange History of a Mysterious Being and the Account of a Remarkable Journey,* published in 1895 by John Uri Lloyd, tells of a journey to the center of

Illustration from *Etidorhpa;* art by John Augustus Knapp

the Earth in the company of a strange androgynous being. (By the way, the name Etidorhpa, spelled backward, is Aphrodite, the name of the Greek goddess of love.)

Baron Trump's exploration of vast and mysterious underground caves in the mountains of Russia provides a clear connection to the hollow Earth idea—and, some would say, to the notorious "Trump-Russia collusion" narrative promoted in the media. Meanwhile, curiously, recent archaeological discoveries in a Russian cave have turned up evidence for technologically advanced civilization, ostensibly Denisovan, dating to over forty-five thousand years ago (see chapter 19).

Others have noticed that the Lockwood books also seem to foreshadow the amazing science of Nikola Tesla. This idea takes on special significance when another little-known fact is considered: As most students of the life of Tesla are aware, when the great inventor died on January 7, 1943, at the age of eighty-six, alone in his room in the New Yorker Hotel, FBI agents immediately swooped in to claim any papers he might have left behind. What many do not know is that among those assigned to evaluate the Tesla materials was John G. Trump, a professor at MIT and well-known electrical engineer serving as a technical aide to the National Defense Research Committee. Trump's nephew, Donald, would go on to become the forty-fifth president of the United States. Donald Trump has spoken often of conversations

John G. Trump

he had with his uncle when he was growing up. "My uncle used to tell me about nuclear before nuclear was nuclear," Trump was quoted as saying in the *New Yorker* magazine.*

While many may see such astonishing coincidences as evidence for the reality of time travel, others may see another possible explanation—a concept called synchronicity, first introduced by pioneering psychoanalyst Carl Jung. Jung argued that the simultaneous occurrence of events with no apparent causal relationship, which are yet meaningfully related, is evidence of synchronicity. This notion may not be any easier for reductionist materialists to explain, but it did have major support from some of the greatest minds of the twentieth century, including physicist Wolfgang Pauli. Inspired by Jung, Pauli came to believe that two events can be connected not by cause and effect but by their mutual presence in the collective unconscious.†

Carl Jung

---

*See Amy Davidson Sorkin, "Donald Trump's Nuclear Uncle," *New Yorker,* April 8, 2016, https://www.newyorker.com/news/amy-davidson/donald-trumps-nuclear-uncle.
†For an examination of the collaborative and complementary work between Jung and Pauli, see Marialuisa Donati, "Beyond Synchronicity: The Worldview of Carl Gustav Jung and Wolfgang Pauli," *Journal of Analytical Psychology* 49, no. 5 (2004): 707–28, https://www.ncbi.nlm.nih.gov/pubmed/15533199.

38

Wheel of the Ages

Is the story of Atlantis written in the stars?

The precession of the equinoxes is the astronomical phenomenon that gives us the so-called astrological ages, where the point of sunrise at the spring equinox appears to move slowly backward through the zodiac at the rate of about one sign every 2,150 years. This, according to most astronomers, is due to a slow wobble in the Earth's axis that takes almost twenty-six thousand years to circle the zodiac.

An hourglass and the passage from ancient to modern worlds; art by Tom Miller for *Atlantis Rising*

427

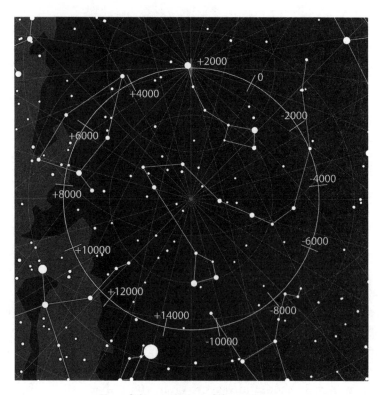

Map of the precession of the equinoxes
as seen in the skies of the northern hemisphere

This change in the stars relative to Earth, forming the Great—or Platonic—Year, is made up of the twelve astrological ages that, like the twelve spokes of a great wheel, slowly turn at the rate of one degree of arc every seventy-two years. We are now at the end of Pisces and, like the song says, "this is the dawning of the age of Aquarius" as the stars that mark the boundaries precess by.

It is worth noting that the very detection of such a slow and subtle movement would require centuries of close, disciplined, and continuous observation—something that, orthodox science maintains, would have been beyond the capability of any primitive ancient society. Precession, according to mainstream academic science, was discovered no earlier than between 190 and 120 BCE by the Greek astronomer Hipparchus, and not everyone accepts that even Hipparchus knew about the precession.

If you could show that, long before the Greeks, "primitive people" knew about precession, you could make a very strong case for the existence of advanced science in prehistory, something that orthodoxy has consistently, even fiercely, denied. Nevertheless, groundbreaking new research on very ancient cave paintings makes exactly the point—that indeed, ancient people had an advanced knowledge of, at the least, astronomy.

According to a University of Edinburgh press release announcing the new study, the artworks found at sites across Europe are not simply depictions of wild animals, as was once thought. Instead, close analysis shows that the animal symbols represent star constellations in the night sky and are used to represent dates and mark events such as comet strikes. They reveal that, perhaps as far back as forty thousand years ago, humans kept track of time using knowledge of how, over thousands of years, the position of the stars imperceptibly changes. The findings suggest that long before the Greeks, ancient people understood the precession of the equinoxes.*

The study shows, moreover, that around the time that Neanderthals became extinct, and perhaps before humankind settled in western Europe, people could define dates to within 250 years. In fact, when the researchers studied details of Paleolithic and Neolithic art featuring animal symbols at sites in Turkey, Spain, France, and Germany, they discovered that all the sites used the same method of date-keeping based on sophisticated astronomy, though the art was separated in time by tens of thousands of years. Even the world's oldest sculpture, the Lion-Man of Hohlenstein-Stadel Cave, from 38,000 BCE, was found to conform to this same ancient time-keeping system.

The researchers clarified earlier findings from a study of stone carvings at Göbekli Tepe in Turkey, which had been interpreted as a memorial to a devastating comet strike around 11,000 BCE, initiating the Younger Dryas mini ice age. They also decoded the famous Lascaux Cave tableau from France. The art, which features a dying man and several animals, may commemorate another comet strike from around 15,200 BCE, the researchers believe.

---

*See the press release from the University of Edinburgh: "Prehistoric Cave Art Reveals Ancient Use of Complex Astronomy," Phys.org (online), November 27, 2018, https:// phys.org/news/2018-11-prehistoric-cave-art-reveals-ancient.html.

The shaft scene from Lascaux Cave in France, featuring a dying man and several animals. It may commemorate a comet strike from around 15,200 BCE, say researchers.

By comparing the age of many examples of cave art—determined by chemically dating the paints used—with the positions of stars in ancient times, as predicted by sophisticated software, the researchers were able to confirm their findings. In other words, the astronomical insights of ancient people were far greater than previously believed. Their knowledge may have even aided in navigation of the open seas, a fact with far-reaching implications for our understanding of prehistoric human migration.*

THE OTHER PRECESSION STORY

Some scholars, like Walter Cruttenden (author of *Lost Star of Myth and Time*), have argued that the twenty-six-thousand-year precession of the equinoxes (a.k.a. the Great Year)—which some, like the Hindu sage Sri Yukteswar, have said tracks the rise and fall of civilizations—exists

---

*See Martin B. Sweatman and Alistair Coombs, "Decoding European Palaeolithic Art: Extremely Ancient Knowledge of Precession of the Equinoxes," *Athens Journal of History* 5, no. 1 (2018): 1–30, https://www.athensjournals.gr/history/2019-5-1-1-Sweatman.pdf.

Hindu saint and scholar
Sri Yukteswar

because our sun is part of a binary star system. Most astronomers think precession, which moves backward through the zodiac, is caused by the slow wobble of Earth's axis, but no one has yet ruled out the possibility that the sun is part of a binary system where two or more stars simultaneously orbit each other. Such a system for our sun would not be uncommon and could also account for the precession of the equinoxes.

Astronomers are now taking another look at the theory that our sun may have a long-lost twin. They haven't found it yet, but nevertheless, they call it Nemesis. The big question is, if the sun is, in fact, a binary star, where is its twin? Cruttenden calls it a "lost star." Others look for a brown dwarf or maybe Planet X, like that proposed by Zecharia Sitchin. A new mathematical model from the University of California at Berkeley says that the hypothetical Nemesis may have migrated out into the Milky Way. It might even be hiding behind the Perseus cloud of gas and dust that appears as a black spot in the sky, concealing whatever is behind it. Sarah Sadavoy and Steven Stahler, coauthors of the study, have found many such binary stars.*

Some observers, though, have begun to argue that the sun's missing

---

*See Sarah I. Sadavoy and Steven W. Stahler, "Embedded binaries and their dense cores," *Monthly Notices of the Royal Astronomical Society* 469, no. 4 (August 2017): 3881–3900, https://doi.org/10.1093/mnras/stx1061.

twin is no longer missing. The sun's long-lost mate, they say, is actually the brightest star in the northern sky: Sirius. The online Sirius Research Group of the Binary Research Institute is dedicated to assembling and analyzing the data for such a proposition.

Astronomy professor Dr. William Brown of Colorado State University at Pueblo supports their view. Brown makes the case that our sun and Sirius have apparently interlocking orbits, and that celestial bodies in our solar system show harmonic resonance with the Sirius system. More significantly, as Brown pointed out, the Sirius Research Group recorded the position of Sirius for over twenty years and did not record any measurable alteration in its location relative to the precession. In other words, it closely fits the requirements.*

If Brown is right, the connection would give new meaning to the clear interest of ancient societies in Sirius, especially in Egypt. One of

Sirius and the constellation Orion

---

*See William Brown, "A Sirius Revolution: The Sun's Astral Companion: A Model for the Sun-Sirius System," *Viewzone Magazine* (online), n.d., http://www.viewzone.com /sirius.html.

the so-called air shafts from the Queen's Chamber (site of the mysterious "Gantenbrink's Door") is, in fact, pointed precisely at Sirius, which the Egyptians identified with the goddess Isis.

Of special interest are the Dogon people of landlocked Mali in western Africa, who have demonstrated an inexplicably advanced knowledge of Sirius and its nearby small twin, Sirius B. Sirius B cannot be seen without a high-power telescope and was not discovered until recently, yet its existence has been known to this supposedly primitive African tribe since ancient times.*

In the developed world, some esoteric wisdom teachings, such as Theosophy, and including teachers like Alice Bailey and Elizabeth Clare Prophet, have long revered Sirius as the home of an interstellar hierarchy of light called the Great White Brotherhood, and in contrast to the common appellation of "Dog Star," they have identified Sirius as the "God Star." Could they have been on to something?

THE SECRETS OF THE STARS

In their classic 1969 study *Hamlet's Mill: An Essay Investigating the Origins of Human Knowledge and Its Transmission through Myth*, Giorgio de Santillana and Hertha von Dechend collected myths and legends from around the world to show how knowledge of the stars was encoded into the stories. The central theme was based on a character named Amlodhi (Hamlet), who owned a mill. In the beginning the mill ground out peace and plenty, but as time passed and circumstances worsened, the mill came to grind out salt. Ultimately, the mill sunk to the bottom of the ocean, where it ground out only rocks and sand, creating a whirlpool—a vast *maelstrom*—the "grinding stream."

The mill here is actually a metaphor for Earth's polar axis, which pierces the center of the Earth and the frame of time and points toward the northern and southern axes of the sky. The authors found that myths from cultures as diverse as Iceland, Norway, Finland, Italy, Persia, India, Mexico, and Greece have a churning mill as their central

---

*See "Was the Sirius Star System Home to the Dogon African Tribe?," Gaia (online), October 13, 2019, https://www.gaia.com/article/did-this-african-tribe-originate-in -another-star-system.

theme and invoke the assistance of gods, goddesses, and the forces of nature to assure that the "mill of heaven" grinds smoothly. The mill, de Santillana and von Dechend believed, was the precession of the equinoxes, and its persistence in myth provides a cosmic timepiece that can be used to study the past.

According to astrologer Julie Loar, in her article "Hamlet's Mill and the Wheel of Heaven" for *Atlantis Rising* #121 (January/February 2017), the slow movement of the sun through the constellations of the zodiac reflects the nature of the world's ages. Each age is said to have a particular character, or dispensation, followed by a "twilight of the gods." At the end of an age, the supporting pillars of that eon collapse and floods and cataclysm trumpet the unfolding of a new age.

During the age of Taurus, bulls were the sacred animals of sacrifice. In Aries, the icon and animal of sacrifice was the ram. During the period of Pisces, the sacrificial symbolism transferred from the lamb of God to the fisher of men, where the figure of Jesus was accompanied by fish symbolism, including the fish as the symbol of Christianity itself.

From this view, the Great Wheel can be imagined as a cycle resembling a day, with a dawn, noon, sunset, and midnight. The wheel of the Hindu *yugas* has a similar approach, but the Satya Yuga, the golden age, is the longest. This great cycle slowly ascends through periods of increasing light and then slowly descends into a time of growing darkness. The Treta Yuga is the second longest, followed by the Dwapara Yuga and then the Kali Yuga, which is the shortest and darkest. It is said we are now still in the Kali Yuga. Unlike the solar year, the darkness is far shorter than in a golden age. Certain times on the wheel are seen as light and others as dark and forbidding because of sun's horizontal proximity to the galactic plane.

If the *yugas* are overlaid on the astrological ages, says Loar, the dark age of the Kali Yuga spans the ages of Aries and Pisces. We are now just leaving the age of Pisces. The Dwapara Yuga, ascending and descending, covers the ages of Aquarius and Taurus. We are entering the age of Aquarius, and according to the Hindu tradition, light is now increasing. Light increases in the Treta Yuga in the ages of Capricorn and Sagittarius, on one side of the wheel, and darkens on the other side, in the ages of Gemini and Cancer. The Satya Yuga covers the four constellations of Scorpio, Libra, Virgo, and Leo.

This is similar to the Greek ages, and the Roman ones that followed, which Ovid called Golden, Silver, Bronze, and Iron. Hesiod saw five ages and included the Age of Heroes between the Bronze Age and the Iron Age. At times these ages are correlated with historical time lines. The Greeks, and the Romans who copied them, are seen as descending from an earlier Golden Age into the darker times in which we now live.

Hamlet's Mill explains that the time when the cogs of the great mill shifted, heralding the beginning of a new age, was seen as especially fraught with peril. How did the ancient knowledge of those who watched the skies long ago determine that this was true? What could be the mechanism driving the timing, character, and overarching lessons of the ages? Perhaps there is some inherent magic in the geometry of twelve that relates to music, vibration, and frequency? Or perhaps it is the stars themselves and their unique energies that drive the influences of the ages and of astrology itself? The Tibetans are said to be custodians of star knowledge that includes awareness of the "personalities" of certain bright stars and the nature of their frequencies. These are mysteries we may well be unable to penetrate, but if we are wise, we will pay attention.

De Santillana and von Dechend made a compelling case for sophisticated knowledge among the ancients. The authors of *Hamlet's Mill* demonstrated repeatedly that myth was never intended to be fiction or fable but rather to serve as a clever mnemonic device, enabling people to recall and transmit complex astronomical information through stories. In other words, using sky lore as the mechanism and the night sky as the canvas, myth became a brilliant device, an astronomical allegory, for teaching and transmitting sky lore over vast periods of time.

In his book *Hero with a Thousand Faces,* Joseph Campbell spoke of a "magic ring of myth" that flows through every culture. He said that a "mythology is a system of images that incorporates a concept of the universe as a divinely energized and energizing ambience within which we live."[*] Myths are single stories in this grand scheme that interlock in some way to create a tapestry. Campbell explained that myths are not created or invented in the way stories are. He said they are inspired, and arise in the same way dreams do, and that they speak to the deep

---

[*]Campbell made this statement in an April 1981 interview with Bill Moyer on the PBS series *Bill Moyers Journal.*

The constellation Leo

of both the individual and all that is. As we face a juncture in our own time of shifting cogs on the Great Wheel, Julie Loar believes that we desperately need new myths, new archetypal stories of a cosmos too big to imagine, in which we are not diminished by its size but are rather ignited by the understanding that we are part of a magnificent creation that can be known. As the age of Aquarius begins in earnest, she thought, so does our journey of exploration.

British historian Arnold Toynbee saw cycles of change unfolding through history, like the processes of nature, including birth, life, and death or transcendence for entire civilizations. In the precession of the equinoxes, the sinking of Atlantis, as recorded by Plato, and the beginning of the Younger Dryas mini ice age would have occurred in the age of Leo about 12,500 years ago at the point on the calendar of the Great Year directly opposite our present position. It is clear that our own time could resonate with it. "History," Mark Twain is purported to have said, "may not repeat itself, but it does rhyme." The cadence may be slow, but for anyone who cares to read it, the poetry is inescapable.